Conservatism in America since 1930

Conservatism in America since 1930

A Reader

EDITED BY

Gregory L. Schneider

New York University Press

NEW YORK AND LONDON

NEW YORK UNIVERSITY PRESS
New York and London

Library of Congress Cataloging-in-Publication Data
Conservatism in America since 1930 : a reader / [edited by] Gregory L. Schneider.
    p. cm.
Includes bibliographical references and index.
ISBN 0-8147-9798-9 (cloth : alk. paper) — ISBN 0-8147-9799-7 (pbk. : alk. paper)
    1. Conservatism—United States—History—20th century.
I. Schneider, Gregory L., 1965–

JC573.2.U6 C64 2003
320.52'0973'0904—dc21   2002043137

New York University Press books are printed on acid-free paper, and
their binding materials are chosen for strength and durability.

Manufactured in the United States of America

10 9 8 7 6 5 4 3 2 1

For my wife, Petra, with love always,
and for Bailey and Balin, with love from Dad.
I also dedicate this book to
Richard M. Fried, University of Illinois at Chicago
Alonzo Hamby, Ohio University
John Lewis Gaddis, Yale University
Three mentors.

Contents

Acknowledgments

A project of this type is necessarily a monastic enterprise, involving the selection and rejection of numerous documents and the—sometimes—tedious process of securing permissions to use them. No edited collection is perfect and not everyone will be happy with what is included herein and what is not. I have strived to include important sources and crucial debates within the modern conservative movement in America, all aimed at reflecting the great diversity within American conservative thought and activity. I am especially grateful to former NYU editor-in-chief Niko Pfund for encouraging this project and the three anonymous reviewers of the manuscript for helping me shape the project in important ways. I also wish to thank the current editor-in-chief Steve Maikowski for responding generously to my request for more time in finishing the manuscript, as well as the staff of NYU Press, particularly Emily Park, for their professionalism in this, my second book, with the press.

My thanks also to my colleagues in the Social Science Department of Emporia State University, for providing a collegial and exciting intellectual environment—you know who you are. Special thanks go to Phil Kelly, my good colleague and friend, who nurtured young academics in his role as chair of our department, providing me (and others) much needed release time from heavy teaching obligations in order to dedicate time to scholarly pursuits. *Gracias.*

The dedication pays tribute to my wife Petra, who provides a nurturing environment for myself and our two children, Bailey and Balin to whom I also dedicate the book, although they remain more interested in reading Dr. Seuss than Dr. Schneider.

The dedication also pays homage to three men who helped shape my career as a historian and a scholar. They served as inspirations when I first read their works as an undergraduate at Drake University, they were my mentors at various phases of my graduate career at Ohio University and the University of Illinois at Chicago, and they continue to inspire me now. It has long been a dream of mine to pay tribute to teachers who contributed to enriching my career as a historian; this is but a small repayment to the tremendous debt of gratitude that I owe from my association with these three fine contemporary historians and teachers. Thank you.

Introduction

"In 1945 no articulate, coordinated, self-consciously conservative intellectual force existed in the United States. There were, at best, scattered voices
of protest, profoundly pessimistic about the future of the country."[1] So
wrote historian George H. Nash in the most influential book on the
formation of American conservatism. As a political and social force in
American life, conservatism was still in its adolescence when Nash wrote,
and as he looked back to document the movement's origins and intellectual roots in the post–World War II period, he found a continuing
struggle for identity as the hallmark of the conservative intellectual movement. It was this quest for identity, for that which defined and shaped
what constituted an American conservatism, that dominated (and still
dominates) the conservative disposition today.

The study of social movements gives pause to historians in search of
clear-cut beginnings and endings. Are there continuities between even the
most vaguely expressed conservative sentiments and the political conservatism dominant in America today? Or, instead, should the historian be
more careful to stress the discontinuities that may exist between past and
present? Students of history are presented with the same dilemma: Does
history move in a steady stream, or are there abrupt and often discon-
certing changes brought about by events and personalities? How does one
choose between continuity and discontinuity when studying something as
amorphous as ideas and their impact on history?

Historians have described the history of conservatism in a linear manner.[2] The story goes something like this. Angry over the growing concentration of power in the federal government, a process that began with the
development of modern liberalism during the Depression years and accelerated with American involvement in World War II, classical liberal
scholars and journalists resurrected the dormant ideas of limited government and individual rights. At the same time the horrors of World War
II helped engender a conservative viewpoint that saw little to admire

about a civilization that could destroy mankind with atomic weapons. The Nazi extermination of the Jews, the aerial bombardment of cities, and the barbarity of war sparked a traditionalist conservative rebirth critical of the modern age. Finally, the beginning of the Cold War led conservatives to fully embrace anticommunism; Stalinism had replaced fascism as the totalitarian enemy. The movement of former communists to the political Right helped faster development of Cold War anticommunist conservatism. By the late 1950s, the fusion of these disparate factions helped create the modern conservative political movement, as politicians like Arizona senator Barry Goldwater and California governor Ronald Reagan proved amenable to conservative factions. A combination of liberal failure and conservative organizing allowed Reagan to draw support from Americans disenchanted with the state of the nation.[3] Reagan's presidential victory in 1980 proved to be the high point of the postwar conservative movement. From the dismal swamp of conservative organizing in the 1930s and 1940s, conservatism had reached its summit in the Reagan years.

Such a linear progression has much to recommend it. What I would call the "Whig interpretation of conservatism" allows historians to document how a relatively powerless group of intellectuals and popularizers could develop their ideas, reach out to constituents, organize effective issue-oriented groups, win political power, and translate their ideas into policy. Yet history—especially intellectual history—rarely proceeds in such a clear-cut pattern. Whiggish historical interpretations minimize conflict. Rancorous disputes over how to translate ideas into action dominate any social or political movement.[4] Among American conservatives, such rancor occurred as regularly as a tidal cycle, typically involving disputes over identity—what conservatism should be and how it should proceed. In the course of post–World War II history, conservatives constantly fought over what their ideas stood for, how and whether political action could bring them to fruition, and what the consequences of political action might mean for the original principles.

The fact that conservatism emerged in an intellectual climate hostile to its core principles helped, as much as it initially hindered, its development. Conservatives, according to cultural critic Lionel Trilling, "with some isolated and ecclesiastical exceptions express themselves . . . only in action or irritable mental gestures which seek to resemble ideas."[5] Liberal historian Arthur M. Schlesinger, Jr., dismissed conservatism as "the politics of nostalgia," while political theorist Louis Hartz argued that *only* the Lockean-liberal tradition was relevant to American political thought.[6] In *The New American Right*, social scientists placed conservatives on the Freudian couch and diagnosed them as suffering from an "authoritarian personality" and practicing the "politics of paranoia," the causes of which, the essayists argued, were rooted in status anxiety. Conservatives were abnormal, representatives of ideological creed, a "pseudo-conservatism" in the words of historian Richard Hofstadter, deviating from the social and economic munificence postwar liberalism provided.[7] As Soviet authorities once imprisoned dissenters from communist orthodoxy on charges of mental illness, liberal intellectuals dismissed conservatives as imbalanced extremists; irritable mental gestures indeed.

Conservatism developed as an intellectual and political movement during the heyday of postwar liberalism. However, it would be inaccurate to conclude that conservatism developed solely in reaction to liberalism. Rather, a conservative intellectual tradition—emphasizing, not exclusively, limited government and veneration for the Constitution, moral traditionalism rooted in a Christian religious heritage, a muscular anti-communism, and the embrace of free-market economics—flowed alongside of, and competed with, modern liberalism for much of the postwar era. At the same time, conservatives developed a critique of modern liberal premises regarding the economy, foreign policy, and culture. The development of such a critique allowed for conservatives to organize politically and to challenge modern liberalism. While the first foray into politics—the 1964 Goldwater campaign—failed disastrously, liberalism's decline in the 1960s and 1970s worked to the advantage of the political Right.

Yet, even at the peak of its political success, conservatism continued to evolve. Sometimes conservatives eschewed older established principles and sometimes they brought old principles back. The essays and documents in this collection display such a development from the 1930s until the *fin de siecle*. The reader displays not only the variety in conservative thought but also the disagreements and conflicts in the construction of a conservative identity. While the essays and documents herein are arranged chronologically, they also reflect the protean nature of American conservatism, how alterations in conservative thought offer a recurrence of debates over identity. Through such an approach the reader will gain insight not only into the most important intellectual contributors to

American conservatism, but also into those forsaken ideas and arguments now considered marginal to mainstream conservatism.

No collection of essays and documents can offer a complete story of the tremendous diversity in conservative thought, and I recognize the limitations in any effort to do so. With that in mind, I have chosen essays that offer an introduction to conservative thought for the general reader and student, as well as essays that will challenge those with a more specialized interest in the study of conservative thought. They all reflect, however, "the quest for self-definition" that George Nash saw in American conservatism more than a generation ago. That such a quest for self-definition continues to this day reflects the intractability of identity in modern American conservative discourse.

Part I

The Old Right

The conservative idea in modern America developed from an unorgan-
ized and diverse collection of individuals. Although no self-described
conservative *movement* existed before World War II, there were groups of
libertarians, agrarians, individualists, collectivists, nationalists, and others
who fit well the postwar label conservative.[1] Never certain where to focus
their energies, conservatives were frustrated by the political success of
Franklin Roosevelt and the New Deal. They were threatened by the growing concentration of power in the central state and in the movement away
from the principles of limited government and separated powers embodied in the Constitution and the tradition of American republican government. Yet, conservatives failed to organize politically against the New
Deal.[2]

Conservatives had other difficulties during the Depression decade. In
an age of mass democracy and the era of the common man, this group
felt a grave threat emanating from the power of the people. The burgeon-
ing labor movement and communist activity within America proved the
danger described as "the revolt of the masses."[3] The Depression years
were, for many conservatives, a "red decade" in which the collapse of
faith in capitalism and republican government allowed for the spread of
communism. Conservatives looked suspiciously on even the most moderate reforms. To a later generation of New Left radicals, the New Deal
preserved the status quo and created a corporate liberal State—it was
hardly reformist. To conservatives, however, it suggested ominous portents of unlimited executive power and statist planning more reminiscent
of the Soviet Union or Nazi Germany.[4]

The problem conservatives faced was determining how to preserve the
last vestiges of the inherited constitutional tradition—and other
traditions—in an age of mass democracy. Unable to develop a democratic
movement capable of challenging the New Deal, conservatives failed to
build a coherent political alternative to modern liberalism. However, they

did argue for principles that, while inoperative at that time politically, would sustain them through the decade and set the stage for a conservative intellectual and political reawakening after World War II.

The chapters in Part I depict a small portion of the concerns and ideas of the old Right. The first chapter, "Southern Agrarians and the Defense of Region," is the "Statement of Principles" contained in *I'll Take My Stand: The South and the Agrarian Tradition* (1930). This essay was written by "Twelve Southerners," professors of literature, poetry, and history, many of whom were from Vanderbilt University in Nashville, Tennessee (including among its more prominent members John Crowe Ransom, Robert Penn Warren, Donald Davidson, and Allen Tate). The Agrarians, as the twelve were soon labeled, argued for a social and economic order founded upon a return to a pre-industrial past. They objected to what they saw as the "evil dispensation" of industrial America, its ruinous effect on culture, economy, and society. Such concerns struck deep chords and inspired many agrarian-based movements during the Depression decade, many of them funded by New Deal agencies.[5] However, none of them ever gained the support of a political party or of the American people. The later effort to broaden the appeal of agrarianism, a collection of essays published as *Who Owns America?* (1936), would fail to generate a political movement. How could America turn back the clock to a pre-industrial past?

One individual who recognized the importance of the agrarian critique was Seward Collins, editor and publisher of the long distinguished *Bookman* which, by the late 1920s, had fallen on difficult times. In the late 1920s, Collins had published the work of the new humanists, primarily Paul Elmer More (1864–1937) and Irving Babbitt (1865–1933). Both were professors of literature, Babbitt at Harvard and More at Princeton. They represented a cultural conservatism and social and cultural philosophy based on veneration of the ancient classics and disdain for modernism.[6] They were influential early in the century for their criticism as well as their mentoring of literary figures like T. S. Eliot. But they seemed hopelessly reactionary—Upton Sinclair referred to them as "literary mummies"—and in publishing their work (almost exclusively), Collins set off a temporary controversy in the late 1920s and early 1930s over the new humanists that was put to rest upon Babbitt's death in 1933.[7]

Collins, continually in search of conservative ideas, turned next to agrarianism and its English counterpart, distributism, best represented by the work of G. K. Chesterton and Hilaire Belloc. Seeking to advance these ideas, Collins renamed his journal *The American Review*, and, for little more than four years (beginning in April 1933), provided a forum for an eclectic mixture of various positions regarding culture, politics, foreign affairs, and social philosophy, which fit nicely with his enigmatic beliefs. But Collins contributed to problems for his magazine when he publicly embraced fascism as a solution to the problems of American life. In so doing, he lost supporters, including agrarian Allen Tate, who stopped publishing in the magazine. His open support for Francisco Franco in the Spanish Civil War and growing anti-Semitism also derailed any chance that the publication could spur a conservative intellectual revival. Yet, *The American Review* remained an important conservative journal, the only truly literate one of the 1930s; I have included Collins' editorial comments as an example of what *The American Review* sought to do, and his defense of monarchy as a model of one rejected conservative viewpoint before World War II.

The last two chapters represent another example of the diversity within the old Right. Albert Jay Nock (1871–1945), whom Michael Wreszin has labeled a "superfluous anarchist," represented a strong individualism associated with a classical liberal tradition hostile to the State.[8] Nock had been an Episcopal minister before divorcing his wife and leaving the cloth, finding sanction in radical journalism. He was dedicated to progressive reform causes but after World War I developed a strong individualist streak which mocked the pretensions of reform. In 1920 he helped start *The Freeman*, one of the finest early liberal-individualist publications, but it stopped publication in 1924. Nock made his living as a journalist and essayist, writing regularly for H. L. Mencken's *The American Mercury* after his own journal's failure, and became particularly enthralled with Thomas Jefferson, whereby he gained insight for his defense of individualism. An eclectic borrower of ideas, Nock was also attracted to the social conservatism of architect Ralph Adams Cram (1863–1942), a defender of social and cultural elitism. In 1936 he published *Our Enemy, the State*, an unapologetic assault on the modern State as the enemy of freedom, from which Chapter 3 is taken. In 1944 he published his entertaining autobiography, *Memoirs of a Superfluous Man*, in which he discussed Cram's idea of a remnant of individuals who were granted the task of defending Western civilization from the barbarities of modernism. Nock was one of the key architects of American conservatism, but his death in 1945 seemed to suggest an end to efforts to restore traditional social order to society.

The final chapter of Part I is a founding statement of the weekly

publication *Human Events*. Founded in 1944, and edited initially by journalists Frank Hanighen, William Henry Chamberlin, and Haverford College president Felix Morley, *Human Events* sought to articulate a noninterventionist, America First conservatism in the postwar world. The effort
to resurrect a postwar noninterventionist foreign policy, a dominant concern of the old Right, failed due to the growing threat of the Soviet Union
and communist expansion in Eastern Europe. *Human Events* remained
committed to the noninterventionist anticommunism until the late 1940s
when American policy seemed to be abetting communist expansion. A
change in editorial policy, one which supported the global Cold War
against communism, led to Morley's resignation and moved *Human
Events* toward the postwar vital center conservatism coming to fruition
by the mid-1950s.

Chapter One

Southern Agrarians and the Defense of Region

The authors contributing to this book are Southerners, well acquainted with one another and of similar tastes, though not necessarily living in the same physical community, and perhaps only at this moment aware of themselves as a single group of men. By conversation and exchange of letters over a number of years it had developed that they entertained many convictions in common, and it was decided to make a volume in which each one should furnish his views upon a chosen topic. This was the general background. But background and consultation as to the various topics were enough; there was to be no further collaboration. And so no single author is responsible for any view outside his own article. It was through the good fortune of some deeper agreement that the book was expected to achieve its unity. All the articles bear in the same sense upon the book's title-subject: all tend to support a Southern way of life against what may be called the American or prevailing way; and all as much as agree that the best terms in which to represent the distinction are contained in the phrase, Agrarian *versus* Industrial.

But after the book was under way it seemed a pity if the contributors, limited as they were within their special subjects, should stop short of showing how close their agreements really were. On the contrary, it seemed that they ought to go on and make themselves known as a group already consolidated by a set of principles which could be stated with a good deal of particularity. This might prove useful for the sake of future reference, if they should undertake any further joint publication. It was then decided to prepare a general introduction for the book which would state briefly the common convictions of the group. This is the statement. To it every one of the contributors in this book has subscribed.

"Introduction: A Statement of Principles" in Twelve Southerners, *I'll Take My Stand: The South and the Agrarian Tradition,* Copyright 1977 by Louis D. Rubin, Jr. Reprinted by permission of Louisiana State University Press.

Nobody now proposes for the South, or for any other community in this country, an independent political destiny. That idea is thought to have been finished in 1865. But how far shall the South surrender its moral, social, and economic autonomy to the victorious principle of Union? That question remains open. The South is a minority section that has hitherto been jealous of its minority right to live its own kind of life. The South scarcely hopes to determine the other sections, but it does propose to determine itself, within the utmost limits of legal action. Of late, however, there is the melancholy fact that the South itself has wavered a little and shown signs of wanting to join up behind the common or American industrial ideal. It is against that tendency that this book is written. The younger Southerners, who are being converted frequently to the industrial gospel, must come back to the support of the Southern tradition. They must be persuaded to look very critically at the advantages of becoming a "new South" which will be only an undistinguished replica of the usual industrial community.

But there are many other minority communities opposed to industrialism, and wanting a much simpler economy to live by. The communities and private persons sharing the agrarian tastes are to be found widely within the Union. Proper living is a matter of the intelligence and the will, does not depend on the local climate or geography, and is capable of a definition which is general and not Southern at all. Southerners have a filial duty to discharge to their own section. But their cause is precarious and they must seek alliances with sympathetic communities everywhere. The members of the present group would be happy to be counted as members of a national agrarian movement.

Industrialism is the economic organization of the collective American society. It means the decision of society to invest its economic resources in the applied sciences. But the word science has acquired a certain sanctitude. It is out of order to quarrel with science in the abstract, or even with the applied sciences when their applications are made subject to criticism and intelligence. The capitalization of the applied sciences has now become extravagant and uncritical; it has enslaved our human energies to a degree now clearly felt to be burdensome. The apologists of industrialism do not like to meet this charge directly; so they often take refuge in saying that they are devoted simply to science! They are really devoted to the applied sciences and to practical production. Therefore it is necessary to employ a certain skepticism even at the expense of the

Cult of Science, and to say, It is an Americanism, which looks innocent and disinterested, but really is not either.

The contribution that science can make to a labor is to render it easier by the help of a tool or a process, and to assure the laborer of his perfect economic security while he is engaged upon it. Then it can be performed with leisure and enjoyment. But the modern laborer has not exactly received this benefit under the industrial regime. His labor is hard, its tempo is fierce, and his employment is insecure. The first principle of a good labor is that it must be effective, but the second principle is that it must be enjoyed. Labor is one of the largest items in the human career; it is a modest demand to ask that it may partake of happiness.

The regular act of applied science is to introduce into labor a labor-saving device or a machine. Whether this is a benefit depends on how far it is advisable to save the labor. The philosophy of applied science is generally quite sure that the saving of labor is a pure gain, and that the more of it the better. This is to assume that labor is an evil, that only the end of labor or the material product is good. On this assumption labor becomes mercenary and servile, and it is no wonder if many forms of modern labor are accepted without resentment though they are evidently brutalizing. The act of labor as one of the happy functions of human life has been in effect abandoned, and is practiced solely for its rewards.

Even the apologists of industrialism have been obliged to admit that some economic evils follow in the wake of the machines. These are such as overproduction, unemployment, and a growing inequality in the distribution of wealth. But the remedies proposed by the apologists are always homeopathic. They expect the evils to disappear when we have bigger and better machines, and more of them. Their remedial programs, therefore, look forward to more industrialism. Sometimes they see the system righting itself spontaneously and without direction: they are Optimists. Sometimes they rely on the benevolence of capital, or the militancy of labor, to bring about a fairer division of the spoils: they are Coöperationists or Socialists. And sometimes they expect to find super-engineers, in the shape of Boards of Control, who will adapt production to consumption and regulate prices and guarantee business against fluctuations: they are Sovietists. With respect to these last it must be insisted that the true Sovietists or Communists—if the term may be used here in the European sense—are the Industrialists themselves. They would have the government set up an economic super-organization, which in turn would become the government. We therefore look upon the Communist menace as a menace indeed, but not as a Red one; because it is simply according to the blind drift of our industrial development to expect in America at last much the same economic system as that imposed by violence upon Russia in 1917.

Turning to consumption, as the grand end which justifies the evil of modern labor, we find that we have been deceived. We have more time in which to consume, and many more products to be consumed. But the tempo of our labors communicates itself to our satisfactions, and these also become brutal and hurried. The constitution of the natural man probably does not permit him to shorten his labor-time and enlarge his consuming-time indefinitely. He has to pay the penalty in satiety and aimlessness. The modern man has lost his sense of vocation.

Religion can hardly expect to flourish in an industrial society. Religion is our submission to the general intention of a nature that is fairly inscrutable; it is the sense of our role as creatures within it. But nature industrialized, transformed into cities and artificial habitations, manufactured into commodities, is no longer nature but a highly simplified picture of nature. We receive the illusion of having power over nature, and lose the sense of nature as something mysterious and contingent. The God of nature under these conditions is merely an amiable expression, a superfluity, and the philosophical understanding ordinarily carried in the religious experience is not there for us to have.

Nor do the arts have a proper life under industrialism, with the general decay of sensibility which attends it. Art depends, in general, like religion, on a right attitude to nature; and in particular on a free and disinterested observation of nature that occurs only in leisure. Neither the creation nor the understanding of works of art is possible in an industrial age except by some local and unlikely suspension of the industrial drive.

The amenities of life also suffer under the curse of a strictly-business or industrial civilization. They consist in such practices as manners, conversation, hospitality, sympathy, family life, romantic love—in the social exchanges which reveal and develop sensibility in human affairs. If religion and the arts are founded on right relations of man-to-nature, these are founded on right relations of man-to-man.

Apologists of industrialism are even inclined to admit that its actual processes may have upon its victims the spiritual effects just described. But they think that all can be made right by extraordinary educational efforts, by all sorts of cultural institutions and endowments. They would cure the poverty of the contemporary spirit by hiring experts to instruct it in spite of itself in the historic culture. But salvation is hardly to be encountered on that road. The trouble with the life-pattern is to be located at its economic base, and we cannot rebuild it by pouring in soft materials from the top. The young men and women in colleges, for example, if they are already placed in a false way of life, cannot make more than an inconsequential acquaintance with the arts and humanities transmitted to them. Or else the understanding of these arts and humanities will but make them the more wretched in their own destitution.

The "Humanists" are too abstract. Humanism, properly speaking, is not an abstract system, but a culture, the whole way in which we live, act, think, and feel. It is a kind of imaginatively balanced life lived out in a definite social tradition. And, in the concrete, we believe that this, the genuine humanism, was rooted in the agrarian life of the older South and of other parts of the country that shared in such a tradition. It was not an abstract moral "check" derived from the classics—it was not soft material poured in from the top. It was deeply founded in the way of life itself—in its tables, chairs, portraits, festivals, laws, marriage customs. We cannot recover our native humanism by adopting some standard of taste that is critical enough to question the contemporary arts but not critical enough to question the social and economic life which is their ground.

The tempo of the industrial life is fast, but that is not the worst of it; it is accelerating. The ideal is not merely some set form of industrialism, with so many stable industries, but industrial progress, or an incessant extension of industrialization. It never proposes a specific goal; it initiates the infinite series. We have not merely capitalized certain industries; we have capitalized the laboratories and inventors, and undertaken to employ all the labor-saving devices that come out of them. But a fresh labor-saving device introduced into an industry does not emancipate the laborers in that industry so much as it evicts them. Applied at the expense of agriculture, for example, the new processes have reduced the part of the population supporting itself upon the soil to a smaller and smaller fraction. Of course no single labor-saving process is fatal; it brings on a period of unemployed labor and unemployed capital, but soon a new industry is devised which will put them both to work again, and a new commodity is thrown upon the market. The laborers were sufficiently embarrassed in the meantime, but, according to the theory, they will eventually be taken care of. It is now the public which is embarrassed; it feels obligated to purchase a commodity for which it had expressed no desire, but it is invited to make its budget equal to the strain. All might yet be well, and stability and comfort might again obtain, but for this: partly because of industrial ambitions and partly because the repressed creative impulse must break out somewhere, there will be a stream of further labor-saving devices in all industries, and the cycle will have to be repeated over and over. The result is an increasing disadjustment and instability.

It is an inevitable consequence of industrial progress that production greatly outruns the rate of natural consumption. To overcome the disparity, the producers, disguised as the pure idealists of progress, must coerce and wheedle the public into being loyal and steady consumers, in order to keep the machines running. So the rise of modern advertising—along with its twin, personal salesmanship—is the most significant development of our industrialism. Advertising means to persuade the consumers to want exactly what the applied sciences are able to furnish them. It consults the happiness of the consumer no more than it consulted the happiness of the laborer. It is the great effort of a false economy of life to approve itself. But its task grows more difficult every day.

It is strange, of course, that a majority of men anywhere could ever as with one mind become enamored of industrialism: a system that has so little regard for individual wants. There is evidently a kind of thinking that rejoices in setting up a social objective which has no relation to the individual. Men are prepared to sacrifice their private dignity and happiness to an abstract social ideal, and without asking whether the social ideal produces the welfare of any individual man whatsoever. But this is absurd. The responsibility of men is for their own welfare and that of their neighbors; not for the hypothetical welfare of some fabulous creature called society.

Opposed to the industrial society is the agrarian, which does not stand in particular need of definition. An agrarian society is hardly one that has no use at all for industries, for professional vocations, for scholars and artists, and for the life of cities. Technically, perhaps, an agrarian society is one in which agriculture is the leading vocation, whether for wealth, for pleasure, or for prestige—a form of labor that is pursued with intelligence and leisure, and that becomes the model to which the other forms approach as well as they may. But an agrarian regime will be secured readily enough where the superfluous industries are not allowed to rise against it. The theory of agrarianism is that the culture of the soil is the best and most sensitive of vocations, and that therefore it should have the economic preference and enlist the maximum number of workers.

These principles do not intend to be very specific in proposing any practical measures. How may the little agrarian community resist the Chamber of Commerce of its county seat, which is always trying to import some foreign industry that cannot be assimilated to the life-pattern of the community? Just what must the Southern leaders do to defend the traditional Southern life? How may the Southern and the Western agrarians unite for effective action? Should the agrarian forces try to capture the Democratic party, which historically is so closely affiliated with the defense of individualism, the small community, the state, the South? Or must the agrarians—even the Southern ones—abandon the Democratic party to its fate and try a new one? What legislation could most profitably be championed by the powerful agrarians in the Senate of the United States? What anti-industrial measures might promise to stop the advances of industrialism, or even undo some of them, with the least harm to those concerned? What policy should be pursued by the educators who have a tradition at heart? These and many other questions are of the greatest importance, but they cannot be answered here.

For, in conclusion, this much is clear: If a community, or a section, or a race, or an age, is groaning under industrialism, and well aware that it is an evil dispensation, it must find the way to throw it off. To think that this cannot be done is pusillanimous. And if the whole community, section, race, or age thinks it cannot be done, then it has simply lost its political genius and doomed itself to impotence.

Chapter Two

Monarch as Alternative

Seward Collins

The American Review is founded to give greater currency to the ideas of a
number of groups and individuals who are radically critical of conditions
prevalent in the modern world, but launch their criticism from a "traditionalist" basis: from the basis of a firm grasp on the immense body of
experience accumulated by men in the past, and the insight which this
knowledge affords. The magazine is a response to the widespread and
growing feeling that the forces and principles which have produced the
modern chaos are incapable of yielding any solution; that the only hope
is a return to fundamentals and tested principles which have been largely
pushed aside. Fortunately, there is no lack of able men to represent this
traditionalist point of view, although they have been forced to work in
isolation from each other and have achieved nothing like the influence to
which their stature entitles them. It should be obvious that a periodical
aiming to bring these groups and individuals together is particularly
needed in this country, where tradition took little root before it was
overridden by the disruptive forces that are now threatening Western
civilization. In Europe the spokesmen for sanity and order are more
numerous and more solidly entrenched: they have built up such a weighty
mass of indictment and prescription that they can be said to have their
modernist foes already on the defensive. For this reason we shall frequently be drawing on European contributors, but the editorial emphasis
will be directed to the needs of this country.

There will be no attempt in this first issue to draw up a "platform" of
the magazine's policy—indeed, the magazine has no policy, strictly speaking, beyond that of providing an organ for writers who represent the

Reprinted from *The American Review* (April 1933): 22–27.

direction described—nor even to state the views of the contributors whom it has enlisted and hopes to enlist: that must be the task of the magazine from issue to issue. But it will make our purpose clearer if we at least mention some of the men we have in mind. Most of our readers are probably already more or less familiar with the work of the American "humanists," Irving Babbitt and Paul Elmer More, and their co-workers, who received considerable attention in the columns of this magazine's predecessor, *The Bookman*. The existence, at least, of their work has become widely known in recent years, but the substance of their profound analysis of modern society, their fresh application of tradition to psychology, ethics, politics, philosophy, religion, literature, has scarcely begun to penetrate contemporary opinion to its clearly destined extent. One main purpose of *The American Review* is to carry on the work of *The Bookman* in making their contribution better known.

Another group on whom *The American Review* hopes to draw extensively are the English "Distributists." The leaders of this group, Hilaire Belloc and G. K. Chesterton, are of course among the best known writers of the day, but their work in the field of economics has received amazingly little attention, considering the fact that they offer a carefully reasoned alternative to the Capitalist-Communist dilemma. Both men are represented in this issue of the magazine, so that we do not need to say more of their viewpoint here, beyond stating that we think there is nothing more important for those who are wrestling with the hideous and apparently hopeless economic conditions of the modern world than giving thoughtful consideration to their work.

Here in this country there is a group of writers who resemble the English Distributists in being able men of letters who have devoted considerable thought to economic problems; and they have arrived at conclusions closely related to those of the Distributists. The Southern Agrarians, as they have been called, published in 1930 a symposium, *I'll Take My Stand*, which drew general attention to their work. But in our opinion its importance as a contribution to economic problems was almost universally underestimated. Their drastic criticism of industrialism, their emphasis on agrarian life, and their praise for the ways of the old South, were dismissed as nostalgia and a hopeless attempt to return to the past. But this is a most superficial judgement of a deeply considered viewpoint that goes to the very heart of American history as well as of contemporary problems. It is becoming increasingly recognized that the Civil War was at bottom an economic war, the industrial North against the agrarian

South; and it should be obvious that while the North won the victory for its way of life, it has spent seventy years in throwing the victory away, until now the industrialism for which it stood has come to the end of its resources and threatens to drag the world down in ruins about it. It is with no futile nostalgia that the Southern group turn to the old Southern ways: it is with a far more acute understanding of the modern dilemma than their critics, who are so limited by the narrow purview of our tottering carpet-bag civilization that they can recognize the merit of no solution that does not talk the shallow language of "planning" or the barbaric jargon of Marxism.

Like the Distributists—and, indeed, like the humanists, though they have devoted less attention to economics—the Southern Agrarians are aware that economic problems are really ethical problems, and that ethics are inseparable from philosophy and religion: the approach of both groups is through a rounded view of life. And if both groups, with their widely differing backgrounds, have arrived at essentially similar conclusions as to the only basis on which civilized living and liberty can be maintained, this confirmatory coincidence should lend emphasis to the need for studying their views with care. Two members of the Southern group, John Donald Wade and Donald Davidson, are represented in this issue. We hope to have contributions from others later.

A fourth group on whom *The American Review* hopes to draw are the neo-scholastics, the men who are carrying on the Aristotelico-thomistic tradition in philosophy and applying it to modern problems. It is being increasingly recognized that they are the spokesmen for a body of thought which was far from exhausted by the little which the moderns salvaged from it when summarily rejecting it, and has much of value to contribute to present-day discussions.

These four groups are representative of the general point of view to which *The American Review* is seeking to give composite expression. It will be observed that there are large differences among them, as is true also of others who have not been mentioned: T. S. Eliot, for example, whose position is familiar to most readers; the French writers, Ernest Seillière, Charles Maurras, Léon Daudet, Henri Massis; in England, Wyndham Lewis and Christopher Dawson. All these men, and others less well known who might be mentioned, differ sharply from one another, while at the same time having so much in common that they clearly represent one general direction in contemporary thought. It is one of the main purposes of this review to afford a place where these differences may be threshed out.

It should be added that while *The American Review* aims at providing a forum for the views of these "Radicals of the Right," or "Revolutionary Conservatives," as they might be called, no effort will be made to have every contribution a part of the main program. On the contrary, few issues of the magazine will be lacking in at least one piece that is included on other grounds than its relation to ideas; there will be room as well for pure diversion and for pure scholarship. In regard to the latter, since the limits of length customary in monthlies will be disregarded, the magazine will in part be able to perform the function formerly belonging to the quarterlies; most quarterlies nowadays being indistinguishable from monthlies except by infrequency and bulk. We shall be able to avail ourselves of much good scholarly work that now goes unpublished or is relegated to the small audience of the learned journals.

In forthcoming issues there will be several more articles which, like Mr. Dawson's this month, afford a criticism of Communism. The conversion to Communism of a number of liberals in this country, and some also in England, will receive particular attention. Mr. Goad's survey of the Corporate State is the first of several articles on the inner workings of the present Italian government. The Fascist economics, in particular, which have received scant treatment by our universally liberal and radical press, are badly in need of sympathetic exposition. The rise of Hitler to power in Germany brings up still further aspects of the Fascist question which will be discussed. The scrapping of the parliamentary system in a growing number of European countries, paralleled by the drift toward increasing the power of the President in this country, especially in times of crisis, raises the whole question of the relative worth of monarchy and republicanism. The collapse of our economic system and the at least partial recession from our insanely top-heavy mechanism of production and distribution which must now take place gives pressing actuality to the matter of regionalism and decentralization, of federalism and its alternatives. On these and other political and economic subjects the collaborators of this review have much to say, from a point of view not current in the vast bulk of contemporary organs of opinion. But the essence of that point of view is the need for approaching these practical questions through morals and through philosophy and religion out of which morals grow. It is by discussions in these fields that *The American Review* hopes to make a contribution toward bringing a measure of order and sanity into our national life.

The Revival of Monarchy

In his short period in office President Roosevelt has handled a banking crisis in masterly fashion, and through his agriculture, reforestation, currency, and other measures, has acted vigorously to alleviate distress and to provide industry with the purchasing power it needs to resume movement. It is a relief to see capacity for action after floundering ineptitude. No man of good will but wishes the President well in his efforts; anything that might restore business along the old lines sufficiently to lessen the hideous suffering and demoralization of unemployment must be tried and must be supported by all citizens at whatever cost to their own comfort or their own hopes and plans for the future of our public life.

It is in no captious spirit, therefore, that this piece is written to point out that the relief of unemployment and the stimulation of business along the old lines are not a cure for our ills or even a beginning of such a cure. The only hint of the fundamental changes needed lies in the unusual powers accorded the President by Congress. Already the cry of "dictator" has been raised in the press, both in rejoicing and in alarm. But it should be obvious that the emergency powers granted President Roosevelt bear only the most superficial resemblance to the dictatorships that have flourished in Europe since the War. The purpose of this article is to analyze the significance of the contemporary dictatorships in relation to the conditions out of which they spring; in the hope not only of making our political thinking more realistic, but also of indicating the needed course of action in our practical politics.

It is a commonplace among all but the blindest of commentators on public life in this country and most of the countries of Europe that whatever the *form* of government has been—democratic, monarchical, or aristocratic—the *essence* of government for several generations has been plutocracy: the wealthy have controlled the State, and the State has been governed in the interests of the wealthy. A plutocracy which preserves itself in power for a long time (through a series of happy accidents), which spreads its gains among a large number, and which achieves popular support by inducing the bulk of the citizens to believe that they may rise to be a part of itself, does not cease to be a plutocracy.

The moral background of plutocracy is greed. Plutocracy is the enthronement of the desire for gain. In summarizing the last hundred and fifty years of Western history, truth would far outweigh exaggeration if one were to say that the moral history of the period has been the progressive emancipation of greed; the intellectual history has been chiefly the finding of ever more powerful agencies for greed to utilize (scientific industrialism); the political history has been, in the national field, the usurpation of government by the most successfully greedy, and in the international field, the strife resulting from greed using the forces of the State to feed itself (imperialism). The moral, intellectual, political, legal, and technical structure built up by the dominance of greed is called Capitalism. Its essence is the destruction of private property and liberty by the concentration of wealth and the sources of wealth in the hands of a few, who act blindly in their own interests at the expense of the interests of society as a whole.

These familiar facts are mentioned here only as an introduction to a study of the cure that is shaping itself before our eyes. For that Capitalism is a disease which must be cured, and cured quickly, is obvious. Capitalism was inhuman and repulsive enough in the heyday of its power; in its decline, and especially since it nearly blew itself and all civilization to pieces in the Great War which it caused, it has become intolerable.

What can be done to reform our plutocratic state called Capitalism? In the first place, a plutocracy cannot reform itself. An oligarchical régime which was not at the beginning of its power that rare historical phenomenon, an aristocracy, cannot make itself an aristocracy as its power and popularity wane. Neither the soil nor the seeds of aristocracy are present. Not only is the *aristocratic* solution impossible, but the *democratic* solution as well. The people are powerless to recover the State from a plutocracy. Nor will a plutocracy voluntarily abdicate in favour of its subjects; only an aristocracy would relinquish power when it realized that it had governed unwisely—or would even realize that it had. A plutocracy will grant concessions, punish flagrant offenders among its members, offer bribes, make promises. But it cannot reform itself, and it will not abdicate.

What recourse remains? Besides aristocracy and democracy there is only one from of government monarchy. The only way to conquer a plutocracy is by means of a monarch. There is no other way possible. Nor is any other necessary.

This will doubtless be unfamiliar and unwelcome language to many readers in this great democracy, founded, as we are told, in revolt from the tyranny of a monarch and aspiring to a higher and freer form of government than that of the kings and tyrants of old. What I mean by monarchy will become clearer in the course of this paper, but let me say at once that I am not speaking of hereditary dynasties, of thrones, sceptres, crowns, courts, and the traditional trappings of royalty. I am speaking of the *monarchical principle.*

What is a monarch? A monarch is a man (or woman, or, formally, child) in whom all governmental responsibility of a State is vested; he governs in the interest of the whole State, and in secular matters stands above all individuals and groups in the State. The ultimate sovereignty of the people is symbolized in him and is by him realized in action. In particular the leading function of the monarch, in the words of Hilaire Belloc, "is to protect the weak against the strong, and therefore to prevent the accumulation of wealth in few hands, the corruption of the Courts of Justice and of the sources of public opinion."

It is worth noting that there is no essential conflict between the monarchical principle, however strongly present, and the full expression of the democratic principle. The democratic *form* is only one way of satisfying the democratic spirit. Those who insist on the absolute superiority of monarchy to other forms of government (my concern here is not with absolute merits but with resolving a particular situation) put the case more emphatically: "There is no People unless there be also a King." When we are confronted with plutocracy, such an apophthegm takes on deep meaning. It is quoted from *Monarchy or Money Power,* the recent valuable book by the Scotch author R. McNair Wilson, who is a Royalist (that is, one who is attached not only to the monarchical principle, but also to its hereditary form and to a particular claimant). His whole passage is worth quoting:

> The story of the Middle Ages is the story of the fight for Kingship, in which the Church, no less than the laity, played a part. The object was to establish Kings secured in their office on the one hand by the grace of God, and on the other by the loyalty of the People, so that power might be assured wherewith to curb the intoxication of privilege and the influence of money. It is evident that the People cannot exert power of itself, for, in truth, there is no People unless there be also a King. Peoples without Kings are ever sundered into parties and factions of which the richest inevitably becomes the most powerful. The triumph of the richest is the occasion of the rewarding of its financial backers.

So much by way of definition. Before coming to the heart of my theme, I shall mention the cure for Capitalism called Communism, apropos of the accession to power in Germany of Hitler and the National Socialist German Workers' Party. One would gather from the fantastic lack of proportion of our press—not to say its gullibility and sensationalism— that the most important aspect of the German revolution was the hard- ships suffered by Jews under the new régime. Even if the absurd atrocity stories were all true, the fact would be almost negligible beside an event that shouts aloud in spite of the journalistic silence: the victory of Hitler signifies the end of the Communist threat, *forever*. Wherever Commu- nism grows strong enough to make a Communist revolution a danger, it will be crushed by a Fascist revolution. This was indicated by the advent of Mussolini. It is now proved by Hitler. A Communist revolution in any large country has become an impossibility. Communism as the successor to Capitalism has been eliminated.

To show the truth of this contention, let us glance at the factors that made the Communist revolution successful in Russia. They were four: Lenin, a commander of supreme genius; disorder in Russia on an almost incredible scale, especially in the army; a surprise technique in *coup d'état*—seizure of the technological nerve-centres of the capital before attempting the seats of government; and the almost total absence in Russia of a middle class, the main strength against Communism. Now it is obvious that such a favourable combination of circumstances can never happen again. Even assuming a parallel state of disorder, the other factors would not be present. A strong middle class exists in every other Capitalist country. The surprise technique is public knowledge, and has been check- mated by the Fascist opposition.

Above all, there can never be another Lenin. Not that he was unique in ability; from this point of view there is probably a Lenin in every generation, and he might at any time turn out to be on the side of revolution. But never again could a man of Lenin's intelligence and stature as a statesman accept the Marxian philosophy, and so lead a *Communist* revolution. It was still possible in Russia, in the eighties and nineties, for a first-rate mind to swallow the whole Hegelo-Marxian- materialistic-deterministic-Utopian fantasy. But with each year since, that has become increasingly difficult. The whole structure is fading into a nineteenth-century period-piece, along with Fourierism, Anarchism, and the Single Tax. Its canonization by the Soviet régime will not suffice to save it. Can one imagine the young men of Russia, with youth's natural tendency to scoff, not beginning to look for the laughable aspects of the philosophy which is being stuffed down their throats by high pressure pedagogy? And when one begins to look for the laughable aspects of Hegelo-Marxism, the end has come. Outside Russia the abler Marxians—like Max Eastman in this country and John Strachey in England—find the official doctrines too thick and seek to graft the economic and political parts onto a more palatable philosophy. In other words, Marxianism is disintegrating. No: there can never again be a great Marxian—let alone one of the unimaginable greatness to have been able to cope with the development in Germany leading to the installation of Hitler as Chancellor.

The danger of Hitler to Communism was several years ago appreciated by Trotsky, and in 1930 he began urging on the Comintern the policy of having the German Communists unite with the Social Democrats and strike before it was too late. His pamphlet at the end of 1931, *Germany, the Key to the International Situation*, contains such warnings as these:

> The coming into power of the German "National Socialists" would mean above all the extermination of the flower of the German proletariat, the disruption of its organizations, the extirpation of its belief in itself and its future.... For the immediate, perceptible future, for the next ten or twenty years, a victory of Fascism in Germany would mean a suspension in the development of revolutionary progress, collapse of the Comintern and the triumph of world imperialism in its most heinous and bloodthirsty forms. ... Make haste, worker-Communists, you have very little time left!

Alas, Trotsky in his exile at Prinkipo was imagining himself in Petrograd in 1917, with chaos under the incompetent Republican government, the city full of army deserters, the navy disloyal, and above all with Lenin at his side to make the revolution. His warnings and prophecies sprang from masterly insight. The Communist revolution in Germany—and everywhere else—*has* been put off by twenty years; which means forever. The Third International *has* collapsed. Such paper existence as it preserves it owes to neglecting Trotsky's advice to order the attempt at power in Germany, which it knew would have been lunacy. But the Comintern has not enhanced its prestige by partially reversing itself and calling for a "united front against Fascism" just *after* Hitler's accession had made the whole question academic; one policy was as good as the other, and consistency would have been wiser. But one policy was as *bad* as the other, also. The Trotskyite criticism of the Comintern's decision to consider the Social Democrats merely milder Fascists, and Brüning as bad as Hitler, was entirely justified, as was his warning that that path instead of the "united front" meant disaster. But the Comintern view that Trotsky was merely indulging in disastrous "putschism" was likewise justified. The point is that the question was not one of this policy or that, of a wrong direction and a possible better reversal: *The task itself was hopeless,* and was bound to get the Comintern into a hopeless mess sooner or later. The opposite policy could have brought the same results, the same bitterness, the same irreconcilable factions. When business goes badly the partners fall out. The Communist revolution has been stopped by Fascism. Germany was its one hope among all the Western nations, "the weakest link in the Capitalist chair." Germany has taken the other road.

But the full significance of Hitler is better understood not by contrasting Fascists and Communists, but by examining as a whole the post-War dictatorships. In the pre-War period numerous cures for Capitalism were attempted, the most important of which were these three: the democratic, the humanitarian, and the moral. The democratic cure was the one tried in this country: the transformation of our limited democracy into a radical democracy by the progressive extension of the franchise, in the hope of curbing the destructive power of wealth. By the humanitarian remedy, I mean Marxism, which springs from an exaggerated sympathy for the weak and an exaggerated blaming of the powerful. Its proposal in essence is to reverse the positions of the weak and the powerful: to "expropriate the expropriators." Socialism, as contrasted with Communism, took its "ideology" from Marx, but preferred ballots to insurrection as the road to the revolution. That is, it combined the ineffectuality of democracy with the inhumanity of Marxism. By the moral cure for Capitalism, I mean the effort of the churches, particularly the Catholic Church, to curb the evils of Capitalism by demonstrating and inveighing against the corrupt ethics at their root.

Of these three principal pre-War remedies for Capitalism, only the remedy of Marx has been able to make conspicuous headway. Why? I come back to the thesis of this paper: the only way to abolish a plutocracy is by establishing a monarchy. The chief significance of the Communist revolution is the same as that of the Fascist revolution and the Nazi revolution: the revival of monarchy. After a long interregnum, Europe is returning to its ancestral form of government. For Europe has at length determined to rid itself of Capitalism, the Usurper.

It will doubtless sound paradoxical to point to Karl Marx as the forerunner of a revival of monarchy—and of aristocracy, too, as will appear in a moment. But his permanent reputation will, I think, be owed to just that fact: that he was the first to see clearly that the only cure for Capitalism was monarchy. He was wrong on everything else—horribly wrong. But on that he was right. To be sure, he called it "the dictatorship of the proletariat," and thought of it as the gateway to socialism, which in turn was to melt blissfully into the rosy dawn of the Communist Utopia. His grasp of human nature was in general distorted to the point of being diseased, and he had no capacity for abstract thought. But the central political problem of the modern world did not elude him. As a devoted follower of Marx, Lenin was able to provide the first successful opposition that Capitalism has had, and to set up the first of the New Monarchies which are altering the course of history.

It should be noted that it is just this principle of monarchy in operation, and not the more distinctively Communist doctrines, which accounts for the high esteem in which the "Soviet experiment" has come to be held by so many foreign observers in recent years. There are, to be sure, other factors to account for the much better press obtained by Soviet Russia than by Fascist Italy, where the same monarchical principle is at work. These are the factors wherein Russia imitates all that is worst in our own society: materialism; the worship of science, pseudo-science, and applied science, humanitarianism, feminism, "modern" education, decadence of religion and family; size, hustle, efficiency, and so on. These as well as monarchy arouse admiration for the Communist State.

When one turns to Italy, seeking to learn the nature of the new monarchies, one gradually comes to realize that Mussolini is the most constructive statesman of our age. Not only did he grasp the need of monarchy, but he joined it to a sound moral system. The value of Mussolini's work passes almost totally unrecognized among us, owing to the liberal and radical domination of our press. The liberals are so beclouded by false ideas of liberty that they remember nothing but castor oil and the suppression of free speech—though they conveniently forget such things when they consider Russia. The radicals—and nearly everyone else—can think only in terms of the opposition between Capitalists and Workers; they can conceive no government *above* them both and zealous to protect the rights of all classes. If it is not a workers' government, it must be an exploiters' government, so down with it. They are led to this unreal contrast and hasty dismissal by their false conception of property: by their answering the Capitalist abuse of the rights of property

with their silly but sinister over-simplification, *abolishing* private ownership of productive property. A State which safeguards property can only
be, for them, an exploiting State. If you told them that property was the
essential condition of liberty, and that was why it was safeguarded, they
would laugh. They would never think of studying the experience of
Italians to see from its application what truth there might be in the
doctrine. I am not contending, let me hasten to add, that in Italy justice
is invariably done and property always distributed equitably. I am saying
that while the Communist conquest of a Capitalist State and the governing of it on a monarchical basis was important, the arrival of a monarch
who does not level all before him but takes over a plutocratic State as a
going concern, preserving its assets while correcting its evils, is an event
of far greater importance. Not the least of its importance is the fact that
it can happen again, whereas the Communist revolution cannot. In fact
it has happened again, in Germany.

But notice the new form which monarchy has taken among us on its
rebirth, a form unknown in European civil history. The old monarchs
lost their power, it is generally agreed, because the aristocracy, the body
of assistants which monarchs need, failed them: the aristocracies did not
adapt themselves to the rise of commerce and the middle classes, but
allowed themselves to be thrust aside or absorbed. Perhaps they could
not have done otherwise; in any case they failed the monarchs, and
monarchy declined. Now it is a familiar fact that the New Monarch comes
into power surrounded by a large body of men devoted to their leader,
and like him determined to rule the State in the interests of the whole
people. In other words, the Communist Party is essentially an aristocracy,
as is the Fascist Party and the Nazi Party.

Another specific note of the new monarchy and the new aristocracy is
that they are not hereditary. It is not yet clear how the monarchical
succession will occur, but it is probable that Russia has already provided
the example: when the monarch dies, his cabinet selects his successor.
This hierarchical election of the monarch, it will be noted, is the form of
succession in the Catholic Church. It seems not unlikely that the oldest
and most powerful organization in existence should have developed forms
of government that could be adapted to civil purposes. The aristocracies,
again, will probably resemble the Church in being publicly recruited,
organized chiefly on an hierarchical basis, with individual devotion and
ability recognized by advancement.

But these are mere speculations, thrown out in an attempt to discover what permanent features the new monarchies will have if they remain in power, as seems likely. They are altering and growing from day to day, and have by no means solved all their problems. But it is obvious that they are wrestling with their problems with an energy and freshness not paralleled in any of the older governments. It would not be surprising if Germany, that master of organization and thoroughness, made some contributions of her own. At its beginning the new German régime is essentially similar to the Italian, with perhaps a more determined conquest of plutocracy than Mussolini was able to attempt when he started. Hitler's first attention is rightly being given to restoring agriculture. But he is the first of the New Monarchs to face the awful problem of a heavily industrialized society. His decisions here may well mark, for better or for worse, a turning point in history. But it is too early to predict much of Germany. It is not even sure yet that the Third Reich will not turn out to be rather a revival of Prussianism than an experiment in the New Monarchy.

In another article I hope to discuss the possibility of the spread of the monarchical revival to countries where it is as yet unknown, particularly this country. My purpose here has been to seek a unifying principle in the political convulsions of the post-War period, and to show its relation to the main task of the immediate future: the destruction of Capitalism and the building of a healthier society, a society in which liberty and the family are safeguarded by widespread opportunity for ownership, in which the working of the land is raised to its rightful place as the first and best of industries, in which the fruits of nature and of man's inventiveness can be equitably shared, in which the spiritual and creative sides of life are richly nourished and given full freedom.

Chapter Three

Radical Individualism
The State as Enemy

Albert Jay Nock

If we look beneath the surface of our public affairs, we can discern one fundamental fact, namely: a great redistribution of power between society and the State. This is the fact that interests the student of civilization. He has only a secondary or derived interest in matters like price-fixing, wage-fixing, inflation, political banking, "agricultural adjustment," and similar items of State policy that fill the pages of newspapers and the mouths of publicists and politicians. All these can be run up under one head. They have an immediate and temporary importance, and for this reason they monopolize public attention, but they all come to the same thing; which is, an increase of State power and a corresponding decrease of social power.

It is unfortunately none too well understood that, just as the State has no money of its own, so it has no power of its own. All the power it has what society gives it, plus what it confiscates from time to time on one pretext or another; there is no other source from which State power can be drawn. Therefore every assumption of State power, whether by gift or seizure, leaves society with so much less power; there is never, nor can be, any strengthening of State power without a corresponding and roughly equivalent depletion of social power.

Moreover, it follows that with any exercise of State power, not only the exercise of social power in the same direction but the disposition to exercise it in that direction, tends to dwindle. . . .

Heretofore in this country sudden crises of misfortune have been met

Reprinted from *Our Enemy, The State* (San Francisco: Fox and Wilkes, 1994), public domain, 3–11, 13–14, 18–21, 23–25.

by a mobilization of social power. In fact (except for certain institutional enterprises like the home for the aged, the lunatic-asylum, city-hospital and county-poorhouse), destitution, unemployment, "depression" and similar ills, have been no concern of the State, but have been relieved by the application of social power. Under Mr. Roosevelt, however, the State assumed this function, publicly announcing the doctrine, brand-new in our history, that the State owes its citizens a living. Students of politics, of course, saw in this merely an astute proposal for a prodigious enhancement of State power; merely what, as long ago as 1794, James Madison called "the old trick of turning every contingency into a resource for accumulating force in the government"; and the passage of time has proved that they were right. The effect of this upon the balance between State power and social power is clear, and also its effect of a general indoctrination with the idea that an exercise of social power upon such matters is no longer called for.

It is largely in this way that the progressive conversion of social power into State power becomes acceptable and gets itself accepted. When the Johnstown flood occurred, social power was immediately mobilized and applied with intelligence and vigour. Its abundance, measured by money alone, was so great that when everything was finally put in order, something like a million dollars remained. If such a catastrophe happened now, not only is social power perhaps too depleted for the like exercise, but the general instinct would be to let the State see to it. Not only has social power atrophied to that extent, but the disposition to exercise it in that particular direction has atrophied with it. If the State has made such matters its business, and has confiscated the social power necessary to deal with them, why, let it deal with them. We can get some kind of rough measure of this general atrophy by our own disposition when approached by a beggar. Two years ago we might have been moved to give him something; today we are moved to refer him to the State's relief-agency. The State has said to society, You are either not exercising enough power to meet the emergency, or are exercising it in what I think is an incompetent way, so I shall confiscate your power, and exercise it to suit myself. Hence when a beggar asks us for a quarter, our instinct is to say that the State has already confiscated our quarter for his benefit, and he should go to the State about it.

Every positive intervention that the State makes upon industry and commerce has a similar effect. When the State intervenes to fix wages or prices, or to prescribe the conditions of competition, it virtually tells the enterpriser that he is not exercising social power in the right way, and therefore it proposes to confiscate his power and exercise it according to the State's own judgment of what is best. . . .

The process of converting social power into State power may perhaps be seen at its simplest in cases where the State's intervention is directly competitive. The accumulation of State power in various countries has been so accelerated and diversified within the last twenty years that we now see the State functioning as telegraphist, telephonist, match-pedlar, radio-operator, cannon-founder, railway-builder and owner, railway-operator, wholesale and retail tobacconist, shipbuilder and owner, chief chemist, harbour-maker and dockbuilder, housebuilder, chief educator, newspaper-proprietor, food-purveyor, dealer in insurance, and so on through a long list. It is obvious that private forms of these enterprises must tend to dwindle in proportion as the energy of the State's encroachments on them increases, for the competition of social power with State power is always disadvantaged, since the State can arrange the terms of competition to suit itself, even to the point of outlawing any exercise of social power whatever in the premises; in other words, giving itself a monopoly. Instances of this expedient are common; the one we are probably best acquainted with is the State's monopoly of letter-carrying. Social power is estopped by sheer fiat from application to this form of enterprise, notwithstanding it could carry it on far cheaper, and, in this country at least, far better. The advantages of this monopoly in promoting the State's interests are peculiar. No other, probably, could secure so large and well-distributed a volume of patronage, under the guise of a public service in constant use by so large a number of people; it plants a lieutenant of the State at every country-crossroad. It is by no means a pure coincidence that an administration's chief almoner and whip-at-large is so regularly appointed Postmaster-general.

Thus the State "turns every contingency into a resource" for accumulating power in itself, always at the expense of social power; and with this it develops a habit of acquiescence in the people. New generations appear, each temperamentally adjusted—or as I believe our American glossary now has it, "conditioned"—to new increments of State power, and they tend to take the process of continuous accumulation as quite in order. All the State's institutional voices unite in confirming this tendency; they unite in exhibiting the progressive conversion of social power into State power as something not only quite in order, but even as wholesome and necessary for the public good.

In the United States at the present time, the principal indexes of the increase of State power are three in number. First, the point to which the centralization of State authority has been carried. Practically all the sovereign rights and powers of the smaller political units—all of them that are significant enough to be worth absorbing—have been absorbed by the federal unit; nor is this all. State power has not only been thus concentrated at Washington, but it has been so far concentrated into the hands of the Executive that the existing regime is a regime of personal government. It is nominally republican, but actually monocratic; a curious anomaly, but highly characteristic of a people little gifted with intellectual integrity. Personal government is not exercised here in the same ways as in Italy, Russia, or Germany, for there is as yet no State interest to be served by so doing, but rather the contrary; while in those countries there is. But personal government is always personal government; the mode of its exercise is a matter of immediate political expediency, and is determined entirely by circumstances.

This regime was established by a *coup d'Etat* of a new and unusual kind, practicable only in a rich country. It was effected, not by violence, like Louis-Napoleon's, or by terrorism, like Mussolini's, but by purchase. It therefore presents what might be called an American variant of the *coup d'Etat*. Our national legislature was not suppressed by force of arms, like the French Assembly in 1851, but was bought out of its functions with public money; and as appeared most conspicuously in the elections of November, 1934, the consolidation of the *coup d'Etat* was effected by the same means; the corresponding functions in the smaller units were reduced under the personal control of the Executive. This is a most remarkable phenomenon; possibly nothing quite like it ever took place; and its character and implications deserve the most careful attention.

A second index is supplied by the prodigious extension of the bureaucratic principle that is now observable. This is attested *prima facie* by the number of new boards, bureaux, and commissions set up at Washington in the last two years. They are reported as representing something like 90,000 new employés appointed outside the civil service, and the total of the federal pay-roll in Washington is reported as something over three million dollars per month. This, however, is relatively a small matter. The pressure of centralization has tended powerfully to convert every official and every political aspirant in the smaller units into a venal and complaisant agent of the federal bureaucracy. This presents an interesting parallel with the state of things prevailing in the Roman Empire in the last days of the Flavian dynasty, and afterwards. The rights and practices of local self-government, which were formerly very considerable in the provinces and much more so in the municipalities, were lost by surrender rather than by suppression. The imperial bureaucracy, which up to the second century was comparatively a modest affair, grew rapidly to great size, and local politicians were quick to see the advantage of being on terms with it. They came to Rome with their hats in their hands, as governors, Congressional aspirants and such-like now go to Washington. Their eyes and thoughts were constantly fixed on Rome, because recognition and preferment lay that way; and in their incorrigible sycophancy they became, as Plutarch says, like hypochondriacs who dare not eat or take a bath without consulting their physician.

A third index is seen in the erection of poverty and mendicancy into a permanent political asset. Two years ago, many of our people were in hard straits; to some extent, no doubt, through no fault of their own, though it is now clear that in the popular view of their case, as well as in the political view, the line between the deserving poor and the undeserving poor was not distinctly drawn. Popular feeling ran high at the time, and the prevailing wretchedness was regarded with undiscriminating emotion, as evidence of some general wrong done upon its victims by society at large, rather than as the natural penalty of greed, folly, or actual misdoings; which in large part it was. The State, always instinctively "turning every contingency into a resource" for accelerating the conversion of social power into State power, was quick to take advantage of this state of mind. All that was needed to organize these unfortunates into an invaluable political property was to declare the doctrine that the State owes all its citizens a living; and this was accordingly done. It immediately precipitated an enormous mass of subsidized voting-power, an enormous resource for strengthening the State at the expense of society.

There is an impression that the enhancement of State power which has taken place since 1932 is provisional and temporary, that the corresponding depletion of social power is by way of a kind of emergency-loan, and therefore is not to be scrutinized too closely. There is every probability that this belief is devoid of foundation. No doubt our present regime will be modified in one way and another; indeed, it must be, for the process of consolidation itself requires it. But any essential change would be quite unhistorical, quite without precedent, and is therefore most unlikely; and by an essential change, I mean one that will tend to redistribute actual power between the State and society. In the nature of things, there is no reason why such a change should take place, and every reason why it should not. We shall see various apparent recessions, apparent compromises, but the one thing we may be quite sure of is that none of these will tend to diminish actual State power.

For example, we shall no doubt shortly see the great pressure-group of politically organized poverty and mendicancy subsidized indirectly instead of directly, because State interest can not long keep pace with the hand-over-head disposition of the masses to loot their own Treasury. The method of direct subsidy, or sheer cash-purchase, will therefore in all probability soon give way to the indirect method of what is called "social legislation"; that is, a multiplex system of State-managed pensions, insurances, and indemnities of various kinds. This is an apparent recession, and when it occurs it will no doubt be proclaimed as an actual recession, no doubt accepted as such; but is it? Does it actually tend to diminish State power and increase social power? Obviously not, but quite the opposite. It tends to consolidate firmly this particular fraction of State power, and opens the way to getting an indefinite increment upon it by the mere continuous invention of new courses and developments of State-administered social legislation, which is an extremely simple business. One may add the observation for whatever its evidential value may be worth, that if the effect of progressive social legislation upon the sum-total of State power were unfavourable or even nil, we should hardly have found Prince de Bismarck and the British Liberal politicians of forty years ago going in for anything remotely resembling it.

When, therefore, the inquiring student of civilization has occasion to observe this or any other apparent recession upon any point of our present regime, he may content himself with asking the one question, *What effect has this upon the sum-total of State power?* The answer he gives himself will show conclusively whether the recession is actual or apparent, and this is all he is concerned to know.

There is also an impression that if actual recessions do not come about of themselves, they may be brought about by the expedient of voting one political party out and another one in. This idea rests upon certain assumptions that experience has shown to be unsound; the first one being that the power of the ballot is what republican political theory makes it out to be, and that therefore the electorate has an effective choice in the matter. It is a matter of open and notorious fact that nothing like this is true. Our nominally republican system is actually built on an imperial model, with our professional politicians standing in the place of the praetorian guards; they meet from time to time, decide what can be "got away with," and how, and who is to do it; and the electorate votes according to their prescriptions. Under these conditions it is easy to provide the appearance of any desired concession of State power, without the reality; our history shows innumerable instances of very easy dealing with problems in practical politics much more difficult than that. One may remark in this connexion also the notoriously baseless assumption that party-designations connote principles, and that party-pledges imply performance. Moreover, underlying these assumptions and all others that faith in "political action" contemplates, is the assumption that the interests of the State and the interests of society are, at least theoretically, identical; whereas in theory they are directly opposed, and this opposition invariably declares itself in practice to the precise extent that circumstances permit.

However, without pursuing these matters further at the moment, it is probably enough to observe here that in the nature of things the exercise of personal government, the control of a huge and growing bureaucracy, and the management of an enormous mass of subsidized voting-power, are as agreeable to one stripe of politician as they are to another. Presumably they interest a Republican or a Progressive as much as they do a Democrat, Communist, Farmer-Labourite, Socialist, or whatever a politician may, for electioneering purposes, see fit to call himself. This was demonstrated in the local campaigns of 1934 by the practical attitude of politicians who represented nominal opposition parties. It is now being further demonstrated by the derisible haste that the leaders of the official opposition are making towards what they call "reorganization" of their party. One may well be inattentive to their words; their actions, however, mean simply that the recent accretions of State power are here to stay, and that they are aware of it; and that, such being the case, they are preparing to dispose themselves most advantageously in a contest for their control and management. This is all that "reorganization" of the Republican party means, and all it is meant to mean; and this is in itself quite enough to show that any expectation of an essential change of regime through a change of party-administration is illusory. On the contrary, it is clear that whatever party-competition we shall see hereafter will be on the same terms as heretofore. It will be a competition for control and management, and it would naturally issue in still closer centralization, still further extension of the bureaucratic principle, and still larger concessions to subsidized voting-power. This course would be strictly historical, and is furthermore to be expected as lying in the nature of things, as it so obviously does.

Indeed, it is by this means that the aim of the collectivists seems likeliest to be attained in this country; this aim being the complete extinction of social power through absorption by the State. Their fundamental doctrine was formulated and invested with a quasi-religious sanction by the idealist philosophers of the last century; and among peoples who have accepted it in terms as well as in fact, it is expressed in formulas almost identical with theirs. Thus, for example, when Hitler says that "the State dominates the nation because it alone represents it," he is only putting into loose popular language the formula of Hegel, that "the State is the general substance, whereof individuals are but accidents." Or, again, when Mussolini says, "Everything for the State; nothing outside the State; nothing against the State," he is merely vulgarizing the doctrine of Fichte, that "the State is the superior power, ultimate and beyond appeal, absolutely independent."

It may be in place to remark here the essential identity of the various extant forms of collectivism. The superficial distinctions of Fascism, Bolshevism, Hitlerism, are the concern of journalists and publicists; the serious student sees in them only the one root-idea of a complete conversion of social power into State power. When Hitler and Mussolini invoke a kind of debased and hoodwinking mysticism to aid their acceleration of this process, the student at once recognizes his old friend, the formula of Hegel, that "the State incarnates the Divine Idea upon earth," and he is not hoodwinked. The journalist and the impressionable traveller may make what they will of "the new religion of Bolshevism"; the student contents himself with remarking clearly the exact nature of the process which this inculcation is designed to sanction.

This process—the conversion of social power into State power—has not been carried as far here as it has elsewhere; as it has in Russia, Italy, or Germany, for example. Two things, however, are to be observed. First, that it has gone a long way, at a rate of progress which has of late been greatly accelerated. What has chiefly differentiated its progress here from its progress in other countries is its unspectacular character. Mr. Jefferson wrote in 1823 that there was no danger he dreaded so much as "the consolidation [i.e., centralization] of our government by the noiseless and therefore unalarming instrumentality of the Supreme Court." These words characterize every advance that we have made in State aggrandizement. Each one has been noiseless and therefore unalarming, especially to a people notoriously preoccupied, inattentive, and incurious. Even the *coup d'Etat* of 1932 was noiseless and unalarming. In Russia, Italy, Germany, the *coup d'Etat* was violent and spectacular; it had to be; but here it was neither. Under cover of a nation-wide, State-managed mobilization of inane buffoonery and aimless commotion, it took place in so unspectacular a way that its true nature escaped notice, and even now is not generally understood. . . .

The second thing to be observed is that certain formulas, certain arrangements of words, stand as an obstacle in the way of our perceiving how far the conversion of social power into State power has actually gone. The force of phrase and name distorts the identification of our own actual acceptances and acquiescences. We are accustomed to the rehearsal of certain poetic litanies, and provided their cadence be kept entire, we are indifferent to their correspondence with truth and fact. When Hegel's doctrine of the State, for example, is restated in terms by Hitler and Mussolini, it is distinctly offensive to us, and we congratulate ourselves on our freedom from the "yoke of a dictator's tyranny." No American politician would dream of breaking in on our routine of litanies with anything of the kind. We may imagine, for example, the shock to popular sentiment that would ensue upon Mr. Roosevelt's declaring publicly that "the State embraces everything, and nothing has value outside the State. The State creates right." Yet an American politician, as long as he does not formulate that doctrine in set terms, may go further with it in a practical way than Mussolini has gone, and without trouble or question. Suppose Mr. Roosevelt should defend his regime by publicly reasserting Hegel's dictum that "the State alone possesses rights, because it is the strongest." One can hardly imagine that our public would get that down without a great deal of retching. Yet how far, really, is that doctrine alien to our public's actual acquiescences? Surely not far. . . .

There appears to be a curious difficulty about exercising reflective thought upon the actual nature of an institution into which one was born and one's ancestors were born. One accepts it as one does the atmosphere; one's practical adjustments to it are made by a kind of reflex. One seldom thinks about the air until one notices some change, favourable or unfavourable, and then one's thought about it is special; one thinks about purer air, lighter air, heavier air, not about air. So it is with certain human institutions. We know that they exist, that they affect us in various ways, but we do not ask how they came to exist, or what their original intention was, or what primary function it is that they are actually fulfilling; and when they affect us so unfavourably that we rebel against them, we contemplate substituting nothing beyond some modification or variant of the same institution. Thus colonial America, oppressed by the monarchical State, brings in the republican State; Germany gives up the republican State for the Hitlerian State; Russia exchanges the monocratic State for the collectivist State; Italy exchanges the constitutionalist State for the "totalitarian" State.

It is interesting to observe that in the year 1935 the average individual's incurious attitude towards the phenomenon of the State is precisely what his attitude was towards the phenomenon of the Church in the year, say, 1500. The State was then a very weak institution; the Church was very strong. The individual was born into the Church, as his ancestors had been for generations, in precisely the formal, documented fashion in which he is now born into the State. He was taxed for the Church's support, as he now is for the State's support. He was supposed to accept the official theory and doctrine of the Church, to conform to its discipline, and in a general way to do as it told him; again, precisely the sanctions that the State now lays upon him. If he were reluctant or recalcitrant, the Church made a satisfactory amount of trouble for him, as the State now does. Notwithstanding all this, it does not appear to have occurred to the Church-citizen of that day, any more than it occurs to the State-citizen of the present, to ask what sort of institution it was that claimed his allegiance. There it was; he accepted its own account of itself, took it as it stood, and at its own valuation. Even when he revolted, fifty years later, he merely exchanged one form or mode of the Church for another, the Roman for the Calvinist, Lutheran, Zuinglian, or what not; again, quite as the modern State-citizen exchanges one mode of the State for another. He did not examine the institution itself, nor does the State-citizen today. . . .

It appears to that with the depletion of social power going on at the rate it is, the State-citizen should look very closely into the essential nature of the institution that is bringing it about. He should ask himself whether he has a theory of the State, and if so, whether he can assure himself that history supports it. He will not find this a matter that can be settled offhand; it needs a good deal of investigation, and a stiff exercise of reflective thought. He should ask, in the first place, how the State originated, and why; it must have come about somehow, and for some purpose. This seems an extremely easy question to answer, but he will not find it so. Then he should ask what it is that history exhibits continuously as the State's primary function. Then, whether he finds that "the State" and "government" are strictly synonymous terms; he uses them as such, but are they? Are there any invariable characteristic marks that differentiate the institution of government from the institution of the State? Then finally he should decide whether, by the testimony of history, the State is to be regarded as, in essence, a social or an anti-social institution? . . .

Aristotle, confusing the idea of the State with the idea of government, thought the State originated out of the natural grouping of the family. Other Greek philosophers, labouring under the same confusion, somewhat anticipated Rousseau in finding its origin in the social nature and disposition of the individual; while an opposing school, which held that the individual is naturally anti-social, more or less anticipated Hobbes by finding it in an enforced compromise among the anti-social tendencies of individuals. Another view, implicit in the doctrine of Adam Smith, is that the State originated in the association of certain individuals who showed a marked superiority in the economic virtues of diligence, prudence, and thrift. The idealist philosophers; variously applying Kant's transcendentalism to the problem, came to still different conclusions; and one or two other views, rather less plausible, perhaps, than any of the foregoing, have been advanced.

The root-trouble with all these views is not precisely that they are conjectural, but that they are based on incompetent observation. They miss the invariable characteristic marks that the subject presents; as, for example, until quite lately, all views of the origin of malaria missed the invariable ministrations of the mosquito, or as opinions about the bubonic plague missed the invariable mark of the rat-parasite. It is only within the last half-century that the historical method has been applied to the problem of the State. This method runs back the phenomenon of the State to its first appearance in documented history, observing its invariable characteristic marks, and drawing inferences as indicated. There are so many clear intimations of this method in earlier writers— one finds them as far back as Strabo—that one wonders why its systematic application was so long deferred; but in all such cases, as with malaria and typhus, when the characteristic mark is once determined, it is so obvious that one always wonders why it was so long unnoticed. Perhaps in the case of the State, the best one can say is that the cooperation of the *Zeitgeist* was necessary, and that it could be had no sooner.

The positive testimony of history is that the State invariably had its origin in conquest and confiscation. No primitive State known to history originated in any other manner. On the negative side, it has been proved beyond peradventure that no primitive State could possibly have had any other origin. Moreover, the sole invariable characteristic of the State is the economic exploitation of one class by another. In this sense, every State known to history is a class-State. Oppenheimer defines the State, in respect of its origin, as an institution "forced on a defeated group by a conquering group, with a view only to systematizing the domination of the conquered by the conquerors, and safeguarding itself against insurrection from within and attack from without. This domination had no other final purpose than the economic exploitation of the conquered group by the victorious group."

An American statesman, John Jay, accomplished the respectable feat of compressing the whole doctrine of conquest into a single sentence. "Nations in general," he said, "will go to war whenever there is a prospect of getting something by it." Any considerable economic accumulation, or any considerable body of natural resources, is an incentive to conquest. The primitive technique was that of raiding the coveted possessions, appropriating them entirely, and either exterminating the possessors, or dispersing them beyond convenient reach. Very early, however, it was seen to be in general more profitable to reduce the possessors to dependence, and use them as labour-motors; and the primitive technique was accordingly modified. Under special circumstances, where this exploitation was either impracticable or unprofitable, the primitive technique is even now occasionally revived, as by the Spaniards in South America, or by ourselves against the Indians. But these circumstances are exceptional; the modified technique has been in use almost from the beginning, and everywhere its first appearance marks the origin of the State. . . .

Everywhere we find the political organization proceeding from the same origin, and presenting the same mark of intention, namely: the economic exploitation of a defeated group by a conquering group.

Everywhere, that is, with but the one significant exception. Wherever economic exploitation has been for any reason either impracticable or unprofitable, the State has never come into existence; government has existed, but the State, never. The American hunting tribes, for example, whose organization so puzzled our observers, never formed a State, for there is no way to reduce a hunter to economic dependence and make him hunt for you. Conquest and confiscation were no doubt practicable, but no economic gain would be got by it, for confiscation would give the aggressors but little beyond what they already had; the most that could come of it would be the satisfaction of some sort of feud. For like reasons primitive peasants never formed a State. The economic accumulations of their neighbours were too slight and too perishable to be interesting; and especially with the abundance of free land about, the enslavement of their neighbours would be impracticable, if only for the police-problems involved.

It may now be easily seen how great the difference is between the institution of government, as understood by Paine and the Declaration of Independence, and the institution of the State. . . .

Based on the idea of natural rights, government secures those rights to the individual by strictly negative intervention, making justice costless and easy of access; and beyond that it does not go. The State, on the other hand, both in its genesis and by its primary intention, is purely anti-social. It is not based on the idea of natural rights, but on the idea that the individual has no rights except those that the State may provisionally grant him. It has always made justice costly and difficult of access, and has invariably held itself above justice and common morality whenever it could advantage itself by so doing. So far from encouraging a wholesome development of social power, it has invariably, as Madison said, turned every contingency into a resource for depleting social power and enhancing State power. As Dr. Sigmund Freud has observed, it can not even be said that the State has ever shown any disposition to suppress crime, but only to safeguard its own monopoly of crime. In Russia and Germany, for example, we have lately seen the State moving with great alacrity against infringement of its monopoly by private persons, while at the same time exercising that monopoly with unconscionable ruthlessness. Taking the State wherever found, striking into its history at any point, one sees no way to differentiate the activities of its founders, administrators, and beneficiaries from those of a professional-criminal class.

*

Such are the antecedents of the institution which is everywhere now so busily converting social power by wholesale into State power. The recognition of them goes a long way towards resolving most, if not all, of the apparent anomalies which the conduct of the modern State exhibits. It is of great help, for example, in accounting for the open and notorious fact that the State always moves slowly and grudgingly towards any purpose that accrues to society's advantage, but moves rapidly and with alacrity towards one that accrues to its own advantage; nor does it ever move towards social purposes on its own initiative, but only under heavy pressure, while its motion towards anti-social purposes is self-sprung. . . .

Thus the individual's sense of his own importance inclines him strongly to resent the suggestion that the State is by nature anti-social. He looks on its failures and misfeasances with somewhat the eye of a parent, giving it the benefit of a special code of ethics. Moreover, he has always the expectation that the State will learn by its mistakes, and do better. Granting that its technique with social purposes is blundering, wasteful, and vicious . . . he sees no reason why, with an increase of experience and responsibility, the State should not improve.

Something like this appears to be the basic assumption of collectivism. Let but the State confiscate *all* social power, and its interests will become identical with those of society. Granting that the State is of anti-social origin, and that it has borne a uniformly anti-social character throughout its history, let it but extinguish social power completely, and its character will change; it will merge with society, and thereby become society's efficient and disinterested organ. The historic State, in short, will disappear, and government only will remain. It is an attractive idea; the hope of its being somehow translated into practice is what, only so few years ago, made "the Russian experiment" so irresistibly fascinating to generous spirits who felt themselves hopelessly State-ridden. A closer examination of the State's activities, however, will show that this idea, attractive though it be, goes to pieces against the iron law of fundamental economics, that *man tends always to satisfy his needs and desires with the least possible exertion.* Let us see how this is so.

There are two methods, or means, and only two, whereby man's needs and desires can be satisfied. One is the production and exchange of wealth; this is the *economic means.* The other is the uncompensated appropriation of wealth produced by others; this is the *political means.*

The primitive exercise of the political means was, as we have seen, by conquest, confiscation, expropriation, and the introduction of a slave-economy. The conqueror parcelled out the conquered territory among beneficiaries, who thenceforth satisfied their needs and desires by exploiting the labour of the enslaved inhabitants. The feudal State, and the merchant-State, wherever found, merely took over and developed successively the heritage of character, intention, and apparatus of exploitation which the primitive State transmitted to them; they are in essence merely higher integrations of the primitive State.

The State, then, whether primitive, feudal, or merchant, is *the organization of the political means*. Now since man tends always to satisfy his needs and desires with the least possible exertion, he will employ the political means whenever he can—exclusively, if possible; otherwise, in association with the economic means. He will, at the present time, that is, have recourse to the State's modern apparatus of exploitation; the apparatus of tariffs, concessions, rent-monopoly, and the like. It is a matter of the commonest observation that this is his first instinct. So long, therefore, as the organization of the political means is available— so long as the highly centralized bureaucratic State stands as primarily a distributor of economic advantage, an arbiter of exploitation, so long will that instinct effectively declare itself. A proletarian State would merely, like the merchant-State, shift the incidence of exploitation, and there is no historic ground for the presumption that a collectivist State would be in any essential respect unlike its predecessors; as we are beginning to see, "the Russian experiment" has amounted to the erection of a highly centralized bureaucratic State upon the ruins of another, leaving the entire apparatus of exploitation intact and ready for use. Hence, in view of the law of fundamental economics just cited, the expectation that collectivism will appreciably alter the essential character of the State appears illusory.

Thus the findings arrived at by the historical method amply support the immense body of practical considerations brought forward by Spencer against the State's inroads upon social power. When Spencer concludes that "in State-organizations, corruption is unavoidable," the historical method abundantly shows cause why, in the nature of things, this should be expected—*vilescit origine tali*. When Freud comments on the shocking disparity between State-ethics and private ethics—and his observations on this point are most profound and searching—the historical method at once supplies the best of reasons why that disparity should be looked for. When Ortega y Gasset says that "Statism is the higher form taken by violence and direct action, when these are set up as standards," the historical method enables us to perceive at once that his definition is precisely that which one would make *a priori*.

The historical method, moreover, establishes the important fact that, as in the case of tabetic or parasitic diseases, the depletion of social power by the State can not be checked after a certain point of progress is passed. History does not show an instance where, once beyond this point, this depletion has not ended in complete and permanent collapse. In some cases, disintegration is slow and painful. Death set its mark on Rome at the end of the second century, but she dragged out a pitiable existence for some time after the Antonines. Athens, on the other hand, collapses quickly. Some authorities think that Europe is dangerously near that point, if not already past it; but contemporary conjecture is probably without much value. That point may have been reached in America, and it may not; again, certainty is unattainable—plausible arguments may be made either way. Of two things, however, we may be certain: the first is, that the rate of America's approach to that point is being prodigiously accelerated; and the second is, that there is no evidence of any disposition to retard it, or any intelligent apprehension of the danger which that acceleration betokens.

Chapter Four

Conservatism Takes Shape
Human Events

It is proposed, on the basis or interest already demonstrated, shortly to begin distribution of a weekly analysis under the above title. This will examine and interpret those international developments which, while wholly beyond the control of our own electorate, are nevertheless holding the future of this Republic and of all its citizens.

There is increasing need for intelligent, coordinated, and continuous consideration of the international scene in relation to those principles and ideals which alone justified the establishment of the United States. Within a quarter century we have been a reluctant and unhappy participant in two world wars. How this could happen is today of loss importance than the absolute necessity that a really constructive peace should follow the ruin and slaughter of the present conflict.

The effect on the United States of two such dislocations in a single generation has been to distort and impoverish our national life without as yet substituting promise of the development of that world community which military victory alone cannot secure. It is realization that we are making our birthright to gain nothing but disillusion which accounts for the growing anxiety of all who have the American tradition and American ideals at heart.

On the one hand, a domestic counterpart of National Socialism is already affecting the freedom of the individual and the vitality of local self-government. On the other hand, a parallel trend towards permanent military alliances threatens to destroy that political independence which in the past encouraged our friendship with all nations and assured that we should bear malice towards none.

Felix Morley, January 1, 1944. Felix Morley Papers, Box 50. Name and Subject Series II (Human Events, Corr. and Minutes), Herbert Hoover Presidential Library, West Branch, Iowa. Reprinted by permission.

True Liberalism will survive neither subordination to a despotic bureaucracy at home, not entanglement in any Balance of Power system
directed from abroad by those over whom American public opinion has
no control.

The present political, social, and economic strains will not be resolved—
they will on the contrary be intensified—if the unconditional surrender
of our present enemies finds the United States implicated in unauthor-
ized, unpredictable, and unlimited military commitments in every quarter
of the globe.

The vast material strength of this country is not directed by the specialized training which has enabled Great Britain to develop and retain
her far-flung Empire. Nor does the overlordship of subject peoples appeal
to Americans as a desirable national ambition. Equally at variance with
American ideals is that ruthless regimentation of the individual whereby
Russia bide fair to become dominant from the Atlantic to the China Sea.

Indeed, all forms of imperial rule, whether Fascist, Communist, or
Capitalist, are inherently antagonistic to that principle of government of
the people, by the people, and for the people to which America gives
allegiance.

The isolationism which most seriously threatens the United States
today is the increasing disregard of that political philosophy which
prompted the establishment and insured the development of this Nation.
It is this type of isolationism which is causing surrender of our basic
concepts in favor of a party line laid down for some in London, for others
in Moscow. The abandonment of a great tradition is illustrated by the
substitution of blundering uncertainty for the constructive leadership
which springs from fidelity to dynamic ideals.

It seems, therefore, high time for careful, objective, and continuous
examination of America's place in the post-war world, undertaken primarily from the viewpoint of the essential American tradition. It is high
time for America to develop broader international understanding, and to
exercise moral leadership in accordance with the principles which have
made us great. But it is also preeminently a time for rededication to our
own neglected creed. If this is lost then we, as a people, will have nothing
but hollow material power to contribute to post-war settlement. And
physical strength alone has never been able yet to construct, far less
maintain, a lasting peace.

"Human Events" takes its title from that part of the Declaration of
Independence which asserts that it was proper for the American people

"to assume, among the powers of the earth" a "separate and equal station." No apologies, therefore, will be offered for studying the course of those events from a distinctly American viewpoint. This does not mean a narrowly nationalistic approach. It does involve the underlying conviction that the development of Man as an individual is more important than the furtherance of totalitarian trends.

The growing threat to our national heritage is the more insidious because it comes to a large extent from within. That danger, at least, can be countered by a careful consideration and interpretation of events from the viewpoint of the average well-disposed American. His natural inclination towards Faith and Hope is, unfortunately, at present almost entirely subordinated to an interpretation which continuously emphasizes Fear and Hate.

"Human Events" will consciously seek to emphasize that Appeal to Reason, tempered by Good Will, which is necessary for both social and individual security. This policy involves the reporting of facts which newspapers overlook. It involves equally the delineation of historical and philosophic background in order to focus the permanent as opposed to the transitory significance of what transpires.

The effort will be thorough. There will be no smart predictions or snap judgments. Only one subject will be treated in each issue. But this correspondence may be filed for reference with assurance that the passage of time will not quickly destroy its validity and with certainty that in later years the opinions currently expressed will never be classifiable as vindictive, misleading, or deliberately propagandistic.

"Human Events" will above all attempt, in the present crisis, to forward unity and understanding for the preservation and development of American ideals, in behalf of human rather than national aggrandizement. It will seek to determine whether this country, in this 168th year of national independence, remains spiritually a nation "dedicated to the proposition that all men are created equal."

Your interest and cooperation are solicited. A sample copy and a trial subscription blank are enclosed.

Part II

Classical Liberalism

•

The Great Depression seemed to confirm, for many economists, the necessity for governmental intervention. With capitalist economies reeling; with unemployment reaching heretofore unheard of levels—as high as 25 percent nationally in 1933, and for some industrial cities like Chicago and Toledo, as high as 70 percent; with the American people in wanton need of relief; only governmental intervention, it was thought, could cure the economic ailments plaguing the nation, and the world. Such intervention, we now know, cured little. While government provided stability to a broken system, a modicum of recovery, and reform—such as Social Security and backing of labor rights—only World War II brought full economic recovery, and that came only as a result of economic planning, wage and price controls, and governmental intervention that made the New Deal look positively laissez-faire.

"War is the health of the State." Critics of war, like Randolph Bourne, have consistently maintained this fundamentally well understood axiom: during wartime, the State grows and accumulates powers it finds difficult to gain in peacetime. In America, a well-developed antistatist tradition going back to anti-Federalist hostility to the Constitution—culminating with the Bill of Rights—prevented the central State from ever becoming too powerful.[1] America's long tradition of nonintervention in the affairs of European nations, and a century of relative European peace after 1815, kept American involvement in foreign wars to a minimum; few American lives were lost in grand campaigns abroad.

The two world wars marked a fundamental departure from this tradition. Modern warfare necessitated a mobilized citizenry; technological changes produced barbarous conflicts which needed direction from a centralized governmental authority. Ideologies like fascism and communism challenged ideals of liberty both at home and abroad, necessitating a more interventionist foreign policy based on doctrines of continued preparedness. Pearl Harbor had caught America off guard; in the post–

World War II nuclear era, such unpreparedness would mean national suicide.

Conservatives, hostile to grand crusades abroad, redirected their energy after World War II to embrace the Cold War against communism. But they also fought against growing state power at home, believing that such an expansion threatened individual liberty and represented a turn toward a planned economy and socialism. Classical liberal economist F. A. Hayek (1899–1992) best represented this view in *The Road to Serfdom*, published in 1944. Hayek wrote his treatise as a warning to England and America about the dangers of state planning. "It is necessary now to state the unpalatable truth that it is Germany whose fate we are in some danger of repeating," Hayek wrote alarmingly.[2] How could England and America, in the midst of defeating Hitler's Germany, be replicating just such a tyranny?

For Hayek, the threat lay in the embrace of state planning. Writing in wartime England, Hayek saw ominous signs of a desire for state planning after the war's end, symbolized by the British Labour Party's calls for nationalization of vital industries like steel, coal mining, and railroads. Such policies, enacted in the Soviet Union and in Nazi Germany, led to diminished individual liberty and an end to the free market. These traditions, vital to civilization, were threatened by the increase in state power which occurred during the war.

Frustrated by his inability to affect politics, Hayek and other like-minded classical liberal economists, philosophers, and journalists, formed the Mont Pelerin Society in 1947, named after the Swiss resort where the first meeting took place. The Society provided a haven for free-market economists, conducting intense seminars where disputes (often) erupted among the participants.[3] Aside from Hayek, Austrian economist Ludwig Van Mises, the author of a massive work on socialism and one of the leading theorists of the Austrian school of economics, was a member.[4] So also were future Nobel Prize-winning economists like George Stigler, Gary Becker, and Milton Friedman. The latter trio possessed a common university address in Chicago and founded the "Chicago school" addressing economic problems through free-market alternatives, rather than statism.

The most impressive member of the Chicago school was Milton Friedman (1912–). Friedman gained notoriety for his theoretical work in price theory and in developing a school of economic thought known as monetarism. The monetarists, with their emphasis on fiscal policy and free-market economics as solutions to the perennial problem of governmental financing and public policy, would eventually challenge, but not displace, the ruling Keynesian consensus on postwar economic thought.[5] Much like Hayek, Friedman became more famous for his contributions to public policy and ruminations on political philosophy. Especially important is the lengthy excerpt included in this reader from *Capitalism and Freedom* (1962), taken from a series of lectures Friedman had given in 1956 at Wabash College in Indiana.

Capitalism and Freedom catapulted Friedman into celebrity consciousness, even though the book was not widely reviewed. Friedman's belief in individual freedom as "the prime objective of social arrangements," and his insistence that capitalism acted as the social system most conducive to the promotion of such freedom, gave Friedman a wide popular audience for his work. It is a classic statement concerning the limitation of governmental power and in particular profoundly affected young conservatives beginning to organize conservative clubs on college campuses.[6] The book sold over 400,000 copies and gave Friedman opportunities to expound on his philosophy in a long-running column in *Newsweek*.[7] In 1976, Friedman received the Nobel Prize for economics and in 1978 was invited to develop a television program, entitled *Free To Choose*, that aired in ten installments to millions of viewers on the Public Broadcasting Service (the book accompanying the program was translated into seventeen languages and the program has aired in many countries, including Russia). Such a philosophy, combined with his work in theoretical economics and as an advisor to presidents and governments, has contributed to Friedman's status as an apostle for individual freedom and capitalism, and assured his stature as one of the preeminent economists of the modern age.

Chapter Five

Resurrecting the Abandoned Road

F. A. Hayek

Contemporary events differ from history in that we do not know the results they will produce. Looking back, we can assess the significance of past occurrences and trace the consequences they have brought in their train. But while history runs its course, it is not history to us. It leads us into an unknown land, and but rarely can we get a glimpse of what lies ahead. It would be different if it were given to us to live a second time through the same events with all the knowledge of what we have seen before. How different would things appear to us; how important and often alarming would changes seem that we now scarcely notice! It is probably fortunate that man can never have this experience and knows of no laws which history must obey.

Yet, although history never quite repeats itself, and just because no development is inevitable, we can in a measure learn from the past to avoid a repetition of the same process. One need not be a prophet to be aware of impending dangers. An accidental combination of experience and interest will often reveal events to one man under aspects which few yet see.

The following pages are the product of an experience as near as possible to twice living through the same period—or at least twice watching a very similar evolution of ideas. While this is an experience one is not likely to gain in one country, it may in certain circumstances be acquired by living in turn for long periods in different countries. Though the influences to which the trend of thought is subject in most civilized

F. A. Hayek, *The Road to Serfdom* (Chicago: University of Chicago Press, 1994 ed.), 3–9, 13–14, 15–25. Reprinted by permission of University of Chicago Press and Estate of F. A. Hayek.

nations are to a large extent similar, they do not necessarily operate at the same time or at the same speed. Thus, by moving from one country to another, one may sometimes twice watch similar phases of intellectual development. The senses have then become peculiarly acute. When one hears for a second time opinions expressed or measures advocated which one has first met twenty or twenty-five years ago, they assume a new meaning as symptoms of a definite trend. They suggest, if not the necessity, at least the probability, that developments will take a similar course.

It is necessary now to state the unpalatable truth that it is Germany whose fate we are in some danger of repeating. The danger is not immediate, it is true, and conditions in England and the United States are still so remote from those witnessed in recent years in Germany as to make it difficult to believe that we are moving in the same direction. Yet, though the road be long, it is one on which it becomes more difficult to turn back as one advances. If in the long run we are the makers of our own fate, in the short run we are the captives of the ideas we have created. Only if we recognize the danger in time can we hope to avert it.

It is not to the Germany of Hitler, the Germany of the present war, that England and the United States bear yet any resemblance. But students of the currents of ideas can hardly fail to see that there is more than a superficial similarity between the trend of thought in Germany during and after the last war and the present current of ideas in the democracies. There exists now in these countries certainly the same determination that the organization of the nation which has been achieved for purposes of defense shall be retained for the purposes of creation. There is the same contempt for nineteenth-century liberalism, the same spurious "realism" and even cynicism, the same fatalistic acceptance of "inevitable trends." And at least nine out of every ten of the lessons which our most vociferous reformers are so anxious we should learn from this war are precisely the lessons which the Germans did learn from the last war and which have done much to produce the Nazi system. There are a large number of other points where at an interval of fifteen to twenty-five years we seem to follow the example of Germany. Although one does not like to be reminded, it is not so many years since the socialist policy of that country was generally held up by progressives as an example to be imitated, just as in more recent years Sweden has been the model country to which progressive eyes were directed. All those whose memory goes further back know how deeply for at least a generation before the last war

German thought and German practice influenced ideals and policy in England and, to some extent, in the United States.

The author has spent about half of his adult life in his native Austria, in close touch with German intellectual life, and the other half in the United States and England. In the latter period he has become increasingly convinced that at least some of the forces which have destroyed freedom in Germany are also at work here and that the character and the source of this danger are, if possible, even less understood than they were in Germany. The supreme tragedy is still not seen that in Germany it was largely people of good will, men who were admired and held up as models in the democratic countries, who prepared the way for, if they did not actually create, the forces which now stand for everything they detest. Yet our chance of averting a similar fate depends on our facing the danger and on our being prepared to revise even our most cherished hopes and ambitions if they should prove to be the source of the danger. There are few signs yet that we have the intellectual courage to admit to ourselves that we may have been wrong. Few are ready to recognize that the rise of fascism and naziism was not a reaction against the socialist trends of the preceding period but a necessary outcome of those tendencies. This is a truth which most people were unwilling to see even when the similarities of many of the repellent features of the internal regimes in communist Russia and National Socialist Germany were widely recognized. As a result, many who think themselves infinitely superior to the aberrations of naziism, and sincerely hate all its manifestations, work at the same time for ideals whose realization would lead straight to the abhorred tyranny.

All parallels between developments in different countries are, of course, deceptive; but I am not basing my argument mainly on such parallels. Nor am I arguing that these developments are inevitable. If they were, there would be no point in writing this. They can be prevented if people realize in time where their efforts may lead. But until recently there was little hope that any attempt to make them see the danger would be successful. It seems, however, as if the time were now ripe for a fuller discussion of the whole issue. Not only is the problem now more widely recognized; there are also special reasons which at this juncture make it imperative that we should face the issues squarely.

It will, perhaps, be said that this is not the time to raise an issue on which opinions clash sharply. But the socialism of which we speak is not a party matter, and the questions which we are discussing have little to do with the questions at dispute between political parties. It does not affect our problem that some groups may want less socialism than others; that some want socialism mainly in the interest of one group and others in that of another. The important point is that, if we take the people whose views influence developments, they are now in the democracies in some measure all socialists. If it is no longer fashionable to emphasize that "we are all socialists now," this is so merely because the fact is too obvious. Scarcely anybody doubts that we must continue to move toward socialism, and most people are merely trying to deflect this movement in the interest of a particular class or group.

It is because nearly everybody wants it that we are moving in this direction. There are no objective facts which make it inevitable. . . . The main question is where this movement will lead us. Is it not possible that if the people whose convictions now give it an irresistible momentum began to see what only a few yet apprehend, they would recoil in horror and abandon the quest which for half a century has engaged so many people of good will? Where these common beliefs of our generation will lead us is a problem not for one party but for every one of us—a problem of the most momentous significance. Is there a greater tragedy imaginable than that, in our endeavor consciously to shape our future in accordance with high ideals, we should in fact unwittingly produce the very opposite of what we have been striving for?

There is an even more pressing reason why at this time we should seriously endeavor to understand the forces which have created National Socialism: that this will enable us to understand our enemy and the issue at stake between us. It cannot be denied that there is yet little recognition of the positive ideals for which we are fighting. We know that we are fighting for freedom to shape our life according to our own ideas. That is a great deal, but not enough. It is not enough to give us the firm beliefs which we need to resist an enemy who uses propaganda as one of his main weapons not only in the most blatant but also in the most subtle forms. It is still more insufficient when we have to counter this propaganda among the people in the countries under his control and elsewhere, where the effect of this propaganda will not disappear with the defeat of the Axis powers. It is not enough if we are to show to others that what we are fighting for is worth their support, and it is not enough to guide us in the building of a new world safe against the dangers to which the old one has succumbed.

It is a lamentable fact that the democracies in their dealings with the dictators before the war, not less than in their attempts at propaganda and in the discussion of their war aims, have shown an inner insecurity and uncertainty of aim which can be explained only by confusion about their own ideals and the nature of the differences which separated them from the enemy. We have been misled as much because we have refused to believe that the enemy was sincere in the profession of some beliefs which we shared as because we believed in the sincerity of some of his other claims. Have not the parties of the Left as well as those of the Right been deceived by believing that the National Socialist party was in the service of the capitalists and opposed to all forms of socialism? How many features of Hitler's system have not been recommended to us for imitation from the most unexpected quarters, unaware that they are an integral part of that system and incompatible with the free society we hope to preserve? The number of dangerous mistakes we have made before and since the outbreak of war because we do not understand the opponent with whom we are faced is appalling. It seems almost as if we did not want to understand the development which has produced totalitarianism because such an understanding might destroy some of the dearest illusions to which we are determined to cling. . . .

When the course of civilization takes an unexpected turn—when, instead of the continuous progress which we have come to expect, we find ourselves threatened by evils associated by us with past ages of barbarism—we naturally blame anything but ourselves. Have we not all striven according to our best lights, and have not many of our finest minds incessantly worked to make this a better world? Have not all our efforts and hopes been directed toward greater freedom, justice, and prosperity? If the outcome is so different from our aims—if, instead of freedom and prosperity, bondage and misery stare us in the face—is it not clear that sinister forces must have foiled our intentions, that we are the victims of some evil power which must be conquered before we can resume the road to better things? However much we may differ when we name the culprit—whether it is the wicked capitalist or the vicious spirit of a particular nation, the stupidity of our elders, or a social system not yet, although we have struggled against it for a half a century, fully overthrown—we all are, or at least were until recently, certain of one thing: that the leading ideas which during the last generation have become common to most people of good will and have determined the major changes in our social life cannot have been wrong. We are ready to accept almost any explanation of the present crisis of our civilization except one: that the present state of the world may be the result of genuine error on our own part and that the pursuit of some of our most cherished ideals has apparently produced results utterly different from those which we expected.

While all our energies are directed to bring this war to a victorious conclusion, it is sometimes difficult to remember that even before the war the values for which we are now fighting were threatened here and destroyed elsewhere. Though for the time being the different ideals are represented by hostile nations fighting for their existence, we must not forget that this conflict has grown out of a struggle of ideas within what, not so long ago, was a common European civilization and that the tendencies which have culminated in the creation of the totalitarian systems were not confined to the countries which have succumbed to them. Though the first task must now be to win the war, to win it will only gain us another opportunity to face the basic problems and to find a way of averting the fate which has overtaken kindred civilizations.

Now, it is somewhat difficult to think of Germany and Italy, or of Russia, not as different worlds but as products of a development of thought in which we have shared; it is, at least so far as our enemies are concerned, easier and more comforting to think that they are entirely different from us and that what happened there cannot happen here. Yet the history of these countries in the years before the rise of the totalitarian system showed few features with which we are not familiar. The external conflict is a result of a transformation of European thought in which others have moved so much faster as to bring them into irreconcilable conflict with our ideals, but which has not left us unaffected.

That a change of ideas and the force of human will have made the world what it is now, though men did not foresee the results, and that no spontaneous change in the facts obliged us thus to adapt our thought is perhaps particularly difficult for the Anglo-Saxon nations to see, just because in this development they have, fortunately for them, lagged behind most of the European peoples. We still think of the ideals which guide us, and have guided us for the past generation, as ideals only to be realized in the future and are not aware how far in the last twenty-five years they have already transformed not only the world but also our own countries. We still believe that until quite recently we were governed by what are vaguely called nineteenth-century ideas or the principle of laissez faire. Compared with some other countries, and from the point of view of those impatient to speed up the change, there may be some justification for such belief. But although until 1931 England and America had followed only slowly on the path on which others had led, even by then they had moved so far that only those whose memory goes back to the years before the last war know what a liberal world has been like.

The crucial point of which our people are still so little aware is, however, not merely the magnitude of the changes which have taken place during the last generation but the fact that they mean a complete change in the direction of the evolution of our ideas and social order. For at least twenty-five years before the specter of totalitarianism became a real threat, we had progressively been moving away from the basic ideas on which Western civilization has been built. That this movement on which we have entered with such high hopes and ambitions should have brought us face to face with the totalitarian horror has come as a profound shock to this generation, which still refuses to connect the two facts. Yet this development merely confirms the warnings of the fathers of the liberal philosophy which we still profess. We have progressively abandoned that freedom in economic affairs without which personal and political freedom has never existed in the past. Although we had been warned by some of the greatest political thinkers of the nineteenth century, by De Tocqueville and Lord Acton, that socialism means slavery, we have steadily moved in the direction of socialism. And now that we have seen a new form of slavery arise before our eyes, we have so completely forgotten the warning that it scarcely occurs to us that the two things may be connected.

How sharp a break not only with the recent past but with the whole evolution of Western civilization the modern trend toward socialism means becomes clear if we consider it not merely against the background of the nineteenth century but in a longer historical perspective. We are rapidly abandoning not the views merely of Cobden and Bright, of Adam Smith and Hume, or even of Locke and Milton, but one of the salient characteristics of Western civilization as it has grown from the foundations laid by Christianity and the Greeks and Romans. Not merely nineteenth- and eighteenth-century liberalism, but the basic individualism inherited by us from Erasmus and Montaigne, from Cicero and Tacitus, Pericles and Thucydides, is progressively relinquished.

The Nazi leader who described the National Socialist revolution as a counter-Renaissance spoke more truly than he probably knew. It was the decisive step in the destruction of that civilization which modern man had built up from the age of the Renaissance and which was, above all, an individualist civilization. Individualism has a bad name today, and the term has come to be connected with egotism and selfishness. But the individualism of which we speak in contrast to socialism and all other forms of collectivism has no necessary connection with these. Only gradually shall we be able to make clear the contrast between the two opposing principles. But the essential features of that individualism which, from elements provided by Christianity and the philosophy of classical antiquity, was first fully developed during the Renaissance and has since grown and spread into what we know as Western civilization— are the respect for the individual man *qua* man, that is, the recognition of his own views and tastes as supreme in his own sphere, however narrowly that may be circumscribed, and the belief that it is desirable that men should develop their own individual gifts and bents. "Freedom" and "liberty" are now words so worn with use and abuse that one must hesitate to employ them to express the ideals for which they stood during that period. "Tolerance" is, perhaps the only word which still preserves the full meaning of the principle which during the whole of this period was in the ascendant and which only in recent times has again been in decline, to disappear completely with the rise of the totalitarian state.

The gradual transformation of a rigidly organized hierarchic system into one where men could at least attempt to shape their own life, where man gained the opportunity of knowing and choosing between different forms of life, is closely associated with the growth of commerce. From the commercial cities of northern Italy the new view of life spread with commerce to the west and north, through France and the southwest of Germany to the Low Countries and the British Isles, taking firm root wherever there was no despotic political power to stifle it. In the Low Countries and Britain it for a long time enjoyed its fullest development and for the first time had an opportunity to grow freely and to become the foundation of the social and political life of these countries. And it was from there that in the late seventeenth and eighteenth centuries it again began to spread in a more fully developed form to the West and East, to the New World and to the center of the European continent, where devastating wars and political oppression had largely submerged the earlier beginnings of a similar growth.

During the whole of this modern period of European history the general direction of social development was one of freeing the individual from the ties which had bound him to the customary or prescribed ways in the pursuit of his ordinary activities. The conscious realization that the spontaneous and uncontrolled efforts of individuals were capable of producing a complex order of economic activities could come only after this development had made some progress. The subsequent elaboration of a consistent argument in favor of economic freedom was the outcome of a free growth of economic activity which had been the undesigned and unforeseen by-product of political freedom.

Perhaps the greatest result of the unchaining of individual energies was the marvelous growth of science which followed the march of individual liberty from Italy to England and beyond. That the inventive faculty of man had been no less in earlier periods is shown by the many highly ingenious automatic toys and other mechanical contrivances constructed while industrial technique still remained stationary and by the development in some industries which, like mining or watch-making, were not subject to restrictive controls. But the few attempts toward a more extended industrial use of mechanical inventions, some extraordinarily advanced, were promptly suppressed, and the desire for knowledge was stifled, so long as the dominant views were held to be binding for all: the beliefs of the great majority on what was right and proper were allowed to bar the way of the individual innovator. Only since industrial freedom opened the path to the free use of new knowledge, only since everything could be tried—if somebody could be found to back it at his own risk— and, it should be added, as often as not from outside the authorities officially intrusted with the cultivation of learning, has science made the great strides which in the last hundred and fifty years have changed the face of the world.

As is so often true, the nature of our civilization has been seen more clearly by its enemies than by most of its friends: "the perennial Western malady, the revolt of the individual against the species," as that nineteenth-century totalitarian, Auguste Comte, has described it, was indeed the force which built our civilization. What the nineteenth century added to the individualism of the preceding period was merely to make all classes conscious of freedom, to develop systematically and continuously what had grown in a haphazard and patchy manner, and to spread it from England and Holland over most of the European continent.

The result of this growth surpassed all expectations. Wherever the barriers to the free exercise of human ingenuity were removed, man became rapidly able to satisfy ever widening ranges of desire. And while the rising standard soon led to the discovery of very dark spots in society, spots which men were no longer willing to tolerate, there was probably no class that did not substantially benefit from the general advance. We cannot do justice to this astonishing growth if we measure it by our present standards, which themselves result from this growth and now make many defects obvious. To appreciate what it meant to those who took part in it, we must measure it by the hopes and wishes men held when it began: and there can be no doubt that its success surpassed man's wildest dreams, that by the beginning of the twentieth century the workingman in the Western world had reached a degree of material comfort, security, and personal independence which a hundred years before had seemed scarcely possible.

What in the future will probably appear the most significant and far-reaching effect of this success is the new sense of power over their own fate, the belief in the unbounded possibilities of improving their own lot, which the success already achieved created among men. With the success grew ambition—and man had every right to be ambitious. What had been an inspiring promise seemed no longer enough, the rate of progress far too slow; and the principles which had made this progress possible in the past came to be regarded more as obstacles to speedier progress, impatiently to be brushed away, than as the conditions for the preservation and development of what had already been achieved.

There is nothing in the basic principles of liberalism to make it a stationary creed; there are no hard-and-fast rules fixed once and for all. The fundamental principle that in the ordering of our affairs we should make as much use as possible of the spontaneous forces of society, and resort as little as possible to coercion, is capable of an infinite variety of applications. There is, in particular, all the difference between deliberately creating a system within which competition will work as beneficially as possible and passively accepting institutions as they are. Probably nothing has done so much harm to the liberal cause as the wooden insistence of some liberals on certain rough rules of thumb, above all the principle of laissez faire. Yet, in a sense, this was necessary and unavoidable. Against the innumerable interests which could show that particular measures would confer immediate and obvious benefits on some, while the harm they caused was much more indirect and difficult to see, nothing short of some hard-and-fast rule would have been effective. And since a strong presumption in favor of industrial liberty had undoubtedly been established, the temptation to present it as a rule which knew no exceptions was too strong always to be resisted.

But, with this attitude taken by many popularizers of the liberal doctrine, it was almost inevitable that, once their position was penetrated at some points, it should soon collapse as a whole. The position was further weakened by the inevitably slow progress of a policy which aimed at a gradual improvement of the institutional framework of a free society. This progress depended on the growth of our understanding of the social forces and the conditions most favorable to their working in a desirable manner. Since the task was to assist, and where necessary to supplement, their operation, the first requisite was to understand them. The attitude of the liberal toward society is like that of the gardener who tends a plant and, in order to create the conditions most favorable to its growth, must know as much as possible about its structure and the way it functions.

No sensible person should have doubted that the crude rules in which the principles of economic policy of the nineteenth century were expressed were only a beginning—that we had yet much to learn and that there were still immense possibilities of advancement on the lines on which we had moved. But this advance could come only as we gained increasing intellectual mastery of the forces of which we had to make use. There were many obvious tasks, such as our handling of the monetary system and the prevention or control of monopoly, and an even greater number of less obvious but hardly less important tasks to be undertaken in other fields, where there could be no doubt that the governments possessed enormous powers for good and evil; and there was every reason to expect that, with a better understanding of the problems, we should some day be able to use these powers successfully.

But while the progress toward what is commonly called "positive" action was necessarily slow, and while for the immediate improvement liberalism had to rely largely on the gradual increase of wealth which freedom brought about, it had constantly to fight proposals which threatened this progress. It came to be regarded as a "negative" creed because it could offer to particular individuals little more than a share in the common progress—a progress which came to be taken more and more for granted and was no longer recognized as the result of the policy of freedom. It might even be said that the very success of liberalism became the cause of its decline. Because of the success already achieved, man became increasingly unwilling to tolerate the evils still with him which now appeared both unbearable and unnecessary.

Because of the growing impatience with the slow advance of liberal policy, the just irritation with those who used liberal phraseology in defense of antisocial privileges, and the boundless ambition seemingly justified by the material improvements already achieved, it came to pass that toward the turn of the century the belief in the basic tenets of liberalism was more and more relinquished. What had been achieved came to be regarded as a secure and imperishable possession, acquired once and for all. The eyes of the people became fixed on the new demands, the rapid satisfaction of which seemed to be barred by the adherence to the old principles. It became more and more widely accepted that further advance could be expected not along the old lines within the general framework which had made past progress possible but only by a complete remodeling of society. It was no longer a question of adding to or improving the existing machinery but of completely scrapping and replacing it. And, as the hope of the new generation came to be centered on something completely new, interest in and understanding of the functioning of the existing society rapidly declined; and, with the decline of the understanding of the way in which the free system worked, our awareness of what depended on its existence also decreased.

   This is not the place to discuss how this change in outlook was fostered by the uncritical transfer to the problems of society of habits of thought engendered by the preoccupation with technological problems, the habits of thought of the natural scientist and the engineer, and how these at the same time tended to discredit the results of the past study of society which did not conform to their prejudices and to impose ideals of organization on a sphere to which they are not appropriate. All we are here concerned to show is how completely, though gradually and by almost imperceptible steps, our attitude toward society has changed. What at every stage of this process of change had appeared a difference of degree only has in its cumulative effect already brought about a fundamental difference between the older liberal attitude toward society and the present approach to social problems. The change amounts to a complete reversal of the trend we have sketched, an entire abandonment of the individualist tradition which has created Western civilization.

   According to the views now dominant, the question is no longer how we can make the best use of the spontaneous forces found in a free society. We have in effect undertaken to dispense with the forces which produced unforeseen results and to replace the impersonal and anonymous mechanism of the market by collective and "conscious" direction of all social forces to deliberately chosen goals. The difference cannot be better illustrated than by the extreme position taken in a widely acclaimed book on whose program of so-called "planning for freedom" we shall have to comment yet more than once. "We have never had to set up and direct," writes Dr. Karl Mannheim, "the entire system of nature as we are forced to do today with society. . . . Mankind is tending more and more to regulate the whole of its social life, although it has never attempted to create a second nature."

Chapter Six

Getting Together

Mont Pelerin Society

After World War II, in which many of the values of western civilization were imperiled, 36 scholars, mostly economists, with some historians and philosophers, were invited by Professor Friedrich Hayek to meet at Mont Pelerin, near Montreux, Switzerland, to discuss the state and the possible fate of liberalism in thinking and practice.

After 10 days of deliberation, it was decided to meet again for further discussion, and on April 10, 1947, the Founding Members composed the following "Statement of Aims":

> The central values of civilization are in danger. Over large stretches of the earth's surface the essential conditions of human dignity and freedom have already disappeared. In others they are under constant menace from the development of current tendencies of policy. The position of the individual and the voluntary group are progressively undermined by extensions of arbitrary power. Even that most precious possession of Western Man, freedom of thought and expression, is threatened by the spread of creeds which, claiming the privilege of tolerance when in the position of a minority, seek only to establish a position of power in which they can suppress and obliterate all views but their own.
>
> The group holds that these developments have been fostered by the growth of a view of history which denies all absolute moral standards and by the growth of theories which question the desirability of the rule of law. It holds further that they have been fostered by a decline of belief in private property and the competitive market; for without the diffused power and initiative associated with these institutions it is difficult to imagine a society in which freedom may be effectively preserved.
>
> Believing that what is essentially an ideological movement must be met by intellectual argument and the reassertion of valid ideals, the group,

having made a preliminary exploration of the ground, is of the opinion that further study is desirable inter alia in regard to the following matters:

1. The analysis and exploration of the nature of the present crisis so as to bring home to other its essential moral and economic origins.
2. The redefinition of the functions of the state so as to distinguish more clearly between the totalitarian and the liberal order.
3. Methods of re-establishing the rule of law and of assuring its development in such manner that individuals and groups are not in a position to encroach upon the freedom of others and private rights are not allowed to become a basis of predatory power.
4. The possibility of establishing minimum standards by means not inimical to initiative and functioning of the market.
5. Methods of combating the misuse of history for the furtherance of creeds hostile to liberty.
6. The problem of the creation of an international order conducive to the safeguarding of peace and liberty and permitting the establishment of harmonious international economic relations.

Chapter Seven

Defining Principles
Capitalism and Freedom

Milton Friedman

In a much quoted passage in his inaugural address, President Kennedy said, "Ask not what your country can do for you—ask what you can do for your country." It is a striking sign of the temper of our times that the controversy about this passage centered on its origin and not on its content. Neither half of the statement expresses a relation between the citizen and his government that is worthy of the ideals of free men in a free society. The paternalistic "what your country can do for you" implies that government is the patron, the citizen the ward, a view that is at odds with the free man's belief in his own responsibility for his own destiny. The organismic, "what you can do for your country" implies that government is the master or the deity, the citizen, the servant, or the votary. To the free man, the country is the collection of individuals who compose it, not something over and above them. He is proud of a common heritage and loyal to common traditions. But he regards government as a means, an instrumentality, neither a grantor of favors and gifts, nor a master or god to be blindly worshipped and served. He recognizes no national goal except as it is the consensus of the goals that the citizens severally serve. He recognizes no national purpose except as it is the consensus of the purposes for which the citizens severally strive.

The free man will ask neither what his country can do for him nor what he can do for his country. He will ask rather "What can I and my compatriots do through government" to help us discharge our individual responsibilities, to achieve our several goals and purposes, and above all,

Milton Friedman, *Capitalism and Freedom* (Chicago: University of Chicago Press, 1962), Reprinted by permission of University of Chicago Press and Milton Friedman.

to protect our freedom? And he will accompany this question with another: How can we keep the government we create from becoming a
Frankenstein that will destroy the very freedom we establish it to protect?
Freedom is a rare and delicate plant. Our minds tell us, and history
confirms, that the great threat to freedom is the concentration of power.
Government is necessary to preserve our freedom, it is an instrument
through which we can exercise our freedom; yet by concentrating power
in political hands, it is also a threat to freedom. Even though the men
who wield this power initially be of good will and even though they be
not corrupted by the power they exercise, the power will both attract and
form men of a different stamp.

How can we benefit from the promise of government while avoiding
the threat to freedom? Two broad principles embodied in our Constitution give an answer that has preserved our freedom so far, though they
have been violated repeatedly in practice while proclaimed as precept.

First, the scope of government must be limited. Its major function
must be to protect our freedom both from the enemies outside our gates
and from our fellow-citizens: to preserve law and order, to enforce private
contracts, to foster competitive markets. Beyond this major function,
government may enable us at times to accomplish jointly what we would
find it more difficult or expensive to accomplish severally. However, any
such use of government is fraught with danger. We should not and cannot
avoid using government in this way. But there should be a clear and large
balance of advantages before we do. By relying primarily on voluntary cooperation and private enterprise, in both economic and other activities,
we can insure that the private sector is a check on the powers of the
governmental sector and an effective protection of freedom of speech, of
religion, and of thought.

The second broad principle is that government power must be dispersed. If government is to exercise power, better in the county than in
the state, better in the state than in Washington. If I do not like what my
local community does, be it in sewage disposal, or zoning, or schools, I
can move to another local community, and though few may take this
step, the mere possibility acts as a check. If I do not like what my state
does, I can move to another. If I do not like what Washington imposes, I
have few alternatives in this world of jealous nations.

The very difficulty of avoiding the enactments of the federal government is of course the great attraction of centralization to many of its
proponents. It will enable them more effectively, they believe, to legislate

programs that—as they see it—are in the interest of the public, whether it be the transfer of income from the rich to the poor or from private to governmental purposes. They are in a sense right. But this coin has two sides. The power to do good is also the power to do harm; those who control the power today may not tomorrow; and, more important, what one man regards as good, another may regard as harm. The great tragedy of the drive to centralization, as of the drive to extend the scope of government in general, is that it is mostly led by men of good will who will be the first to rue its consequences.

The preservation of freedom is the protective reason for limiting and decentralizing governmental power. But there is also a constructive reason. The great advances of civilization, whether in architecture or painting, in science or literature, in industry or agriculture, have never come from centralized government. Columbus did not set out to seek a new route to China in response to a majority directive of a parliament, though he was partly financed by an absolute monarch. Newton and Leibnitz; Einstein and Bohr; Shakespeare, Milton, and Pasternak; Whitney, McCormick, Edison, and Ford; Jane Addams, Florence Nightingale, and Albert Schweitzer; no one of these opened new frontiers in human knowledge and understanding, in literature, in technical possibilities, or in the relief of human misery in response to governmental directives. Their achievements were the product of individual genius, of strongly held minority views, of a social climate permitting variety and diversity.

Government can never duplicate the variety and diversity of individual action. At any moment in time, by imposing uniform standards in housing, or nutrition, or clothing, government could undoubtedly improve the level of living of many individuals; by imposing uniform standards in schooling, road construction, or sanitation, central government could undoubtedly improve the level of performance in many local areas and perhaps even on the average of all communities. But in the process, government would replace progress by stagnation, it would substitute uniform mediocrity for the variety essential for that experimentation which can bring tomorrow's laggards above today's mean. . . .

An abstract statement can conceivably be complete and exhaustive, though this ideal is certainly far from realized in the two [sections] that follow. The application of the principles cannot even conceivably be exhaustive. Each day brings new problems and new circumstances. That is why the role of the state can never be spelled out once and for all in terms of specific functions. It is also why we need from time to time to re-examine the bearing of what we hope are unchanged principles on the problems of the day. A by-product is inevitably a retesting of the principles and a sharpening of our understanding of them.

It is extremely convenient to have a label for the political and economic viewpoint elaborated in this book. The rightful and proper label is liberalism. Unfortunately, "As a supreme, if unintended compliment, the enemies of the system of private enterprise have thought it wise to appropriate its label," so that liberalism has, in the United States, come to have a very different meaning than it did in the nineteenth century or does today over much of the Continent of Europe.

As it developed in the late eighteenth and early nineteenth centuries, the intellectual movement that went under the name of liberalism emphasized freedom as the ultimate goal and the individual as the ultimate entity in the society. It supported laissez faire at home as a means of reducing the role of the state in economic affairs and thereby enlarging the role of the individual; it supported free trade abroad as a means of linking the nations of the world together peacefully and democratically. In political matters, it supported the development of representative government and of parliamentary institutions, reduction in the arbitrary power of the state, and protection of the civil freedoms of individuals.

Beginning in the late nineteenth century, and especially after 1930 in the United States, the term liberalism came to be associated with a very different emphasis, particularly in economic policy. It came to be associated with a readiness to rely primarily on the state rather than on private voluntary arrangements to achieve objectives regarded as desirable. The catchwords became welfare and equality rather than freedom. The nineteenth-century liberal regarded an extension of freedom as the most effective way to promote welfare and equality; the twentieth-century liberal regards welfare and equality as either prerequisites of or alternatives to freedom. In the name of welfare and equality, the twentieth-century liberal has come to favor a revival of the very policies of state intervention and paternalism against which classical liberalism fought. In the very act of turning the clock back to seventeenth-century mercantilism, he is fond of castigating true liberals as reactionary!

The change in the meaning attached to the term liberalism is more striking in economic matters than in political. The twentieth-century liberal, like the nineteenth-century liberal, favors parliamentary institutions, representative government, civil rights, and so on. Yet even in political matters, there is a notable difference. Jealous of liberty, and hence fearful of centralized power, whether in governmental or private hands, the nineteenth-century liberal favored political decentralization. Committed to action and confident of the beneficence of power so long as it is in the hands of a government ostensibly controlled by the electorate, the twentieth-century liberal favors centralized government. He will resolve any doubt about where power should be located in favor of the state instead of the city, of the federal government instead of the state, and of a world organization instead of a national government.

Because of the corruption of the term liberalism, the views that formerly went under that name are now often labeled conservatism. But this is not a satisfactory alternative. The nineteenth-century liberal was a radical, both in the etymological sense of going to the root of the matter, and in the political sense of favoring major changes in social institutions. So too must be his modern heir. We do not wish to conserve the state interventions that have interfered so greatly with our freedom, though, of course, we do wish to conserve those that have promoted it. Moreover, in practice, the term conservatism has come to cover so wide a range of views, and views so incompatible with one another, that we shall no doubt see the growth of hyphenated designations, such as libertarian-conservative and aristocratic-conservative.

Partly because of my reluctance to surrender the term to proponents of measures that would destroy liberty, partly because I cannot find a better alternative, I shall resolve these difficulties by using the word liberalism in its original sense—as the doctrines pertaining to a free man.

The Relation between Economic Freedom and Political Freedom

It is widely believed that politics and economics are separate and largely unconnected; that individual freedom is a political problem and material welfare an economic problem; and that any kind of political arrangements can be combined with any kind of economic arrangements. The chief contemporary manifestation of this idea is the advocacy of "democratic socialism" by many who condemn out of hand the restrictions on individual freedom imposed by "totalitarian socialism" in Russia, and who are persuaded that it is possible for a country to adopt the essential features of Russian economic arrangements and yet to ensure individual freedom through political arrangements. The thesis of this [section] is that such a view is a delusion, that there is an intimate connection between economics and politics, that only certain combinations of political and economic arrangements are possible, and that in particular, a society which is socialist cannot also be democratic, in the sense of guaranteeing individual freedom.

Economic arrangements play a dual role in the promotion of a free society. On the one hand, freedom in economic arrangements is itself a component of freedom broadly understood, so economic freedom is an end in itself. In the second place, economic freedom is also an indispensable means toward the achievement of political freedom.

The first of these roles of economic freedom needs special emphasis because intellectuals in particular have a strong bias against regarding this aspect of freedom as important. They tend to express contempt for what they regard as material aspects of life, and to regard their own pursuit of allegedly higher values as on a different plane of significance and as deserving of special attention. For most citizens of the country, however, if not for the intellectual, the direct importance of economic freedom is at least comparable in significance to the indirect importance of economic freedom as a means to political freedom.

The citizen of Great Britain, who after World War II was not permitted to spend his vacation in the United States because of exchange control, was being deprived of an essential freedom no less than the citizen of the United States, who was denied the opportunity to spend his vacation in Russia because of his political views. The one was ostensibly an economic limitation on freedom and the other a political limitation, yet there is no essential difference between the two.

The citizen of the United States who is compelled by law to devote something like 10 percent of his income to the purchase of a particular kind of retirement contract, administered by the government, is being deprived of a corresponding part of his personal freedom. How strongly this deprivation may be felt and its closeness to the deprivation of religious freedom, which all would regard as "civil" or "political" rather than "economic," were dramatized by an episode involving a group of farmers of the Amish sect. On grounds of principle, this group regarded compulsory federal old age programs as an infringement of their personal individual freedom and refused to pay taxes or accept benefits. As a result, some of their livestock were sold by auction in order to satisfy claims for social security levies. True, the number of citizens who regard compulsory old age insurance as a deprivation of freedom may be few, but the believer in freedom has never counted noses.

A citizen of the United States who under the laws of various states is not free to follow the occupation of his own choosing unless he can get a license for it, is likewise being deprived of an essential part of his freedom. So is the man who would like to exchange some of his goods with, say, a Swiss for a watch but is prevented from doing so by a quota. So also is the Californian who was thrown into jail for selling Alka Seltzer at a price below that set by the manufacturer under so-called "fair trade" laws. So also is the farmer who cannot grow the amount of wheat he wants. And so on. Clearly, economic freedom, in and of itself, is an extremely important part of total freedom.

Viewed as a means to the end of political freedom, economic arrangements are important because of their effect on the concentration or dispersion of power. The kind of economic organization that provides economic freedom directly, namely, competitive capitalism, also promotes political freedom because it separates economic power from political power and in this way enables the one to offset the other.

Historical evidence speaks with a single voice on the relation between political freedom and a free market. I know of no example in time or place of a society that has been marked by a large measure of political freedom, and that has not also used something comparable to a free market to organize the bulk of economic activity.

Because we live in a largely free society, we tend to forget how limited is the span of time and the part of the globe for which there has ever been anything like political freedom: the typical state of mankind is tyranny, servitude, and misery. The nineteenth century and early twentieth century in the Western world stand out as striking exceptions to the general trend of historical development. Political freedom in this instance clearly came along with the free market and the development of capitalist institutions. So also did political freedom in the golden age of Greece and in the early days of the Roman era.

History suggests only that capitalism is a necessary condition for political freedom. Clearly it is not a sufficient condition. Fascist Italy and Fascist Spain, Germany at various times in the last seventy years, Japan before World Wars I and II, tzarist Russia in the decades before World War I—are all societies that cannot conceivably be described as politically free. Yet, in each, private enterprise was the dominant form of economic organization. It is therefore clearly possible to have economic arrangements that are fundamentally capitalist and political arrangements that are not free.

Even in those societies, the citizenry had a good deal more freedom than citizens of a modern totalitarian state like Russia or Nazi Germany, in which economic totalitarianism is combined with political totalitarianism. Even in Russia under the Tzars, it was possible for some citizens, under some circumstances, to change their jobs without getting permission from political authority because capitalism and the existence of private property provided some check to the centralized power of the state.

The relation between political and economic freedom is complex and by no means unilateral. In the early nineteenth century, Bentham and the Philosophical Radicals were inclined to regard political freedom as a means to economic freedom. They believed that the masses were being hampered by the restrictions that were being imposed upon them, and that if political reform gave the bulk of the people the vote, they would do what was good for them, which was to vote for laissez faire. In retrospect, one cannot say that they were wrong. There was a large measure of political reform that was accompanied by economic reform in the direction of a great deal of laissez faire. An enormous increase in the well-being of the masses followed this change in economic arrangements.

The triumph of Benthamite liberalism in nineteenth-century England was followed by a reaction toward increasing intervention by government in economic affairs. This tendency to collectivism was greatly accelerated, both in England and elsewhere, by the two World Wars. Welfare rather than freedom became the dominant note in democratic countries. Recognizing the implicit threat to individualism, the intellectual descendants of the Philosophical Radicals—Dicey, Mises, Hayek, and Simons, to mention only a few—feared that a continued movement toward centralized control of economic activity would prove *The Road to Serfdom,* as Hayek entitled his penetrating analysis of the process. Their emphasis was on economic freedom as a means toward political freedom.

Events since the end of World War II display still a different relation between economic and political freedom. Collectivist economic planning has indeed interfered with individual freedom. At least in some countries, however, the result has not been the suppression of freedom, but the reversal of economic policy. England again provides the most striking example. The turning point was perhaps the "control of engagements" order which, despite great misgivings, the Labour party found it necessary to impose in order to carry out its economic policy. Fully enforced and carried through, the law would have involved centralized allocation of individuals to occupations. This conflicted so sharply with personal liberty that it was enforced in a negligible number of cases, and then repealed after the law had been in effect for only a short period. Its repeal ushered in a decided shift in economic policy, marked by reduced reliance on centralized "plans" and "programs," by the dismantling of many controls, and by increased emphasis on the private market. A similar shift in policy occurred in most other democratic countries.

The proximate explanation of these shifts in policy is the limited success of central planning or its outright failure to achieve stated objectives. However, this failure is itself to be attributed, at least in some measure, to the political implications of central planning and to an unwillingness to follow out its logic when doing so requires trampling rough-shod on treasured private rights. It may well be that the shift is only a temporary interruption in the collectivist trend of this century. Even so, it illustrates the close relation between political freedom and economic arrangements.

Historical evidence by itself can never be convincing. Perhaps it was sheer coincidence that the expansion of freedom occurred at the same time as the development of capitalist and market institutions. Why should there be a connection? What are the logical links between economic and political freedom? In discussing these questions we shall consider first the market as a direct component of freedom, and then the indirect relation between market arrangements and political freedom. A by-product will be an outline of the ideal economic arrangements for a free society.

As liberals, we take freedom of the individual, or perhaps the family, as our ultimate goal in judging social arrangements. Freedom as a value in this sense has to do with the interrelations among people; it has no meaning whatsoever to a Robinson Crusoe on an isolated island (without his Man Friday). Robinson Crusoe on his island is subject to "constraint," he has limited "power," and he has only a limited number of alternatives, but there is no problem of freedom in the sense that is relevant to our discussion. Similarly, in a society freedom has nothing to say about what an individual does with his freedom; it is not an all-embracing ethic. Indeed, a major aim of the liberal is to leave the ethical problem for the individual to wrestle with. The "really" important ethical problems are those that face an individual in a free society—what he should do with his freedom. There are thus two sets of values that a liberal will emphasize—the values that are relevant to relations among people, which is the context in which he assigns first priority to freedom; and the values that are relevant to the individual in the exercise of his freedom, which is the realm of individual ethics and philosophy.

The liberal conceives of men as imperfect beings. He regards the problem of social organization to be as much a negative problem of preventing "bad" people from doing harm as of enabling "good" people to do good; and, of course, "bad" and "good" people may be the same people, depending on who is judging them.

The basic problem of social organization is how to co-ordinate the economic activities of large numbers of people. Even in relatively backward societies, extensive division of labor and specialization of function is required to make effective use of available resources. In advanced societies, the scale on which co-ordination is needed, to take full advantage of the opportunities offered by modern science and technology, is enormously greater. Literally millions of people are involved in providing one another with their daily bread, let alone with their yearly automobiles. The challenge to the believer in liberty is to reconcile this widespread interdependence with individual freedom.

Fundamentally, there are only two ways of co-ordinating the economic activities of millions. One is central direction involving the use of coercion—the technique of the army and of the modern totalitarian state. The other is voluntary co-operation of individuals—the technique of the market place.

The possibility of co-ordination through voluntary co-operation rests on the elementary—yet frequently denied—proposition that both parties to an economic transaction benefit from it, *provided the transaction is bilaterally voluntary and informed.*

Exchange can therefore bring about co-ordination without coercion. A working model of a society organized through voluntary exchange is a *free private enterprise exchange economy*—what we have been calling competitive capitalism.

In its simplest form, such a society consists of a number of independent households—a collection of Robinson Crusoes, as it were. Each household uses the resources it controls to produce goods and services that it exchanges for goods and services produced by other households, on terms mutually acceptable to the two parties to the bargain. It is thereby enabled to satisfy its wants indirectly by producing goods and services for others, rather than directly by producing goods for its own immediate use. The incentive for adopting this indirect route is, of course, the increased product made possible by division of labor and specialization of function. Since the household always has the alternative of producing directly for itself, it need not enter into any exchange unless it benefits from it. Hence, no exchange will take place unless both parties do benefit from it. Co-operation is thereby achieved without coercion.

Specialization of function and division of labor would not go far if the ultimate productive unit were the household. In a modern society, we have gone much farther. We have introduced enterprises which are intermediaries between individuals in their capacities as suppliers of service and as purchasers of goods. And similarly, specialization of function and division of labor could not go very far if we had to continue to rely on the barter of product for product. In consequence, money has been introduced as a means of facilitating exchange, and of enabling the acts of purchase and of sale to be separated into two parts.

Despite the important role of enterprises and of money in our actual economy, and despite the numerous and complex problems they raise, the central characteristic of the market technique of achieving coordination is fully displayed in the simple exchange economy that contains neither enterprise nor money. As in that simple model, so in the complex enterprise and money exchange economy, co-operation is strictly individual and voluntary *provided:* (a) that enterprises are private, so that the ultimate contracting parties are individuals, and (b) that individuals are effectively free to enter or not to enter into any particular exchange, so that every transaction is strictly voluntary.

It is far easier to state these provisos in general terms than to spell them out in detail, or to specify precisely the institutional arrangements most conducive to their maintenance. Indeed, much of technical economic literature is concerned with precisely these questions. The basic requisite is the maintenance of law and order to prevent physical coercion of one individual by another and to enforce contracts voluntarily entered into, thus giving substance to "private." Aside from this, perhaps the most difficult problems arise from monopoly—which inhibits effective freedom by denying individuals alternatives to the particular exchange—and from "neighborhood effects"—effects on third parties for which it is not feasible to charge or recompense them. These problems will be discussed in more detail in the following chapter.

So long as effective freedom of exchange is maintained, the central feature of the market organization of economic activity is that it prevents one person from interfering with another in respect of most of his activities. The consumer is protected from coercion by the seller because of the presence of other sellers with whom he can deal. The seller is protected from coercion by the consumer because of other consumers to whom he can sell. The employee is protected from coercion by the employer because of other employers for whom he can work, and so on. And the market does this impersonally and without centralized authority.

Indeed, a major source of objection to a free economy is precisely that it does this task so well. It gives people what they want instead of what a particular group thinks they ought to want. Underlying most arguments against the free market is a lack of belief in freedom itself.

The existence of a free market does not of course eliminate the need for government. On the contrary, government is essential both as a forum for determining the "rules of the game" and as an umpire to interpret and enforce the rules decided on. What the market does is to reduce greatly the range of issues that must be decided through political means, and thereby to minimize the extent to which government need participate directly in the game. The characteristic feature of action through political channels is that it tends to require or enforce substantial conformity. The great advantage of the market, on the other hand, is that it permits wide diversity. It is, in political terms, a system of proportional representation. Each man can vote, as it were, for the color of tie he wants and get it; he does not have to see what color the majority wants and then, if he is in the minority, submit.

It is this feature of the market that we refer to when we say that the market provides economic freedom. But this characteristic also has implications that go far beyond the narrowly economic. Political freedom means the absence of coercion of a man by his fellow men. The fundamental threat to freedom is power to coerce, be it in the hands of a monarch, a dictator, an oligarchy, or a momentary majority. The preservation of freedom requires the elimination of such concentration of power to the fullest possible extent and the dispersal and distribution of whatever power cannot be eliminated—a system of checks and balances. By removing the organization of economic activity from the control of political authority, the market eliminates this source of coercive power. It enables economic strength to be a check to political power rather than a reinforcement.

Economic power can be widely dispersed. There is no law of conservation which forces the growth of new centers of economic strength to be at the expense of existing centers. Political power, on the other hand, is more difficult to decentralize. There can be numerous small independent governments. But it is far more difficult to maintain numerous equipotent small centers of political power in a single large government than it is to have numerous centers of economic strength in a single large economy. There can be many millionaires in one large economy. But can there be more than one really outstanding leader, one person on whom the energies and enthusiasms of his countrymen are centered? If the central government gains power, it is likely to be at the expense of local governments. There seems to be something like a fixed total of political power to be distributed. Consequently, if economic power is joined to political power, concentration seems almost inevitable. On the other hand, if economic power is kept in separate hands from political power, it can serve as a check and a counter to political power.

The force of this abstract argument can perhaps best be demonstrated by example. Let us consider first, a hypothetical example that may help to bring out the principles involved, and then some actual examples from recent experience that illustrate the way in which the market works to preserve political freedom.

One feature of a free society is surely the freedom of individuals to advocate and propagandize openly for a radical change in the structure of the society—so long as the advocacy is restricted to persuasion and does not include force or other forms of coercion. It is a mark of the political freedom of a capitalist society that men can openly advocate and work for socialism. Equally, political freedom in a socialist society would require that men be free to advocate the introduction of capitalism. How could the freedom to advocate capitalism be preserved and protected in a socialist society?

In order for men to advocate anything, they must in the first place be able to earn a living. This already raises a problem in a socialist society, since all jobs are under the direct control of political authorities. It would take an act of self-denial whose difficulty is underlined by experience in the United States after World War II with the problem of "security" among Federal employees, for a socialist government to permit its employees to advocate policies directly contrary to official doctrine.

But let us suppose this act of self-denial to be achieved. For advocacy of capitalism to mean anything, the proponents must be able to finance their cause—to hold public meetings, publish pamphlets, buy radio time, issue newspapers and magazines, and so on. How could they raise the funds? There might and probably would be men in the socialist society with large incomes, perhaps even large capital sums in the form of government bonds and the like, but these would of necessity be high public officials. It is possible to conceive of a minor socialist official retaining his job although openly advocating capitalism. It strains credulity to imagine the socialist top brass financing such "subversive" activities.

The only recourse for funds would be to raise small amounts from a large number of minor officials. But this is no real answer. To tap these sources, many people would already have to be persuaded, and our whole problem is how to initiate and finance a campaign to do so. Radical movements in capitalist societies have never been financed this way. They have typically been supported by a few wealthy individuals who have become persuaded—by a Frederick Vanderbilt Field, or an Anita McCormick Blaine, or a Corliss Lamont, to mention a few names recently prominent, or by a Friedrich Engels, to go farther back. This is a role of inequality of wealth in preserving political freedom that is seldom noted— the role of the patron.

In a capitalist society, it is only necessary to convince a few wealthy people to get funds to launch any idea, however strange, and there are many such persons, many independent foci of support. And, indeed, it is not even necessary to persuade people or financial institutions with available funds of the soundness of the ideas to be propagated. It is only necessary to persuade them that the propagation can be financially successful; that the newspaper or magazine or book or other venture will be profitable. The competitive publisher, for example, cannot afford to publish only writing with which he personally agrees; his touchstone must be the likelihood that the market will be large enough to yield a satisfactory return on his investment.

In this way, the market breaks the vicious circle and makes it possible ultimately to finance such ventures by small amounts from many people without first persuading them. There are no such possibilities in the socialist society; there is only the all-powerful state.

Let us stretch our imagination and suppose that a socialist government is aware of this problem and is composed of people anxious to preserve freedom. Could it provide the funds? Perhaps, but it is difficult to see how. It could establish a bureau for subsidizing subversive propaganda. But how could it choose whom to support? If it gave to all who asked, it would shortly find itself out of funds, for socialism cannot repeal the elementary economic law that a sufficiently high price will call forth a large supply. Make the advocacy of radical causes sufficiently remunerative, and the supply of advocates will be unlimited.

Moreover, freedom to advocate unpopular causes does not require that such advocacy be without cost. On the contrary, no society could be stable if advocacy of radical change were costless, much less subsidized. It is entirely appropriate that men make sacrifices to advocate causes in which they deeply believe. Indeed, it is important to preserve freedom only for people who are willing to practice self-denial, for otherwise freedom degenerates into license and irresponsibility. What is essential is that the cost of advocating unpopular causes be tolerable and not prohibitive.

But we are not yet through. In a free market society, it is enough to have the funds. The suppliers of paper are as willing to sell it to the *Daily Worker* as to the *Wall Street Journal*. In socialist society, it would not be enough to have the funds. The hypothetical supporter of capitalism would have to persuade government factory making paper to sell to him, the government printing press to print his pamphlets, a government post-office to distribute them among the people, a government agency to rent him a hall in which to talk, and so on.

Perhaps there is some way in which one could overcome these difficulties and preserve freedom in a socialist society. One can not say it is utterly impossible. What is clear, however, is that there are very real difficulties in establishing institutions that will effectively preserve the possibility of dissent. So far as I know, none of the people who have been in favor of socialism and also in favor of freedom have really faced up to this issue, or made even a respectable start at developing the institutional arrangements that would permit freedom under socialism. By contrast, it is clear how a free market capitalist society fosters freedom.

A striking practical example of these abstract principles is the experience of Winston Churchill. From 1933 to the outbreak of World War II, Churchill was not permitted to talk over the British radio, which was, of course, a government monopoly administered by the British Broadcasting Corporation. Here was a leading citizen of his country, a Member of Parliament, a former cabinet minister, a man who was desperately trying by every device possible to persuade his countrymen to take steps toward off the menace of Hitler's Germany. He was not permitted to talk over the radio to the British people because the BBC was a government monopoly and his position was too "controversial."

Another striking example, reported in the January 26, 1959 issue of *Time*, has to do with the "Blacklist Fadeout." Says the *Time* story,

> The Oscar-awarding ritual is Hollywood's biggest pitch for dignity, but two years ago dignity suffered. When one Robert Rich was announced as top writer for the *The Brave One*, he never stepped forward. Robert Rich was pseudonym, masking one of about 150 writers . . . blacklisted by the industry since 1947 as suspected Communists or fellow travelers. The case was particularly embarrassing because the Motion Picture Academy had barred any Communist or Fifth Amendment pleader from Oscar competition. Last week both the Communist rule and the mystery of Rich's identity were suddenly rescripted.
>
> Rich turned out to be Dalton *(Johnny Got His Gun)* Trumbo, one of the original "Hollywood Ten" writers who refused to testify at the 1947 hearings on Communism in the movie industry. Said producer Frank King, who had stoutly insisted that Robert Rich was "a young guy in Spain with a beard": "We have an obligation to our stockholders to buy the best script we can. Trumbo brought us *The Brave One* and we bought it." . . .
>
> In effect it was the formal end of the Hollywood black list. For barred writers, the informal end came long ago. At least 15% of current Hollywood films are reportedly written by blacklist members. Said Producer King, "There are more ghosts in Hollywood than in Forest Lawn. Every company in town has used the work of blacklisted people. We're just the first to confirm what everybody knows."

One may believe, as I do, that communism would destroy all of our freedoms, one may be opposed to it as firmly and as strongly as possible, and yet, at the same time, also believe that in a free society it is intolerable for a man to be prevented from making voluntary arrangements with others that are mutually attractive because he believes in or is trying to promote communism. His freedom includes his freedom to promote communism. Freedom also, of course, includes the freedom of others not to deal with him under those circumstances. The Hollywood blacklist was an unfree act that destroys freedom because it was a collusive arrangement that used coercive means to prevent voluntary exchanges. It didn't work precisely because the market made it costly for people to preserve the blacklist. The commercial emphasis, the fact that people who are running enterprises have an incentive to make as much money as they can, protected the freedom of the individuals who were blacklisted by providing them with an alternative form of employment, and by giving people an incentive to employ them.

If Hollywood and the movie industry had been government enterprises or if in England it had been a question of employment by the British Broadcasting Corporation it is difficult to believe that the "Hollywood Ten" or their equivalent would have found employment. Equally, it is difficult to believe that under those circumstances, strong proponents of individualism and private enterprise—or indeed strong proponents of any view other than the status quo—would be able to get employment.

Another example of the role of the market in preserving political freedom was revealed in our experience with McCarthyism. Entirely aside from the substantive issues involved, and the merits of the charges made, what protection did individuals, and in particular government employees, have against irresponsible accusations and probings into matters that it went against their conscience to reveal? Their appeal to the Fifth Amendment would have been a hollow mockery without an alternative to government employment.

Their fundamental protection was the existence of a private market economy in which they could earn a living. Here again, the protection was not absolute. Many potential private employers were, rightly or wrongly, averse to hiring those pilloried. It may well be that there was far less justification for the costs imposed on many of the people involved than for the costs generally imposed on people who advocate unpopular causes. But the important point is that the costs were limited and not prohibitive, as they would have been if government employment had been the only possibility.

It is of interest to note that a disproportionately large fraction of the people involved apparently went into the most competitive sectors of the economy—small business, trade, farming—where the market approaches most closely the ideal free market. No one who buys bread knows whether the wheat from which it is made was grown by a Communist or a Republican, by a constitutionalist or a Fascist, or, for that matter, by a Negro or a white. This illustrates how an impersonal market separates economic activities from political views and protects men from being discriminated against in their economic activities for reasons that are irrelevant to their productivity—whether these reasons are associated with their views or their color.

As this example suggests, the groups in our society that have the most at stake in the preservation and strengthening of competitive capitalism are those minority groups which can most easily become the object of the distrust and enmity of the majority—the Negroes, the Jews, the foreign-born, to mention only the most obvious. Yet, paradoxically enough, the enemies of the free market—the Socialists and Communists—have been recruited in disproportionate measure from these groups. Instead of recognizing that the existence of the market has protected them from the attitudes of their fellow countrymen, they mistakenly attribute the residual discrimination to the market.

In the 1920s and the 1930s intellectuals in the United States were overwhelmingly persuaded that capitalism was a defective system inhibiting economic well-being and thereby freedom and that the hope for the future lay in a greater measure of deliberate control by political authorities over economic affairs. The conversion of the intellectuals was not achieved by the example of any actual collectivist society, though it undoubtedly was much hastened by the establishment of a communist society in Russia and the glowing hopes placed in it. The conversion of the intellectuals was achieved by a comparison between the existing state of affairs, with all its injustices and defects and a hypothetical state of affairs as it might be. The actual was compared with the ideal.

At the time, not much else was possible. True, mankind had experienced many epochs of centralized control, of detailed intervention by the state into economic affairs. But there had been a revolution in politics, in science, and in technology. Surely, it was argued, we can do far better with a democratic political structure, modern tools, and modern science than was possible in earlier ages.

The attitudes of that time are still with us. There is still a tendency to regard any existing government intervention as desirable, to attribute all evils to the market, and to evaluate new proposals for government control in their ideal form, as they might work if run by able, disinterested men, free from the pressure of special interest groups. The proponents of limited government and free enterprise are still on the defensive.

Yet, conditions have changed. We now have several decades of experience with governmental intervention. It is no longer necessary to compare the market as it actually operates and government intervention as it ideally might operate. We can compare the actual with the actual.

If we do so, it is clear that the difference between the actual operation of the market and its ideal operation—great though it undoubtedly is—is as nothing compared to the difference between the actual effects of government intervention and their intended effects. Who can now see any great hope for the advancement of men's freedom and dignity in the massive tyranny and despotism that hold sway in Russia? Wrote Marx and Engels in *The Communist Manifesto:* "The proletarians have nothing to lose but their chains. They have a world to win." Who today can regard the chains of the proletarians in the Soviet Union as weaker than the chains of the proletarians in the United States, or Britain or France or Germany or any Western state?

Let us look closer to home. Which if any of the great "reforms" of past decades has achieved its objectives? Have the good intentions of the proponents of these reforms been realized?

Regulation of the railroads to protect the consumer quickly became an instrument whereby the railroads could protect themselves from the competition of newly emerging rivals—at the expense, of course, of the consumer.

An income tax initially enacted at low rates and later seized upon as a means to redistribute income in favor of the lower classes has become a facade, covering loopholes and special provisions that render rates that are highly graduated on paper largely ineffective. A flat rate of 23½ percent on presently taxable income would yield as much revenue as the present rates graduated from 20 to 91 percent. An income tax intended to reduce inequality and promote the diffusion of wealth has in practice fostered reinvestment of corporate earnings, thereby favoring the growth of large corporations, inhibiting the operation of the capital market, and discouraging the establishment of new enterprises.

Monetary reforms, intended to promote stability in economic activity and prices, exacerbated inflation during and after World War I and fostered a higher degree of instability thereafter than had ever been experienced before. The monetary authorities they established bear primary responsibility for converting a serious economic contraction into the catastrophe of the Great Depression from 1929–33. A system established largely to prevent bank panics produced the most severe banking panic in American history.

An agricultural program intended to help impecunious farmers and to remove what were alleged to be basic dislocations in the organization of agriculture has become a national scandal that has wasted public funds, distorted the use of resources, riveted increasingly heavy and detailed controls on farmers, interfered seriously with United States foreign policy and withal has done little to help the impecunious farmer.

A housing program intended to improve the housing conditions of the poor, to reduce juvenile delinquency, and to contribute to the removal of urban slums, has worsened the housing conditions of the poor, contributed to juvenile delinquency, and spread urban blight.

In the 1930s, "labor" was synonymous with "labor union," the intellectual community; faith in the purity and virtue of labor unions was on a par with faith in home and motherhood. Extensive legislation was enacted to favor labor unions and to foster "fair" labor relation. Labor unions waxed in strength. By the 1950s, "labor union" was almost a dirty word; it was no longer synonymous with "labor," no longer automatically to be taken for granted as on the side of the angels.

Social security measures were enacted to make receipt of assistance a matter of right, to eliminate the need for direct relief and assistance. Millions now receive social security benefits. Yet the relief rolls grow and the sums spent on direct assistance mount.

The list can easily be lengthened: the silver purchase program of the 1930s, public power projects, foreign aid programs of the post-war years, F.C.C., urban redevelopment programs, the stockpiling program—these and many more have had effects very different and generally quite opposite from those intended.

There have been some exceptions. The expressways crisscrossing the country, magnificent dams spanning great rivers, orbiting satellites are all tributes to the capacity of government to command great resources. The school system, with all its defects and problems, with all the possibility of improvement through bringing into more effective play the forces of the market, has widened the opportunities available to American youth and contributed to the extension of freedom. It is a testament to the public-spirited efforts of the many tens of thousands who have served on local school boards and to the willingness of the public to bear heavy taxes for what they regarded as a public purpose. The Sherman antitrust laws, with all their problems of detailed administration, have by their very existence fostered competition. Public health measures have contributed to the reduction of infectious disease. Assistance measures have relieved suffering and distress. Local authorities have often provided facilities essential to the life of communities. Law and order have been maintained, though in many a large city the performance of even this elementary function of government has been far from satisfactory. As a citizen of Chicago, I speak feelingly.

If a balance be struck, there can be little doubt that the record is dismal. The greater part of the new ventures undertaken by government in the past few decades have failed to achieve their objectives. The United

States has continued to progress; its citizens have become better fed, better clothed, better housed, and better transported; class and social distinctions have narrowed; minority groups have become less disadvantaged; popular culture has advanced by leaps and bounds. All this has been the product of the initiative and drive of individuals co-operating through the free market. Government measures have hampered not helped this development. We have been able to afford and surmount these measures only because of the extraordinary fecundity of the market. The invisible hand has been more potent for progress than the visible hand for retrogression.

Is it an accident that so many of the governmental reforms of recent decades have gone awry, that the bright hopes have turned to ashes? Is it simply because the programs are faulty in detail?

I believe the answer is clearly in the negative. The central defect of these measures is that they seek through government to force people to act against their own immediate interests in order to promote a supposedly general interest. They seek to resolve what is supposedly a conflict of interest, or a difference in view about interests, not by establishing a framework that will eliminate the conflict, or by persuading people to have different interests, but by forcing people to act against their own interest. They substitute the values of outsiders for the values of participants; either some telling others what is good for them, or the government taking from some to benefit others. These measures are therefore countered by one of the strongest and most creative forces known to man—the attempt by millions of individuals to promote their own interests, to live their lives by their own values. This is the major reason why the measures have so often had the opposite of the effects intended. It is also one of the major strengths of a free society and explains why governmental regulation does not strangle it.

The interests of which I speak are not simply narrow self-regarding interests. On the contrary, they include the whole range of values that men hold dear and for which they are willing to spend their fortunes and sacrifice their lives. The Germans who lost their lives opposing Adolph Hitler were pursuing their interests as they saw them. So also are the men and women who devote great effort and time to charitable, educational, and religious activities. Naturally, such interests are the major ones for few men. It is the virtue of a free society that it nonetheless permits these interests full scope and does not subordinate them to the narrow materialistic interests that dominate the bulk of mankind. That is why capitalist societies are less materialistic than collectivist societies.

Why is it, in light of the record, that the burden of proof still seems to rest on those of us who oppose new government programs and who seek to reduce the already unduly large role of government? Let Dicey answer: "The beneficial effect of State intervention, especially in the form of legislation, is direct, immediate, and, so to speak, visible, whilst its evil effects are gradual and indirect, and lie out of sight. . . . Nor . . . do most people keep in mind that State inspectors may be incompetent, careless, or even occasionally corrupt . . . ; few are those who realize the undeniable truth that State help kills self-help. Hence the majority of mankind must almost of necessity look with undue favor upon governmental intervention. This natural bias can be counteracted only by the existence, in a given society, . . . of a presumption or prejudice in favor of individual liberty, that is, of laissez-faire. The mere decline, therefore, of faith in self-help—and that such a decline has taken place is certain—is of itself sufficient to account for the growth of legislation tending towards socialism."

The preservation and expansion of freedom are today threatened from two directions. The one threat is obvious and clear. It is the external threat coming from the evil men in the Kremlin who promise to bury us. The other threat is far more subtle. It is the internal threat coming from men of good intentions and good will who wish to reform us. Impatient with the slowness of persuasion and example to achieve the great social changes they envision, they are anxious to use the power of the state to achieve their ends and confident of their own ability to do so. Yet if they gained the power, they would fail to achieve their immediate aims and, in addition, would produce a collective state from which they would recoil in horror and of which they would be among the first victims. Concentrated power is not rendered harmless by the good intentions of those who create it.

The two threats unfortunately reinforce one another. Even if we avoid a nuclear holocaust, the threat from the Kremlin requires us to devote a sizable fraction of our resources to our military defense. The importance of government as a buyer of so much of our output, and the sole buyer of the output of many firms and industries, already concentrates a dangerous amount of economic power in the hands of the political authorities, changes the environment in which business operates and the criteria relevant for business success, and in these and other ways endangers a free market. This danger we cannot avoid. But we needlessly intensify it by continuing the present widespread governmental intervention in areas unrelated to the military defense of the nation and by undertaking ever new governmental programs—from medical care for the aged to lunar exploration.

As Adam Smith once said, "There is much ruin in a nation." Our basic structure of values and the interwoven network of free institutions will withstand much. I believe that we shall be able to preserve and extend freedom despite the size of the military programs and despite the economic powers already concentrated in Washington. But we shall be able to do so only if we awake to the threat that we face, only if we persuade our fellow men that free institutions offer a surer, if perhaps at times a slower, route to the ends they seek than the coercive power of the state. The glimmerings of change that are already apparent in the intellectual climate are a hopeful augury.

Part III

Traditionalism

While World War II played a role in the resurrection of classical liberalism in America and throughout the world, it also contributed to a revived traditionalism, which its critics would label the "new conservatism." The devastation wrought by the war, particularly the aerial bombardment of cities, the atomic bombing of Japan, and the revelation of atrocities on an unimaginable scale—such as the Nazi slaughter of the Jews and the tens of millions killed worldwide in the war—required explanation, particularly as politicians and intellectuals continued to proclaim the contemporary age as the summit of human progress. How did mankind descend into madness? What could explain the barbarism of the first half of the twentieth century?

One person who felt compelled to explain such events was Richard M. Weaver (1910–1963), a professor of English at the University of Chicago. Weaver was a Southerner and reflected the heritage of his upbringing in that region. Originally inclined toward socialism when a student at the University of Kentucky during the early years of the Great Depression, Weaver went on to Vanderbilt for graduate studies, and eventually eschewed radicalism. At Vanderbilt he fell easily into the circle of the agrarians and was greatly influenced by their defense of southern regionalism and dedication to traditional order. Upon graduation, he took a teaching position at Texas A & M University and by 1939 had shed his left-wing views. Miserable in Texas, Weaver entered the doctoral program at Louisiana State University, completing a dissertation entitled "The Confederate South, 1865–1910: A Study in the Survival of a Mind and a Culture" (published posthumously as *The Southern Tradition at Bay*).[1] He received a teaching position in English at the University of Chicago, where he remained until his death in 1963.[2]

Weaver was disillusioned by the war, and this disillusionment formed the basis for his writing what would become *Ideas Have Consequences*. Weaver told one correspondent:

I have become convinced in the past few years that the essence of civilization is ethical. . . . And never has the power of ethical discrimination been
as low as it is today. The atomic bomb was the final blow to the code of
humanity. I cannot help thinking that we will suffer retribution for this.
For a long time to come I believe my chief interest is going to be the
restoration of civilization, of the distinctions that make life intelligible.[3]

Weaver's goal was to root the "dissolution of the western world" he
everywhere saw evident and to put forth a solution to the crisis of
mankind's moral decline.

The first chapter of Part III is the introduction from the resulting
work, *Ideas Have Consequences*, a title Weaver never liked. Weaver lays
out the reasons for man's decline, how man "became a moral idiot." He
then argues that this decline goes back further than the barbarisms of the
twentieth century; indeed, they are rooted in the Christian heresy of
nominalism propounded by the English monk William of Occam in the
fourteenth century (the doctrine that "man is the measure of all things"
as Weaver described it). Weaver's book was greeted with mixed reviews
when it was published in 1948, with liberal reviewers heaping opprobrium
on such a reactionary viewpoint.[4] But the book had a profound influence
on a growing philosophical conservatism in America. It is no wonder,
then, that eminent conservative thinkers credit Weaver's slim little volume as being representative, in the words of Frank Meyer, of "the *fons et
origo* of the contemporary American conservative movement," or for
publisher Henry Regnery, as one of the works providing "the intellectual
basis for the modern conservative movement."[5]

One person greatly influenced by Weaver was Russell Kirk (1918–1996).
Kirk was the son of a railroad worker, born in Plymouth, Michigan.
Except for a stint in the army during World War II, college, and sabbati-
cals abroad (typically to his beloved Scottish countryside), Kirk would
spend few years outside of Michigan, residing in an ancestral home
named Piety Hill in Mecosta for the remainder of his life.[6] A man deeply
at odds with the modern age's worship of industrialism and technology,
Kirk lived the idyllic life of a conservative sage from some premodern
past, writing on his own terms, free from the constraints of an academic
life in the modern university. (He was briefly employed by Michigan State
University, which he referred to, derisively, as "behemoth university.")

Kirk received his doctorate of letters from St. Andrews University in
Scotland, the first American to be accorded this degree. While stationed

in the deserts of Utah as a soldier in World War II, Kirk had read major conservative and classical liberal writers (he was influenced by Albert Jay Nock's description of the remnant in his *Memoirs of a Superfluous Man*). Most prominently, Edmund Burke, the great English-Irish statesman whose *Reflections on the Revolution in France* remains the classic statement of the pernicious effects of revolutionary nihilism (Burke supported the American Revolution), inspired Kirk. Burke's conservatism represented the politics of a prescriptive tradition, a social order based on inherited traditions, whether embodied by religion, the rule of law, or an aristocratic order. For Kirk, such a tradition was sadly lacking in American politics. Much like Weaver, Kirk was horrified by the failures of modernity; unlike Weaver, Kirk saw a return to Burkean principles as a possible path for society to emulate ("a renewed preference for the old and tried, against the new and untried"). His tone was cautiously optimistic, pointing to a normative conception of politics that it would be possible to replicate. As he later wrote, Burke provided "the modern understanding that the great problem of politics is the maintenance of a tolerable tension between the claims of order and the claims of freedom."[7]

Kirk's dissertation was published in 1953 by Regnery Publishing, a firm begun in 1946 by Henry Regnery, one of the founders of *Human Events,* and himself a contributor to postwar traditionalism (Regnery's firm gained notoriety for its publication of William F. Buckley, Jr.'s *God and Man at Yale* in 1951). *The Conservative Mind,* from which Chapter 9 is taken, established Kirk as the preeminent scholar of the conservative disposition in Anglo-American thought. Not only did he employ, explicitly, the term conservative to describe the "literature of order" which he described, but he also developed six canons of conservatism. While religion is one of the canons of this conservatism, the book itself is remarkably free of a religious perspective; rather, Kirk depicted a wide variety of conservatives who embraced and contributed to the postulates of a traditional social order.

The book contributed to the rebirth of the term conservatism in national consciousness; the name conservative was employed to describe not only the intellectual position Kirk espoused but also to describe any opponent of liberalism, modernism, and the State. Kirk's book was widely reviewed, much like Weaver's, and sparked a controversy concerning the "new conservatism," as the traditionalist viewpoint was labeled.[8] The controversy grew heated with the publication of Frank Meyer's "Collectivism Rebaptized" in the July 16, 1955 issue of *The Freeman*, a libertarian monthly published by the Foundation for Economic Education in New York.

Frank Meyer, an ex-communist, would become the foremost theoretician of conservatism in the late 1950s and early 1960s. He was responsible for the "fusion" of both traditionalism and classical liberalism which transformed conservatism from a disconnected body of ideas into a political ideology.[9] But in the mid-1950s, Meyer was still in the process of shifting from the collectivist ideology of communism to a defense of liberal individualism. Influenced greatly by nineteenth-century English classical liberal philosopher John Stuart Mill, Meyer felt threatened by what he saw as the unprincipled abstractions of the new conservatism. Kirk, Weaver, and others represented a threat to individual liberty through their insistence on prescriptive tradition and social order. What social order was Kirk interested in defending? Could not the communist insistence on defending the primacy of the State represent a similar, albeit fallacious, defense of social order? While Kirk was not defending the central state, neither was he defending the primacy of individualism over society. Meyer defended the value of the individual person above all else. As an *ex*-communist, it should not be surprising that he did so. In so doing, he pointed out some of the theoretical problems with the new conservatism and paved the way for a reconciliation between a traditional social order and individual liberty, a reconciliation that would allow conservatism to "plunge into politics" (see Part V).

Chapter Eight

The Quest for Order

Richard M. Weaver

In considering the world to which these matters are addressed, I have been chiefly impressed by the difficulty of getting certain initial facts admitted. This difficulty is due in part to the widely prevailing Whig theory of history, with its belief that the most advanced point in time represents the point of highest development, aided no doubt by theories of evolution which suggest to the uncritical a kind of necessary passage from simple to complex. Yet the real trouble is found to lie deeper than this. It is the appalling problem, when one comes to actual cases, of getting men to distinguish between better and worse. Are people today provided with a sufficiently rational scale of values to attach these predicates with intelligence? There is ground for declaring that modern man has become a moral idiot. So few are those who care to examine their lives, or to accept the rebuke which comes of admitting that our present state may be a fallen state, that one questions whether people now understand what is meant by the superiority of an ideal. One might expect abstract reasoning to be lost upon them; but what is he to think when attestations of the most concrete kind are set before them, and they are still powerless to mark a difference or to draw a lesson? For four centuries every man has been not only his own priest but his own professor of ethics, and the consequence is an anarchy which threatens even that minimum consensus of value necessary to the political state.

Surely we are justified in saying of our time: If you seek the monument to our folly, look about you. In our own day we have seen cities obliterated and ancient faiths stricken. We may well ask, in the words of Mat-

Richard M. Weaver, *Ideas Have Consequences* (Chicago: University of Chicago Press, 1948), 1–17. Reprinted by permission of University of Chicago Press.

thew, whether we are not faced with "great tribulation, such as was not since the beginning of the world," We have for many years moved with a brash confidence that man had achieved a position of independence which rendered the ancient restraints needless. Now, in the first half of the twentieth century, at the height of modern progress, we behold unprecedented outbreaks of hatred and violence; we have seen whole nations desolated by war and turned into penal camps by their conquerors; we find half of mankind looking upon the other half as criminal. Everywhere occur symptoms of mass psychosis. Most portentous of all, there appear diverging bases of value, so that our single planetary globe is mocked by worlds of different understanding. These signs of disintegration arouse fear, and fear leads to desperate unilateral efforts toward survival, which only forward the process.

Like Macbeth, Western man made an evil decision, which has become the efficient and final cause of other evil decisions. Have we forgotten our encounter with the witches on the heath? It occurred in the late fourteenth century, and what the witches said to the protagonist of this drama was that man could realize himself more fully if he would only abandon his belief in the existence of transcendentals. The powers of darkness were working subtly, as always, and they couched this proposition in the seemingly innocent form of an attack upon universals. The defeat of logical realism in the great medieval debate was the crucial event in the history of Western culture; from this flowed those acts which issue now in modern decadence.

One may be accused here of oversimplifying the historical process, but I take the view that the conscious policies of men and governments are not mere rationalizations of what has been brought about by unaccountable forces. They are rather deductions from our most basic ideas of human destiny, and they have a great, though not unobstructed, power to determine our course.

For this reason I turn to William of Occam as the best representative of a change which came over man's conception of reality at this historic juncture. It was William of Occam who propounded the fateful doctrine of nominalism, which denies that universals have a real existence. His triumph tended to leave universal terms mere names serving our convenience. The issue ultimately involved is whether there is a source of truth higher than, and independent of, man; and the answer to the question is decisive for one's view of the nature and destiny of humankind. The practical result of nominalist philosophy is to banish the reality which is perceived by the intellect and to posit as reality that which is perceived by the senses. With this change is the affirmation of what is real, the whole orientation of culture takes a turn, and we are on the road to modern empiricism.

It is easy to be blind to the significance of a change because it is remote in time and abstract in character. Those who have not discovered that world view is the most important thing about a man, as about the men composing a culture, should consider the train of circumstances which have with perfect logic proceeded from this. The denial of universals carries with it the denial of everything transcending experience. The denial of everything transcending experience means inevitably—though ways are found to hedge on this—the denial of truth. With the denial of objective truth there is no escape from the relativism of "man the measure of all things." The witches spoke with the habitual equivocation of oracles when they told man that by this easy choice he might realize himself more fully, for they were actually initiating a course which cuts one off from reality. Thus began the "abomination of desolation" appearing today as a feeling of alienation from all fixed truth.

Because a change of belief so profound eventually influences every concept, there emerged before long a new doctrine of nature. Whereas nature had formerly been regarded as imitating a transcendent model and as constituting an imperfect reality, it was henceforth looked upon as containing the principles of its own constitution and behavior. Such revision has had two important consequences for philosophical inquiry. First, it encouraged a careful study of nature, which has come to be known as science, on the supposition that by her acts she revealed her essence. Second, and by the same operation, it did away with the doctrine of forms imperfectly realized. Aristotle had recognized an element of unintelligibility in the world, but the view of nature as a rational mechanism expelled this element. The expulsion of the element of unintelligibility in nature was followed by the abandonment of the doctrine of original sin. If physical nature is the totality and if man is of nature, it is impossible to think of him as suffering from constitutional evil; his defections must now be attributed to his simple ignorance or to some kind of social deprivation. One comes thus by clear deduction to the corollary of the natural goodness of man.

And the end is not yet. If nature is a self-operating mechanism and man is a rational animal adequate to his needs, it is next in order to elevate rationalism to the rank of a philosophy. Since man proposed now not to go beyond the world, it was proper that he should regard as his highest intellectual vocation methods of interpreting data supplied by the senses. There followed the transition to Hobbes and Locke and the eighteenth-century rationalists, who taught that man needed only to reason correctly upon evidence from nature. The question of what the world was made for now becomes meaningless because the asking of it presupposes something prior to nature in the order of existents. Thus it is not the mysterious fact of the world's existence which interests the new man but explanations of how the world works. This is the rational basis for modern science, whose systemization of phenomena is, as Bacon declared in the *New Atlantis,* a means to dominion.

At this stage religion begins to assume an ambiguous dignity, and the question of whether it can endure at all in a world of rationalism and science has to be faced. One solution was deism, which makes God the outcome of a rational reading of nature. But this religion, like all those which deny antecedent truth, was powerless to bind; it merely left each man to make what he could of the world open to the senses. There followed references to "nature and nature's God," and the anomaly of a "humanized" religion.

Materialism loomed next on the horizon, for it was implicit in what had already been framed. Thus it soon became imperative to explain man by his environment, which was the work of Darwin and others in the nineteenth century (it is further significant of the pervasive character of these changes that several other students were arriving at similar explanations when Darwin published in 1859). If man came into this century trailing clouds of transcendental glory, he was now accounted for in a way that would satisfy the positivists.

With the human being thus firmly ensconced in nature, it at once became necessary to question the fundamental character of his motivation. Biological necessity, issuing in the survival of the fittest, was offered as the *causa causans,* after the important question of human origin had been decided in favor of scientific materialism.

After it has been granted that man is molded entirely by environmental pressures, one is obligated to extend the same theory of causality to his institutions. The social philosophers of the nineteenth century found in Darwin powerful support for their thesis that human beings act always out of economic incentives, and it was they who completed the abolishment of freedom of the will. The great pageant of history thus became reducible to the economic endeavors of individuals and classes; and elaborate prognoses were constructed on the theory of economic conflict and resolution. Man created in the divine image, the protagonist of a great drama in which his soul was at stake, was replaced by man the wealth-seeking and -consuming animal.

Finally came psychological behaviorism, which denied not only freedom of the will but even such elementary means of direction as instinct. Because the scandalous nature of this theory is quickly apparent, it failed to win converts in such numbers as the others; yet it is only a logical extension of them and should in fairness be embraced by the upholders of material causation. Essentially, it is a reduction to absurdity of the line of reasoning which began when man bade a cheerful goodbye to the concept of transcendence.

There is no term proper to describe the condition in which he is now left unless it be "abysmality." He is in the deep and dark abysm, and he has nothing with which to raise himself. His life is practice without theory. As problems crowd upon him, he deepens confusion by meeting them with *ad hoc* policies. Secretly he hungers for truth but consoles himself with the thought that life should be experimental. He sees his institutions crumbling and rationalizes with talk of emancipation. Wars have to be fought, seemingly with increased frequency; therefore he revives the old ideals—ideals which his present assumptions actually render meaningless—and, by the machinery of state, forces them again to do service. He struggles with the paradox that total immersion in matter unfits him to deal with the problems of matter.

His decline can be represented as a long series of abdications. He has found less and less ground for authority at the same time he thought he was setting himself up as the center of authority in the universe; indeed, there seems to exist here a dialectic process which takes away his power in proportion as he demonstrates that his independence entitles him to power.

This story is eloquently reflected in changes that have come over education. The shift from the truth of the intellect to the facts of experience followed hard upon the meeting with the witches. A little sign appears, "a cloud no bigger than a man's hand," in a change that came over the study of logic in the fourteenth century—the century of Occam. Logic became grammaticized, passing from a science which taught men *vere loqui* to one which taught *recte loqui* or from an ontological division by categories to a study of signification, with the inevitable focus upon historical meanings. Here begins the assault upon definition: if words no longer correspond to objective realities, it seems no great wrong to take liberties with words. From this point on, faith in language as a means of arriving at truth weakens, until our own age, filled with an acute sense of doubt, looks for a remedy in the new science of semantics.

So with the subject matter of education. The Renaissance increasingly adapted its course of study to produce a successful man of the world, though it did not leave him without philosophy and the graces, for it was still, by heritage, at least, an ideational world and was therefore near enough transcendental conceptions to perceive the dehumanizing effects of specialization. In the seventeenth century physical discovery paved the way for the incorporation of the sciences, although it was not until the nineteenth that these began to challenge the very continuance of the ancient intellectual disciplines. And in this period the change gained momentum, aided by two developments of overwhelming influence. The first was a patent increase in man's dominion over nature which dazzled all but the most thoughtful; and the second was the growing mandate for popular education. The latter might have proved a good in itself, but it was wrecked on equalitarian democracy's unsolvable problem of authority: none was in a position to say what the hungering multitudes were to be fed. Finally, in an abject surrender to the situation, in an abdication of the authority of knowledge, came the elective system. This was followed by a carnival of specialism, professionalism, and vocationalism, often fostered and protected by strange bureaucratic devices, so that on the honored name of university there traded a weird congeries of interests, not a few of which were anti-intellectual even in their pretensions. Institutions of learning did not check but rather contributed to the decline by losing interest in *Homo sapiens* to develop *Homo faber*.

Studies pass into habits, and it is easy to see these changes reflected in the dominant type of leader from epoch to epoch. In the seventeenth century it was, on the one side, the royalist and learned defender of the faith and, on the other, aristocratic intellectuals of the type of John Milton and the Puritan theocrats who settled New England. The next century saw the domination of the Whigs in England and the rise of encyclopedists and romanticists on the Continent, men who were not without intellectual background but who assiduously cut the mooring strings to reality as they succumbed to the delusion that man is by nature good. Frederick the Great's rebuke to a sentimentalist, *"Ach, mein lieber Sulzer, er kennt nicht diese verdammte Rasse,"* epitomizes the difference between the two outlooks. The next period witnessed the rise of the popular leader and demagogue, the typical foe of privilege, who broadened the franchise in England, wrought revolution on the Continent, and in the United States replaced the social order which the Founding Fathers had contemplated with demagogism and the urban political machine. The twentieth century ushered in the leader of the masses, though at this point there occurs a split whose deep significance we shall have occasion to note. The new prophets of reform divide sharply into sentimental humanitarians and an elite group of remorseless theorists who pride themselves on their freedom from sentimentality. Hating this world they never made, after its debauchery of centuries, the modern Communists—revolutionaries and logicians—move toward intellectual rigor. In their decision lies the sharpest reproach yet to the desertion of intellect by Renaissance man and his successors. Nothing is more disturbing to modern men of the West than the logical clarity with which the Communists face all problems. Who shall say that this feeling is not born of a deep apprehension that here are the first true realists in hundreds of years and that no dodging about in the excluded middle will save Western liberalism?

This story of man's passage from religious or philosophical transcendentalism has been told many times, and, since it has usually been told as a story of progress, it is extremely difficult today to get people in any number to see contrary implications. Yet to establish the fact of decadence is the most pressing duty of our time because, until we have demonstrated that cultural decline is a historical fact—which can be established—and that modern man has about squandered his estate, we cannot combat those who have fallen prey to hysterical optimism.

Such is the task, and our most serious obstacle is that people traveling this downward path develop an insensibility which increases with their degradation. Loss is perceived most clearly at the beginning; after habit becomes implanted, one beholds the anomalous situation of apathy mounting as the moral crisis deepens. It is when the first faint warnings come that one has the best chance to save himself; and this, I suspect, explains why medieval thinkers were extremely agitated over questions which seem to us today without point or relevance. If one goes on, the monitory voices fade out, and it is not impossible for him to reach a state in which his entire moral orientation is lost. Thus in the face of the enormous brutality of our age we seem unable to make appropriate response to perversions of truth and acts of bestiality. Multiplying instances show complacency in the presence of contradiction which denies the heritage of Greece, and a callousness to suffering which denies the spirit of Christianity. Particularly since the great wars do we observe this insentience. We approach a condition in which we shall be amoral without the capacity to perceive it and degraded without means to measure our descent.

That is why, when we reflect upon the cataclysms of the age, we are chiefly impressed with the failure of men to rise to the challenge of them. In the past, great calamities have called forth, if not great virtues, at least heroic postures; but after the awful judgments pronounced against men and nations in recent decades, we detect notes of triviality and travesty. A strange disparity has developed between the drama of these actions and the conduct of the protagonists, and we have the feeling of watching actors who do not comprehend their roles.

Hysterical optimism will prevail until the world again admits the existence of tragedy, and it cannot admit the existence of tragedy until it again distinguishes between good and evil. Hope of restoration depends upon recovery of the "ceremony of innocence," of that clearness of vision and knowledge of form which enable us to sense what is alien or destructive, what does not comport with our moral ambition. The time to seek this is now, before we have acquired the perfect insouciance of those who prefer perdition. For, as the course goes on, the movement turns centrifugal; we rejoice in our abandon and are never so full of the sense of accomplishment as when we have struck some bulwark of our culture a deadly blow.

In view of these circumstances, it is no matter for surprise that, when we ask people even to consider the possibility of decadence, we meet incredulity and resentment. We must consider that we are in effect asking for a confession of guilt and an acceptance of sterner obligation; we are making demands in the name of the ideal or the suprapersonal, and we cannot expect a more cordial welcome than disturbers of complacency have received in any other age. On the contrary, our welcome will rather be less today, for a century and a half of bourgeois ascendancy has produced a type of mind highly unreceptive to unsettling thoughts. Added to this is the egotism of modern man, fed by many springs, which will scarcely permit the humility needed for self-criticism.

The apostles of modernism usually begin their retort with catalogues of modern achievement, not realizing that here they bear witness to their immersion in particulars. We must remind them that we cannot begin to enumerate until we have defined what is to be sought or proved. It will not suffice to point out the inventions and processes of our century unless it can be shown that they are something other than a splendid efflorescence of decay. Whoever desires to praise some modern achievement should wait until he has related it to the professed aims of our civilization as rigorously as the Schoolmen related a corollary to their doctrine of the nature of God. All demonstrations lacking this are pointless.

If it can be agreed, however, that we are to talk about ends before means, we may begin by asking some perfectly commonplace questions about the condition of modern man. Let us, first of all, inquire whether he knows more or is, on the whole, wiser than his predecessors.

This is a weighty consideration, and if the claim of the modern to know more is correct, our criticism falls to the ground, for it is hardly to be imagined that a people who have been gaining in knowledge over the centuries have chosen an evil course.

Naturally, everything depends on what we mean by knowledge. I shall adhere to the classic proposition that there is no knowledge at the level of sensation, that therefore knowledge is of universals, and that whatever we know as a truth enables us to predict. The process of learning involves interpretation, and the fewer particulars we require in order to arrive at our generalization, the more apt pupils we are in the school of wisdom.

The whole tendency of modern thought, one might say its whole moral impulse, is to keep the individual busy with endless induction. Since the time of Bacon the world has been running away from, rather than toward, first principles, so that, on the verbal level, we see "fact" substituted for "truth," and on the philosophic level, we witness attack upon abstract ideas and speculative inquiry. The unexpressed assumption of empiricism is that experience will tell us what we are experiencing. In the popular arena one can tell from certain newspaper columns and radio programs that the average man has become imbued with this notion and imagines that an industrious acquisition of particulars will render him a man of knowledge. With what pathetic trust does he recite his facts! He has been told that knowledge is power, and knowledge consists of a great many small things.

Thus the shift from speculative inquiry to investigation of experience has left modern man so swamped with multiplicities that he no longer sees his way. By this we understand Goethe's dictum that one may be said to know much only in the sense that he knows little. If our contemporary belongs to a profession, he may be able to describe some tiny bit of the world with minute fidelity, but still he lacks understanding. There can be no truth under a program of separate sciences, and his thinking will be invalidated as soon as *ab extra* relationships are introduced.

The world of "modern" knowledge is like the universe of Eddington, expanding by diffusion until it approaches the point of nullity.

What the defenders of present civilization usually mean when they say that modern man is better educated than his forebears is that he is literate in larger numbers. The literacy can be demonstrated; yet one may question whether there has ever been a more deceptive panacea, and we are compelled, after a hundred years of experience, to echo Nietzsche's bitter observation: "Everyone being allowed to learn to read, ruineth in the long run not only writing but also thinking." It is not what people can read; it is what they do read, and what they can be made, by any imaginable means, to learn from what they read, that determine the issue of this noble experiment. We have given them a technique of acquisition; how much comfort can we take in the way they employ it? In a society where expression is free and popularity is rewarded they read mostly that which debauches them and they are continuously exposed to manipulation by controllers of the printing machine—as I shall seek to make clear in a later passage. It may be doubted whether one person in three draws what may be correctly termed knowledge from his freely chosen reading matter. The staggering number of facts to which he today has access serves only to draw him away from consideration of first principles, so that his orientation becomes peripheral. And looming above all as a reminder of this fatuity is the tragedy of modern Germany, the one totally literate nation.

Now those who side with the Baconians in preferring shoes to philosophy will answer that this is an idle complaint, because the true glory of modern civilization is that man has perfected his material estate to a point at which he is provided for. And probably it could be shown statistically that the average man today, in countries not desolated by war, has more things to consume than his forebears. On this, however, there are two important comments to be made.

The first is that since modern man has not defined his way of life, he initiates himself into an endless series when he enters the struggle for an "adequate" living. One of the strangest disparities of history lies between the sense of abundance felt by older and simpler societies and the sense of scarcity felt by the ostensibly richer societies of today. Charles Péguy has referred to modern man's feeling of "slow economic strangulation," his sense of never having enough to meet the requirements which his pattern of life imposes on him. Standards of consumption which he cannot meet, and which he does not need to meet, come virtually in the guise of duties. As the abundance for simple living is replaced by the scarcity for complex living, it seems that in some way not yet explained we have formalized prosperity until it is for most people only a figment of the imagination. Certainly the case of the Baconians is not won until it has been proved that the substitution of covetousness for wantlessness, of an ascending spiral of desires for a stable requirement of necessities, leads to the happier condition.

Suppose, however, we ignore this feeling of frustration and turn our attention to the fact that, by comparison, modern man has more. This very circumstance sets up a conflict, for it is a constant law of human nature that the more a man has to indulge in, the less disposed he is to endure the discipline of toil—that is to say, the less willing he is to produce that which is to be consumed. Labor ceases to be functional in life; it becomes something that is grudgingly traded for that competence, or that superfluity, which everyone has a "right" to. A society spoiled in this manner may be compared to a drunkard: the more he imbibes the less is he able to work and acquire the means to indulge his habit. A great material establishment, by its very temptation to luxuriousness, unfits the owner for the labor necessary to maintain it, as has been observed countless times in the histories of individuals and of nations.

But let us waive all particular considerations of this sort and ask whether modern man, for reasons apparent or obscure, feels an increased happiness. We must avoid superficial conceptions of this state and look for something fundamental. I should be willing to accept Aristotle's "feeling of conscious vitality." Does he feel equal to life; does he look upon it as does a strong man upon a race?

First, one must take into account the deep psychic anxiety, the extraordinary prevalence of neurosis, which make our age unique. The typical modern has the look of the hunted. He senses that we have lost our grip upon reality. This, in turn, produces disintegration, and disintegration leaves impossible that kind of reasonable prediction by which men, in eras of sanity, are able to order their lives. And the fear accompanying it unlooses the great disorganizing force of hatred, so that states are threatened and wars ensue. Few men today feel certain that war will not wipe out their children's inheritance; and, even if this evil is held in abeyance, the individual does not rest easy, for he knows that the Juggernaut technology may twist or destroy the pattern of life he has made for himself. A creature designed to look before and after finds that to do the latter has gone out of fashion and that to do the former is becoming impossible. Added to this is another deprivation. Man is constantly being assured today that he has more power than ever before in history, but his daily experience is one of powerlessness. Look at him today somewhere in the warren of a great city. If he is with a business organization, the odds are great that he has sacrificed every other kind of independence in return for that dubious one known as financial. Modern social and corporate organization makes independence an expensive thing; in fact, it may make common integrity a prohibitive luxury for the ordinary man, as Stuart Chase has shown. Not only is this man likely to be a slavey at his place of daily toil, but he is cribbed, cabined, and confined in countless ways, many of which are merely devices to make possible physically the living together of masses. Because these are deprivations of what is rightful, the end is frustration, and hence the look, upon the faces of those whose souls have not already become minuscule, of hunger and unhappiness.

These are some questions that should be put to the eulogists of progress. It will certainly be objected that the decadence of a present age is one of the permanent illusions of mankind; it will be said that each generation feels it with reference to the next in the same way that parents can never quite trust the competence of their children to deal with the great world. In reply we must affirm that, given the conditions described, each successive generation does show decline in the sense that it stands one step nearer the abysm. When change is in progress, every generation will average an extent of it, and that some cultures have passed from a high state of organization to dissolution can be demonstrated as objectively as anything in history. One has only to think of Greece, of Venice, of Germany. The assertion that changes from generation to generation are illusory and that there exist only cycles of biological reproduction is another form of that denial of standards, and ultimately of knowledge, which lies at the source of our degradation.

Civilization has been an intermittent phenomenon; to this truth we have allowed ourselves to be blinded by the insolence of material success. Many late societies have displayed a pyrotechnic brilliance and a capacity for refined sensation far beyond anything seen in their days of vigor. That such things may exist and yet work against that state of character concerned with choice, which is the anchor of society, is the great lesson to be learned. . . .

Chapter Nine

The Conservative Mind

Russell Kirk

"The stupid party": this is John Stuart Mill's description of conservatives.
Like certain other summary dicta which nineteenth-century liberals
thought to be forever triumphant, this judgment needs review in our age
of disintegrating liberal and radical theories. Certainly many dull and
unreflecting people have lent their inertia to the cause of conservatism:
"It is commonly sufficient for practical purposes if conservatives, without
saying anything, just sit and think, or even if they merely sit," F. J. C.
Hearnshaw observed. Edmund Burke, the greatest of modern conservative
thinkers, was not ashamed to acknowledge the allegiance of humble men
whose sureties are prejudice and prescription; for, with affection, he
likened them to cattle under the English oaks, deaf to the insects of radical
innovation. Yet the conservative principle has been defended, these past
hundred and fifty years, by men of learning and genius. To review conservative ideas, examining their validity for this perplexed age, is the
purpose of this book, which does not pretend to be a history of conservative parties. This study is a prolonged essay in definition. What is the
essence of British and American conservatism? What system of ideas,
common to England and the United States, has sustained men of conservative instincts in their resistance against radical theories and social transformation ever since the beginning of the French Revolution?

Walk beside the Liffey in Dublin, a little way west of the dome of the
Four Courts, and you come to an old doorway in a blank wall. This is
the roof-less wreck of an eighteenth-century house, and until recently the

house still was here, inhabited although condemned: Number 12, Arran Quay, formerly a brick building of three stories, which began as a gentleman's residence, sank to the condition of a shop, presently was used as a governmental office of the meaner sort, and was demolished in 1950—a history suggestive of changes on a mightier scale since 1729, in Irish society. For in that year, Edmund Burke, the greatest native of Ireland, was born here. Modern Dublin's memories do not extend much beyond the era of O'Connell, and the annihilation of Burke's birthplace seems to have stirred up no protest. Across the river you see what was once the town house of the Earls of Moira and is now the office of a society for suppressing mendicity; and beyond that, the gigantic Guinness brewery. Behind Burke's house (or the sad scrap of it that remains), toward the old church of St. Michan in which, they say, he was baptised, stretch tottering brick slums where barefoot children scramble over broken walls. If you turn toward O'Connell Street, an easy stroll takes you to the noble façade of Trinity College and the statues of Burke and Goldsmith; northward, near Parnell Square, you may hear living Irish orators proclaiming through amplifiers that they have succeeded in increasing sevenfold the pensions of widows, a mere earnest of their intent. And you may reflect, with Burke, "What shadows we are, and what shadows we pursue!"

Since Burke's day, there have been alterations aplenty in Dublin. Yet to the visitor, Ireland sometimes seems a refuge of tradition amidst the flux of our age, and Dublin a conservative old city; and so they are. A world that damns tradition, exalts equality, and welcomes change; a world that has clutched at Rousseau, swallowed him whole, and demanded prophets yet more radical; a world smudged by industrialism, standardized by the masses, consolidated by government; a world crippled by war, trembling between the colossi of East and West, and peering over a smashed barricade into the gulf of dissolution: this, our era, is the society Burke foretold, with all the burning energy of his rhetoric, in 1790. By and large, radical thinkers have won the day. For a century and a half, conservatives have yielded ground in a manner which, except for occasionally successful rear-guard actions, must be described as a rout.

As yet the causes of their shattering defeat are not wholly clear. Two general explanations are possible, however: first, that throughout the modern world "*things* are in the saddle," and conservative ideas, however sound, cannot resist the unreasoning forces of industrialism, centralization, secularism, and the levelling impulse; second, that conservative thinkers have lacked perspicacity sufficient to meet the conundrums of modern times. And either explanation has some foundation. . . .

The Conservative Mind, then, is limited to British and American thinkers who have stood by tradition and old establishments. Only Britain and America, among the great nations, have escaped revolution since 1790, which seems attestation that their conservatism is a sturdy growth and that investigation of it may be rewarding. To confine the field more narrowly still, this book is an analysis of thinkers in the line of Burke. Convinced that Burke's is the true school of conservative principle, I have left out of consideration most anti-democratic liberals like Lowe, most anti-governmental individualists like Spencer, most anti-parliamentary writers like Carlyle. Every conservative thinker discussed in the following chapters—even the Federalists who were Burke's contemporaries—felt the influence of the great Whig, although sometimes the ideas of Burke penetrated to them only through a species of intellectual filter.

Conscious conservatism, in the modern sense, did not manifest itself until 1790, with the publication of *Reflections on the Revolution in France*. In that year the prophetic powers of Burke defined in the public consciousness, for the first time, the opposing poles of conservation and innovation. The Carmagnole announced the opening of our era, and the smoky energy of coal and steam in the north of England was the signal for another revolution. If one attempts to trace conservative ideas back to an earlier time in Britain, soon he is enmeshed in Whiggery, Toryism, and intellectual antiquarianism; for the modern issues, though earlier taking substance, were not yet distinct. Nor does the American struggle between conservatives and radicals become intense until Citizen Genêt and Tom Paine transport across the Atlantic enthusiasm for French liberty: the American Revolution, substantially, had been a conservative reaction, in the English political tradition, against royal innovation. If one really must find a preceptor for conservatism who is older than Burke, he cannot rest satisfied with Bolingbroke, whose skepticism in religion disqualifies him, or with the Machiavellian Hobbes, or that old-fangled absolutist Filmer. Falkland, indeed, and Clarendon and Halifax and Strafford, deserve study; still more, in Richard Hooker one discovers profound conservative observations which Burke inherited with his Anglicanism and which Hooker drew in part from the Schoolmen and their authorities; but already one is back in the sixteenth century, and then in the thirteenth, and this book is concerned with modern problems. In any practical sense, Burke is the founder of our conservatism. . . .

Any informed conservative is reluctant to condense profound and intricate intellectual systems to a few pretentious phrases; he prefers to leave that technique to the enthusiasm of radicals. Conservatism is not a fixed and immutable body of dogma, and conservatives inherit from Burke a talent for reexpressing their convictions to fit the time. As a working premise, nevertheless, one can observe here that the essence of social conservatism is preservation of the ancient moral traditions of humanity. Conservatives respect the wisdom of their ancestors . . . they are dubious of wholesale alteration. They think society is a spiritual reality, possessing an eternal life but a delicate constitution: it cannot be scrapped and recast as if it were a machine. "What is conservatism?" Abraham Lincoln inquired once. "Is it not adherence to the old and tried, against the new and untried?" It is that, but it is more . . .

I think that there are six canons of conservative thought—

(1) Belief that a divine intent rules society as well as conscience, forging an eternal chain of right and duty which links great and obscure, living and dead. Political problems, at bottom, are religious and moral problems. A narrow rationality, what Coleridge calls the Understanding, cannot of itself satisfy human needs. "Every Tory is a realist," says Keith Feiling: "he knows that there are great forces in heaven and earth that man's philosophy cannot plumb or fathom. We do wrong to deny it, when we are told that we do not trust human reason: we do not and we may not. Human reason set up a cross on Calvary, human reason set up the cup of hemlock, human reason was canonised in Nôtre Dame." Politics is the art of apprehending and applying the Justice which is above nature.

(2) Affection for the proliferating variety and mystery of traditional life, as distinguished from the narrowing uniformity and equalitarianism and utilitarian aims of most radical systems. This is why Quintin Hogg (Lord Hailsham) and R. J. White describe conservatism as "enjoyment." It is this buoyant view of life which Walter Bagehot called "the proper source of an animated Conservatism."

(3) Conviction that civilized society requires orders and classes. The only true equality is moral equality; all other attempts at levelling lead to despair, if enforced by positive legislation. Society longs for leadership, and if a people destroy natural distinctions among men, presently Buonaparte fills the vacuum.

(4) Persuasion that property and freedom are inseparably connected, and that economic levelling is not economic progress. Separate property from private possession, and liberty is erased.

(5) Faith in prescription and distrust of "sophisters and calculators." Man must put a control upon his will and his appetite, for conservatives know man to be governed more by emotion than by reason. Tradition and sound prejudice provide checks upon man's anarchic impulse.

(6) Recognition that change and reform are not identical, and that innovation is a devouring conflagration more often than it is a torch of progress. Society must alter, for slow change is the means of its conservation, like the human body's perpetual renewal; but Providence is the proper instrument for change, and the test of a statesman is his cognizance of the real tendency of Providential social forces.

Various deviations from this system of ideas have occurred, and there are numerous appendages to it; but in general conservatives have adhered to these articles of belief with a consistency rare in political history. To catalogue the principles of their opponents is more difficult. At least five major schools of radical thought have competed for public favor since Burke entered politics: the rationalism of the *philosophies,* the romantic emancipation of Rousseau and his allies, the utilitarianism of the Benthamites, the positivism of Comte's school, and the collectivistic materialism of Marx and other socialists. This list leaves out of account those scientific doctrines, Darwinism chief among them, which have done so much to undermine the first principles of a conservative order. To express these several radicalisms in terms of a common denominator probably is presumptuous, foreign to the philosophical tenets of conservatism. All the same, in a hastily generalizing fashion one may say that radicalism since 1790 has tended to attack the prescriptive arrangement of society on the following grounds—

(1) The perfectibility of man and the illimitable progress of society: meliorism. Radicals believe that education, positive legislation, and alteration of environment can produce men like gods; they deny that humanity has a natural proclivity toward violence and sin.

(2) Contempt for tradition. Reason, impulse, and materialistic determinism are severally preferred as guides to social welfare, trustier than the wisdom of our ancestors. Formal religion is rejected and a variety of anti-Christian systems are offered as substitutes.

(3) Political levelling. Order and privilege are condemned; total democ-

racy, as direct as practicable, is the professed radical ideal. Allied with this spirit, generally, is a dislike of old parliamentary arrangements and an eagerness for centralization and consolidation.

(4) Economic levelling. The ancient rights of property, especially property in land, are suspect to almost all radicals; and collectivistic reformers hack at the institution of private property root and branch.

As a fifth point, one might try to define a common radical view of the state's function; but here the chasm of opinion between the chief schools of innovation is too deep for any satisfactory generalization. One can only remark that radicals unite in detesting Burke's description of the state as a divinely ordained moral essence, a spiritual union of the dead, the living, and those yet unborn.

So much for preliminary delineation. The radical, when all is said, is a neoterist, in love with change; the conservative, a man who says with Joubert, *Ce sont les crampons qui unissent une génération à une autre*— these ancient institutions of politics and religion. *Conservez ce qu'ont vu vos pères.* If one seeks by way of definition more than this, the sooner he turns to particular thinkers, the safer ground he is on. . . .

In a revolutionary epoch, sometimes men taste every novelty, sicken of them all, and return to ancient principles so long disused that they seem refreshingly hearty when they are rediscovered. History often appears to resemble a roulette wheel; there is truth in the old Greek idea of cycles, and round again may come the number which signifies a conservative order. One of those flaming clouds which we deny to the Deity but arrogate to our own employment may erase our present elaborate constructions as abruptly as the tocsin in the Faubourg St. Germain terminated an age equally tired of itself. Yet this roulette-wheel simile would be repugnant to Burke (or to John Adams), who knew history to be the unfolding of a Design. The true conservative thinks of this process, which looks like chance or fate, as, rather, the Providential operation of a moral law of polarity. And Burke, could he see our century, never would concede that a consumption-society, so near to suicide, is the end for which Providence has prepared man. If a conservative order is indeed to return, we ought to know the tradition which is attached to it, so that we may rebuild society; if it is not to be restored, still we ought to understand conservative ideas so that we may rake from the ashes what scorched fragments of civilization escape the conflagration of unchecked will and appetite. . . .

In both great English-speaking nations, conservatism has manifested a political and intellectual continuity for nearly one hundred and sixty-five years, while the radical parties that detested tradition have dissolved in succession, adhering as a movement to no common principle except hostility to whatever is established. British Socialism, though three times successful in attaining power, three times has grown sick of itself and surrendered political leadership to the Conservatives. In America, not a single public man of importance confesses himself to be a socialist; and when one prominent politician, Mr. Henry Wallace, flirted with doctrinaire collectivism, he was repudiated by his former admirers. Liberalism and Populism and Fascism and Syndicalism and nearly every other organized political manifestation of the "party of progress" has been discredited in Britain and America. Conservatives have retreated a long way since the French Revolution began; now and then they have fled headlong; but they have not despaired when they were beaten. The radicals have been able to rouse the appetite for novelty and the passion of envy among modern peoples; the conservatives have been able to fortify themselves within the inertia and the tradition of man; and these latter are powerful walls still. Certainly the conservatives have been routed, forced back from ditch to palisade; but they never have surrendered; and today, when the ranks of radicalism are decimated, timorous, and afflicted by internecine ferocity, conservatism has such an opportunity for regaining ground as it has not seen since that day when modern radicalism issued its challenge to traditional society by decorating "this hell-porch of a Hotel de Ville" with human heads on pikes.

How much conservatives have lost since July 14, 1789, has been suggested in the previous chapters of this prolonged essay. What they have retained, in Britain and America, remains immensely greater than what they have forfeited. The celebrants of the Feast of Reason, could they see the Anglo-American civilization of 1960, would be astonished to find Christianity still enduring on either side of the Atlantic—in the form of established churches in England and Scotland, in the form of diligent churchgoing and public affirmation of Christian morality in America. If the churches of Britain and America are not altogether in a sound condition, still they are healthier than they were in 1789. The latitudinarian parsons (more than half of whom, as Burke knew, had revolutionary sympathies at the beginning of the troubles in France) have been replaced, often, by diligent modern clergymen who take their duties earnestly; the America that Jefferson complacently told a Barbary potentate was "not a Christian nation" is simultaneously the home of muscular Protestantism and a chief prop of Rome. As Tocqueville predicted, democratic times have altered the practice of religion, but they have not worked the ruin of religious conviction. Thus the indispensable basis of any conservative order, religious sanction, remains reasonably secure.

As for political institutions, the outward shape of things has altered little in either Britain or the United States; and even the inward constitution has changed only in an orderly and harmonious fashion. The British Constitution still recognizes Crown, Lords, and Commons; it still acknowledges the ancient rights of Englishmen, even when they are violated under the apology of pressing necessity. The House of Commons remains a powerful body of critics, able to check the encroachments of government; the House of Lords, however reduced in authority, still admits the principle of aristocracy—and, possibly, may be so reformed as actually to increase its influence; the Queen and the idea of monarchy are respected by every important political faction. In America, the Federal Constitution has endured as the most sagacious conservative document in the history of Western civilization; the balance of interests and powers which John Adams and the Southern statesmen defended still operates, however threatened by centralization in this century; and no one advocates a radical revision of political establishments in America, despite the numerous abuses that shelter themselves behind federal and state constitutions.

Private property, which both aristocratic and middle-class elements in conservatism believe to be indispensable to an orderly society, remains an influence of vast power in Britain and America, and no faction dares to propose its abolition. "Nationalization" has lost its appeal in Britain; general appetite for durable private possessions never was greater in America than it is today. Income taxes and inheritance levies have injured the foundation of private ownership, but the edifice is in no immediate danger of collapse.

Respect for established usage and longing for continuity are not dead among English-speaking peoples, either. Despite the disruptive forces of mass-communication, rapid transportation, industrial standardization, a cheap press, and Gresham's Law working in affairs of the mind, despite the radical effects of vulgarized scientific speculation and weakened private morality, despite the decay of family economy and family affections, most men and women in the twentieth century still feel veneration for what their ancestors have believed, and express a pathetic eagerness to find stability in a time of flux. Thus the uprooting of humanity by proletarianization is not yet irreparable, and conservatives may appeal to an unsatisfied emotion of gigantic potency. The very triumph of the psychiatrist and the pseudo-religious sect in our century illustrates the fumbling of humanity for conservative values.

Of the six premises for conservative belief which are listed in the introductory chapter of this book *[Conservative Mind]*, then, four at least continue to animate the social impulses of a great many people in America and Britain. The conservatives' rout has been most serious where the principle of leadership, the idea of order and class, is concerned, and also in the necessity for combining reverence with the spirit of self-reliance, moral and social. Conservatism's most conspicuous difficulty in our time is that it confronts a people who have come to look upon society, vaguely, as a homogeneous mass of identical individuals, with indistinguishable abilities and needs, whose happiness may be secured by direction from above, through legislation or some manner of public instruction. Conservatism must teach humanity once more that the germ of public affections (in Burke's words) is "to love the little platoon we belong to in society." Somehow our conservative leaders must contrive to reconcile individualism (which sustained nineteenth-century life at the same time it starved the soul of the nineteenth century) with the sense of community that inspired Burke and Adams. If conservatives cannot redeem the modern masses from the sterile modern mass-mind, then a miserable collectivism which impoverishes both soul and body impends over Britain and America—the collectivism that now has deluged Europe east of the Elbe and the Austrian Alps, the collectivism (as Orwell wrote) of "the streamlined men who think in slogans and talk in bullets."

The prospect of this collectivism, affrighting even the obdurate radicals of the West, is the immediate impulse behind the revival of popular conservatism in Britain and the United States. The horror of life and death under Russian communism has produced a reaction which, perhaps, thinking conservatives must discount somewhat, even while they utilize its effect to re-establish the importance of conservative values. For although the triumph of the proletarian revolution and the absolute state, equalitarian and atheistic, everywhere would be disastrous to civilization, its particular forms probably would not always be identical with its present manifestation in eastern Europe. The enthusiastic liberal and the doctrinaire radical generally tend to forget the influence of national tradition and local political habits upon even revolutionary movements; any conservative, however, knows that France remains France whether ruled by Louis XIV or by Robespierre, and that the Russia of Stalin is still, beneath the surface, the Russia of Conrad's *Under Western Eyes*. British total collectivism, or American, would assume certain distinct character-istics peculiar to either nation, in some respects more nearly tolerable than Russian communism, in some other respects possibly even less endurable. . . .

The intelligent conservative, then, will not attempt to convince the public that political collectivism may be moderated; for it cannot stop short of a barbarous social demoralization; but he will endeavor to show men precisely how, and under what guise, the menace of collectivism impends over Western society. If popular opinion in Britain and America fails properly to apprehend the problem, all reaction against the ponder-ous tyranny of communism will be in vain; for in their anxiety to resist the Russian manifestation of this system, Britain and America may impose upon themselves their own particular oppression of mass-mind and mass-action. In our world, only intelligent conservatives retain the conviction and the clarity of purpose required to delineate the outlines of the vague system by which we are dismayed. By liberals and socialists, the shape of the new collectivism is scarcely better descried than Tweedledum's and Tweedledee's "monstrous crow, as big as a tar-barrel," though quite as alarming as that shadow. . . .

However moribund liberalism and old-style socialism may have be-come, the lust for change never lacks agents. Throughout the world, a new revolutionary theory and system seem to be taking substance: what Tocqueville predicted long ago as "democratic despotism," but harsher than he expected even that tyranny to be; in some sense, what Mr. James Burnham calls "the managerial revolution"; super-bureaucracy, arrogat-ing to itself functions that cannot properly appertain to the bureau or the cabinet; the planned economy, encompassing not merely the economy proper, however, but the whole moral and intellectual range of human activities; the grand form of *Plannwirtschaft*, state planning for its own sake, state socialism devoid of the sentimental aims which originally characterized socialism. In a confused way, mixed up with the notion of some mysterious deliberate conspiracy against democratic freedom, George Orwell succeeded in awakening the dread of the British and the American public against this conception of society by his novel *Nineteen-Eighty-Four*, much as Aldous Huxley had stirred up a vague alarm earlier by his *Brave New World*. Ideas of the efficacy and beneficence of "plan-ning" for socialistic ends have helped to clear the way for this Behemoth; but its reality would be crueller to the old-style socialist than his worst visions of capitalism. New-style socialists, all the same, are embracing this prospect with avidity. . . . Power is loved for its own disciplinary sake; regulation becomes an end, more than a means.

Democracy, in the old sense, must be sacrificed to the New Society; freedom, in the old sense, must be forgotten. How long will the planned society retain the theory and form of socialism? Is it possible that the new order may serve ends so foreign to the old humanitarian socialism as to be no more socialistic than the "people's democracies" of Rumania and Albania are democratic? George Orwell described the classes and occupations from which the managers and planners of the new absolute state are being recruited, "made up from the most part of bureaucrats, scientists, technicians, trade-union organizers, publicity experts, sociologists, teachers, journalists, and professional politicians . . . whose origins lay in the salaried middle class and the upper grades of the working class" and who "had been shaped and brought together by the barren world of monopoly industry and centralized government," schooled beyond their proper worldly prospects or, indeed, beyond their intellectual capacities, lacking property, lacking religious faith, lacking ancestors or expectation of posterity, seeking to gratify by the acquisition of power their loneliness and their nameless hungers . . .

Saint-Simon and Comte were the fathers of this planned society (some seeds of it may be detected in Utilitarianism, too, despite the individualism of the Benthamites); Professor Wilhelm Röpke, that penetrating social thinker in the line of Burckhardt, calls the planners' ideal "eternal Saint-Simonism," and he describes their dream as "that attitude of mind which is the outcome of a mixture of the hubris of the natural scientist and engineer mentality of those who, with the cult of the 'Colossal,' combine their egotistical urge to assert themselves; those who would construct and organize economics, the State, and society according to supposedly scientific laws and blueprints, while mentally reserving for themselves the principal *porte-feuilles*. And so we observe those collectivist social engineers of the type of a Wells or a Mannheim who quite openly admit the point of view of 'society as a machine' and who would thus seriously like to see realized the nightmare of a veritable Hell of civilization brought about by the complete instrumentation and functionalization of humanity." This would not be capitalism, nor yet socialism; it is the colossal state created chiefly for its own sake. Socialists may help to erect this structure; they will not endure to administer or enjoy it.

The New Society, if constructed on this model, at first may seem a convenient arrangement for enforcing equality of condition; but its structure—as if a diabolical instinct had inspired its building—especially facilitates ends quite different, the gratification of a lust for power and the destruction of all ancient political institutions in the interest of the new dominant elites. The great Plan requires that the public be kept constantly in an emotional state closely resembling that of a nation at war; this lacking, obedience and co-operation shrivel, for the old motives to duty are lost to sight in the machine-society. . . .

When faith in God, duty to ramily, hope of advancement, and satisfaction with one's task have vanished from the routine of life, Big Brother remains to show the donkey the stick instead of the carrot. A powerful new interest in society hopes to play the role of Big Brother, to be the managers of the Managerial Revolution. "There are many in all parties who look forward to the time when virtually the whole of the population will be dependent on the State for the whole of the amenities of life," says Mr. Douglas Jerrold. "Those who do so are the representatives of the most powerful class of the present day who, like the ruling classes which have preceded them, work in unspoken alliance toward common ends. This class is the new aristocracy of the pen and the desk, the professional organizers and administrators, who not only control the executive government (itself a province of vastly increasing importance), but also the machinery of organized labour and organized capital, and who now wish to assume not only the direction of all our great productive undertakings but, through the control of education and doctoring, of the private lives of all the citizens." . . .

During the remaining half of the present century, the principal endeavor of intelligent conservatives is likely to be resistance to the idea of a planned society, through restoration of an order which will make the planned society unnecessary and impracticable. But simple expostulation and lamentation will not suffice to impede the growth of *Plannwirtschaft;* conservative parties have committed that error too often. If, by the year 1984, justice, liberty, and hope still are general characteristics of Western social thought, the credit for this conservation of traditional values may belong to the school of genuinely reformatory and critical conservatism which is a growing influence in America and Britain and western Europe, making itself felt in the universities, expressing its convictions with a renewed vigor in the periodical press. The chief problems which intelligent conservatives of this century must endeavor to solve or to moderate may be grouped, with tolerable precision, in four categories:

(1) The problem of spiritual and moral regeneration; the restoration of the ethical system and the religious sanction upon which any life worth living is founded. This is conservatism at its highest; but it cannot be accomplished as a deliberate program of social reform, "political Christianity." "There is a tendency, especially among the English-speaking Protestant peoples, to treat religion as a kind of social tonic that can be used in times of national emergency in order to extract a further degree of moral effort from the people," Mr. Christopher Dawson observes. If the conservatives' effort comes to no more than this, it will fail. Spiritual restoration cannot be a means to social restoration: it must be its own end.

(2) The problem of leadership, which has two aspects: the preservation of some measure of veneration, discipline, order, and class; and the purgation of our system of education, so that learning once again may become truly liberal.

(3) The problem of the proletariat. The mass of men must find status and hope within society: true family, respect for the past, responsibility for the future, private property, duty as well as right, inner resources that matter more than the mass-amusements and mass-vices with which the modern proletarian seeks to forget his lack of an object. The degeneration of the family to mere common house-tenancy menaces the very essence of recognizable human character; and the phenomenon of social boredom, spreading in ever-widening circles to every level of civilized existence, promises a future more dreary than the round of life in the decaying Roman system. To restore purpose to labor and domestic existence, to give men back old hopes and long views and thought of posterity, will require the bold imagination which Burke infused into conservative ideas.

(4) The problem of economic stability. This does not mean the securing of plenty for everyone: no social program, least of all the planned economy of the welfare state, is likely to succeed in gratifying the material appetites of all humanity. But it does mean the establishment of a rational relationship between endeavor and reward. It means the adjustment of the British economy, for instance, to an age of diminished empire and intensified foreign competition; it means the adjustment of the American economy to the real capacities of American production, which cannot

permanently supply the demands of half the world with a flow of manufactures and agricultural commodities.

The immediate perplexities with which the newspapers and the radio incessantly deluge the public are not mentioned in this summary of the conservatives' task—the conundrum of atomic energy and new weapons of war, the success or failure of international organizations, the menace of Russian power. But these are not problems for conservative thought, or radical thought either, strictly speaking: they are problems of expediency, to be met by the soldier and the diplomat. The methods by which they may be solved will originate in some larger system of thought than the arts of diplomacy and publicity. A conservative is not tied hard and fast, by his philosophy, to any particular view of international relations, or any particular techniques of foreign offices. If the four great conservative necessities listed above can be satisfied with reasonable success, then the problems of war and peace are likely to fall into some manner of settlement, so far as the issues of war and peace ever can be settled among men. The conservative believes that a people to whom religious veneration, proper leadership, continuity of life, and material stability have been restored can meet nearly any temporary exigency; and that a people vexed by incessant change, carping radicalism, and ignorance of final causes can solve satisfactorily no social problem. An intelligent conservative feels that the ills of the world cannot be cured by any single ingenious system of improvisation or any solemn political contrivance. Each problem must be considered upon its own terms, but in the light of the wisdom of our ancestors. "And the more thoroughly we understand our own political tradition, the more readily its whole resources are available to us, the less likely we shall be to embrace the illusions which wait for the ignorant and the unwary," remarks a brilliant disciple of Burke, Mr. Michael Oakeshott, in his inaugural lecture upon assuming the professorial chair at the London School of Economics and Political Science which previously had been occupied by radical thinkers, Graham Wallas and Harold Lask—"the illusion that in politics we can get on without a tradition of behaviour, the illusion that the abridgement of a tradition is itself a sufficient guide, and the illusion that in politics there is anywhere a safe harbour, a destination to be reached or even a delectable strand of progress. The world is the best of all possible worlds, and *everything* in it is a necessary evil." Upon such assumptions the aristocratic old diplomacy was conducted, before the glorious attainment of "open covenants openly arrived at" and the interesting futilities pursued in the United Nations headquarters; as statesmen return to this conservative system of conduct, perplexities that all the heat of radical passion cannot resolve may surrender to the influence of an older complex of beliefs.

"As a negative impulse, conservatism is based on a certain distrust of human nature, believing that the immediate impulses of the heart and visions of the brain are likely to be misleading guides." So said Paul Elmer More in 1915. "But this distrust of human nature is closely connected with another and more positive factor of conservatism—its trust in the controlling power of the imagination." In this same essay on Disraeli, More observed that "conservatism is in general the intuition of genius, whereas liberalism is the efficiency of talent." By the middle of the twentieth century, conservatives were displaying once more those powers of imagination and intuition. They saw with the poet's vision.

The true conservative understands that the regeneration of society cannot be an undertaking purely social; for it is a problem spiritual and moral. Having lost the spirit of consecration, the modern masses are without expectation of anything better than a bigger slice of what they possess already. Dante tells us that damnation is a terribly simple state: the deprivation of hope—or, as the unknown author of the York Mysteries put it,

> Ye cursed caitiffs, from me flee,
> In hell to dwell without an end.
> There shall ye nought but sorrow see
> And sit by Sathanas the fiend.

How to restore a living faith to the routine of existence among the lonely crowd, how to remind men that life has ends—this conundrum the thinking conservative has to face. . . .

Chapter Ten

A Rebel in Search of Tradition

Frank S. Meyer

When two or three years ago Russell Kirk, then a member of the faculty of Michigan State College, published a volume called *The Conservative Mind*, he hardly expected, it is to be presumed, that within a short time it would make him the major prophet of a flourishing new movement. But the emergence of the New Conservatism, which has for some time filled the columns of the quarterlies and magazines of opinion and is now spilling out into the larger world, can indeed be accurately correlated with the appearance of that book.

There were, it is true, earlier premonitions—the shrill cries of Peter Viereck, scattered articles here and there on a more urbane pitch, and other books of the serious caliber of Dr. Kirk's own writing, such as Robert A. Nisbet's *The Quest for Community*. But it was *The Conservative Mind* which precipitated the New Conservatism.

The speed of its development has been enormous, even for a time like ours, when ideas are packaged into trends and movements long before they have had a chance to cure properly. Within the past year or so a multitude of books has appeared, carrying the general theme. To mention only a few, Dr. Kirk himself has produced two more volumes (in descending order of quality, as he grapples with more concrete problems), *A Program for Conservatives* and *Academic Freedom*. Walter Lippmann in *The Public Philosophy* has jumped on the bandwagon, although without explicit acknowledgment, giving a more journalistic twist and more practical momentum to the movement. And the real proof that Dr. Kirk's donnish speculations have brought forth a gusher is the recent appearance, under the aegis of a publisher whose scent for current intellectual

Reprinted by permission from *Freeman* (July 1955): 559–62.

fashion is second to none and with the seal of approval of the Charles Austin Beard Prize, of *Conservatism in America* by Clinton Rossiter. This book, hailed as "an eloquent appeal for a new conservatism to sustain the Republic in the troubled years ahead," presents nothing in its essential principles and program with which Arthur Schlesinger, Jr., or Adlai Stevenson would seriously disagree.

This fundamental compatibility with the collectivist trend of the time which comes out so blatantly in Mr. Rossiter has been implicit in the New Conservatism from the beginning, despite much just and tonic criticism of positivist ethics and the blatant centralizing *tone* of the "liberal" atmosphere by Russell Kirk and his more serious colleagues. Why, then, the tendency, in circles usually strongly critical of collectivism, to receive the New Conservatism as a valid theoretical foundation for a movement of opposition to it?

This is perhaps partly a matter of words, of labels. The term "liberal" has for some time now been captured by the proponents of a powerful state and a controlled economy and has been corrupted into the opposite of its true meaning. To be conservative has, therefore, by usage and consent come to mean to be an opponent of that false "liberalism." From a certain point of view there has been logic to this custom, when by conservative was understood loyalty to the established traditions of the Constitution and to a free American social structure, as over against the Roosevelt revolution.

A Difference of Principle

In fact, conservatism is not a body of principles, but a tone, an attitude. That attitude does indeed tend to conduce towards a respect for the wisdom acquired by human beings through long ages and towards skepticism of social blueprints, of utopias, of the approach of the Socialist and the social worker. It carries with it, however, no built-in defense against the acceptance, grudging though it may be, of institutions which reason and prudence would otherwise reject, if only those institutions are sufficiently firmly established.

The fundamental political issue today is that between, on the one hand, collectivism and statism which merge gradually into totalitarianism and, on the other, what used to be called liberalism, what we may perhaps call individualism: the principles of the primacy of the individual, the division of power, the limitation of government, the freedom of the economy. This is not a problem of tone or attitude, not a difference between the conservative and the radical temperament; *it is a difference of principle.* What is at stake are fundamental concepts of the relationship of individual men to a society and the institutions of a society.

On this issue, Dr. Kirk, and others who are seriously interested in the fundamental questions which concern him, are at the best equivocal, while the more journalistic New Conservatives, Viereck, Lippmann, Rossiter, seize upon the attitude of conservatism to justify conservation of the New Deal and its works. This kind of conservative must, in Clinton Rossiter's words, reject the "indecent anti-statism of laissez-faire individualism." For the New Conservative must not forget man's "need for both voluntary and submissive association with other men. The individualism of the Right has not been an inspiration for all Americans, but a clever weapon with which the rich could defend their riches and the powerful their power."

"Liberalism" is wearing a bit thin, fraying at the edges. Provided the fundamental realities of power—group and state over the individual, "sober community responsibility" over "laissez-faire anarchy"—are retained (and consolidated), the mantle of the conservative tone can well befit the established order of the welfare society. After all, that order is in its twenty-third year since the fateful election of 1932. The New Conservatism is, on an intellectual level, a natural complement to the Eisenhower version of Rooseveltism. Conservatism, after all, is a relative term. The question is: what do you want to conserve?

What, then, do the New Conservatives want to conserve? What is the content of their position and the principles for which they stand? To answer that question in a brief article requires at the best some simplification. There are different men and different emphases among the New Conservatives. It would hardly be fair to take as representative Clinton Rossiter's vulgarizations of the New Conservatism, or the tired platitudes of Walter Lippmann, or the strident diatribes of Peter Viereck as his New Conservatism leads him to the glorification of Adlai Stevenson. However a doctrine may be perverted or misused, its essential value stands or falls on its own merit. That it can be misused is of course a primary reason for examining very carefully its pretensions; but in the end, whatever is made of them, it is the ideas themselves with which we have to come to grips.

The Thinking of Russell Kirk

Therefore, it is to the effective thinkers of the movement that analysis and criticism should be directed. Of these Russell Kirk is undoubtedly the most significant. But it is not an easy matter to pin down Dr. Kirk's thinking. There is no doubt as to his general tone and attitude nor as to the source and content of his ultimate values; but in the field of human action—the area of ethics, politics, and economics—it is almost impossible to find clear and distinct principle.

To suggest the quality of his tone, one can perhaps do no better than to quote Dr. Kirk himself: "Now, in sober reality, conservatives are . . . a number of persons, of all classes and occupations, whose view of life is reverential, and who tend to be guided by the wisdom of their ancestors, instead of abstract speculation."

The source of his ultimate values is the accumulated wisdom of Western civilization, impinging upon his imagination most strongly, it would seem, in the forms achieved by the English eighteenth and nineteenth centuries and with the spiritual content of High Anglican Christianity. Those ultimate values can be and have been the starting point for many modes of action in the world, but integrally they lead to a belief in the unique value of every individual person, a belief which is the first principle of any philosophy of freedom (and which can, of course, also be arrived at in other ways).

But it is only the first principle. However deeply it is held, it is not by itself sufficient to guarantee the freedom of men in society. Too many interpretations are possible as to what the "integrity of the individual person" consists of. And, given the persuasiveness of one of these interpretations, men will always be found who, if they possess the power, will attempt to enforce their interpretation on other men. The only way the freedom of individuals can be protected against this ever-present danger is through a second set of principles. While these principles have for their aim the actualization of the philosophical and spiritual end, the freedom and integrity of the individual, they are themselves derived not only from this end but also from the realities of human life. They are framed with full awareness of the propensity of human beings to translate the freedom of other human beings into their freedom to do what those with power think is right and just.

In the ethical, the political, the economic spheres, these practical principles are as vital as the general philosophical principle, if freedom is to be transformed from a dream into the actual situation in which men live. They can be rather simply stated, and they are the criteria by which the pretensions of a political philosophy, by whatever name it calls itself, must be judged.

The first of these principles is no more than the restatement of the innate value of the individual person in political and social terms: *all* value resides in the individual; *all* social institutions derive their value and, in fact, their very being from individuals and are justified only to the extent that they serve the needs of individuals.

From this fundamental axiom of the good society are developed two others which arise from experience and from understanding of the dangers to freedom which lie in the very nature of human beings. Since power is the instrumentality of control by men and groups of men over other men and since in this imperfect world, in the end, the only check upon power is power, the division of power (both within the political sphere and between the political sphere and other spheres) and unceasing vigilance to keep it divided are the essential safeguards of freedom.

With this goes the other and corollary principle, a special case of the principle of division of power, but of the greatest importance: the entire sphere of economic activity must remain free of political control. For only the strict separation of the sources of a man's material existence— property, employment, provision for illness and old age—from political institutions can enable him to maintain his independence of them. And further, if the state, which is the legal repository of force for the preservation of the conditions of peaceful civil life and for defense against external enemies, gains control over any other sphere of human activity, the very possibility of effective division of power is gone.

Rejects the Tradition of Individualism

If Dr. Kirk's thinking is judged by these principles, it becomes apparent that he lacks the standards to effectuate politically and socially his undoubtedly genuine concern for the integrity of the individual person as a philosophical and spiritual truth. He can criticize with great cogency the dehumanizing aspects of the federal social security program. He can stigmatize the totalitarian implications of the federal school lunch program. But on these, as on a dozen other practical issues of growing collectivism and the state's encroachment, he shows no sign of under-standing the problems of principle reflected. He can write feelingly of the dangers of concentration of power without ever indicating by what stan-dards overconcentration is to be judged and to what limits it is to be restrained. His books are full of just and shrewd critiques of aspect after aspect of the contemporary world, but for every such critique there is, implied or explicit, a condemnation of the ideas and the institutional frameworks which are essential to the reversal of the trend.

Nor is he merely neutral or undecided in his attitude towards these principles. Once they are stated clearly and unequivocally, he castigates them as the abstractions of "defecated intellectuals." He detests them and the men who formulated them and the whole tradition of individualism as heartily as he does Marxism and contemporary materialist collectivism.

If Dr. Kirk is so concerned about the evils he sees around us, the fruits of developing collectivism, and nevertheless rejects the principles of a free society, what does he propose, what does he stand for positively? Since he presents himself and his beliefs always rhetorically, never on a reasoned basis, he can succeed in establishing the impression that he has a strong and coherent outlook without ever taking a systematic and consistent position. In justice to him, it must be said that he would make a virtue of this. He pours scorn on all the systematic positions he discusses as being "abstract," "radical," "Jacobin," "liberal"; and he exalts, as the model of conservative statesmanship, disdain for systematic thought and respect for "prejudice and prescription," that is, for the traditionally accepted.

Dr. Kirk takes as his guide the English statesman, Edmund Burke, and puts him forward as the paragon of conservatism. But what he forgets is that Burke was fighting against the radical principles of centralization of the French Revolution in defense of a society whose traditions themselves incorporated a systematic, if incomplete, theory of freedom—the modes of the common law, a considerable degree of division of power, long-established rights of the individual and of property, the principles of 1688. His reliance upon tradition, upon prescription, upon prejudice in the circumstances of 1790 would, in the crisis of 1688, have made him the supporter of a very different policy and of very different principles. How-ever much one may respect Burke's stand as a practical statesman, it is impossible to derive a firm political position from him. As Richard Wea-ver has said: "Of clear rational principle he had a mortal distrust . . . it would be blindness to take him as a mentor."

It can be admitted that the long experience crystallized in traditional human wisdom is a necessary make-weight to the conclusions which reason would seem to dictate to a single group or even to the conscience of a whole generation. But to make tradition, "prejudice and prescription," not along with reason but *against* reason, the sole foundation of one's position is to enshrine the maxim, "Whatever is, is right," as the first principle of thought about politics and society. Such a position is immoral from any point of view; and actually Dr. Kirk could not accept it, for it is particularly inconsonant with that Christian vision of the freedom of the soul and the will which he holds. But we can only find what he does believe by strenuously digging it out of the rhetorical flow. What he believes seems to be that the particular strand of tradition which appeals to him, and which he presumptuously considers the only one compatible with Christianity, is right and is the only guide to a good society.

It will not imitate Dr. Kirk's own arrogance when he pontificates that "individualism is anti-Christian. It is possible logically to be a Christian, and possible logically to be an individualist; it is not possible to be the two simultaneously." No doubt his political position is compatible with Christianity, but so are many other positions. For Christianity, or any other religious vision, is concerned with the relations between the individual man and God. And while it certainly can, by affecting the inner being of individuals, affect the way in which they go about solving the problem of creating tolerable social conditions, it does not pretend to dictate a single form of these conditions valid for all ages and all times.

Dr. Kirk, however, seems to insist that a certain kind of society is the only tolerable one, and this not because *he* believes in it and puts forward arguments to support his concept. This certainly would be his privilege, however wrong he might be. But he pretends instead to have no principles personally arrived at. He merely recognizes what is ordained by Providential prescription.

The social pattern which emerges from the hints and suggestions in his writings (for he never tells us exactly what he wants and certainly never gives any idea of what it would mean in modern circumstances) is shaped by such words as "Authority," "order," "community," "duty," "obedience." "Freedom" is a rare word; "the individual" is anathema. The qualities of this suggested society are a mixture of those of eighteenth-century England and medieval Europe—or perhaps, more aptly, they are those of Plato's Republic with the philosopher-king replaced by the squire and the vicar.

No wonder that Dr. Kirk never describes concretely what such a society would be like under modern conditions, with the enormous strength of modern industry and modern arms, the decrease in distance and the ease of communication—in a word, with the technological facilities for power and centralization which exist today. Such societies of "authority and order," societies of status, have in the past, under the scattered and decentralized nature of power then, sometimes involved a considerable measure of freedom. But, quite apart from the essential and principled superiority of a society of contract to a society of status in terms of freedom, any society of status today, with the increased potentialities of power of our times, could only move inevitably to totalitarianism.

As all around us we see signs of regression from contract to status and the growing predominance of society and state over the individual, when this is indeed the characteristic form that the attack upon freedom takes today, Dr. Kirk in the peroration of *The Conservative Mind* can complacently write: "Our world may be passing from contract back to status. Whether that process is good or evil, conservatives must prepare society for Providential change. . . ."

If indeed our society ever completes the fearful voyage on which it has embarked "from contract back to status"—from freedom to slavery, not to put too fine a point upon it—it will not be the doing of Providence but of men. And alongside those men who have consciously substituted for the principles of freedom those of socialism and collectivism, the responsibility will be shared by those who, while they long for the conditions of our free ancestors, reject as abstract and doctrinaire the very principles which made them free. Dr. Kirk might well reread the passage from a speech of Randolph of Roanoke which begins the fourth chapter of his own book on that great statesman: "There are certain great principles, which if they be not held inviolate, at all seasons, our liberty is gone. If we give them up, it is perfectly immaterial what is the character of our Sovereign; whether he be King or President, elective or hereditary—it is perfectly immaterial what is his character—we shall be slaves. . . ."

Part IV

Anticommunism

The Cold War helped regenerate a fear of communism in America that contributed to the unification of disparate strands of conservative belief and served as the fulcrum on which the conservative movement was balanced for much of the postwar era. For traditionalists like Richard Weaver and Russell Kirk, communism represented a heretical desire for utopia, the idea that human nature was perfectible and that heaven could be made on Earth.[1] Communism destroyed traditional social order—family, religion, and community—and established the State, under the banner of the communist party, as the final arbiter of all decisions affecting individuals. Classical liberals also rejected communist tyranny and what it entailed for the demise of the rule of law and individual freedom. Communist governments were totalitarian, ruled by the iron will of the dictatorship of the proletariat, and in the end, were murderous, destroying not only lives in pursuit of their utopian premises, but also morality and belief in God.[2]

Conservatives in Congress found some difficulty in the early years of the Cold War supporting Harry Truman's policy of containment of the Soviet Union. Led by noninterventionists in Congress like Arthur Vanderberg (R-Mich.) and Robert A. Taft (R-Ohio), conservative senators initially rejected Truman's claims for American involvement abroad, at least until the threat of Soviet expansion was made clear to them. After 1947, the skeptical, noninterventionist Republican majority endorsed the Cold War, authorizing military and economic aid to Greece and Turkey, passing the Marshall Plan, developing the national security apparatus (the Central Intelligence Agency, National Security Agency, Department of Defense), and ratifying the North Atlantic Treaty Organization (NATO), America's first military alliance since an alliance with France was abrogated in 1800. Noninterventionism was dead.

Some conservatives remained skeptical of Cold War internationalism, believing there was less to fear from Soviet expansion in Europe than in subversive communist espionage at home.[3] For awhile, individuals associated with *Human Events,* particularly Felix Morley, attempted to keep conservatives focused on America First-styled principles rather than pursuing global crusades against communism. Increasingly, Morley found this to be an impossible task. With fear of communist subversion leading to congressional investigations into communist spy rings within the United States; with the Truman administration "scaring the hell" out of the Republican Congress in order to gain its support for its foreign policy; with Soviet leader Joseph Stalin's blundering foreign policy in Europe (especially his role in engineering the Czechoslovakian coup d'etat in 1948 and his blockade of western access routes to Berlin, precipitating a year-long crisis); and, especially, with the fall of China to communism in 1949, conservatives once dedicated to the proposition of noninterventionism became alarmed at the menace of international communism and advocates of a global Cold War.[4]

Those most alarmed at the inroads of communism were former communists themselves. A growing number of postwar conservatives, including Frank Meyer, James Burnham, John Dos Passos, and Max Eastman, had been passionate believers in, if not active members of, the communist party, or its Trotskyite offshoot. This first generation of "neoconservatives" became supporters of anticommunist foreign policies and efforts to investigate communist influence at home. Indeed, James Burnham articulated a liberation strategy later adopted by the Eisenhower administration.[5] The ex-communists proved their disenchantment with "the god that failed" by dedicating themselves wholeheartedly to expose the tyranny and evil of communist regimes.[6]

One of these converts to anticommunism—and the use of the spiritual metaphor of conversion is most appropriate in his case—was Whittaker Chambers (1901–1961). Chambers had been a contributor to *The New Masses* and *The Daily Worker,* and eventually worked as an underground operative in the Soviet Union's spy apparatus in Washington, D.C. during the 1930s, recruiting potential agents from the ranks of New Deal agencies. He found many willing participants, One of his recruits was Alger Hiss, a lawyer then employed by the Agricultural Adjustment Agency and later by the Department of State. In a famous 1947 congressional hearing, Chambers named Hiss as an individual who was involved in espionage in the 1930s, even providing intimate details of Hiss's apartment and his love of birdwatching. Several days later Hiss denied he knew Chambers. Under intense pressure, Chambers produced evidence to support his claims, in the form of documents typed on a typewriter later identified as belonging to Hiss.[7] Hiss had lied to Congress and was eventually convicted of perjury (the statute of limitations on espionage had run out). Still, Chambers was vilified in the press and by liberals (including Secretary of State Dean Acheson) for his allegations against Hiss (evidence from Soviet archives has proven Hiss's connection to Soviet military intelligence, but such evidence did not come to light until 1995). Chambers spent the remainder of his days working in somber reflection on his Maryland farm. He wrote his memoirs, *Witness*, from which the excerpt included in Chapter 11 is taken. Chambers became a Christian, a conversion that helped him rediscover the spiritual dimension of man's existence absent in communism. His lament for the spiritual crisis that plagued the modern age, not simply overt in communism, but also manifest in the materialism of the West, depicted a pessimism about the modern condition that epitomized a soul in turmoil (he believed the West did not possess the moral capability needed to defeat communism). Both a lamentation and a prayer, *Witness* profoundly influenced the conservative movement.

A more scholarly analysis of communism from a conservative perspective is provided in the selection from Gerhart Niemeyer (1907–1994). A professor of political science, Niemeyer was born in Germany, educated at Cambridge and at the Universities of Munich and Kiel. He emigrated to the United States in 1937 and taught at Princeton, Oglethorpe, Yale, and Columbia before settling at Notre Dame in 1955. An expert on political ideology, Niemeyer wrote many works on communism, including *An Inquiry into Soviet Mentality* (1956), *Facts on Communism, Volume I: The Communist Ideology* (1959), and myriad essays published in scholarly and conservative journals. Chapter 12, "The Communist Mind," is from a pamphlet published in 1963 by the Intercollegiate Society of Individualists (now known as the Intercollegiate Studies Institute, or ISI), a conservative organization founded in 1951 to propagate on behalf of conservative ideas on campus.

ISI's first president was William F. Buckley, Jr. (1925–). Buckley was an anti-red diaper baby, a cradle conservative who had been taught to fear revolution by his father, an oil executive and financial contributor to conservative and libertarian causes. A young supporter of America First before World War II, Buckley served in the army at the end of the war and matriculated at Yale in 1946. There, he distinguished himself in journalism and in debate. He also was greatly disturbed by Yale's instruction in economics and religion, and in 1951, he published an exposé of his alma mater, *God and Man at Yale,* which attacked the Yale administration for condoning the teaching of collectivism in economics, and agnosticism, if not atheism, in religion. The book turned the young Buckley into a celebrity and for the next four years he sought to develop an outlet for conservative views. His persistence resulted in the formation of the weekly magazine *National Review,* the first issue appearing in November 1955.[8]

Buckley represented the growing fusion of conservative ideas and wanted *National Review* to be a home for all factions of conservatism. He was especially dedicated to anticommunism and hired many ex-communists to be editors and contributors to the new weekly (including Frank Meyer, James Burnham, Whittaker Chambers, and Max Eastman). The Catholic Buckley, along with college friend turned brother-in-law L. Brent Bozell (also Catholic), supported Joseph McCarthy's investigations, writing a defense of the Senator entitled *McCarthy and His Enemies* (published by Regnery in 1954). Even after McCarthy's 1955 censure in the Senate, Buckley remained loyal to the senator. The speech included here was given by Buckley in 1959 upon Soviet leader Nikita Khrushchev's visit to New York. The Khrushchev-Eisenhower summit, heralded by most of the media as a crucial development in easing tensions in the Cold War, was seen by conservatives as a betrayal of those people held captive in communist nations. The other document included in this chapter displays some of the conservative hostility toward communism; the Hungary Pledge (published in *National Review* in 1956) is just one example of conservative antipathy toward peaceful coexistence with communist governments. Such a viewpoint would remain a consistent theme of conservative anticommunism well into the Reagan era.

Chapter Eleven

A Witness

Whittaker Chambers

Beloved Children,

I am sitting in the kitchen of the little house at Medfield, our second farm which is cut off by the ridge and a quarter-mile across the fields from our home place, where you are. I am writing a book. In it I am speaking to you. But I am also speaking to the world. To both I owe an accounting.

It is a terrible book. It is terrible in what it tells about men. If anything, it is more terrible in what it tells about the world in which you live. It is about what the world calls the Hiss-Chambers Case; or even more simply, the Hiss Case. It is about a spy case. All the props of an espionage case are there—foreign agents, household traitors, stolen documents, microfilm, furtive meetings, secret hideaways, phony names, an informer, investigations, trials, official justice.

But if the Hiss Case were only this, it would not be worth my writing about or your reading about. It would be another fat folder in the sad files of the police, another crime drama in which the props would be mistaken for the play (as many people have consistently mistaken them). It would not be what alone gave it meaning, what the mass of men and women instinctively sensed it to be, often without quite knowing why. It would not be what, at the very beginning, I was moved to call it: "a tragedy of history."

For it was more than human tragedy. Much more than Alger Hiss or Whittaker Chambers was on trial in the trials of Alger Hiss. Two faiths were on trial. Human societies, like human beings, live by faith and die when faith dies. At issue in the Hiss Case was the question whether this sick society, which we call Western civilization, could in its extremity still cast up a man whose faith in it was so great that he would voluntarily abandon those things which men hold good, including life, to defend it. At issue was the question whether this man's faith could prevail against a man whose equal faith it was that this society is sick beyond saving, and that mercy itself pleads for its swift extinction and replacement by another. At issue was the question whether, in the desperately divided society, there still remained the will to recognize the issues in time to offset the immense rally of public power to distort and pervert the facts.

At heart, the Great Case was this critical conflict of faiths; that is why it was a great case. On a scale personal enough to be felt by all, but big enough to be symbolic, the two irreconcilable faiths of our time—Communism and Freedom—came to grips in the persons of two conscious and resolute men. Indeed, it would have been hard, in a world still only dimly aware of what the conflict is about, to find two other men who knew so clearly. Both had been schooled in the same view of history (the Marxist view). Both were trained by the same party in the same selfless, semisoldierly discipline. Neither would nor could yield without betraying, not himself, but his faith; and the different character of these faiths was shown by the different conduct of the two men toward each other throughout the struggle. For, with dark certitude, both knew, almost from the beginning, that the Great Case could end only in the destruction of one or both of the contending figures, just as the history of our times (both men had been taught) can end only in the destruction of one or both of the contending forces.

But this destruction is not the tragedy. The nature of tragedy is itself misunderstood. Part of the world supposes that the tragedy in the Hiss Case lies in the acts of disloyalty revealed. Part believes that the tragedy lies in the fact that an able, intelligent man, Alger Hiss, was cut short in the course of a brilliant public career. Some find it tragic that Whittaker Chambers, of his own will, gave up a $30,000-a-year job and a secure future to haunt for the rest of his days the ruins of his life. These are shocking facts, criminal facts, disturbing facts: they are not tragic.

Crime, violence, infamy are not tragedy. Tragedy occurs when a human soul awakes and seeks, in suffering and pain, to free itself from crime, violence, infamy, even at the cost of life. The struggle is the tragedy—not defeat or death. That is why the spectacle of tragedy has always filled men, not with despair, but with a sense of hope and exaltation. That is why this terrible book is also a book of hope. For it is about the struggle of the human soul—of more than one human soul. It is in this sense that the Hiss Case is a tragedy. This is its meaning beyond the headlines, the revelations, the shame and suffering of the people involved. But this tragedy will have been for nothing unless men understand it rightly, and from it the world takes hope and heart to begin its own tragic struggle with the evil that besets it from within and from without, unless it faces the fact that the world, the whole world, is sick unto death and that, among other things, this Case has turned a finger of fierce light into the suddenly opened and reeking body of our time.

My children, as long as you live, the shadow of the Hiss Case will brush you. In every pair of eyes that rests on you, you will see pass, like a cloud passing behind a woods in winter, the memory of your father—dissembled in friendly eyes, lurking in unfriendly eyes. Sometimes you will wonder which is harder to bear: friendly forgiveness or forthright hate. In time, therefore, when the sum of your experience of life gives you authority, you will ask yourselves the question: What was my father?

I will give you an answer: I was a witness. I do not mean a witness for the Government or against Alger Hiss and the others. Nor do I mean the short, squat, solitary figure, trudging through the impersonal halls of public buildings to testify before Congressional committees, grand juries, loyalty boards, courts of law. A man is not primarily a witness *against* something. That is only incidental to the fact that he is a witness *for* something. A witness, in the sense that I am using the word, is a man whose life and faith are so completely one that when the challenge comes to step out and testify for his faith, he does so, disregarding all risks, accepting all consequences.

One day in the great jury room of the Grand Jury of the Southern District of New York, a juror leaned forward slightly and asked me: "Mr. Chambers, what does it mean to be a Communist?" I hesitated for a moment, trying to find the simplest, most direct way to convey the heart of this complex experience to men and women to whom the very fact of the experience was all but incomprehensible. Then I said:

"When I was a Communist, I had three heroes. One was a Russian. One was a Pole. One was a German Jew.

"The Pole was Felix Djerjinsky. He was ascetic, highly sensitive, intelligent. He was a Communist. After the Russian Revolution, he became head of the Tcheka and organizer of the Red Terror. As a young man, Djerjinsky had been a political prisoner in the Paviak Prison in Warsaw. There he insisted on being given the task of cleaning the latrines of the other prisoners. For he held that the most developed member of any community must take upon himself the lowliest tasks as an example to those who are less developed. That is one thing that it meant to be a Communist.

"The German Jew was Eugen Leviné. He was a Communist. During the Bavarian Soviet Republic in 1919, Leviné was the organizer of the Workers and Soldiers Soviets. When the Bavarian Soviet Republic was crushed, Leviné was captured and court-martialed. The court-martial told him: 'You are under sentence of death.' Leviné answered: 'We Communists are always under sentence of death.' That is another thing that it meant to be a Communist.

"The Russian was not a Communist. He was a pre-Communist revolutionist named Kalyaev. (I should have said Sazonov.) He was arrested for a minor part in the assassination of the Tsarist prime minister, von Plehve. He was sent into Siberian exile to one of the worst prison camps, where the political prisoners were flogged. Kalyaev sought some way to protest this outrage to the world. The means were few, but at last he found a way. In protest against the flogging of other men, Kalyaev drenched himself in kerosene, set himself on fire and burned himself to death. That also is what it meant to be a Communist."

That also is what it means to be a witness.

But a man may also be an involuntary witness. I do not know any way to explain why God's grace touches a man who seems unworthy of it. But neither do I know any other way to explain how a man like myself— tarnished by life, unprepossessing, not brave—could prevail so far against the powers of the world arrayed almost solidly against him, to destroy him and defeat his truth. In this sense, I am an involuntary witness to God's grace and to the fortifying power of faith.

It was my fate to be in turn a witness to each of the two great faiths of our time. And so we come to the terrible word, Communism. My very dear children, nothing in all these pages will be written so much for you, though it is so unlike anything you would want to read. In nothing shall I be so much a witness, in no way am I so much called upon to fulfill my task, as in trying to make clear to you (and to the world) the true nature of Communism and the source of its power, which was the cause of my ordeal as a man, and remains the historic ordeal of the world in the 20th century. For in this century, within the next decades, will be decided for generations whether all mankind is to become Communist, whether the whole world is to become free, or whether, in the struggle, civilization as we know it is to be completely destroyed or completely changed. It is our fate to live upon that turning point in history.

The world has reached that turning point by the steep stages of a crisis mounting for generations. The turning point is the next to the last step. It was reached in blood, sweat, tears, havoc, and death in World War II. The chief fruit of the First World War was the Russian Revolution and the rise of Communism as a national power. The chief fruit of the Second World War was our arrival at the next to the last step of the crisis with the rise of Communism as a world power. History is likely to say that these were the only decisive results of the world wars.

The last war simplified the balance of political forces in the world by reducing them to two. For the first time, it made the power of the Communist sector of mankind (embodied in the Soviet Union) roughly equal to the power of the free sector of mankind (embodied in the United States). It made the collision of these powers all but inevitable. For the world wars did not end the crisis. They raised its tensions to a new pitch. They raised the crisis to a new stage. All the politics of our time, including the politics of war, will be the politics of this crisis.

Few men are so dull that they do not know that the crisis exists and that it threatens their lives at every point. It is popular to call it a social crisis. It is in fact a total crisis—religious, moral, intellectual, social, political, economic. It is popular to call it a crisis of the Western world. It is in fact a crisis of the whole world. Communism, which claims to be a solution of the crisis, is itself a symptom and an irritant of the crisis.

In part, the crisis results from the impact of science and technology upon mankind which, neither socially nor morally, has caught up with the problems posed by that impact. In part, it is caused by men's efforts to solve those problems. World wars are the military expression of the crisis. World-wide depressions are its economic expression. Universal desperation is its spiritual climate. This is the climate of Communism. Communism in our time can no more be considered apart from the crisis than a fever can be acted upon apart from an infected body.

I see in Communism the focus of the concentrated evil of our time. You will ask: Why, then, do men become Communists? How did it happen that you, our gentle and loved father, were once a Communist?

Were you simply stupid? No, I was not stupid. Were you morally depraved? No, I was not morally depraved. Indeed, educated men become Communists chiefly for moral reasons. Did you not know that the crimes and horrors of Communism are inherent in Communism? Yes, I knew that fact. Then why did you become a Communist? It would help more to ask: How did it happen that this movement, once a mere muttering of political outcasts, became this immense force that now contests the mastery of mankind? Even when all the chances and mistakes of history are allowed for, the answer must be: Communism makes some profound appeal to the human mind. You will not find out what it is by calling Communism names. That will not help much to explain why Communism whose horrors, on a scale unparalleled in history, are now public knowledge, still recruits its thousands and holds its millions—among them some of the best minds alive. Look at Klaus Fuchs, standing in the London dock, quiet, doomed, destroyed, and say whether it is possible to answer in that way the simple question: Why?

First, let me try to say what Communism is not. It is not simply a vicious plot hatched by wicked men in a sub-cellar. It is not just the writings of Marx and Lenin, dialectical materialism, the Politburo, the labor theory of value, the theory of the general strike, the Red Army, secret police, labor camps, underground conspiracy, the dictatorship of the proletariat, the technique of the coup d'état. It is not even those chanting, bannered millions that stream periodically, like disorganized armies, through the heart of the world's capitals: Moscow, New York, Tokyo, Paris, Rome. These are expressions of Communism, but they are not what Communism is about.

In the Hiss trials, where Communism was a haunting specter, but which did little or nothing to explain Communism, Communists were assumed to be criminals, pariahs, clandestine men who lead double lives under false names, travel on false passports, deny traditional religion, morality, the sanctity of oaths, preach violence and practice treason. These things are true about Communists, but they are not what Communism is about.

The revolutionary heart of Communism is not the theatrical appeal: "Workers of the world, unite. You have nothing to lose but your chains. You have a world to gain." It is a simple statement of Karl Marx, further simplified for handy use: "Philosophers have explained the world; it is necessary to change the world." Communists are bound together by no secret oath. The tie that binds them across the frontiers of nations, across barriers of language and differences of class and education, in defiance of religion, morality, truth, law, honor, the weaknesses of the body and the irresolutions of the mind, even unto death, is a simple conviction: It is necessary to change the world. Their power, whose nature baffles the rest of the world, because in a large measure the rest of the world has lost that power, is the power to hold convictions and to act on them. It is the same power that moves mountains; it is also an unfailing power to move men. Communists are that part of mankind which has recovered the power to live or die—to bear witness—for its faith. And it is a simple, rational-faith that inspires men to live or die for it.

It is not new. It is, in fact, man's second oldest faith. Its promise was whispered in the first days of the Creation under the Tree of the Knowledge of Good and Evil: "Ye shall be as gods." It is the great alternative faith of mankind. Like all great faiths, its force derives from a simple vision. Other ages have had great visions. They have always been different versions of the same vision: the vision of God and man's relationship to God. The Communist vision is the vision of Man without God.

It is the vision of man's mind displacing God as the creative intelligence of the world. It is the vision of man's liberated mind, by the sole force of its rational intelligence, redirecting man's destiny and reorganizing man's life and the world. It is the vision of man, once more the central figure of the Creation, not because God made man in His image, but because man's mind makes him the most intelligent of the animals. Copernicus and his successors displaced man as the central fact of the universe by proving that the earth was not the central star of the universe. Communism restores man to his sovereignty by the simple method of denying God.

The vision is a challenge and implies a threat. It challenges man to prove by his acts that he is the masterwork of the Creation—by making thought and act one. It challenges him to prove it by using the force of his rational mind to end the bloody meaninglessness of man's history—by giving it purpose and a plan. It challenges him to prove it by reducing the meaningless chaos of nature, by imposing on it his rational will to order, abundance, security, peace. It is the vision of materialism. But it threatens, if man's mind is unequal to the problems of man's progress, that he will sink back into savagery (the A and the H bombs have raised the issue in explosive forms), until nature replaces him with a more intelligent form of life.

It is an intensely practical vision. The tools to turn it into reality are at hand—science and technology, whose traditional method, the rigorous exclusion of all supernatural factors in solving problems, has contributed to the intellectual climate in which the vision flourishes, just as they have contributed to the crisis in which Communism thrives. For the vision is shared by millions who are not Communists (they are part of Communism's secret strength). Its first commandment is found, not in the *Communist Manifesto,* but in the first sentence to the physics primer: "All of the progress of mankind to date results from the making of careful measurements." But Communism, for the first time in history, has made this vision the faith of a great modern political movement.

Hence the Communist Party is quite justified in calling itself the most revolutionary party in history. It has posed in practical form the most revolutionary question in history: God or Man? It has taken the logical next step which three hundred years of rationalism hesitated to take, and said what millions of modern minds think, but do not dare or care to say: If man's mind is the decisive force in the world, what need is there for God? Henceforth man's mind is man's fate.

This vision *is* the Communist revolution, which, like all great revolutions, occurs in man's mind before it takes form in man's acts. Insurrection and conspiracy are merely methods of realizing the vision; they are merely part of the politics of Communism. Without its vision, they, like Communism, would have no meaning and could not rally a parcel of pickpockets. Communism does not summon men to crime or to utopia, as its easy critics like to think. On the plane of faith, it summons mankind to turn its vision into practical reality. On the plane of action, it summons men to struggle against the inertia of the past which, embodied in social, political, and economic forms, Communism claims, is blocking the will of mankind to make its next great forward stride. It summons men to overcome the crisis, which, Communism claims, is in effect a crisis of rending frustration, with the world, unable to stand still, but unwilling to go forward along the road that the logic of a technological civilization points out—Communism.

This is Communism's moral sanction, which is twofold. Its vision points the way to the future; its faith labors to turn the future into present reality. It says to every man who joins it: the vision is a practical problem of history; the way to achieve it is a practical problem of politics, which is the present tense of history. Have you the moral strength to take upon yourself the crimes of history so that man at last may close his chronicle of age-old, senseless suffering, and replace it with purpose and a plan?

The answer a man makes to this question is the difference between the Communist and those miscellaneous socialists, liberals, fellow travelers, unclassified progressives and men of good will, all of whom share a similar vision, but do not share the faith because they will not take upon themselves the penalties of the faith. The answer is the root of that sense of moral superiority which makes Communists, though caught in crime, berate their opponents with withering self-righteousness.

The Communist vision has a mighty agitator and a mighty propagandist. They are the crisis. The agitator needs no soap box. It speaks insistently to the human mind at the point where desperation lurks. The propagandist writes no Communist gibberish. It speaks insistently to the human mind at the point where man's hope and man's energy fuse to fierceness.

The vision inspires. The crisis impels. The workingman is chiefly moved by the crisis. The educated man is chiefly moved by the vision. The workingman, living upon a mean margin of life, can afford few visions—even practical visions. An educated man, peering from the Harvard Yard, or any college campus, upon a world in chaos, finds in the vision the two certainties for which the mind of man tirelessly seeks: a reason to live and a reason to die. No other faith of our time presents them with the same practical intensity. That is why Communism is the central experience of the first half of the 20th century, and may be its final experience—will be, unless the free world, in the agony of its struggle with Communism, overcomes its crisis by discovering, in suffering and pain, a power of faith which will provide man's mind, at the same intensity, with the same two certainties: a reason to live and a reason to die. If it fails, this will be the century of the great social wars. If it succeeds, this will be the century of the great wars of faith.

You will ask: Why, then, do men cease to be Communists? One answer is: Very few do. Thirty years after the Russian Revolution, after the known atrocities, the purges, the revelations, the jolting zigzags of Communist politics, there is only a handful of ex-Communists in the whole world. By ex-Communists I do not mean those who break with Communism over differences of strategy and tactics (like Trotsky) or organization (like Tito). Those are merely quarrels over a road map by people all of whom are in a hurry to get to the same place.

Nor, by ex-Communists, do I mean those thousands who continually drift into the Communist Party and out again. The turnover is vast. These are the spiritual vagrants of our time whose traditional faith has been leached out in the bland climate of rationalism. They are looking for an intellectual night's lodging. They lack the character for Communist faith because they lack the character for any faith. So they drop away, though Communism keeps its hold on them.

By an ex-Communist, I mean a man who knew clearly why he became a Communist, who served Communism devotedly and knew why he served it, who broke with Communism unconditionally and knew why he broke with it. Of these there are very few—an index to the power of the vision and the power of the crisis.

History very largely fixes the patterns of force that make men Communists. Hence one Communist conversion sounds much like another— rather impersonal and repetitious, awesome and tiresome, like long lines of similar people all stolidly waiting to get in to see the same movie. A man's break with Communism is intensely personal. Hence the account of no two breaks is likely to be the same. The reasons that made one Communist break may seem without force to another ex-Communist.

It is a fact that a man can join the Communist Party, can be very active in it for years, without completely understanding the nature of Communism or the political methods that follow inevitably from its vision. One day such incomplete Communists discover that the Communist Party is not what they thought it was. They break with it and turn on it with the rage of an honest dupe, a dupe who has given a part of his life to a swindle. Often they forget that it takes two to make a swindle.

Others remain Communists for years, warmed by the light of its vision, firmly closing their eyes to the crimes and horrors inseparable from its practical politics. One day they have to face the facts. They are appalled at what they have abetted. They spend the rest of their days trying to explain, usually without great success, the dark clue to their complicity. As their understanding of Communism was incomplete and led them to a dead end, their understanding of breaking with it is incomplete and leads them to a dead end. It leads to less than Communism, which was a vision and a faith. The world outside Communism, the world in crisis, lacks a vision and a faith. There is before these ex-Communists absolutely nothing. Behind them is a threat. For they have, in fact, broken not with the vision, but with the politics of the vision. In the name of reason and intelligence, the vision keeps them firmly in its grip—self-divided, paralyzed, powerless to act against it.

Hence the most secret fold of their minds is haunted by a terrifying thought: What if we were wrong? What if our inconstancy is our guilt? That is the fate of those who break without knowing clearly that Communism is wrong because something else is right, because to the challenge: *God or Man?*, they continue to give the answer: *Man*. Their pathos is that not even the Communist ordeal could teach them that man without God is just what Communism said he was: the most intelligent of the animals, that man without God is a beast, never more beastly than when he is most intelligent about his beastliness. *"Er nennt's Vernunft,"* says the Devil in Goethe's *Faust*, *"und braucht's allein, nur tierischer als jedes Tier zu sein"*—Man calls it reason and uses it simply to be more beastly than any beast. Not grasping the source of the evil they sincerely hate, such ex-Communists in general make ineffectual witnesses against it. They are witnesses against something; they have ceased to be witnesses for anything.

Yet there is one experience which most sincere ex-Communists share, whether or not they go only part way to the end of the question it poses. The daughter of a former German diplomat in Moscow was trying to explain to me why her father, who, as an enlightened modern man, had been extremely pro-Communist, had become an implacable anti-Communist. It was hard for her because, as an enlightened modern girl, she shared the Communist vision without being a Communist. But she loved her father and the irrationality of his defection embarrassed her. "He was immensely pro-Soviet," she said, "and then—you will laugh at me—but you must not laugh at my father—and then—one night—in Moscow—he heard screams. That's all. Simply one night he heard screams."

A child of Reason and the 20th century, she knew that there is a logic of the mind. She did not know that the soul has a logic that may be more compelling than the mind's. She did not know at all that she had swept away the logic of the mind, the logic of history, the logic of politics, the myth of the 20th century, with five annihilating words: one night he heard screams.

What Communist has not heard those screams? They come from husbands torn forever from their wives in midnight arrests. They come, muffled, from the execution cellars of the secret police, from the torture chambers of the Lubianka, from all the citadels of terror now stretching from Berlin to Canton. They come from those freight cars loaded with men, women, and children, the enemies of the Communist State, locked in, packed in, left on remote sidings to freeze to death at night in the

Russian winter. They come from minds driven mad by the horrors of mass starvation ordered and enforced as a policy of the Communist State. They come from the starved skeletons, worked to death, or flogged to death (as an example to others) in the freezing filth of sub-arctic labor camps. They come from children whose parents are suddenly, inexplicably, taken away from them—parents they will never see again.

What Communist has not heard those screams? Execution, says the Communist code, is the highest measure of social protection. What man can call himself a Communist who has not accepted the fact that Terror is an instrument of policy, right if the vision is right, justified by history, enjoined by the balance of forces in the social wars of this century? Those screams have reached every Communist's mind. Usually they stop there. What judge willingly dwells upon the man the laws compel him to condemn to death—the laws of nations or the laws of history?

But one day the Communist really hears those screams. He is going about his routine party tasks. He is lifting a dripping reel of microfilm from a developing tank. He is justifying to a Communist fraction in a trade union an extremely unwelcome directive of the Central Committee. He is receiving from a trusted superior an order to go to another country and, in a designated hotel, at a designated hour, meet a man whose name he will never know, but who will give him a package whose contents he will never learn. Suddenly, there closes around that Communist a separating silence, and in that silence he hears screams. He hears them for the first time. For they do not merely reach his mind. They pierce beyond. They pierce to his soul. He says to himself: "Those are not the screams of man in agony. Those are the screams of a soul in agony." He hears them for the first time because a soul in extremity has communicated with that which alone can hear it—another human soul.

Why does the Communist ever hear them? Because in the end there persists in every man, however he may deny it, a scrap of soul. The Communist who suffers this singular experience then says to himself: "What is happening to me? I must be sick." If he does not instantly stifle that scrap of soul, he is lost. If he admits it for a moment, he has admitted that there is something greater than Reason, greater than the logic of mind, of politics, of history, of economics, which alone justifies the vision. If the party senses his weakness, and the party is peculiarly cunning at sensing such weakness, it will humiliate him, degrade him, condemn him, expel him. If it can, it will destroy him. And the party will be right. For he has betrayed that which alone justifies its faith—the vision of Almighty

Man. He has brushed the only vision that has force against the vision of Almighty Mind. He stands before the fact of God.

The Communist Party is familiar with this experience to which its members are sometimes liable in prison, in illness, in indecision. It is recognized frankly as a sickness. There are ways of treating it—if it is confessed. It is when it is not confessed that the party, sensing a subtle crisis, turns upon it savagely. What ex-Communist has not suffered this experience in one form or another, to one degree or another? What he does about it depends on the individual man. That is why no ex-Communist dare answer for his sad fraternity the question: Why do men break with Communism? He can only answer the question: How did you break with Communism? My answer is: Slowly, reluctantly, in agony.

Yet my break began long before I heard those screams. Perhaps it does for everyone. I do not know how far back it began. Avalanches gather force and crash, unheard, in men as in the mountains. But I date my break from a very casual happening. I was sitting in our apartment on St. Paul Street in Baltimore. It was shortly before we moved to Alger Hiss's apartment in Washington. My daughter was in her high chair. I was watching her eat. She was the most miraculous thing that had ever happened in my life. I liked to watch her even when she smeared porridge on her face or dropped it meditatively on the floor. My eye came to rest on the delicate convolutions of her ear—those intricate, perfect ears. The thought passed through my mind: "No, those ears were not created by any chance coming together of atoms in nature (the Communist view). They could have been created only by immense design." The thought was involuntary and unwanted. I crowded it out of my mind. But I never wholly forgot it or the occasion. I had to crowd it out of my mind. If I had completed it, I should have had to say: Design presupposes God. I did not then know that, at that moment, the finger of God was first laid upon my forehead.

One thing most ex-Communists could agree upon: they broke because they wanted to be free. They do not all mean the same thing by "free." Freedom is a need of the soul, and nothing else. It is in striving toward God that the soul strives continually after a condition of freedom. God alone is the inciter and guarantor of freedom. He is the only guarantor. External freedom is only an aspect of interior freedom. Political freedom, as the Western world has known it, is only a political reading of the Bible. Religion and freedom are indivisible. Without freedom the soul dies. Without the soul there is no justification for freedom. Necessity is the only ultimate justification known to the mind. Hence every sincere break with Communism is a religious experience, though the Communist fail to identify its true nature, though he fail to go to the end of the experience. His break is the political expression of the perpetual need of the soul whose first faint stirring he has felt within him, years, months, or days before he breaks. A Communist breaks because he must choose at last between irreconcilable opposites—God or Man, Soul or Mind, Freedom or Communism.

Communism is what happens when, in the name of Mind, men free themselves from God. But its view of God, its knowledge of God, its experience of God, is what alone gives character to a society or a nation, and meaning to its destiny. Its culture, the voice of this character, is merely that view, knowledge, experience, of God, fixed by its most intense spirits in terms intelligible to the mass of men. There has never been a society or a nation without God. But history is cluttered with the wreckage of nations that became indifferent to God, and died.

The crisis of Communism exists to the degree in which it has failed to free the peoples that it rules from God. Nobody knows this better than the Communist Party of the Soviet Union. The crisis of the Western world exists to the degree in which it is indifferent to God. It exists to the degree in which the Western world actually shares Communism's materialist vision, is so dazzled by the logic of the materialist interpretation of history, politics, and economics, that it fails to grasp that, for it, the only possible answer to the Communist challenge: Faith in God or Faith in Man? is the challenge: Faith in God.

Economics is not the central problem of this century. It is a relative problem which can be solved in relative ways. Faith is the central problem of this age. The Western world does not know it, but it already possesses the answer to this problem—but only provided that its faith in God and the freedom He enjoins is as great as Communism's faith in Man. . . .

Chapter Twelve

The Communist Mind

Gerhart Niemeyer

The west is still groping to comprehend the nature of the Communist threat. By and large, the effort at understanding our enemy is still lacking in system and purpose. Most writings on Communism presuppose, rather than aspire at, knowledge of what it is that endangers us. Uncritically held assumptions about Communism separate schools of thought from each other. Thus, one school of thought posits that the Communist threat is that of an ambitious great power pursuing an expansive policy in the style of nineteenth-century imperialism. Another presupposes that the threat stems from the existence of the "Communist system," meaning the collectivized economy as such. These are the assumptions underlying our various approaches to the Communist problem. This essay is an attempt to challenge both of the already mentioned presuppositions, even though both point to important elements in the situation. It is submitted that neither the power of Russia nor a foreign collectivist economy endangers our national security and way of life, but that the threat stems from the mentality of the people who are organized in the Communist Party and, through choice, association, and discipline, acquire attitudes of profound and irremediable irrationality. Such people, when in possession of political power, constitute a perennial disturbance to the peace of nations and of the world.

What is it that shapes and orients the Communist mind? Communists feel linked to each other and to the Party by the tenets of belief which go under the name of the Communist ideology. This is a complex structure

Gerhart Niemeyer Papers, Box 1, Folder 1 (Speeches and Writings), Hoover Institution on War, Revolution and Peace, Stanford University, Palo Alto, Calif. Reprinted by permission of Intercollegiate Studies Institute, Wilmington, Del.

with many component elements of which the socialist, or collectivist, element has attracted Western attention more than any other. And yet, if one asks whether there is one thing in the ideology that constitutes the key to the Communist mind, it would be the theory of history rather than the doctrine of collectivist economy. Characteristically, the theory of history of Communism is the part that has encountered little objection and less intellectual resistance in the West, even though, for the Communist, it is the doctrine of historical necessity which replaces religion, ethics, and philosophy.

One can reduce the Marxist-Leninist speculation about history to a simple formula: History is a chain of cause-and-effect successions of certain types of society, each following the preceding one with inexorable necessity. The entire course of history thus is said to obey objective "laws" which can be "scientifically" known. Knowledge of these "laws" enables man not only to understand the past, but to gauge the future, and thus to find the "correct" line of action for the present. Surveying the whole of history from beginning to end, Communism avers that history moves not merely forward but also upward, toward a climax which will constitute the fulfillment of everything that has gone before. Communists believe that history culminates in the fight of the proletariat against capitalism, of which the Communist Party considers itself the cadre organization.

Communists thus look at history in a way which radically differs from that of other people: From the vantage point of the ultimate end, retrospecting the present from the future. The certainty of things to come furnishes the Communist point of view for all problems of the present. Communists claim to know, with "scientific" accuracy, where mankind must eventually arrive. The present and all its aspects assume in this perspective the character of a mere period of transition. To Communists, the future is more real than the present, because it is the ultimate destiny toward which everything present is moving. This way of reversing the normal human perspective of present and future marks a turn from rational to irrational thinking about politics. Something that exists, like man, cannot look upon its own existence from the point of view of a future completion of time, as the Danish philosopher Kierkegaard has reminded us. Existence means to have an open future with a variety of possibilities. To regard the whole of history as if it were already realized, retrospectively, is something not given to man. It is the prerogative of

God. Communists, in claiming a foreknowledge that can only be that of a Being above and beyond time, cast themselves in a role not befitting the human situation. This is the deepest source of Communist irrationality. Let us observe that irrationality in some of its applications.

The future is knowable—but only to those trained in its "science": Marxism-Leninism. Marxist analysis has "proved" that a fully human life can be expected not in the present but only in the future that will emerge from the victory of the proletariat over its enemies. The Party has styled itself the "Vanguard" of the proletariat, the organization that is doing unremitting battle against the resisting forces of the present. The Party and its forces are "good," its use of force is justified, its wars are holy, its cause triumphant. Instead of judging in terms of criteria of intrinsic goodness, the Communists judge themselves and others by the yardstick of the "forward movement of history." If anything or anyone is identified with the anticipated future, the verdict is "progressive," meaning "good" because justified by history. Identification with the present or even the past results in a judgment of "reactionary," meaning bad because condemned by history. Motion in time has taken the place of ethics.

The future is already known—that means that, for the Communist in the present, the future is not a matter of open possibilities. Only one kind of road leads from here to the anticipated there. To know this road is the task of political thinking. All Communist thinking therefore turns on the problem of the "correct" choice, the choice of that one road to the future. Compared with all others, the Communist Party claims to know most about this "correct" choice. Being the "Vanguard," the element that is furthest advanced in consciousness of the future course of history, the Party is ahead of others in the motion toward the destined goal. It can see what is yet hidden from others. From its insights into things to come, it knows the "true" interests of peoples, classes, and nations, and has the right to overrule the illusory interests which people mistakenly assume to be theirs. The truth unfolds as history moves on. All those who dissent from the Party today will not be able to realize their mistake until the morrow has vindicated its Communist servants.

The "Party Line" is thus more than expediency. It appears to Communists like the blazing of a trail by a competent guide who alone is familiar with the terrain and aware of the detours that must be taken to arrive at the yet unseen goal. Communists would not necessarily claim that the Party is above mistakes. But they do regard it as in fact infallible, for in comparison with the Party there is nobody who could claim to be more "advanced," nobody with even equally valid insights into the road to be traveled, nobody who could conceivably improve on the Party's judgment. Because the truth that is history becomes accessible through struggle against the forces of reaction, the body which leads in this struggle must, by virtue of its forward position, have superior knowledge. The Party, in Communist eyes, is therefore more than a mere power organization. It is the fountainhead of truth, a truth which, in Lenin's words, is "always concrete." It is a spiritual home. It is the only available framework for meaningful individual action, if the meaning of human action is tied to the promotion of mankind's future destiny. It is the sole structure of order in an otherwise chaotic world. Outside of the Party, there is nothing but darkness, reaction, corruption, and hopelessness. Thus even a Communist who has come to doubt the Party's ideology finds it a matter of heartbreaking difficulty to sever himself from the Party and from there to go out into a world where no similar organization links his daily action with universal meaning and a hopeful future.

"The party and the masses" is a chapter by itself. Only the Party can have knowledge of the anticipated future and the road leading there. The masses, caught up in the present and its concerns, cannot sufficiently detach themselves from reactionary influences. The Party, therefore, must "lead and not follow." It must never adjust to people and their interests but, rather adjust people to itself and its interests. The proper role for the masses is one of "support" for Party policies. Being unable to appeal to the masses in terms of what the Party alone can know by virtue of Marxism-Leninism, the Party can gain mass support only by playing on the masses' present grievances, discontentments, and needs. One could call this a kind of adjustment of the Party to people and their feelings. But the adjustment is not made in good faith. The Communists are fully and articulately aware that they arouse hopes and make promises which they intend to deny once their strategic objective has been attained thanks to the masses' support. The Party's faithlessness, however, does not trouble the Communist conscience. If the Party deceives and manipulates the masses, it will eventually turn out to have been for the good, as all increases in the Party's power will move history nearer to the anticipated future. The masses, who are incapable of being moved by the "truth," must be led by the Party as children are led by parents.

A similar relationship exists between Party leadership and Party rank and file. The Communist term for this relationship is "democratic centralism." It means in practice that all Party members take part in endless debates and discussions about foregone conclusions. The Communists cannot approach the process of discussion as one of open possibilities, which approach would alone guarantee respect for the minds that converge in give-and-take. Since for the Communists history admits of only one "correct" road, the discussion can also have only one "correct" outcome, and the discussion process is one of attunement to this single choice. Any failure to take "the" correct path is for him necessarily a "deviation," and a deviation is a betrayal of "progress," and thus "reaction." A discussion is for Communists not a process of finding the materials for a forthcoming decision, but rather one of making the members understand the necessity and rationalization of a decision already taken. This is logical only when one pretends to have scientific knowledge of history's "Laws."

The same orientation underlies the typical Communist "toughness." Present shortcomings or setbacks cannot daunt a mind that has made its habitat entirely in the future. The present, from this perspective, must appear nothing but imperfect, hostile, and transitory. From here to the future the road is one of struggle, and the struggle is a "protracted" one, replete with victories and defeats, periods of contention and of lull, battles and campaigns, advances and retreats. The Communist manages to see in present imperfections the expected perfection of the future, as did the Russian lecturer who told Professor Gollwitzer a report on Russia saying that Russians live in beautiful new homes was true, even though at present many Russians do not yet live that way. "To see the future in the present means to think dialectically" (Gollwitzer, *Und Fuehren Wohin Du Nicht Willst*). For a Communist it is one of the basic facts of life that the Party, as long as it exists, must expect to struggle against enemies of superior strength. No campaign, no battle can be considered final except the one that puts its last enemy at its feet. Since the Party has been appointed by History as the instrument to move mankind forward toward the fulfillment of its destiny, the Party's eventual victory is assured. Khrushchev's "We shall bury you!" was meant not as a declaration of intention but as a confident reference to fact, a statement of "knowledge" concerning what will be the end of it all.

The Party's leadership consists of those people who, by virtue of their ideological "correctness," know most about the road that history must take. These people, and the small minority that belongs to the Party, are assumed to be surrounded by hostile influences of vastly superior strength. Organization and strict Party discipline are considered the recipe to the Party's eventual success over even the strongest enemy. Communists trust nobody and believe in nothing, except the Party and its mission. Thus the highest Communist duty is discipline. It is this discipline, permeating the entire personality, which renders Communists so formidable as enemies. The Communists' discipline has its roots in ideological convictions, for the ultimate enforcement consists in the threat of expulsion from the Party. Only those who assume that the Party alone is the enterprise of Progress, and that outside of the Party there is nothing but selfishness and Reaction, will fear expulsion as the Christian fears excommunication. The secret of Communist discipline is the Communists' belief in a world divided between bourgeois reaction and socialist revolution in which the Party leads the forces of progress.

The communist attitude toward people is based on the assumption that, as there are two ages, the present of capitalism and the future of socialism, there are two ideologies and two kinds of people, the "progressives" and the "reactionaries." The "progressives" are those who help the revolution which is the path toward the future age. All others are reactionary. The Communists' condemnation of all people classified as "reactionaries" follows from their total rejection of present-day society. They compare the present bourgeois and the future socialist society. Of these two, only the future one is considered real human life. It is seen as an age in which all tensions, disharmonies, and shortcomings of human existence will disappear. Man will be fully himself, his thoughts will be one with his actions, his individuality will harmonize with society, his days will no longer be darkened by poverty, oppression, and war. The future alone is the full realization of truth, freedom, and humanity. By contrast, the present age is for Communists totally "false." It is an existence characterized by exploitation, wars, the rule of money, political and economic oppression. Philosophy, religion, and government do not represent truth but merely the interests of the ruling class strife. Each individual's life is distorted by false institutions and hostile powers. His labor belongs to someone else. His mind is enslaved by false notions. Thus all those who have their interests in the present age rather than in the socialist future are seen as the enemies of truth and humanity. The dividing line between revolutionaries and reactionaries is razor sharp. For, as Lenin did not tire to point out, there are only two ideologies in the world, bourgeois and socialist, since "mankind has not created a third ideology." Anyone who fails to be socialist, even unwittingly, actually stands on the side of the bourgeoisie. Whether one is "progressive" or not is thus not a matter of intention but "objective" identification—either with the interests of the Party, or else with those of the class enemy.

In Communist eyes, the world is thus bipolarized. This is the characteristic feature of the period of "transition" or "protracted struggle" between Communists and their enemies, a period that constitutes for Communists the framework of their lives and actions. The "period of transition" is filled with the struggle between "two camps." This notion splits everything in two: classes—the bourgeoisie and the proletariat; ideologies—the bourgeois and the socialist ideology; people—the progressives and the reactionaries; nations—the "peace-loving" and the "imperialist" nations; wars—imperialist wars and wars of liberation, and, similarly, laws, philosophies, even methods of science. The criterion of distinction is objective support. He who by his thoughts and actions supports the bourgeoisie does not deserve respect or even existence. He who objectively supports the Party is approved. Since the Party Line, by design, zigs and zags, mere revolutionary conviction alone will not do. One must be able to step fast when the Party changes tactics and to guess right while the change is taking place. What is more the Communists recognize and accept the support of non-Communist elements. These are officially called "vacillating" elements, who, purely for tactical purposes, constitute a kind of third force between the battle lines. According to the Communists, a third force cannot endure long, for sooner or later it will split, one part coming down on the bourgeois and the other on the Communist side. Until then, these "vacillating" elements can be effectively "neutralized" or even used as allies, albeit with the full knowledge that eventually they must be fought and liquidated as ideological enemies.

There are only two ideologies, the bourgeois and the socialist ideology, but of these the bourgeois is still considered by far stronger. Lenin established the dogma that bourgeois ideological influences would powerfully linger long after the abolition of private property and that they constituted a besetting temptation even to Communist Party members. Hence the proper attitude of Communists toward all people is a basic universal suspicion. The bourgeois ideology is seen lurking under every bed, in every human foible, behind every appearance of slackness or self-interest. Communists characteristically struggle not merely on external battle lines but also against the "enemy within." All people deserve to be distrusted:

Trust must be earned by unwavering Party loyalty and can never be securely enjoyed. On the same showing, one can call the Communist attitude toward people one of basic and primary hostility. The Party imagines itself surrounded by enemies on all sides. There may be occasional allies, which are even considered essential to the Party's strategic achievements, but every ally, according to Lenin's admonition, must be "watched as if he were an enemy." In the entire world, only those who have succeeded in fully detaching themselves from the present and its lure can be considered reliable. All others are enemies, if not open, then disguised. The latter, in order to be fought, must first be "unmasked."

Communists have put between themselves and all other people a deliberate and profound alienation, or estrangement. They postulate that all who have not cast their will and thought into the mold of the socialist future cannot live in the same world with Communists. Communists cannot and will not accept the world in which, on their showing, all non-Communists actually live. Thus their design with respect to these other people is to re-make them into the Communist image. Communists adopt a totalitarian attitude toward people under their rule because they deny the right of these people to be what they are and want to be, and aim at the forceful creation of an entirely "new man." This is a long educational process, for the duration of which the human material under Communist hands is still considered shaped by bourgeois influences and thus hostile to the Party. The totalitarian plan of recreating man must therefore be supplemented by the Party's dictatorial power, that is, power "organized for war" (Lenin). The Communist quest for power is thus no ordinary desire to enjoy the distinctions and perquisites of command. It is an enterprise to create the world according to the Communists' idea of what it should have been, and to make men into something which they are not now, never have been, and do not want to be. Communist totalitarianism springs from the arrogation of the role of God.

A Communist, even though he might not be able to quote Marxist scripture and verse for his statements, might sum up his own view of the world as follows: A future socialist society is a certainty. The present bourgeois society must be rejected as totally unworthy and inhuman. Among all men, only a small group, the Communists, possess clear and scientific knowledge of the future while all others are still captive to the prejudices of the present. Between Communists and non-Communists there is thus no community of values. Under these conditions, life, and all politics, must be a continuous struggle. To assume that there could be harmony and unity in the present world would be but a reactionary illusion. Revolutionary realism emphasizes rather than mitigates the conflict. This does not bar stratagems of "coexistence" with the enemy, with the purpose of capturing, through the enemy's own institutions, the loyalties of people still under his influence. No inner reconciliation with the present society and its defending forces, however, can be considered anything else but treason of the Revolution. The good life can come only in the future. The future that is good will emerge from the victorious struggle of the Party against its reactionary enemies. The Party's power, its militant enterprise, its strategies and tactics, its use of force and ruse, its ongoing conquest of loyalties and institutions are sacred, as the entire revolutionary course of history is sacred. Any resistance to the Party is utterly unjustifiable. One does not measure the Party and its opponents with the same yardstick. The Party alone represents progress and hope; its enemies represent the total evil of the present. Thus, there can be no right to resist the Revolution. Khrushchev, in this sense, told Walter Lippmann that Western opposition to the ongoing Communist world Revolution is impermissible "interference."

A Communist is a man who has the outlook just described. He has steeped himself in it by inclination, choice, and ceaseless indoctrination. The outlook is also bolstered by official Party enforcement. The combination of attraction, semi-rational persuasion, and enforcement is extremely strong. To see people and situations, the Party, and oneself in the perspectives laid down by dogmatized ideology, becomes second nature to a Communist. The grip of the ideology is all the firmer since Communists are not likely to be confronted with any articulate alternative. At one point alone a different set of ideas might make an opposing claim on him: The traditional standards of morality, demanding good will, charity, veracity, and faithfulness, pose a conflict with the Communist norm of the class struggle. The struggle-hardened Communist is likely to win this argument with his conscience by persuading himself that since the course of history is known as certain, helping the course of history is the only moral conduct, compared with which traditional morality is nothing but bourgeois sentimentality. Once he commits himself to the belief that history treads an objectively knowable path, all the other arguments of the Party ideology follow with grim but inescapable logic. With regard to this fundamental dogma, the Communist not only finds no alternative view available in the contemporary world, but actually finds himself aided and abetted by Western thought. Positivism, Progressivism, Historicism have left deep marks on most Western intellectuals. These intellectual patterns are first cousin to the Communist ideology in that they, too, posit a knowable and predictable course of historical causality, the progressive movement of history to higher forms of life, the key role of revolutions, the struggle against the heritage of the past in the name of the future. Opposite views have not yet been sufficiently articulated in the West.

One can say, therefore, that in the West, too, ideologies hold sway and that between the prevailing ideologies in the West and Communism there are certain affinities and similarities. From all other ideologies the Communists differ by a trait of character which under different circumstances would be considered admirable: They take their beliefs seriously and expect at all times to act upon them. The Communists are above all ideological activists. This is why they constitute a more deadly threat than others whose thinking may also be irrationally distorted. Any ideology, since it proceeds from irrational premises, is apt to cause profound disturbances in the social order. In the Communist case, the character of the disturbance is a militant hostility towards men and existing institutions, a design to subvert, uproot, and destroy everything that exists. This flows from the fact that Communists live in a dreamworld, of the coming realization of which they are yet "scientifically" convinced. When dreams are carried over into the sober light of the day and become confused with reality, human action loses the quality of sobriety and adopts quixotic features. The substitution of a fictitious future age for the world of actual experience must entail irrationality of action. The irrationality of Communists manifests itself in their self-willed alienation from the world in which, after all, they also live.

One must distinguish between substantive and pragmatic rationality, the first concerning basic views of man, society, nature, and life, the second concerning the suitability of means to given ends. The Communists are irrational in a substantive sense. It is their construction of ends, and the realities on which ends are based, which is arbitrarily distorted and contrived. The pragmatic conclusions drawn from these ideological assumptions, however, are quite rational, given the basic postulates. The Communists, in daily life, are concerned almost exclusively with the full range of these pragmatic principles. Their problems are those of the protracted struggle, the Party and its leadership, the strength and weaknesses of the enemy, the assessment of various social forces from the point of view of the strategy, and the expediency of this or that policy to be adopted by the Soviet Union. Assuming the need to destroy the present-day world, the Communists have developed the art of destroying social structures to a previously unknown high level. This one must call pragmatic rationality of a sort, just as the "perfect crime" is a variety of pragmatic rationality. What is more, a certain amount of constructive rationality has room within the substantive irrationality of the Communist world view. Even a ruler committed to a dreamworld can succeed in commanding resources and skills which produce missiles, spaceships, and steel presses. Political madness is capable of creating an illusion of genuine and rational purpose and may even spur the output of great energy applied to ways, means, and instruments.

No amount of technical rationality, though, can remedy a deficiency of substantive rationality. The Communists are and remain in a basic and irremediable conflict with reality. It is, of course, impossible to escape from reality, and the Communists run their head against its walls all the time. On those occasions, they have a choice of trying to suppress resistant reality by sheer power or making concessions in the interest of continuing their struggle. By and large, they have preferred the second course, a course that was initiated by Lenin when he accepted the Peace of Brest Litovsk and, three years later, instituted the NEP. But Lenin also taught them that such concessions must never be made in the spirit of a change of mind. Rather, they are mere temporary retreats. This determination to continue believing in a world of their fancy rather than accepting the lessons taught them by reality bars the Communists forever from the achievement of peace. Not even where they have established total power over men and society have they created anything that could be honored by the name of order. Wherever Communists are organized for power there is hostility, suspicion, insecurity, and disintegration. Nor have they accomplished even within their own Party anything like relations of trust and friendship.

The present age of humanity is deeply disturbed, nations are threatened, institutions and traditions subverted, humanity suppressed, because a movement given to a cult of unreality has organized itself as a political army. There is a widespread misconception that Communists are engendered by conditions of social misery. This is quite contrary to the The truth is that Communists are made by Communists. Tempted by visions of fancy, bribed by a pseudo-scientism, they come to believe the reality of dreams, submerge themselves in a world of their own intellectual making, and pretend to be masters of creation. As long as such people are effectively organized for political action, the world can have no peace. Socialism might be conceived as an order of society. The might of Russia may disturb the sleep of other nations' rulers. Neither, however, can be called a fundamental threat to human order and peoples' existence. That threat comes solely from the irrational, alienated, destructive mind that has taken political shape in the Communist Party.

Chapter Thirteen

Khrushchev at the UN
The Damage We Have Done to Ourselves

William F. Buckley, Jr.

Ladies and gentlemen:

The damage Khrushchev can do to us on this trip is not comparable to the damage we have done to ourselves. Khrushchev is here. And his being here profanes the nation. But the harm we have done, we have done to ourselves; and for that we cannot hold Khrushchev responsible. There is nothing he is in a position to do, as he passes through our land, that can aggravate the national dishonor. We can only dishonor ourselves. Mr. Eisenhower invited him to come. But that was a transient damage that might have been laid to the vagaries of personal diplomacy. The lasting damage is related to the national acquiescence in Mr. Eisenhower's aberration. That acquiescence required the lapse of our critical and moral faculties. And for so long as they are in suspension, regeneration is not possible.

I deplore the fact that Khrushchev travels about this country—having been met at the frontier by our own prince, who arrived with his first string of dancing girls, and a majestic caravan of jewels and honey and spires; I mind that he will wend his lordly way from city to city, where the Lilliputians will fuss over his needs, weave garlands through the ring in his nose, shiver when he belches out his threats, and labor in panic to sate his imperial appetites. I mind that Khrushchev is here; but I mind more that Eisenhower invited him. I mind that Eisenhower invited him, but I mind much more the defense of that invitation by the *thought-leaders* of the nation. Khrushchev cannot by his presence here perma-

From *National Review*, September 26, 1959, pp. 349–351. Copyright 1959 by National Review, Inc., 215 Lexington Avenue, New York, NY 10016. Reprinted by permission.

nently damage us, I repeat; and neither can Mr. Eisenhower by inviting him. But we are gravely damaged if it is true that in welcoming Khrushchev, Eisenhower speaks for America; for in that case the people have lost their reason; and we cannot hope to live down the experience until we have recovered our reason, and regained our moral equilibrium.

I mind, in a word, the so-called "reasons" that have been advanced—and accepted—as to why Mr. Eisenhower issued the invitation. I mind first that "reasons" are being put forward, but mostly that they are being accepted. Khrushchev's visit has been successfully transmuted into a "diplomatic necessity"; and many even speak of it as a stroke of diplomatic genius. If the invitation had been rendered by President Eisenhower in his capacity as principal agent of American foreign policy, the deed would have been explosive enough. But the true dimensions of our national crisis became visible upon the appearance of the concentric ripples of assent that followed upon the issuance of the invitation. *A splendid idea,* said the chairman of the Foreign Relations Committee of the Senate, having presumably first consulted the editorial columns of the *New York Times* to make sure his compass was properly oriented.

And in a matter of days, we were being solemnly advised by the majority of the editorial writers of the nation that (a) the invitation was bound to meet with the approval of all those who favor peace in the world and good will towards men; and that (b) in any event, those who opposed the invitation have no alternative save to abide by the spirit that moved the President—as a matter of loyalty. "If you have to throw something at him," said Mr. Nixon upon touching ground after his visit to Moscow, "throw flowers." And then Mr. Gallup confirmed the popularity of the President's decision—which, it turns out, exceeds even the popularity of the President himself.

I do not recall that six months ago Mr. Gallup canvassed the American people on the question whether Mr. Khrushchev should be invited to this country, but I doubt that anyone would dispute my guess that as emphatic a majority would then have voted against the visit.

What happened? The sheer cogency of the invitation evidently struck the people as forcibly as the superiority of round as against square wheels is said one day to have struck our primitive ancestors. *Obviously* the visit is in order, the people seem to have grasped, giving way before the intuitions and analyses of their leaders. How mischievous is the habit of adducing reasons behind everything that is done! I can, happily and unassailably, delight in lobster and despise crabmeat; all my life—as long as I refrain from giving *reasons* why the one food suits and the other sickens. But when I seek rationally to motivate my preferences, I lose my authority. If only the publicists had refrained from shoring up the President's caprice with a Gothic rational structure! But no. We are a rational people. We do nothing without cause. There must be cause behind the invitation; and so the reasons for it are conjured up.

I have not heard a "reason" why Khrushchev should come to this country that is not in fact a reason why he should *not* come to this country. *He will see for himself the health and wealth of the land?* Very well; and having confirmed the fact, what are we to expect? That he will weaken in his adherence to his maniacal course? Because the average American has the use of one and two-thirds toilets? One might as well expect the Bishop of Rome to break the apostolic succession upon being confronted by the splendid new YMCA in Canton, Ohio. Does Khrushchev really *doubt* that there are 67 million automobiles in this country? What is he to do now that he is here? Count them? And if it is true that he doubts the statistics on American production and the American way of life, statistics that have been corroborated by his own technicians— then what reason is there to believe that he will trust the evidence of his own eyes as more reliable? And what will he do if there is a discrepancy? Fire Alger Hiss?

If Khrushchev were a man to be moved by empirical brushes with reality, how could he continue to believe in Communism? He cannot turn a corner in the Soviet Union without colliding against stark evidence of the fraudulence of Marxist theory. Where is the workers' paradise? In the two-room apartments that house five families? In the frozen reaches where he commits to slavery the millions upon millions who fail to appreciate the fact that under the Marxist prescription they have been elevated to a state of total freedom? In the headquarters of the secret police, where files are kept on every citizen of the Soviet Union on the *presumption* that every citizen is an enemy of the proletarian state?

Any man who is capable of being affected by the evidence of things as they are need not leave Russia to discover that the major premises of Karl Marx are mistaken. Dante cultivated a love of heaven by demonstrating the horrors of hell. It did not occur to him that the devil might be converted by taking him around the glories of the Court of the Medici. What reason have we to believe that a man who knows Russia and *still* has not rejected Marx, will be moved by the sight of Levittown?

But even if Khrushchev fails to readjust his views after witnessing the economic miracles wrought by capitalism—in which connection it is relevant to recall the amazement of American industrial leaders on learning last winter that Mikoyan knew more about American industrial accomplishments than they did—even if Khrushchev finds out that Mikoyan was right all along, will he learn that other great lesson which the President advanced as a principal "reason" why Khrushchev should come? Is he going to encounter that firmness of American resolution which will cause him, when he returns to Russia, to furrow his brow in anxiety on resuming the war against us?

I suggest that this brings us to the major reason why Khrushchev should *not* have been invited. If indeed the nation is united behind Mr. Eisenhower in this invitation, then the nation is united behind an act of diplomatic sentimentality which can only confirm Khrushchev in the contempt he feels for the dissipated morale of a nation far gone, as the theorists of Marxism have all along contended, in decrepitude. That he should be invited to visit here as though he were susceptible to a rational engagement! That he should achieve orthodox diplomatic recognition not three years after shocking history itself by the brutalities of Budapest; months after endorsing the shooting down of an unarmed American plane; only weeks since he last shrieked his intention of demolishing the West should it show any resistance to the march of socialism; only days since publishing in an American magazine his undiluted resolve to enslave the citizens of Free Berlin—that such an introduction should end up constituting his credentials for a visit to America will teach him something about the West some of us wish he might never have known.

What is it stands in the way of Communism's march? The little homilies of American capitalism? A gigantic air force which depends less on gasoline than on the pronouncements of the Committee for a Sane Nuclear Policy to know whether it can ever be airborne? Have we not something more to face Khrushchev with? Is this indeed the nature of the enemy, Khrushchev is entitled to wonder exultantly, after twelve days of giddy American cameraderie—will he not cherish as never before the pronouncements of Marx about the weakness of the capitalist opposition? Will he not return convinced that behind the modulated hubbub at the White House, in the State Department, at the city halls, at the economic clubs, at the industrial banquets, he heard—*with his own ears*—the death rattle of the West? Is there a *reason* why we should voluntarily expose to the enemy the great lesion of the West—our deficient understanding—

which saps the will without which we can never save the world for freedom? Will Khrushchev respect us more as, by our deeds, we proclaim and proclaim again and again our hallucinations, in the grinding teeth of the evidence, that we and the Soviet Union can work together for a better world?

It is the imposture of irrationality in the guise of rationality that frightens. The visit is timely, we are told. Why? State one reason. Why was it not timely, if it is timely now, a year ago? If Eisenhower is correct now in welcoming Khrushchev, then was he not wrong yesterday in not welcoming him? But we were all pro-Eisenhower yesterday—when he declared he would not meet with the Soviet leaders while under pressure of blackmail in regard to Berlin. And yet we are pro-Eisenhower today—when he proceeds to meet with Khrushchev, with the threat still hanging over us. If it is so very urgent that we should acquaint Khrushchev with the highways and byways of the United States, why is Eisenhower doing it seven long years after he first had the opportunity? Why has the same nation that implicitly endorsed the social boycott of Soviet leaders changed its mind so abruptly—to harmonize with so dissonant a change in position by our lackadaisical President? (The social history of the White House under Mr. Eisenhower will after all record only one exclusion and one addition during his tenure. Khrushchev was added, Senator McCarthy was ejected. And both times, the thousands cheered.) Is it a mark of loyalty to go along? What if Mr. Eisenhower had announced that upon reflection, Red-China should be invited into the United Nations? Would it be a mark of loyalty for us to assent? Or if he had decided to yield Quemoy and Matsu? A mark of loyalty to go along? And Berlin?

This afternoon Mayor Robert Wagner danced attendance upon Mr. Khrushchev. Did he do so because Premier Khrushchev is head of a foreign state and so entitled ex-officio, to the hospitality of New York's mayor? It isn't that simple, as we pointed out in the *National Review Bulletin* last week. Last year Mayor Wagner ostentatiously announced his refusal to greet Ibn Saud—on the grounds that Ibn Saud discriminates against Jews in Saudi Arabia, and no man who discriminates against Jews in Saudi Arabia is by God going to be handled courteously by Bob Wagner, mayor of New York. Now, as everybody knows, Nikita Khrushchev not only discriminates against Jews, he kills them. On the other hand, he does much the same thing to Catholics and Protestants. Could *that* be why Mr. Wagner consented to honor Khrushchev? Khrushchev murders people without regard to race, color, or creed, that is; on straight

FEPC lines; and therefore, whatever he is guilty of, he is not guilty of discrimination, and so he is entitled to Robert Wagner's hospitality? Is that the shape of the new rationality?

Ladies and gentlemen, we deem it the central revelation of Western experience that man cannot ineradicably stain himself, for the wells of regeneration are infinitely deep. No temple has ever been so profaned that it cannot be purified; no man is ever truly lost; no nation irrevocably dishonored. Khrushchev cannot take permanent advantage of our temporary disadvantage, for it is the West he is fighting. And in the West there lie, however encysted, the ultimate resources, which are moral in nature. Khrushchev is *not* aware that the gates of hell shall not prevail against us. Even out of the depth despair, we take heart in the knowledge that it cannot matter how deep we fall, for there is always hope. In the end, we will bury him.

Chapter Fourteen

The Hungary Pledge

The Soviet regime having by the Hungarian massacre demonstrated once again its isolation from the moral community, I pledge that until all Soviet troops and police are withdrawn from Hungary, I will enter into no economic, social, political, or cultural relations with that regime, or any of its domestic adherents or institutions, or with any Soviet citizens abroad (since these must act whether voluntarily or not as representatives of the regime), or with any persons or institutions freely condoning the Hungarian massacre, except for the sole purpose of persuading such individuals to defect.

(Signed)

The editors of National Review understand the Hungary Pledge to affirm, in effect, a total quarantine, or—in the broadest sense—a cultural boycott, of the Soviet Union, to be maintained at least until all Soviet forces are withdrawn from Hungary. They do not understand it to precommit them in any way to a softened view of Soviet Communism even should the troops be withdrawn from Hungary.

Specifically, though not exclusively, we interpret the Pledge to mean, in the terms relevant to the vocation of each person who accepts it, a resolution; to buy no Soviet products; to sell no product or service directly or indirectly to any Soviet principal (including Soviet legations, consulates, and other agencies abroad); not to load or unload from ships, planes, trains, or trucks goods from or directed to Soviet sources; not to attend any reception, party, dinner, or other gathering at which individuals subject to the quarantine are present, and to leave any gathering if such individuals appear; not to purchase any phonograph record of Soviet manufacture, and not to manufacture or purchase any record featuring music by any Soviet musician; not to produce, show, or attend any concert, theater, movie, ballet, or other such performance on the program of which any Soviet artist figures; not to appear on any platform, radio or TV show with any Soviet citizen or any Communist; not to publish, distribute, sell, or purchase (except for necessary scholarly or intelligence purposes) Soviet or

Communist books or articles; not to engage in any sport or athletic competition with Soviet athletes, or any other competition such as chess; to
boycott completely any and all Soviet "visitors," "exchange delegations,"
etc., in every field—whether agronomists, teachers, architects, scientists, or
whatever.

The editors of *National Review* have individually subscribed to the
Hungary Pledge. We commend it to our readers.

*(If you desire to subscribe formally to the Hungary Pledge, please sign below
the text above, cut it out, and mail it to us, or directly to the American
Friends of the Captive Nations, 62 W. 45th St., New York 36, N.Y. Or write
or type a facsimile of the pledge; or send in to the American Friends for a
copy of it.)*

Part V

Fusion

National Review would contribute to the fusion of conservatism into a unified movement. However, this was no easy task. While William F. Buckley could get both traditionalists and classical liberals to contribute to *National Review*, the two positions were not readily commutable. Traditionalists, with their insistence on social order typically based on religious belief or prescriptive tradition, did not mesh easily with classical liberal insistence on the primacy of the individual. Traditionalists typically ran in their own circles and founded their own journal, *Modern Age* (first published in 1957) dedicated to "conserving the best elements in our civilization."[1] Classical liberals also developed their own organizations, the aforementioned Mont Pelerin Society being foremost, and published in their own journals as well, like *The Freeman*. How could the impasse between these distinctive viewpoints ever be bridged?

Frank S. Meyer (1909–1972) attempted to span the chasm, in the process laying the theoretical foundations for the politicization of conservatism. Meyer was an Oxford-trained political theorist and a member of the communist party. During World War II he broke with the party and moved to the political Right, joining Buckley as an editor of *National Review* in 1955 (where he also contributed a column, "Principles and Heresies"). Meyer was a convert to classical liberalism and especially the idea of individualism at the heart of the later libertarian tradition. Yet he bristled at the cult of Ayn Rand that developed in the 1950s and 1960s and felt libertarian principles of individual rights still needed grounding in a social order. Throughout the 1950s, Meyer worked on developing a theoretical basis for modern conservatism that could help unify the disparate strands of traditionalists and classical liberals.

In 1962, Henry Regnery published *In Defense of Freedom: A Conservative Credo*, from which Chapter 15 is taken. In abbreviated form here, Meyer lays out his argument that conservatives and classical liberals have much in common, a defense of the tradition of freedom upon which social order and individual rights are based. Careful readers will discern evidence of themes in this chapter which he explored in the essay, "Collectivism Rebaptized" (see Part III). Still critical of the "new conservatism," Meyer sought to develop an inherent understanding of the primacy of the individual person against the "heresy" of collectivism.

In Chapter 16, F. A. Hayek's essay "Why I Am Not a Conservative," shows that Meyer's efforts to fuse conservatism into a political ideology would never amount to more than marriage of tactical convenience. Hayek's undisguised hostility to conservatism is displayed herein. Conservatism "is not a social program; in its paternalistic, nationalist and power-adoring tendencies it is often closer to socialism than true liberalism." Hayek clearly identified his position with classical liberalism in this essay (he called himself an "old Whig"); yet he remained, for all practical purposes, a conservative within the fused movement created by Frank Meyer that achieved political influence with the Barry Goldwater presidential campaign and Ronald Reagan's presidency.[2] Both politicians saw much to welcome in Hayek's principles of individual freedom, especially in their efforts to combat both communism and welfare state liberalism. While Hayek remained committed to the individualist views contained in both *The Road to Serfdom* and *The Constitution of Liberty* (from which the essay is taken), his acceptance by conservative politicians contributed to his identification with "the Right," his hostility toward them notwithstanding.

Chapter 17 is from a proposal for a new weekly journal of opinion, written by William F. Buckley, Jr., to gain support for what would become *National Review*. The document gives a clear indication of Buckley's thinking concerning the need for a new magazine that could represent the conservative viewpoint. It also shows his willingness to embrace various positions and bridge the gap between the classical liberals and traditionalists. Chapter 18, the "Credenda" from the first issue of *National Review*, describes the task of the new magazine.

Chapter Fifteen

A Rebel Finds His Tradition

Frank S. Meyer

My intention in writing this book is to vindicate the freedom of the person as the central and primary end of political society. I am also concerned with demonstrating the integral relationship between freedom as a political end and the basic beliefs of contemporary American conservatism.

Liberalism was indeed once, in the last century, the proponent and defender of freedom. But that which is called liberalism today has deserted its heritage of defense of the freedom of the person, to become the peculiarly American form of what in Europe is called democratic socialism. This transformation was the result of a fatal flaw in the philosophical underpinnings of 19th-century liberalism. It stood for individual freedom, but its utilitarian philosophical attitude denied the validity of moral ends firmly based on the constitution of being. Thereby, with this denial of an ultimate sanction for the inviolability of the person, liberalism destroyed the very foundations of its defense of the person as primary in political and social matters.

The complex story of the actual transformation of liberalism—a transformation unfolding out of this profound original defect—is a fascinating chapter in intellectual history. That is not, however, the subject of this book. Although I shall touch upon it from time to time, my concern here is not with the history of liberalism, but with what is today called liberalism—alike by those who are hostile to it and by those who consciously write and act as "liberals." This usage is the only meaning the word retains in common discourse. Therefore, to distinguish contempo-

Frank S. Meyer, *In Defense of Freedom and Related Essays* (Indianapolis, Ind.: Liberty Fund, 1996, 33–40, 149–151). Reprinted by permission.

rary "liberalism" from the liberalism of the 19th century—and in piety towards the 19th-century liberals to whom the freedom of the person was a dear concern—I shall throughout this book refer to what is today called liberalism as "collectivist liberalism."

If, however, 19th-century liberalism by its fundamental philosophical errors gave birth to that form of 20th-century collectivism which passes under the name of liberalism, there was in 19th-century conservatism an inherent flaw of another sort. The conservatives of the last century were sound in their fundamental philosophical position, upholding the objective existence of values based upon the unchanging constitution of being as the criteria for moral thought and action. They staunchly held the line against the assault of utilitarianism, positivism, and scientism, but, on another level they failed philosophically, deeply misreading the nature of man. They would not or they could not see the correlative to their fundamental philosophical position: acceptance of the moral authority derived from transcendent criteria of truth and good must be voluntary if it is to have meaning; if it is coerced by human force, it is meaningless. They were willing, if only the right standards were upheld, to accept an authoritarian structure of state and society. They were, at the best, indifferent to freedom in the body politic; at the worst, its enemies.

There are in the contemporary American scene those who take their inspiration from these 19th-century conservative beliefs. Although they do not compose an organized political group (some of them, indeed, in their practical political influence are essentially part of the "liberal" establishment, while others are allied with the American conservative movement), they do hold a common theoretical position. This position is generally described by the term "The New Conservatism." Although that phrase is sometimes also used more broadly, to refer to the whole contemporary American conservative movement, it is in the specific and limited sense that I shall employ it in this book.

The concepts on which the New Conservatives base themselves can be directly traced to 19th-century conservatism and to certain aspects of the thinking of Edmund Burke, who is explicitly recognized by most of them as a major source of their guiding ideas. Their position is characterized by an organic view of society; by a subordination of the individual person to society; and, therefore, by a denial that the freedom of the person is the decisive criterion of a good polity.

This subordination of freedom, this exaltation of the claims of society, differentiates them from the implicit consensus of contemporary American conservatism. That consensus, it is true, does agree with the New Conservatives on the moral obligation of all men to seek and to respect the norms of virtue objectively based upon an eternal order of truth and good; but, in contradistinction to them, it posits as a necessary corollary that the freedom of the person, not the asserted authority of "society," of some "mysterious incorporation of the human race," is primary in political thought and action.

Should the question be raised, by what right do I maintain against the New Conservatives and the other heirs of 19th-century conservatism that the position which I am defending is essentially the consensus of contemporary American conservatism, I point first to the empirical evidence—and on several levels. At the source to which American conservatism inevitably returns—The Declaration of Independence, the Constitution, and the debates at the time of its adoption—this simultaneous belief in objectively existing moral value and in the freedom of the individual person was promulgated in uncompromising terms. From that source it irradiates the active present scene of American conservatism. The broadly acknowledged political symbol of American conservatism, Barry Goldwater, and its broadly acknowledged intellectual spokesman, William F. Buckley, Jr., share this twin belief. As M. Stanton Evans, in *Revolt on the Campus*, has shown in copious quotations from the leaders of the conservative student movement, it is their guiding light. What is true of the young, is also true of the great majority of adult conservatives. A serious examination of the publications of the various groups among conservatives will, I am convinced, prove this contention to the disinterested reader.

The position taken in this book is, I believe, an accurate representation, a crystallization on the theoretical level, of the empirical attitudes of the widespread and developing American conservative movement. But this very combination of freedom and moral authority—which in the ideological history of the European 19th century were the symbols of opposed liberal and conservative forces—has been the target of sharp theoretical attack by collectivist-liberal writers, and even by some conservatives of the 19th-century tradition. We are told that what is not in the tradition of Burke—or of the medieval synthesis—or of Plato—cannot call itself conservatism: anyone who insists upon freedom in the political and economic sphere, together with "legitimate" conservative beliefs, is really half liberal, half conservative, a sad case of intellectual schizophrenia. Such criticisms might be answered by simply pointing to actuality, asserting that, whether European intellectual history blesses us or not, this is the way the average contemporary American conservative thinks and feels; or by citing the founding documents of the Republic as authority—the authority of another, an American, intellectual history.

But, in candor, this is not enough. It has to be shown that the two aspects of the position are fundamentally in accord, that they are grounded both in the nature of men and in the very constitution of being. It is my aim to make this demonstration, to vindicate on theoretical grounds the native belief of American conservatives that freedom as a prime criterion in the political and social sphere is not alien to the conservative view of man's nature and destiny; that it arises naturally from conservative assumptions; and that it can be effectively defended only upon the basis of those assumptions.

Therefore, the concern of these pages is with establishing the theoretical soundness of this position. I am not primarily concerned with the details or the limitations of present-day political reality, but rather with developing a conservative criterion for a good society, a good polity. That being my intent, the standard of judgment of political questions here presented is just that: a standard, not a program for immediate achievement. I would add, however, that without something in the nature of an ideal image of what a good society should be, without an end which political action can strive to approximate, there is no basis for judging the rights and wrongs of the practical alternatives that constantly present themselves.

The specific character of the concrete political forms indicated by this criterion for any given society will vary immensely depending on the civilizational development and the experience with free institutions of the nation or culture concerned. In the United States, with our Constitutional tradition and Constitutional experience, a comparatively close approximation to the ideal is possible, despite the attrition of several decades of liberal-collectivist ascendancy. For ours is the most effective effort ever made to articulate in *political* terms the Western understanding of the interrelation of the freedom of the person and the authority of an objective moral order. The other nations of Western civilization—all respecters of the person, but without the rock-bound theory of limited government that inspired the American Founders—hold, in varying degree, the preeminence of the person in their tradition; and therefore they approximate, if less closely, to the political ideal here presented. The tradition of the Oriental and Middle Eastern civilizations is still further removed from it; and pre-civilized cultures, such as those of Africa, are at an enormous remove from it.

I realize that such a ranking of nations and cultures, particularly one which places one's own country at the head, will be regarded in the relativist atmosphere of the day as extraordinarily unenlightened and arrogant. Be that as it may, by the criterion I hope to establish, it is the truth; and it is therefore primarily to the United States and secondarily to Western civilization that my analysis has direct relevance.

Furthermore, I should add, lest specious conclusions be drawn from the defense of the freedom of the person, that there is here no advocacy of that equalitarianism which would forbid to men the acquisition of unequal goods, influence, or honor, and the right to pass these "inequalities" on to their heirs if they can. The only equality that can be legitimately derived from the premises of the freedom of the person is the equal right of all men to be free from coercion exercised against their life, liberty, and property. This is the touchstone of a free society. For the rest, the capabilities of men, specific and inherited, should determine their position, their influence, and the respect in which they are held.

Nor does it follow from my thesis that any particular type of political institution is in itself either demanded by, or a guarantee of, development towards a free society. The representative democratic institutions, combined with constitutional guarantees of freedom, which have been the matrix for the development of free societies in the United States, England, and some other Western nations, may not be the best political forms for the achievement of an approximation to a good society even in all countries of Western civilization, much less elsewhere.

But, although there is more than one possible form of political institution for the development of a good society, there are also forms which are totally negative to any such development. Nazism, which was inspired by the concept of reducing the person to nothingness before the state, was destroyed in the war of 1939–45; but Communism, its older brother, today dominates a third of the world and advances with messianic zeal and cold scientific strategy towards the domination of the whole world. Consequently, everything projected in this book presupposes the defeat of this monstrous, atavistic attack upon the survival of the very concepts of moral order and individual freedom. If I do not deal with Communism, it is because I am here concerned with the development of ideas within the Western and American tradition. With Communism, which bases itself on a set of values radically hostile in their very foundation to the Western view of man, there is no common ground for theoretical discussion. Determination and force will decide the issue, and our determination and force—which can be expressed only in terms of counter-attack—will depend upon the depth with which we understand, and, understanding, are loyal to, the truths incarnate in Western civilization and the American republic.

To the drawing out and clarification of these truths, this book is dedicated. In that effort, my central endeavor is to validate the individual person as the decisive concern of political action and political theory. The individual person and social institutions are the polar points to which every political philosophy is oriented. And as men's political arrangements reflect their consciousness, it is by the emphasis placed upon one or the other of these poles by the prevalent political philosophy that the characteristics of a political society are established and perpetuated.

It is my general contention that, despite the weight of the tradition of our civilization on the side of the individual person, the predominant intellectual tendency of this century has brought about a deep derangement of the tension between these two poles of human existence, towards the submergence of the person. It is my particular contention that the criticism by the New Conservatives of this prevailing collectivist dogma itself suffers from an inner error of political understanding.

Against both the prevailing mode of thought and the New Conservative criticism, which are, each in its own way, appeals to experience, I propose the claims of reason and the claims of the tradition of reason. I do not assume that reason is the sole possession of a single living generation, or of any man in any generation. I do assume that it is the active quality whereby men (starting with a due respect for the fundamental moral knowledge of ends and values incorporated in tradition) have the power to distinguish what ought to be from what is, the ideal from the dictates of power. Upon these assumptions, I shall attempt to reestablish, in contemporary contexts, principles drawn from the nature of man, and by these principles to criticize both the prevalent collectivist-liberal orthodoxy and the New Conservatism.

Both, I hope to show, share in political matters a common error, which brings them much closer together than the polemics exchanged between them would seem to indicate. Both are radically affected by the derangement of the tension between the person and social institutions necessary to a good society. Both give so high a place to the concept of society that the freedom of the person is reduced to a subordinate position and becomes transformed from a real end into a pious hope—invoked on suitable occasions, but to be achieved as the implicit result of the establishment of the "right" social pattern, not to be striven for directly. Both reduce the person to a secondary being, whose dignity and rights become dependent upon the gift and grace of society or the state.

Belief in the primacy of the person was inherent from the beginning in the vision which formed Western civilization. The complementary concept of freedom as the determining criterion of the good political and social order was, however, only partially realized, either theoretically or practically, until the foundation of the American republic and the framing of our Constitution. Here for the first time a polity was established based upon the freedom of the person as its end, and upon firm limitation of the powers of the state as the means to achieve that end.

For half a century or more the idea was clearly and firmly held, and the practice of the American republic closely approximated the idea. But a process of retrogression set in, first slowly, then faster and faster—a process in which the decisive moments were the introduction of mass democratism by Andrew Jackson, the undermining of the sovereignty of the several states by Abraham Lincoln, and the naturalization in the United States of 20th-century collectivist principles and methods by Franklin D. Roosevelt. During the past thirty years that process has been frighteningly accelerated. A polity which represented the drive of men towards the full potentialities of their being has been defiled; that drive, more magnificent than any drive in the physical universe towards the moon, the planets or beyond, has been slowed down, cut short, reversed.

That there should set in a retreat from the vision of a truly free social order, and from the difficult and demanding endeavor to realize a polity that makes such an order possible, was perhaps to be expected. Before the advent of the Western concept of the person, men had lived for thousands of years of civilization and tens of thousands of years of pre-civilized human existence under conditions in which freedom was only an occasional and barely grasped concept, only a fugitive reality. But, however harsh the pressures of life, they lived in the deep security of the enveloping social womb. Freedom brings men rudely and directly face to face with their own personal responsibility for their own free actions. This is a shock. Remembrance of the fleshpots of enveloping security ever tugs insidiously at the souls of free men. But where mind and will have been clear and firm, the temptation has been rejected.

It is confusion of mind and consequent debilitation of will that have brought the United States to our present condition. It is not, however, the men and women who make up the citizenry of America, the constituency of those who lead the nation, who have raised the cry for return to the fleshpots. It is and has been the leaders in the social order themselves, the possessors of intellectual and moral authority, who have blinded themselves to the truths of their heritage and rejected the moral responsibility of freedom. They have confused and bewildered those to whom it is their duty to give guidance and leadership. But the old truths, the old understanding still live in the hearts, the basic moral instincts, the fundamental beliefs of ordinary Americans. The established leaders can make them feel ashamed, ignorant, "backward," but they have not been able to eradicate their essential soundness.

The right instincts are there, the energy is there. For the shackling of Leviathan, the limitation of the state's invasion of the free domain of individual persons, those instincts await only intellectual articulation, that energy needs only organization. Here lies the challenge to resurgent conservatism in America: simultaneously to create a new intellectual and spiritual leadership, and on the basis of that leadership to move forward to the defeat of collectivist liberalism in the political sphere. Intellectually and spiritually, it has twin tasks: to come to grips with the prevailing relativist and positivist philosophy and confute it; and to vindicate the great tradition of freedom of the person, exposing collectivist theory, however attenuated and whatever its source, in all its insidious menace. Politically, it must organize the power of the consensus of Americans to bring to the helm of the state men devoted to limiting the power of the state, to freeing the energies of individual persons from bureaucratic encroachment—and to directing the rightful power of the state against the ravening drive of the armed and messianic collectivism of Communism.

The issue rests upon the question: can the new and rising conservative leadership release and guide the pent-up energies, the intuitive understanding of their heritage, the love of freedom and virtue in the hearts of the American people, before the converging forces of cloying collectivism at home and armed collectivism abroad destroy the very meaning of freedom? That issue rests, as every important human issue always rests, in the hands of individual persons. Nothing in history is determined. The decision hangs upon our understanding of the tradition of Western civilization and the American republic, our devotion to freedom and to truth, the strength of our will and of our determination to live as free and virtuous men.

Chapter Sixteen

Why I Am Not a Conservative

F. A. Hayek

At a time when most movements that are thought to be progressive advocate further encroachments on individual liberty,[1] those who cherish freedom are likely to expend their energies in opposition. In this they find themselves much of the time on the same side as those who habitually resist change. In matters of current politics today they generally have little choice but to support the conservative parties. But, though the position I have tried to define is also often described as "conservative," it is very different from that to which this name has been traditionally attached. There is danger in the confused condition which brings the defenders of liberty and the true conservatives together in common opposition to developments which threaten their different ideals equally. It is therefore important to distinguish clearly the position taken here from that which has long been known—perhaps more appropriately— as conservatism.

Conservatism proper is a legitimate, probably necessary, and certainly widespread attitude of opposition to drastic change. It has, since the French Revolution, for a century and a half played an important role in European politics. Until the rise of socialism its opposite was liberalism. There is nothing corresponding to this conflict in the history of the United States, because what in Europe was called "liberalism" was here the common tradition on which the American polity had been built: thus the defender of the American tradition was a liberal in the European sense.[2] This already existing confusion was made worse by the recent

F. A. Hayek, *The Constitution of Liberty* (Chicago: University of Chicago Press, 1959), 397–411, 529–531. Reprinted by permission of University of Chicago Press and Estate of F. A. Hayek.

attempt to transplant to America the European type of conservatism, which, being alien to the American tradition, has acquired a somewhat odd character. And some time before this, American radicals and socialists began calling themselves "liberals." I will nevertheless continue for the moment to describe as liberal the position which I hold and which I believe differs as much from true conservatism as from socialism. Let me say at once, however, that I do so with increasing misgivings, and I shall later have to consider what would be the appropriate name for the party of liberty. The reason for this is not only that the term "liberal" in the United States is the cause of constant misunderstandings today, but also that in Europe the predominant type of rationalistic liberalism has long been one of the pacemakers of socialism.

Let me now state what seems to me the decisive objection to any conservatism which deserves to be called such. It is that by its very nature it cannot offer an alternative to the direction in which we are moving. It may succeed by its resistance to current tendencies in slowing down undesirable developments, but, since it does not indicate another direction, it cannot prevent their continuance. It has, for this reason, invariably been the fate of conservatism to be dragged along a path not of its own choosing. The tug of war between conservatives and progressives can only affect the speed, not the direction, of contemporary developments. But, though there is need for a "brake on the vehicle of progress,"[3] I personally cannot be content with simply helping to apply the brake. What the liberal must ask, first of all, is not how fast or how far we should move, but where we should move. In fact, he differs much more from the collectivist radical of today than does the conservative. While the last generally holds merely a mild and moderate version of the prejudices of his time, the liberal today must more positively oppose some of the basic conceptions which most conservatives share with the socialists.

The picture generally given of the relative position of the three parties does more to obscure than to elucidate their true relations. They are usually represented as different positions on a line, with the socialists on the left, the conservatives on the right, and the liberals somewhere in the middle. Nothing could be more misleading. If we want a diagram, it would be more appropriate to arrange them in a triangle with the conservatives occupying one corner, with the socialists pulling toward the second and the liberals toward the third. But, as the socialists have for a long time been able to pull harder, the conservatives have tended to follow the socialist rather than the liberal direction and have adopted at appropriate intervals of time those ideas made respectable by radical propaganda. It has been regularly the conservatives who have compromised with socialism and stolen its thunder. Advocates of the Middle Way[4] with no goal of their own, conservatives have been guided by the belief that the truth must lie somewhere between the extremes—with the result that they have shifted their position every time a more extreme movement appeared on either wing.

The position which can be rightly described as conservative at any time depends, therefore, on the direction of existing tendencies. Since the development during the last decades has been generally in a socialist direction, it may seem that both conservatives and liberals have been mainly intent on retarding that movement. But the main point about liberalism is that it wants to go elsewhere, not to stand still. Though today the contrary impression may sometimes be caused by the fact that there was a time when liberalism was more widely accepted and some of its objectives closer to being achieved, it has never been a backward-looking doctrine. There has never been a time when liberal ideals were fully realized and when liberalism did not look forward to further improvement of institutions. Liberalism is not averse to evolution and change; and where spontaneous change has been smothered by government control, it wants a great deal of change of policy. So far as much of current governmental action is concerned, there is in the present world very little reason for the liberal to wish to preserve things as they are. It would seem to the liberal, indeed, that what is most urgently needed in most parts of the world is a thorough sweeping-away of the obstacles to free growth.

This difference between liberalism and conservatism must not be obscured by the fact that in the United States it is still possible to defend individual liberty by defending long-established institutions. To the liberal they are valuable not mainly because they are long established or because they are American but because they correspond to the ideals which he cherishes. . . .

This brings me to the first point on which the conservative and the liberal dispositions differ radically. As has often been acknowledged by conservative writers, one of the fundamental traits of the conservative attitude is a fear of change, a timid distrust of the new as such,[5] while the liberal position is based on courage and confidence, on a preparedness to let change run its course even if we cannot predict where it will lead. There would not be much to object to if the conservatives merely disliked too rapid change in institutions and public policy; here the case for caution and slow process is indeed strong. But the conservatives are inclined to use the powers of government to prevent change or to limit its rate to whatever appeals to the more timid mind. In looking forward, they lack the faith in the spontaneous forces of adjustment which makes the liberal accept changes without apprehension, even though he does not know how the necessary adaptations will be brought about. It is, indeed, part of the liberal attitude to assume that, especially in the economic field, the self-regulating forces of the market will somehow bring about the required adjustments to new conditions, although no one can foretell how they will do this in a particular instance. There is perhaps no single factor contributing so much to people's frequent reluctance to let the market work as their inability to conceive how some necessary balance, between demand and supply, between exports and imports, or the like, will be brought about without deliberate control. The conservative feels safe and content only if he is assured that some higher wisdom watches and supervises change, only if he knows that some authority is charged with keeping the change "orderly."

This fear of trusting uncontrolled social forces is closely related to two other characteristics of conservatism: its fondness for authority and its lack of understanding of economic forces. Since it distrusts both abstract theories and general principles,[6] it neither understands those spontaneous forces on which a policy of freedom relies nor possesses a basis for formulating principles of policy. Order appears to the conservatives as the result of the continuous attention of authority, which, for this purpose, must be allowed to do what is required by the particular circumstances and not be tied to rigid rule. A commitment to principles presupposes an understanding of the general forces by which the efforts of society are co-ordinated, but it is such a theory of society and especially of the economic mechanism that conservatism conspicuously lacks. So unproductive has conservatism been in producing a general conception of how a social order is maintained that its modern votaries, in trying to construct a theoretical foundation, invariably find themselves appealing almost exclusively to authors who regarded themselves as liberal. Macaulay, Tocqueville, Lord Acton, and Lecky certainly considered themselves liberals, and with justice; and even Edmund Burke remained an Old Whig to the end and would have shuddered at the thought of being regarded as a Tory.

Let me return, however, to the main point, which is the characteristic complacency of the conservative toward the action of established authority and his prime concern that this authority be not weakened rather than that its power be kept within bounds. This is difficult to reconcile with the preservation of liberty. In general, it can probably be said that the conservative does not object to coercion or arbitrary power so long as it is used for what he regards as the right purposes. He believes that if government is in the hands of decent men, it ought not be too much restricted by rigid rules. Since he is essentially opportunist and lacks principles, his main hope must be that the wise and the good will rule— not merely by example, as we all must wish, but by authority given to them and enforced by them.[7] Like the socialist, he is less concerned with the problem of how the powers of government should be limited than with that of who wields them; and, like the socialist, he regards himself as entitled to force the value he holds on other people.

When I say that the conservative lacks principles, I do not mean to suggest that he lacks moral conviction. The typical conservative is indeed usually a man of very strong moral convictions. What I mean is that he has no political principles which enable him to work with people whose moral values differ from his own for a political order in which both can obey their convictions. It is the recognition of such principles that permits the coexistence of different sets of values that makes it possible to build a peaceful society with a minimum of force. The acceptance of such principles means that we agree to tolerate much that we dislike. There are many values of the conservative which appeal to me more than those of the socialists; yet for a liberal the importance he personally attaches to specific goals is no sufficient justification for forcing others to serve them. . . .

To live and work successfully with others requires more than faithfulness to one's concrete aims. It requires an intellectual commitment to a type of order in which, even on issues which to one are fundamental, others are allowed to pursue different ends.

It is for this reason that to the liberal neither moral nor religious ideals are proper objects of coercion, while both conservatives and socialists recognize no such limits. I sometimes feel that the most conspicuous attribute of liberalism that distinguishes it as much from conservatism as from socialism is the view that moral beliefs concerning matters of conduct which do not directly interfere with the protected sphere of other persons do not justify coercion. This may also explain why it seems to be so much easier for the repentant socialist to find a new spiritual home in the conservative fold than in the liberal.

In the last resort, the conservative position rests on the belief that in any society there are recognizably superior persons whose inherited standards and values and position ought to be protected and who should have a greater influence on public affairs than others. The liberal, of course, does not deny that there are some superior people—he is not an egalitarian—but he denies that anyone has authority to decide who these superior people are. While the conservative inclines to defend a particular established hierarchy and wishes authority to protect the status of those whom he values, the liberal feels that no respect for established values can justify the resort to privilege or monopoly or any other coercive power of the state in order to shelter such people against the forces of economic change. Though he is fully aware of the important role that cultural and intellectual elites have played in the evolution of civilization, he also believes that these elites have to prove themselves by their capacity to maintain their position under the same rules that apply to all others.

Closely connected with this is the usual attitude of the conservative to democracy. I have made it clear earlier that I do not regard majority rule as an end but merely as a means, or perhaps even as the least evil of those forms of government from which we have to choose. But I believe that the conservatives deceive themselves when they blame the evils of our time on democracy. The chief evil is unlimited government, and nobody is qualified to wield unlimited power.[8] The powers which modern democracy possesses would be even more intolerable in the hands of some small elite.

Admittedly, it was only when power came into the hands of the majority that further limitation of the power of government was thought unnecessary. In this sense democracy and unlimited government are connected. But it is not democracy but unlimited government that is objectionable, and I do not see why the people should not learn to limit the scope of majority rule as well as that of any other form of government. At any rate, the advantages of democracy as a method of peaceful change and of political education seem to be so great compared with those of any other system that I can have no sympathy with the anti-democratic strain of conservatism. It is not who governs but what government is entitled to do that seems to me the essential problem.

That the conservative opposition to too much government control is not a matter of principle but is concerned with the particular aims of government is clearly shown in the economic sphere. Conservatives usually oppose collectivist and directivist measures in the industrial field, and here the liberal will often find allies in them. But at the same time conservatives are usually protectionists and have frequently supported socialist measures in agriculture. Indeed, though the restrictions which exist today in industry and commerce are mainly the result of socialist views, the equally important restrictions in agriculture were usually introduced by conservatives at an even earlier date. And in their efforts to discredit free enterprise many conservative leaders have vied with the socialists.[9]

I have already referred to the differences between conservatism and liberalism in the purely intellectual field, but I must return to them because the characteristic conservative attitude here not only is a serious weakness of conservatism but tends to harm any cause which allies itself with it. Conservatives feel instinctively that it is new ideas more than anything else that cause change. But, from its point of view rightly, conservatism fears new ideas because it has no distinctive principles of its own to oppose to them; and, by its distrust of theory and its lack of imagination concerning anything except that which experience has already proved, it deprives itself of the weapons needed in the struggle of ideas. Unlike liberalism with its fundamental belief in the long-range power of ideas, conservatism is bound by the stock of ideas inherited at a given time. And since it does not really believe in the power of argument, its last resort is generally a claim to superior wisdom, based on some self-arrogated superior quality.

This difference shows itself most clearly in the different attitudes of the two traditions to the advance of knowledge. Though the liberal certainly does not regard all change as progress, he does regard the advance of knowledge as one of the chief aims of human effort and expects from it the gradual solution of such problems and difficulties as we can hope to solve. Without preferring the new merely because it is new, the liberal is aware that it is of the essence of human achievement that it produces something new; and he is prepared to come to terms with new knowledge, whether he likes its immediate effects or not.

Personally, I find that the most objectionable feature of the conservative attitude is its propensity to reject well-substantiated new knowledge because it dislikes some of the consequences which seem to follow from it—or, to put it bluntly, its obscurantism. I will not deny that scientists as much as others are given to fads and fashions and that we have much reason to be cautious in accepting the conclusions that they draw from their latest theories. But the reasons for our reluctance must themselves be rational and must be kept separate from our regret that the new theories upset our cherished beliefs. I can have little patience with those who oppose, for instance, the theory of evolution or what are called "mechanistic" explanations of the phenomena of life simply because of certain moral consequences which at first seem to follow from these theories, and still less with those who regard it as irreverent or impious to ask certain questions at all. By refusing to face the facts, the conservative only weakens his own position. Frequently the conclusions which rationalist presumption draws from new scientific insights do not at all follow from them. But only by actively taking part in the elaboration of the consequences of new discoveries do we learn whether or not they fit into our world picture and, if so, how. Should our moral beliefs really prove to be dependent on factual assumptions shown to be incorrect, it would be hardly moral to defend them by refusing to acknowledge facts.

Connected with the conservative distrust of the new and the strange is its hostility to internationalism and its proneness to a strident nationalism. Here is another source of its weakness in the struggle of ideas. It cannot alter the fact that the ideas which are changing our civilization respect no boundaries. But refusal to acquaint one's self with new ideas merely deprives one of the power of effectively countering them when necessary. The growth of ideas is an international process, and only those who fully take part in the discussion will be able to exercise a significant influence. It is no real argument to say that an idea is un-American, un-British, or un-German, nor is a mistaken or vicious ideal better for having been conceived by one of our compatriots.

A great deal more might be said about the close connection between conservatism and nationalism, but I shall not dwell on this point because it may be felt that my personal position makes me unable to sympathize with any form of nationalism. I will merely add that it is this nationalistic bias which frequently provides the bridge from conservatism to collectivism: to think in terms of "our" industry or resource is only a short step away from demanding that these national assets be directed in the national interest. But in this respect the Continental liberalism which derives from the French Revolution is little better than conservatism. I need hardly say that nationalism of this sort is something very different from patriotism and that an aversion to nationalism is fully compatible with a deep attachment to national traditions. But the fact that I prefer and feel reverence for some of the traditions of my society need not be the cause of hostility to what is strange and different.

Only at first does it seem paradoxical that the anti-internationalism of the conservative is so frequently associated with imperialism. But the more a person dislikes the strange and thinks his own ways superior, the more he tends to regard it as his mission to "civilize" others[10]—not by the voluntary and unhampered intercourse which the liberal favors, but by bringing them the blessings of efficient government. . . .

There is one respect, however, in which there is justification for saying that the liberal occupies a position midway between the socialist and the conservative: he is as far from the crude rationalism of the socialist, who wants to reconstruct all social institutions according to a pattern pre-scribed by his individual reason, as from the mysticism to which the conservative so frequently has to resort. What I have described as the liberal position shares with conservatism a distrust of reason to the extent that the liberal is very much aware that we do not know all the answers and that he is not sure that the answers he has are certainly the right ones or even that we can find all the answers. He also does not disdain to seek assistance from whatever non-rational institutions or habits have proved their worth. The liberal differs from the conservative in his willingness to face this ignorance and to admit how little we know, without claiming the authority of supernatural sources of knowledge where his reason fails him. It has to be admitted that in some respects the liberal is fundamen-tally a skeptic[11]—but it seems to require a certain degree of diffidence to let others seek their happiness in their own fashion and to adhere consis-tently to that tolerance which is an essential characteristic of liberalism.

There is no reason why this need mean an absence of religious belief on the part of the liberal. Unlike the rationalism of the French Revolution, true liberalism has no quarrel with religion, and I can only deplore the militant and essentially illiberal antireligionism which animated so much of nineteenth-century Continental liberalism. That this is not essential to liberalism is clearly shown by its English ancestors, the Old Whigs, who, if anything, were much too closely allied with a particular religious belief. What distinguishes the liberal from the conservative here is that, however profound his own spiritual beliefs, he will never regard himself as entitled to impose them on others and that for him the spiritual and the temporal are different spheres which ought not to be confused.

*

What I have said should suffice to explain why I do not regard myself as a conservative. Many people will feel, however, that the position which emerges is hardly what they used to call "liberal." I must, therefore, now face the question of whether this name is today the appropriate name for the party of liberty. I have already indicated that, though I have all my life described myself as a liberal, I have done so more recently with increasing misgivings—not only because in the United States this term constantly gives rise to misunderstanding, but also because I have become more and more aware of the great gulf that exists between my position and the rationalistic Continental liberalism or even the English liberalism of the utilitarians. . . .

It is thus necessary to recognize that what I have called "liberalism" has little to do with any political movement that goes under that name today. It is also questionable whether the historical associations which that name carries today are conducive to the success of any movement. Whether in these circumstances one ought to make an effort to rescue the term from what one feels is its misuse is a question on which opinions may well differ. I myself feel more and more that to use it without long explanations causes too much confusion and that as a label it has become more of a ballast than a source of strength.

In the United States, where it has become almost impossible to use "liberal" in the sense in which I have used it, the term "libertarian" has been used instead. It may be the answer; but for my part I find it singularly unattractive. For my taste it carries too much the flavor of a manufactured term and of a substitute. What I should want is a word which describes the party of life, the party that favors free growth and spontaneous evolution. But I have racked my brain unsuccessfully to find a descriptive term which commends itself.

We should remember, however, that when the ideals which I have been trying to restate first began to spread through the Western world, the party which represented them had a generally recognized name. It was the ideals of the English Whigs that inspired what later came to be known as the liberal movement in the whole of Europe[12] and that provided the conceptions that the American colonists carried with them and which guided them in their struggle for independence and in the establishment of their constitution.[13] Indeed, until the character of this tradition was altered by the accretions due to the French Revolution, with its totalitarian democracy and socialist leanings, "Whig" was the name by which the party of liberty was generally known.

The name died in the country of its birth partly because for a time the principles for which it stood were no longer distinctive of a particular party, and partly because the men who bore the name did not remain true to those principles. The Whig parties of the nineteenth century, in both Britain and the United States, finally brought discredit to the name among the radicals. But it is still true that, since liberalism took the place of Whiggism only after the movement for liberty had absorbed the crude and militant rationalism of the French Revolution, and since our task must largely be to free that tradition from the overrationalistic, nationalistic, and socialistic influences which have intruded into it, Whiggism is historically the correct name for the ideas in which I believe. The more I learn about the evolution of ideas, the more I have become aware that I am simply an unrepentant Old Whig—with the stress on the "old."

To confess one's self an Old Whig does not mean, of course, that one wants to go back to where we were at the end of the seventeenth century. . . .

It is the doctrine which is at the basis of the common tradition of the Anglo-Saxon countries. It is the doctrine from which Continental liberalism took what is valuable in it. It is the doctrine on which the American system of government is based. In its pure form it is represented in the United States, not by the radicalism of Jefferson, nor by the conservatism of Hamilton or even of John Adams, but by the ideas of James Madison, the "father of the Constitution."[14]

I do not know whether to revive that old name is practical politics. That to the mass of people, both in the Anglo-Saxon world and elsewhere, it is today probably a term without definite associations is perhaps more an advantage than a drawback. To those familiar with the history of ideas it is probably the only name that quite expresses what the tradition means. That, both for the genuine conservative and still more for the many socialists turned conservative, Whiggism is the name for their pet aversion shows a sound instinct on their part. It has been the name for the only set of ideals that has consistently opposed all arbitrary power.

It may well be asked whether the name really matters so much. In a country like the United States, which on the whole still has free institutions and where, therefore, the defense of the existing is often a defense of freedom, it might not make so much difference if the defenders of freedom call themselves conservatives, although even here the association with the conservatives by disposition will often be embarrassing. Even when men approve of the same arrangements, it must be asked whether they approve of them because they exist or because they are desirable in themselves. The common resistance to the collectivist tide should not be allowed to obscure the fact that the belief in integral freedom is based on an essentially forward-looking attitude and not on any nostalgic longing for the past or a romantic admiration for what has been.

The need for a clear distinction is absolutely imperative, however, where, as is true in many parts of Europe, the conservatives have already accepted a large part of the collectivist creed—a creed that has governed policy for so long that many of its institutions have come to be accepted as a matter of course and have become a source of pride to "conservative" parties who created them.[15] Here the believer in freedom cannot but conflict with the conservative and take an essentially radical position, directed against popular prejudices, entrenched positions, and firmly established privileges. Follies and abuses are no better for having long been established principles of policy.

Though *quieta non movere* may at times be a wise maxim for the statesman, it cannot satisfy the political philosopher. He may wish policy to proceed gingerly and not before public opinion is prepared to support it, but he cannot accept arrangements merely because current opinion sanctions them. In a world where the chief need is once more, as it was at the beginning of the nineteenth century, to free the process of spontaneous growth from the obstacles and encumbrances that human folly has erected, his hopes must rest on persuading and gaining the support of those who by disposition are "progressives," those who, though they may now be seeking change in the wrong direction, are at least willing to examine critically the existing and to change wherever necessary. . . .

The question of how the principles I have tried to reconstruct by piecing together the broken fragments of a tradition can be translated into a program with mass appeal, the political philosopher must leave to "that insidious and crafty animal, vulgarly called a statesman or politician, whose councils are directed by the momentary fluctuations of affairs."[16] The task of the political philosopher can only be to influence public opinion, not to organize people for action. He will do so effectively only if he is not concerned with what is now politically possible but consistently defends the "general principles which are always the same."[17] In this sense I doubt whether there can be such a thing as a conservative political philosophy. Conservatism may often be a useful practical maxim, but it does not give us any guiding principles which can influence long-range developments.

NOTES

1. This has now been true for over a century, and as early as 1855 J. S. Mill could say (see my *John Stuart Mill and Harriet Taylor* [London and Chicago, 1951], p. 216) that "almost all the projects of social reformers of these days are really *liberticide.*"

2. B. Crick, "The Strange Quest for an American Conservatism," *Review of Politics,* XVII (1955), 365, says rightly that "the normal American who calls himself 'A Conservative' is, in fact, a liberal." It would appear that the reluctance of these conservatives to call themselves by the more appropriate name dates only from its abuse during the New Deal era.

3. The expression is that of R. G. Collingwood, *The New Leviathan* (Oxford: Oxford University Press, 1942), p. 209.

4. Cf. the characteristic choice of this title for the programmatic book by the present British Prime Minister Harold Macmillan, *The Middle Way* (London, 1938).

5. Cf. Lord Hugh Cecil, *Conservatism* ("Home University Library" [London, 1912]), p. 9: "Natural Conservatism . . . is a disposition averse from change; and it springs partly from a distrust of the unknown."

6. Cf. the revealing self-description of a conservative in K. Feiling, *Sketches in Nineteenth Century Biography* (London, 1930), p. 174: "Taken in bulk, the Right have a horror of ideas, for is not the practical man, in Disraeli's words, 'one who practises the blunders of his predecessors'? For long tracts of their history they have indiscriminately resisted improvement, and in claiming to reverence their ancestors often reduce opinion to aged individual prejudice. Their position becomes safer, but more complex, when we add that this Right wing is incessantly overtaking the Left; that it lives by repeated inoculation of liberal ideas, and thus suffers from a never-perfected state of compromise."

7. I trust I shall be forgiven for repeating here the words in which on an earlier occasion I stated an important point: "The main merit of the individualism which [Adam Smith] and his contemporaries advocated is that it is a system under which bad men can do least harm. It is a social system which does not depend for its functioning on our finding good men for running it, or on all men becoming better than they now are, but which makes use of men in all their given variety and complexity, sometimes good and sometimes bad, sometimes intelligent and more often stupid" (*Individualism and Economic Order* [London and Chicago 1948], p. 11).

8. Cf. Lord Acton in *Letters of Lord Acton to Mary Gladstone,* ed. H. Paul (London, 1913), p. 73: "The danger is not that a particular class is unfit to govern. Every class is unfit to govern. The law of liberty tends to abolish the reign of race over race, of faith over faith, of class over class."

9. J. R. Hicks has rightly spoken in this connection of the "caricature drawn alike by the young Disraeli, by Marx and by Goebbels" ("The Pursuit of Economic Freedom," *What We Defend,* ed. E. F. Jacob [Oxford: Oxford University Press, 1942], p. 96). On the role of the conservatives in this connection see also my Introduction to *Capitalism and the Historians* (Chicago: University of Chicago Press, 1954), pp. 19ff.

10. Cf. J. S. Mill, *On Liberty,* ed. R. B. McCallum (Oxford, 1946), p. 83: "I am not aware that any community has a right to force another to be civilised."

11. Cf. Learned Hand, *The Spirit of Liberty,* ed. I. Dilliard (New York, 1952), p. 190: "The Spirit of liberty is the spirit which is not too sure that it is right." See also Oliver Cromwell's often quoted statement in his *Letter to the General Assembly of the Church of Scotland,* August 3, 1650: "I beseech you, in the bowels of Christ, think it possible you may be mistaken." It is significant that this should be the probably best-remembered saying of the only "dictator" in British history!

12. As early as the beginning of the eighteenth century, an English observer could remark that he "scarce ever knew a foreigner settled in England, whether of Dutch, German, French, Italian, or Turkish growth, but became a Whig in a little time after his mixing with us" (quoted by G. H. Guttridge, *English Whiggism and the American Revolution* [Berkeley: University of California Press, 1942], p. 3).

13. In the United States the nineteenth-century use of the term "Whig" has unfortunately obliterated the memory of the fact that in the eighteenth it stood for the principles which guided the revolution, gained independence, and shaped the Constitution. It was in Whig societies that the young James Madison and John Adams developed their political ideals (cf. E. M. Burns, *James Madison* [New Brunswick, N.J.: Rutgers University Press, 1938], p. 4); it was Whig principles which, as Jefferson tells us, guided all the lawyers who constituted such a strong majority among the signers of the Declaration of Independence and among the members of the Constitutional Convention (see *Writings of Thomas Jefferson* ["Memorial ed." (Washington, 1905)], XVI, 156). The profession of Whig principles was carried to such a point that even Washington's soldiers were clad in the traditional "blue and buff" colors of the Whigs, which they shared with the Foxites in the British Parliament and which was preserved down to our own days on the covers of the *Edinburgh Review.* If a socialist generation has made Whiggism its favorite target, this is all the more reason for the opponents of socialism to vindicate the name. It is today the only name which correctly describes the beliefs of the Gladstonian liberals, of the men of the generation of Maitland, Acton, and Bryce, the last generation for whom liberty rather than equality or democracy was the main goal.

14. Cf. S. K. Padover in his Introduction to *The Complete Madison* (New York, 1953), p. 10: "In modern terminology, Madison would be labeled a middle-of-the-road liberal and Jefferson a radical." This is true and important, though we must remember what E. S. Corwin ("James Madison: Layman, Publicist, and Exegete," *New York University Law Review*, XXVII [1952], 285) has called Madison's later "surrender to the overweening influence of Jefferson."

15. Cf. the British Conservative party's statement of policy, *The Right Road for Britain* (London, 1950), pp. 41–42, which claims, with considerable justification, that "this new conception [of the social services] was developed [by] the Coalition Government with a majority of Conservative Ministers and the full approval of the Conservative majority in the House of Commons. . . . [We] set out the principle for the schemes of pensions, sickness and unemployment benefit, industrial injuries benefit and a national health scheme."

16. A. Smith, *W.o.N.*, I, 432.

17. Ibid.

Chapter Seventeen

National Review
Statement of Intentions

William F. Buckley, Jr.

I propose to found a magazine, which will be called *National Weekly*. This magazine will forthrightly oppose the prevailing trend of public opinion; its purpose, indeed, is to *change* the nation's intellectual and political climate. Such tall ambitions are not wholly attributable, I earnestly believe, to the natural enthusiasm and bombast of a would-be publisher; they are based on a rational and prudent survey of the job, its requirements, and its possibilities.

The magazine will begin publication as a minority voice—only in the sense that America's "respectable" press has ordained that such voices as ours are of the past, and are not worth serious attention. But events in the very recent past positively establish that there is a widening gulf between the "respectable" press and the American people, that they look upon each other, increasingly, as strangers. The dogged refusal of the Liberal intelligentsia to concern themselves with the welfare of the American people, the awful crises into which they have lightheartedly hurled the nation and, indeed, the world, have exhausted the faith of many Americans who once responded to the urgings of our Social Engineers. Heavy support for a journal with the orientation and skills of *National Weekly* is already here; our job is to harness that support, which we will do.

National Weekly's opinions are, basically, these:

From Henry Regnery Papers, Box 10, Folder 14 (William F. Buckley Corr., 1944–54), Hoover Institution on War, Revolution and Peace, Stanford University, Palo Alto, Calif. Reprinted by permission of William F. Buckley, Jr.

1. Middle-of-the-Road, *qua* Middle of the Road, is politically, intellectually, and morally repugnant. We shall recommend policies for the simple reason that we consider them right (rather than "non-controversial"); and we consider them right because they are based on principles we deem right (rather than on popularity polls).

2. Among our convictions:

   a. It is the job of centralized government (in peacetime) to protect its citizens' lives, liberty, and property. All other activities of government tend to diminish freedom and hamper progress. The growth of government—the dominant social feature of this century—must be fought relentlessly. In this great social conflict of the era, we are, without reservations, on the libertarian side.

   b. The profound crisis of our era is, in essence, the conflict between the Social Engineers, who seek to adjust mankind to conform with scientific utopias, and the disciples of Truth, who defend the organic moral order. We believe that truth is neither arrived at nor illuminated by monitoring election results, binding though these are for other purposes, but by other means, including a study of human experience. On this point we are, without reservations, on the conservative side.

   c. The century's most blatant force of satanic utopianism is Communism. We consider "co-existence" with Communism neither desirable nor possible, nor honorable; we find ourselves irrevocably at war with Communism and shall oppose any substitute for victory. In this global conflict we are militantly and implacably anti-Communist.

   d. The largest cultural menace in America is the conformity of the intellectual cliques which, in education as well as the arts, are out to impose upon the nation their modish fads and fallacies, and have nearly succeeded in doing so. In this cultural issue, we are, without reservations, on the side of excellence (rather than "newness") and of honest intellectual combat (rather than conformity).

   e. The most alarming single danger to the American political system lies in the fact that an identifiable team of Fabian operators is bent on controlling both our major political parties—under the sanction of such fatuous and unreasoned slogans as "national unity," "middle-of-the-road," "progres-sivism," and "bipartisanship." Clever intriguers are reshaping both parties in the image of Babbitt, gone Social-Democrat. When and where this political issue arises, we are, without reservations, on the side of the traditional two-party system that fights its feuds in public and honestly; and we shall ad-vocate the restoration of the two-party system at all costs.

f. The competitive price system is indispensable to liberty and material progress. It is threatened not only by the growth of Big Brother government, but by the pressure of monopolies—including union monopolies. What is more, some labor unions have clearly identified themselves with doctrinaire so-cialist objectives. The characteristic problems of harassed busi-ness have gone unreported for years, with the result that the public has been taught to assume—almost instinctively—that conflicts between labor and management are generally tracea-ble to greed and intransigence part of management. Some-times they are; often they are not. *National Weekly* will explore and oppose the inroads upon the market economy caused by monopolies in general, and politically oriented unionism in particular; and it will tell the violated businessman's side of the story.

g. No superstition has more effectively bewitched America's Lib-eral elite than the fashionable concepts of world government, the United Nations, internationalism, international atomic pools, etc. Perhaps the most important and readily demonstra-ble lesson of history is that freedom goes hand in hand with a state of political decentralization, that remote government is irresponsible government. It would make greater sense to grant independence to each of our 48 states than to surrender U.S. sovereignty to a world organization. America must choose between a policy that secures American freedom, and a policy that subordinates our country and its interests to those of foreign powers.

3. *National Weekly* will endeavor, in short, to counteract the repre-hensible journalistic trend toward a genteel uniformity of opin-ion, and even of style. This nation, we contend, is not yet ready for that decadent, lukewarm mood of indifference which perme-ates our Liberal press and, insofar as editorial convictions are

concerned, makes most national journals indistinguishable from one another. *National Weekly* is committed to what once was called personal journalism—the manly presentation of deeply felt convictions. It loves controversy. Dedicated to reason, it despises the cant of sweet reasonableness. It has no patience with those certified gentlemen who deem themselves, and their sentimental uniformity, above and beyond intellectual attack. *National Weekly*, in short, will never join the mutual-admiration society of complacent American journalism.

The intellectual (and, consequently, the political) climate of an era is fashioned by the educators, only some of whom are engaged in classroom work. Others are active publicists who express themselves through virtually every medium of communication. But the essence of their ideas is always to be found in the nation's few serious journals which, in modern history, have provided every society with its truly formative influences. The New Deal revolution, for instance, could hardly have happened save for the cumulative impact of *The Nation* and *The New Republic*, and a few other publications, on several American college generations during the twenties and thirties. And the passiveness with which the citizenry at large submitted to so total a revolution as Mr. Roosevelt's would have been inconceivable but for the labors of such characteristic media of contemporary journalism as *Time* and *The New Yorker*—both of which, significantly, were born in the mid-twenties, and both of which, despite diversified editorial intent, have assumed (and, indirectly, urged) exactly that attitude of submission to "the trend."

What is readily demonstrable with respect to the New Deal is equally true of any other revolutionary movement of modern times. While not *conceived* by journalists (that is the philosopher's job), all these movements have been, as all future movements will be, intellectually popularized and politically begotten by a few easily identifiable journals. And the influence of these journals has been decisive not because their circulation was awesome (in most cases it was not), but because they applied their intellectual and moral standards to the events and problems of the day with intelligence, dedication, and consistency. I do not mean to pass over or belittle other highly effective forces that have helped shape history; but the relevant point, in this context, is the undeniable historic effectiveness of formative journalism.

What makes one journalistic effort "formative" and another historically irrelevant is too large a problem to discuss fully in a brief memorandum. But I should like to set down here the basic premises in this area on which I propose to act.

Just as certain magazines help form an era, an era tends to generate for itself the magazines it needs. There seems, for instance, to be an exactly right time for a magazine to be born. The formative magazines of each era appear more or less simultaneously, in cycles of twenty or thirty years, probably because the intellectual demands they create need a certain time to spend themselves, at which point they either peter out, or become accepted and graduate to the status of institutions.

Only when a prevailing opinion is on its way out will a next cycle start auspiciously; and we, I contend, are now living in such a moment. New Deal journalism has degenerated into a jaded defense of the status quo. If we competently and resourcefully attack it at this time with the vigor of true conviction, we can rout it intellectually. If, on the other hand, this fateful moment is not turned to such a use, it will prove irretrievable, and the Fabian-socialist response will develop into America's conditioned reflex.

The after-effects of World War I produced the journalistic era of *The Nation* and *The New Republic*, of *Time* and *The New Yorker*. The after-effects of World War II and Korea have generated conditions auspicious for a change in the nation's attitude. And a number of observable signs point to the possibility of our bringing about that change. Potsdam and Yalta are finally conceded, by virtually all intellectually responsible men, to be landmarks of shame; in 1952, America defeated the Party that founded the New Deal; a new dissatisfaction with the current leftist academic conformity begins to stir in the young college population; best-seller lists occasionally assume a "reactionary" complexion absolutely unheard of throughout the preceding twenty years. In short, the brain-trust of *The Nation* and *The New Republic* no longer monopolizes America's articulate mind.

And yet, recent attempts to rally these newly awakened forces around a new national magazine have not succeeded. Why? Not because of the editors' or contributors' professional shortcomings. I submit. Several such publications have published magnificent material, magnificently prepared, and have performed their task with extraordinary dedication. If they nevertheless have proved unable to break through their suffocating isolation, the reason is, I believe, that they suffer from the handicaps inherent in the psychology of ventures so constituted; many were conceived, and are being promoted, as more or less subsidized missionary endeavors in the interest of The Cause. Others have voluntarily limited their scope, satisfied to organize commando raids on the Left, at decent intervals. Still others have gravitated to the fort-nightly or monthly formula, and have accepted the limitations inherent in journals that cannot, for technical reasons, do the job day-to-day.

Chapter Eighteen

National Review
Credenda and Statement of Principles

William F. Buckley, Jr.

There is, we like to think, solid reason for rejoicing. Prodigious efforts, by many people, are responsible for *National Review*. But since it will be the policy of this magazine to reject the hypodermic approach to world affairs, we may as well start out at once, and admit that the joy is not unconfined.

Let's face it: Unlike Vienna, it seems altogether possible that did *National Review* not exist, no one would have invented it. The launching of a conservative weekly journal of opinion in a country widely assumed to be a bastion of conservatism at first glance looks like a work of supererogation, rather like publishing a royalist weekly within the walls of Buckingham Palace. It is not that of course; if *National Review* is superfluous, it is so for very different reasons: It stands athwart history, yelling Stop, at a time when no one is inclined to do so, or to have much patience with those who so urge it.

National Review is out of place, in the sense that the United Nations and the League of Women Voters and the *New York Times* and Henry Steele Commager are *in* place. It is out of place because, in its maturity, literate America rejected conservatism in favor of radical social experimentation. Instead of covetously consolidating its premises, the United States seems tormented by its tradition of fixed postulates having to do with the meaning of existence, with the relationship of the state to the individual, of the individual to his neighbor, so clearly enunciated in the enabling documents of our Republic.

"I happen to prefer champagne to ditchwater," said the benign old wrecker of the ordered society, Oliver Wendell Holmes, "but there is no reason to suppose that the cosmos does." We have come around to Mr. Holmes' view, so much so that we feel gentlemanly doubts when asserting the superiority of capitalism to socialism, of republicanism to centralism, of champagne to ditchwater—of anything to anything. (How curious that one of the doubts one is *not* permitted is whether, at the margin, Mr. Holmes was a useful citizen!) The inroads that relativism has made on the American soul are not so easily evident. One must recently have lived on or close to a college campus to have a vivid intimation of what has happened. It is there that we see how a number of energetic social innovators, plugging their grand designs, succeeded over the years in capturing the liberal intellectual imagination. And since ideas rule the world, the ideologues, having won over the intellectual class, simply walked in and started to run things.

Run just about *everything*. There never was an age of conformity quite like this one, or a camaraderie quite like the Liberals'. Drop a little itching powder in Jimmy Wechaler's bath and before he has scratched himself for the third time, Arthur Schlesinger will have denounced you in a dozen books and speeches, Archibald MacLeish will have written ten heroic cantos about our age of terror, *Harper's* will have published them, and everyone in sight will have been nominated for a Freedom Award. Conservatives in this country—at least those who have not made their peace with the New Deal, and there is serious question whether there are others—are non-licensed nonconformists; and this is dangerous business in a Liberal world, as every editor of this magazine can readily show by pointing to his scars. Radical conservatives in this country have an interesting time of it, for when they are not being suppressed or mutilated by the Liberals, they are being ignored or humiliated by a great many of those of the well-fed. Right, whose ignorance and amorality have never been exaggerated for the same reason that one cannot exaggerate infinity.

There are, thank Heaven, the exceptions. There are those of generous impulse and a sincere desire to encourage a responsible dissent from the Liberal orthodoxy. And there are those who recognize that when all is said and done, the market place depends for a license to operate freely on the men who issue licenses—on the politicians. They recognize, therefore, that efficient getting and spending is itself impossible except in an atmosphere that encourages efficient getting and spending. And back of all political institutions there are moral and philosophical concepts, implicit or defined. Our political economy and our high-energy industry run on large, general principles, on ideas—not by day-to-day guess work, expedients, and improvisations. Ideas have to go into exchange to become or remain operative; and the medium of such exchange is the printed word. A vigorous and incorruptible journal of conservative opinion is—dare we say it?—as necessary to better living as Chemistry.

We begin publishing, then, with a considerable stock of experience with the irresponsible Right, and a despair of the intransigence of the Liberals, who run this country; and all this in a world dominated by the jubilant single-mindedness of the practicing Communist, with his inside track to History. All this would not appear to augur well for *National Review.* Yet we start with a considerable—and considered—*optimism.*

After all, we crashed through. More than one hundred and twenty investors made this magazine possible, and over fifty men and women of small means, invested less than one thousand dollars apiece in it. Two men and one woman, all three with overwhelming personal and public commitments, worked round the clock to make publication possible. A score of professional writers pledged their devoted attention to its needs, and hundreds of thoughtful men and women gave evidence that the appearance of such a journal as we have in mind would profoundly affect their lives.

Our own views, as expressed in a memorandum drafted a year ago, and directed to our investors, are set forth in an adjacent column. We have nothing to offer but the best that is in us. That, a thousand Liberals who read this sentiment will say with relief, is clearly not enough! It isn't enough. But it is at this point that we steal the march. For we offer, besides ourselves, a position that has not grown old under the weight of a gigantic, parasitic bureaucracy, a position untempered by the doctoral dissertations of a generation of Ph.D's in social architecture, unattenuated by a thousand vulgar promises to a thousand different pressure groups, uncorroded by a cynical contempt for human freedom. And that, ladies and gentlemen, leaves us just about the hottest thing in town.

Among our convictions:

a. It is the job of centralized government (in peace-time) to protect its citizens' lives, liberty, and property. All other activities of government tend to diminish freedom and hamper progress. The growth of government—the dominant social feature of this century—must be fought relentlessly. In this great social conflict of the era, we are, without reservations, on the libertarian side.

b. The profound crisis of our era is, in essence, the conflict between the Social Engineers, who seek to adjust mankind to conform with scientific utopias, and the disciples of Truth, who defend the organic moral order. We believe that truth is neither arrived at nor illuminated by monitoring election results, binding though these are for other purposes, but by other means, including a study of human experience. On this point we are, without reservations, on the conservative side.

c. The century's most blatant force of satanic utopianism is communism. We consider "coexistence" with communism neither desirable nor possible, nor honorable; we find ourselves irrevocably at war with communism and shall oppose any substitute for victory.

d. The largest cultural menace in America is the conformity of the intellectual cliques which, in education as well as the arts, are out to impose upon the nation their modish fads and fallacies, and have nearly succeeded in doing so. In this cultural issue, we are, without reservations, on the side of excellence (rather than "newness") and of honest intellectual combat (rather than conformity).

e. The most alarming single danger to the American political system lies in the fact that an identifiable team of Fabian operators is bent on controlling both our major political parties—under the sanction of such fatuous and unreasoned slogans as "national unity," "middle-of-the-road," "progressivism," and "bipartisanship." Clever intriguers are reshaping both parties in the image of Babbitt, gone Social-Democrat. When and where this political issue arises, we are, without reservations, on the side of the traditional two-party system that fights its feuds in public and honestly; and we shall advocate the restoration of the two-party system at all costs.

f. The competitive price system is indispensable to liberty and material progress. It is threatened not only by the growth of Big Brother government, but by the pressure of monopolies—including union monopolies. What is more, some labor unions have clearly identified themselves with doctrinaire socialist objectives. The characteristic problems of harassed business have gone unreported for years, with the result that the public has been taught to assume—almost instinctively—that conflicts between labor and management are generally traceable to greed and intransigence on the part of management. Sometimes they are; often they are not.

National Review will explore and oppose the inroads upon the market economy caused by monopolies in general, and politically oriented unionism in particular; and it will tell the violated businessman's side of the story.

g. No superstition has more effectively bewitched America's Liberal elite than the fashionable concepts of world government, the United Nations, internationalism, international atomic pools, etc. Perhaps the most important and readily demonstrable lesson of history is that freedom goes hand in hand with a state of political decentralization, that remote government is irresponsible government. It would make greater sense to grant independence to each of our 48 states than to surrender U.S. sovereignty to a world organization.

Part VI

The Plunge into Politics

Conservatives had long sought political power. Robert A. Taft, the son of President William Howard Taft, and senator from Ohio, had failed three times in his quest for the Republican nomination. A foe of the New Deal and a noninterventionist, Taft's last attempt to win the GOP nomination came in 1952 when he was defeated at the convention by the better organized, and more unscrupulous, candidacy of Dwight D. Eisenhower. Taft's death a year later assured a time in the wilderness for conservatives as Joseph McCarthy, a favorite of old Right conservatives, was censured by the Senate in 1954, his power crushed and his political career ruined. Who could take Taft's place and emerge as the standard bearer for conservatism?

The answer came like a hot blast from the Arizona desert. Barry Morris Goldwater, the junior Senator from Arizona, young, dynamic, handsome— his chin seemingly chiseled from the desert rock of his beloved state— proved to be the rising star of conservatism. His growing name recognition, due to his senatorial record, his outspoken support for the Cold War and for defense, and his handling of political duties as the head of the Republican Senatorial Campaign Committee, contributed to a widespread mood among conservatives that, at the very least, Goldwater could make a good vice presidential candidate in 1960. (He was not widely enough known to be the presidential candidate; Richard M. Nixon, Eisenhower's equally young vice president, was considered the shooin for that job.)

Throughout 1959, conservatives, led by former University of Notre Dame law school dean Clarence "Pat" Manion, whose syndicated radio show, the *Manion Forum*, was broadcast nationally, assigned himself the task of collecting Goldwater's views on government and communism into a book. Published in March 1960 as *Conscience of a Conservative*, the book, ghostwritten from Goldwater position papers by *National Review* editor L. Brent Bozell, became an instant bestseller among conservatives, selling thousands of copies (millions by 1964), and contributing to the possibility, especially among young people, that maybe Goldwater could be more than *vice*-presidential material.[1]

Goldwater's presidential candidacy never emerged (and neither was he chosen for the vice-presidency). Young people had fought for Goldwater throughout the spring and summer, organizing Youth for Goldwater clubs on various campuses and attending the August Republican national convention in Chicago, where, they hoped, Goldwater would be chosen as Nixon's running mate. The week before the convention, however, Nixon visited Nelson Rockefeller, the liberal Republican governor of New York, and, in what Goldwater himself would later call "a domestic Munich," arranged to have Massachusetts Republican Henry Cabot Lodge, Jr., named Nixon's running mate in return for Rockefeller's support. When Goldwater addressed the convention, conservatives booed the nominees. Goldwater told conservatives to "grow up" and to "take back the Republican Party." Those in attendance would proceed to do just that.[2]

Young conservatives led the way. Frustrated by the inability of conservatives to influence national politics and, at the same time, hopeful they could do so, young people set about to form a national organization that could serve as a vehicle for developing cadres for conservatism. In September 1960, only two weeks after the Chicago convention, around ninety young conservatives met at William F. Buckley's ancestral home in Sharon, Connecticut, and formed Young Americans for Freedom. The Sharon Statement, and Buckley's editorial announcing the formation of YAF, which appeared in *National Review*, are contained herein. The Sharon Statement, drafted en route to the conference by *Indianapolis News* editor M. Stanton Evans, was a succinct statement of conservative principles, well representative of the fusionist views Frank Meyer had been articulating. YAF would be the largest conservative student organization (it would claim over 60,000 members by the late 1960s), and throughout the 1960s would be a recruiting ground for conservative activists, many of whom would go on to prominence within the conservative movement and in government.[3]

YAF and other conservative organizations, like the anticommunist John Birch Society founded in 1958 by Boston candy manufacturer Robert Welch, articulated a muscular anticommunism throughout the early

1960s. Welch had even labeled Dwight Eisenhower, in a self-published book, *The Politician*, a "conscious agent of the communist conspiracy."[4] The John Birch Society drew tremendous critical press coverage, and the media depicted its founder and society members as extremists. The Kennedy administration investigated anticommunist groups in the early 1960s and there was a general cultural fear, conditioned by films like *Seven Days in May* (1962)—depicting a rabid anticommunist general organizing a coup against the president—that right-wing extremists were a dangerous threat to American democracy.[5]

Certainly there was anger on the Right at the failings of American foreign policy under Eisenhower and Kennedy, but most conservative opposition was channeled into legitimate and constructive purposes. In 1961, a group of former politicos in the Young Republicans organized a draft of Goldwater for the presidency in 1964. Goldwater was hostile to the draft, but in the fall of 1963, after a summer full of activities on behalf of the senator, he changed his mind. He looked forward to debating with Kennedy in the campaign, about offering a clear alternative to the regnant liberalism in American politics. But then Kennedy was assassinated and Goldwater, heartbroken over the loss of his friend, announced his candidacy even though he knew he could not win.[6]

Throughout 1964 conservatives fought for Goldwater. One of the more impassioned treatises on behalf of the Arizonan was Phyllis Schlafly's *A Choice, Not An Echo* (reprinted here in Chapter 22). The president of the Illinois Federation of Republican Women and a former delegate to GOP conventions, Schlafly (1924–) put forth the conservative view that a group of establishment figures within the GOP, primarily East Coast figures like Rockefeller, acted as kingmakers and moved the party from its populist, conservative base of support. In a jeremiad against the reigning "me-tooism" within the Republican Party that sacrificed principle for power, Schlafly made a strong case for Goldwater in 1964. She would later, most famously, use her organizational abilities to help defeat the feminist-supported Equal Rights Amendment in the 1970s and established the Eagle Forum as a vehicle for defending traditionalism in America.

Chapter 23 is Goldwater's acceptance speech at the Republican convention. Goldwater, angry at the liberal Republicans, many of whom would do little to help their candidate get elected in 1964, struck out at those elements at the convention who refused to support him. In the process, he contributed to a divided party in the fall and his devastating defeat in

November to Lyndon Johnson (the biggest landslide in political history to that time). The convention speech depicts well both Goldwater's principles and his stubbornness. His defeat, however, rather than destroying political conservatism in its cradle, would be but the first small step in conservatism's rise to power.

Chapter Nineteen

The Conscience of a Conservative

Barry M. Goldwater

I have been much concerned that so many people today with Conservative instincts feel compelled to apologize for them. Or if not to apologize directly, to qualify their commitment in a way that amounts to breast-beating. "Republican candidates," Vice President Nixon has said, "should be economic conservatives, but conservatives with a heart." President Eisenhower announced during his first term, "I am conservative when it comes to economic problems but liberal when it comes to human problems." Still other Republican leaders have insisted on calling themselves "progressive" Conservatives.[1] These formulations are tantamount to an admission that Conservatism is a narrow, mechanistic *economic* theory that may work very well as a book-keeper's guide, but cannot be relied upon as a comprehensive political philosophy.

The same judgment, though in the form of an attack rather than an admission, is advanced by the radical camp. "We liberals," they say, "are interested in *people*. Our concern is with human beings, while you Conservatives are preoccupied with the preservation of economic privilege and status." Take them a step further, and the Liberals will turn the accusations into a class argument: it is the little people that concern us, not the "malefactors of great wealth."

Such statements, from friend and foe alike, do great injustice to the Conservative point of view. Conservatism is *not* an economic theory, though it has economic implications. The shoe is precisely on the other foot: it is Socialism that subordinates all other considerations to man's material well-being. It is Conservatism that puts material things in their proper place—that has a structured view of the human being and of human society, in which economics plays only a subsidiary role.

The root difference between the Conservatives and the Liberals of today is that Conservatives take account of the *whole* man, while the Liberals tend to look only at the material side of man's nature. The Conservative believes that man is, in part, an economic, an animal creature; but that he is also a spiritual creature with spiritual needs and spiritual desires. What is more, these needs and desires reflect the *superior* side of man's nature, and thus take precedence over his economic wants. Conservatism therefore looks upon the enhancement of man's spiritual nature as the primary concern of political philosophy. Liberals, on the other hand—in the name of a concern for "human beings"—regard the satisfaction of economic wants as the dominant mission of society. They are, moreover, in a hurry. So that their characteristic approach is to harness the society's political and economic forces into a collective effort to *compel* "progress." In this approach, I believe they fight against Nature.

Surely the first obligation of a political thinker is to understand the nature of man. The Conservative does not claim special powers of perception on this point, but he does claim a familiarity with the accumulated wisdom and experience of history, and he is not too proud to learn from the great minds of the past.

The first thing he has learned about man is that each member of the species is a unique creature. Man's most sacred possession is his individual soul—which has an immortal side, but also a mortal one. The mortal side establishes his absolute differentness from every other human being. *Only a philosophy that takes into account the essential differences between men, and, accordingly, makes provision for developing the different potentialities of each man can claim to be in accord with Nature.* We have heard much in our time about "the common man." It is a concept that pays little attention to the history of a nation that grew great through the initiative and ambition of uncommon men. The Conservative knows that to regard man as part of an undifferentiated mass is to consign him to ultimate slavery.

Secondly, the Conservative has learned that the economic and spiritual aspects of man's nature are inextricably intertwined. He cannot be economically free, or even economically efficient, if he is enslaved politically; conversely, man's political freedom is illusory if he is dependent for his economic needs on the State.

The Conservative realizes, thirdly, that man's development, in both its spiritual and material aspects, is not something that can be directed by outside forces. Every man, for his individual good and for the good of his society, is responsible for his *own* development. The choices that govern his life are choices that *he* must make: they cannot be made by any other human being, or by a collectivity of human beings. If the Conservative is less anxious than his Liberal brethren to increase Social Security "benefits," it is because he is more anxious than his Liberal brethren that people be free throughout their lives to spend their earnings when and as they see fit.

So it is that Conservatism, throughout history, has regarded man neither as a potential pawn of other men, nor as a part of a general collectivity in which the sacredness and the separate identity of individual human beings are ignored. Throughout history, true Conservatism has been at war equally with autocrats and with "democratic" Jacobins. The true Conservative was sympathetic with the plight of the hapless peasant under the tyranny of the French monarchy. And he was equally revolted at the attempt to solve that problem by a mob tyranny that paraded under the banner of egalitarianism. The conscience of the Conservative is pricked by *anyone* who would debase the dignity of the individual human being. Today, therefore, he is at odds with dictators who rule by terror, and equally with those gentler collectivists who ask our permission to play God with the human race.

With this view of the nature of man, it is understandable that the Conservative looks upon politics as the art of achieving the maximum amount of freedom for individuals that is consistent with the maintenance of social order. The Conservative is the first to understand that the practice of freedom requires the establishment of order: it is impossible for one man to be free if another is able to deny him the exercise of his freedom. But the Conservative also recognizes that the political power on which order is based is a self-aggrandizing force; that its appetite grows with eating. He knows that the utmost vigilance and care are required to keep political power within its proper bounds.

In our day, order is pretty well taken care of. The delicate balance that ideally exists between freedom and order has long since tipped against freedom practically everywhere on earth. In some countries, freedom is altogether down and order holds absolute sway. In our country the trend is less far advanced, but it is well along and gathering momentum every day. Thus, for the American Conservative, there is no difficulty in identifying the day's overriding political challenge: it is *to preserve and extend freedom*. As he surveys the various attitudes and institutions and laws that currently prevail in America, many questions will occur to him, but the Conservative's first concern will always be: *Are we maximizing freedom?* I suggest we examine some of the critical issues facing us today with this question in mind.

The New Deal, Dean Acheson wrote approvingly in a book called *A Democrat Looks at His Party*, "conceived of the federal government as the whole people organized to do what had to be done." A year later Mr. Larson wrote *A Republican Looks at His Party*, and made much the same claim in his book for Modern Republicans. The "underlying philosophy" of the New Republicanism, said Mr. Larson, is that "if a job has to be done to meet the needs of the people, and no one else can do it, then it is the proper function of the federal government."

Here we have, by prominent spokesmen of both political parties, an unqualified repudiation of the principle of limited government. There is no reference by either of them to the Constitution, or any attempt to define the legitimate functions of government. The government can do whatever *needs* to be done; note, too, the implicit but necessary assumption that it is the government itself that determines *what* needs to be done. We must not, I think, underrate the importance of these statements. They reflect the view of a majority of the leaders of one of our parties, and of a strong minority among the leaders of the other, and they propound the first principle of totalitarianism: that the State is competent to do all things and is limited in what it actually does only by the will of those who control the State.

It is clear that this view is in direct conflict with the Constitution, which is an instrument, above all, for *limiting* the functions of government, and which is as binding today as when it was written. But we are advised to go a step further and ask why the Constitution's framers restricted the scope of government. Conservatives are often charged, and in a sense rightly so, with having an overly mechanistic view of the Constitution: "It is America's enabling document; we are American citizens; therefore," the Conservatives' theme runs, "we are morally and legally obliged to comply with the document." All true. But the Constitution has a broader claim on our loyalty than that. The founding fathers had a *reason* for endorsing the principle of limited government; and this reason recommends defense of the constitutional scheme even to those who take their citizenship obligations lightly. The reason is simple, and it lies at the heart of the Conservative philosophy.

Throughout history, government has proved to be the chief instrument for thwarting man's liberty. Government represents power in the hands of some men to control and regulate the lives of other men. And power, as Lord Acton said, *corrupts* men. "Absolute power," he added, "corrupts absolutely."

State power, considered in the abstract, need not restrict freedom: but absolute state power always does. The *legitimate* functions of government are actually conducive to freedom. Maintaining internal order, keeping foreign foes at bay, administering justice, removing obstacles to the free interchange of goods—the exercise of these powers makes it possible for men to follow their chosen pursuits with maximum freedom. But note that the very instrument by which these desirable ends are achieved *can* be the instrument for achieving undesirable ends—that government can, instead of extending freedom, restrict freedom. And note, secondly, that the "can" quickly becomes "will" the moment the holders of government power are left to their own devices. This is because of the corrupting influence of power, the natural tendency of men who possess *some* power to take unto themselves *more* power. The tendency leads eventually to the acquisition of *all* power—whether in the hands of one or many makes little difference to the freedom of those left on the outside.

Such, then, is history's lesson, which Messrs. Acheson and Larson evidently did not read: release the holders of state power from any restraints other than those they wish to impose upon themselves, and you are swinging down the well-travelled road to absolutism.

The framers of the Constitution had learned the lesson. They were not only students of history, but victims of it: they knew from vivid, personal experience that freedom depends on effective restraints against the accumulation of power in a single authority. And that is what the Constitution is: *a system of restraints against the natural tendency of government to expand in the direction of absolutism.* We all know the main components of the system. The first is the limitation of the federal government's authority to specific, delegated powers. The second, a corollary of the first, is the reservation to the States and the people of all power not delegated to the federal government. The third is a careful division of the federal government's power among three separate branches. The fourth is a prohibition against impetuous alteration of the system—namely, Article V's tortuous, but wise, amendment procedures.

Was it then a *Democracy* the framers created? Hardly. The system of restraints, on the face of it, was directed not only against individual tyrants, but also against a tyranny of the masses. The framers were well aware of the danger posed by self-seeking demagogues—that they might persuade a majority of the people to confer on government vast powers in return for deceptive promises of economic gain. And so they forbade such a transfer of power—first by declaring, in effect, that certain activities are outside the natural and legitimate scope of the public authority, and secondly by dispersing public authority among several levels and branches of government in the hope that each seat of authority, jealous of its own prerogatives, would have a natural incentive to resist aggression by the others.

But the framers were not visionaries. They knew that rules of government, however brilliantly calculated to cope with the imperfect nature of man, however carefully designed to avoid the pitfalls of power, would be no match for men who were determined to disregard them. In the last analysis their system of government would prosper only if the governed were sufficiently determined that it should. "What have you given us?" a woman asked Ben Franklin toward the close of the Constitutional Convention. "A Republic," he said, *"if you can keep it!"*

We have not kept it. The Achesons and Larsons have had their way. The system of restraints has fallen into disrepair. The federal government has moved into every field in which it believes its services are needed. The state governments are either excluded from their rightful functions by federal preemption, or they are allowed to act at the sufferance of the federal government. Inside the federal government both the executive and judicial branches have roamed far outside their constitutional boundary lines. And all of these things have come to pass without regard to the amendment procedures prescribed by Article V. The result is a Leviathan, a vast national authority out of touch with the people, and out of their control. This monolith of power is bounded only by the will of those who sit in high places.

There are a number of ways in which the power of government can be measured.

One is the size of its financial operations. Federal spending is now approaching a hundred billion dollars a year (compared with three and one-half billion less than three decades ago).

Another is the scope of its activities. A study recently conducted by the *Chicago Tribune* showed that the federal government is now the "biggest

land owner, property manager, renter, mover and hauler, medical clini-
cian, lender, insurer, mortgage broker, employer, debtor, taxer and
spender in all history."

Still another is the portion of the peoples' earnings government appro-
priates for its own use: nearly a third of earnings are taken every year in
the form of taxes.

A fourth is the extent of government interference in the daily lives of
individuals. The farmer is told how much wheat he can grow. The wage
earner is at the mercy of national union leaders whose great power is a
direct consequence of federal labor legislation. The businessman is hampered by a maze of government regulations, and often by direct government competition. The government takes 6 percent of most payrolls in
Social Security Taxes and thus compels millions of individuals to post-
pone until later years the enjoyment of wealth they might otherwise enjoy
today. Increasingly, the federal government sets standards of education,
health, and safety.

How did it happen? How did our national government grow from a
servant with sharply limited powers into a master with virtually unlimited
power?

In part, we were swindled. There are occasions when we have elevated
men and political parties to power that promised to restore limited government and then proceeded, after their election, to expand the activities
of government. But let us be honest with ourselves. Broken promises are
not the major causes of our trouble. *Kept* promises are. All too often we
have put men in office who have suggested spending a little more on this,
a little more on that, who have proposed a new welfare program, who
have thought of another variety of "security." We have taken the bait,
preferring to put off to another day the recapture of freedom and the
restoration of our constitutional system. We have gone the way of many
a democratic society that has lost its freedom by persuading itself that if
"the people" rule, all is well.

The Frenchman, Alexis de Tocqueville, probably the most clairvoyant
political observer of modern times, saw the danger when he visited this
country in the 1830s. Even then he foresaw decay for a society that tended
to put more emphasis on its democracy than on its republicanism. He
predicted that America would produce, not tyrants, but "guardians." And
that the American people would "console themselves for being in tutelage
by the reflection that they have chosen their own guardians. Every man
allows himself to be put in lead-strings, because he sees that it is not a

person nor a class of persons, but the people at large that hold the end of his chain."

Our tendency to concentrate power in the hands of a few men deeply concerns me. We can be conquered by bombs or by subversion; but we can also be conquered by neglect—by ignoring the Constitution and disregarding the principles of limited government. Our defenses against the accumulation of unlimited power in Washington are in poorer shape, I fear, than our defenses against the aggressive designs of Moscow. Like so many other nations before us, we may succumb through internal weakness rather than fall before a foreign foe.

I am convinced that most Americans now want to reverse the trend. I think that concern for our vanishing freedoms is genuine. I think that the people's uneasiness in the stifling omnipresence of government has turned into something approaching alarm. But bemoaning the evil will not drive it back, and accusing fingers will not shrink government.

The turn will come when we entrust the conduct of our affairs to men who understand that their first duty as public officials is to divest themselves of the power they have been given. It will come when Americans, in hundreds of communities throughout the nation, decide to put the man in office who is pledged to enforce the Constitution and restore the Republic. Who will proclaim in a campaign speech: "I have little interest in streamlining government or in making it more efficient, for I mean to reduce its size. I do not undertake to promote welfare, for I propose to extend freedom. My aim is not to pass laws, but to repeal them. It is not to inaugurate new programs, but to cancel old ones that do violence to the Constitution, or that have failed in their purpose, or that impose on the people an unwarranted financial burden. I will not attempt to discover whether legislation is 'needed' before I have first determined whether it is constitutionally permissible. And if I should later be attacked for neglecting my constituents' 'interests,' I shall reply that I was informed their main interest is liberty and that in that cause I am doing the very best I can."

The Governor of New York, in 1930, pointed out that the Constitution does not empower the Congress to deal with "a great number of . . . vital problems of government, such as the conduct of public utilities, of banks, of insurance, of business, of agriculture, of education, of social welfare, and a dozen other important features." And he added that "Washington must not be encouraged to interfere" in these areas.

Franklin Roosevelt's rapid conversion from Constitutionalism to the doctrine of unlimited government is an oft-told story. But I am here concerned not so much by the abandonment of States' Rights by the national Democratic Party—an event that occurred some years ago when that party was captured by the Socialist ideologues in and about the labor movement—as by the unmistakable tendency of the Republican Party to adopt the same course. The result is that today *neither* of our two parties maintains a meaningful commitment to the principle of States' Rights. Thus, the cornerstone of the Republic, our chief bulwark against the encroachment of individual freedom by Big Government, is fast disappearing under the piling sands of absolutism.

The Republican Party, to be sure, gives lip-service to States' Rights. We often *talk* about "returning to the States their rightful powers"; the Administration has even gone so far as to sponsor a federal-state conference on the problem. But deeds are what count, and I regret to say that in actual practice, the Republican Party, like the Democratic Party, summons the coercive power of the federal government whenever national leaders conclude that the States are not performing satisfactorily.

Let us focus attention on one method of federal interference—one that tends to be neglected in much of the public discussion of the problem. In recent years the federal government has continued, and in many cases has increased, federal "grants-in-aid" to the States in a number of areas in which the Constitution recognizes the exclusive jurisdiction of the States. These grants are called "matching funds" and are designed to "stimulate" state spending in health, education, welfare, conservation or any other area in which the federal government decides there is a need for national action. If the States agree to put up money for these purposes, the federal government undertakes to match the appropriation according to a ratio prescribed by Congress. Sometimes the ratio is fifty-fifty; often the federal government contributes over half the cost.

There are two things to note about these programs. The first is that they are *federal* programs—they are conceived by the federal government both as to purpose and as to extent. The second is that the "stimulative" grants are, in effect, a mixture of blackmail and bribery. The States are told to go along with the program "or else." Once the federal government has offered matching funds, it is unlikely, as a practical matter, that a member of a State Legislature will turn down his State's fair share of revenue collected from all of the States. Understandably, many legislators feel that to refuse aid would be political suicide. This is an indirect form of coercion, but it is effective nonetheless.

A more direct method of coercion is for the federal government to *threaten* to move in unless state governments take action that Washington deems appropriate. Not so long ago, for example, the Secretary of Labor gave the States a lecture on the wisdom of enacting "up-to-date" unemployment compensation laws. He made no effort to disguise the alternative: if the States failed to act, the federal government would.

Here are some examples of the "stimulative" approach. Late in 1957 a "Joint Federal-State Action Committee" recommended that certain matching funds programs be "returned" to the States on the scarcely disguised grounds that the States, in the view of the Committee, had learned to live up to their responsibilities. These are the areas in which the States were learning to behave: "vocational education" programs in agriculture, home economics, practical nursing, and the fisheries trade; local sewage projects; slum clearance and urban renewal; and enforcement of health and safety standards in connection with the atomic energy program.

Now the point is not that Congress failed to act on these recommendations, or that the Administration gave them only half-hearted support; but rather that the federal government had no business entering these fields in the first place, and thus had no business taking upon itself the prerogative of judging the States' performance. The Republican Party should have said this plainly and forthrightly and demanded the immediate withdrawal of the federal government.

We can best understand our error, I think, by examining the theory behind it. I have already alluded to the book, *A Republican Looks At His Party*, which is an elaborate rationalization of the "Modern Republican" approach to current problems. (It does the job just as well, I might add, for the Democrats' approach.) Mr. Larson devotes a good deal of space to the question of States' Rights. He contends that while there is "a general presumption" in favor of States' Rights, thanks to the Tenth Amendment, this presumption must give way whenever it appears to the federal authorities that the States are not responding satisfactorily to "the needs of the people." This is a paraphrase of his position but not, I think, an unjust one. And if this approach appears to be a high-handed way of dealing with an explicit constitutional provision, Mr. Larson justifies the argument by summoning the concept that "for every right there is a corresponding duty." "When we speak of States' Rights," he writes, "we should never forget to add that there go with those rights the corresponding States' responsibilities." Therefore, he concludes, if the States fail to do their duty, they have only themselves to blame when the federal government intervenes.

The trouble with this argument is that it treats the Constitution of the United States as a kind of handbook in political theory, to be heeded or ignored depending on how it fits the plans of contemporary federal officials. The Tenth Amendment is *not* "a general assumption," but a prohibitory rule of law. The Tenth Amendment recognizes the States' *jurisdiction* in certain areas. States' Rights means that the States have a right to act or *not to act,* as they see fit, in the areas reserved to them. The States may have duties corresponding to these rights, but the duties are owed to the people of the States, not to the federal government. Therefore, the recourse lies not with the federal government, which is not sovereign, but with the people, who are, and who have full power to take disciplinary action. If the people are unhappy with, say, their State's disability insurance program, they can bring pressure to bear on their state officials and, if that fails, they can elect a new set of officials. And if, in the unhappy event they should wish to divest themselves of this responsibility, they can amend the Constitution. The Constitution, I repeat, draws a sharp and clear line between federal jurisdiction and state jurisdiction. The federal, government's failure to recognize that line has been a crushing blow to the principle of limited government.

But again, I caution against a defensive, or apologetic, appeal to the Constitution. There is a *reason* for its reservation of States' Rights. Not only does it prevent the accumulation of power in a central government that is remote from the people and relatively immune from popular restraints; it also recognizes the principle that essentially local problems are best dealt with by the people most directly concerned. Who knows better than New Yorkers how much and what kind of publicly financed slum clearance in New York City is needed and can be afforded? Who knows better than Nebraskans whether that State has an adequate nursing program? Who knows better than Arizonans the kind of school program that is needed to educate their children? The people of my own State— and I am confident that I speak for the majority of them—have long since seen through the spurious suggestion that federal aid comes "free." They know that the money comes out of their own pockets, and that it is returned to them minus a broker's fee taken by the federal bureaucracy. They know, too, that the power to decide how that money shall be spent is withdrawn from them and exercised by some planning board deep in the caverns of one of the federal agencies. They understand this represents a great and perhaps irreparable loss—not only in their wealth, but in their priceless liberty.

Nothing could so far advance the cause of freedom as for state officials throughout the land to assert their rightful claims to lost state power; and for the federal government to withdraw promptly and totally from every jurisdiction which the Constitution reserved to the states.

An attempt has been made in recent years to disparage the principle of States' Rights by equating it with defense of the South's position on racial integration. I have already indicated that the reach of States' Rights is much broader than that—that it affects Northerners as well as Southerners, and concerns many matters that have nothing to do with the race question. Still, it is quite true that the integration issue is affected by the States' Rights principle, and that the South's position on the issue is, today, the most conspicuous expression of the principle. So much so that the country is now in the grips of a spirited and sometimes ugly controversy over an imagined conflict between States' Rights, on the one hand, and what are called "civil rights" on the other.

I say an imagined conflict because I deny that there *can* be a conflict between States' Rights, properly defined—and civil rights, properly defined. If States' "Rights" are so asserted as to encroach upon individual rights that are protected by valid federal laws, then the exercise of state power is a nullity. Conversely, if individual "rights" are so asserted as to infringe upon valid state power, then the assertion of those "rights" is a nullity. The rights themselves do not clash. The conflict arises from a failure to define the two categories of rights correctly, and to assert them lawfully.

States' Rights are easy enough to define. The Tenth Amendment does it succinctly: "The powers not delegated to the United States by the Constitution nor prohibited by it to the States are reserved to the States respectively, or to the people."

Civil rights should be no harder. In fact, however—thanks to extravagant and shameless misuse by people who ought to know better—it is one of the most badly understood concepts in modern political usage. Civil rights is frequently used synonymously with "human rights"—or with "natural rights." As often as not, it is simply a name for describing an activity that someone deems politically or socially desirable. A sociologist writes a paper proposing to abolish some inequity, or a politician makes a speech about it—and, behold, a new "civil right" is born! The Supreme Court has displayed the same creative powers.

A *civil* right is a right that is asserted and is therefore protected by some valid law. It may be asserted by the common law, or by local or federal statutes, or by the Constitution; *but unless a right is incorporated in the law, it is not a civil right and is not enforceable by the instruments of the civil law.* There may be some rights—"natural," "human," or otherwise—that *should* also be civil rights. But if we desire to give such rights the protection of the law, our recourse is to a legislature or to the amendment procedures of the Constitution. We must not look to politicians, or sociologists—or the courts—to correct the deficiency.

In the field of racial relations, there are some rights that are clearly protected by valid laws and are therefore "civil" rights. One of them is the right to vote. The Fifteenth Amendment provides that no one shall be denied the franchise on account of race, color, or previous condition of servitude. Similarly with certain legal privileges enforced by the Fourteenth Amendment. The legislative history of that amendment makes it clear (I quote from the Civil Rights Act of 1866 which the Amendment was designed to legitimize) that people of all races shall be equally entitled "to make and enforce contracts, to sue, be parties, and give evidence, to inherit, to purchase, lease, sell, hold and convey real and personal property and to full and equal benefit of all laws and proceedings for the security of persons and property." After the passage of that Act and the Amendment, all persons, Negroes included, had a "civil" right to these protections.

It is otherwise, let us note, with education. For the federal Constitution does *not* require the States to maintain racially mixed schools. Despite the recent holding of the Supreme Court, I am firmly convinced—not only that integrated schools are not required—but that the Constitution does not permit any interference whatsoever by the federal government in the field of education. It may be just or wise or expedient for negro children to attend the same schools as white children, but they do not have a civil right to do so which is protected by the federal constitution, or which is enforceable by the federal government.

The intentions of the founding fathers in this matter are beyond any doubt: *no powers regarding education were given the federal government.* Consequently, under the Tenth Amendment, jurisdiction over the entire field was reserved to the States. The remaining question is whether the

Fourteenth Amendment—concretely, that amendment's "equal protection" clause—modified the original prohibition against federal intervention.

To my knowledge it has never been seriously argued—the argument certainly was not made by the Supreme Court—that the authors of the Fourteenth Amendment intended to alter the Constitutional scheme with regard to education. Indeed, in the famous school integration decision, *Brown v. Board of Education* (1954), the Supreme Court justices expressly acknowledged that they were not being guided by the intentions of the amendment's authors. *"In approaching this problem,"* Chief Justice Warren said, *"we cannot turn the clock back to 1868 when the amendment was adopted . . . We must consider public education in the light of its full development and in its present place in American life throughout the nation."* In effect, the Court said that what matters is not the ideas of the men who wrote the Constitution, but the *Court's* ideas. It was only by engrafting its own views onto the established law of the land that the Court was able to reach the decision it did.

The intentions of the Fourteenth Amendment's authors are perfectly clear. Consider these facts. 1. During the entire congressional debate on the Fourteenth Amendment it was never once suggested by any proponent of the amendment that it would outlaw segregated schools. 2. At the same time that it approved the Fourteenth Amendment, Congress established schools in Washington in Georgetown "for the sole use of . . . colored children." 3. In all the debates on the amendment by the State Legislatures there was only one legislator, a man in Indiana, who thought the amendment would affect school. 4. The great majority of the States that approved the amendment permitted or required segregated schools at the very time they approved the amendment. There is not room here for exhaustive treatment of this evidence, but the facts are well documented, and they are all we have to know about the Fourteenth Amendment's bearing on this problem. The amendment was not intended to, and therefore it did not outlaw racially separate schools. It was not intended to, and therefore it did not, authorize *any* federal intervention in the field of education.

I am therefore not impressed by the claim that the Supreme Court's decision on school integration is the law of the land. *The Constitution, and the laws "made in pursuance thereof," are the "supreme law of the land."* The Constitution is what its authors intended it to be and said it was—not what the Supreme Court says it is. If we condone the practice of substituting our own intentions for those of the Constitution's framers, we reject, in effect, the principle of Constitutional Government: we endorse a rule of men, not of laws.

I have great respect for the Supreme Court as an institution, but I cannot believe that I display that respect by submitting abjectly to abuses of power by the Court, and by condoning its unconstitutional trespass into the legislative sphere of government. The Congress and the States, equally with the Supreme Court, are obliged to interpret and comply with the Constitution according to their own lights. I therefore support all efforts by the States, excluding violence of course, to preserve their rightful powers over education.

As for the Congress, I would hope that the national legislature would help clarify the problem by proposing to the States a Constitutional amendment that would reaffirm the States' exclusive jurisdiction in the field of education. This amendment would, in my judgment, assert what is already provided unmistakably by the Constitution; but it would put the matter beyond any further question.

It so happens that I am in agreement with the *objectives* of the Supreme Court as stated in the *Brown* decision. I believe that it *is* both wise and just for negro children to attend the same schools as whites, and that to deny them this opportunity carries with it strong implications of inferiority. I am not prepared, however, to impose that judgment of mine on the people of Mississippi or South Carolina, or to tell them what methods should be adopted and what pace should be kept in striving toward that goal. That is their business, not mine. I believe that the problem of race relations, like all social and cultural problems, is best handled by the people directly concerned. Social and cultural change, however desirable, should not be effected by the engines of national power. Let us, through persuasion and education, seek to improve institutions we deem defective. But let us, in doing so, respect the orderly processes of the law. Any other course enthrones tyrants and dooms freedom.

NOTE

1. This is a strange label indeed: it implies that "ordinary" Conservatism is opposed to progress. Have we forgotten that America made its greatest progress when Conservative principles were honored and preserved?

Chapter Twenty

The Young Americans for Freedom

William F. Buckley. Jr.

A new organization was born last week and just possibly it will influence the political future of this country, as why should it not, considering that its membership is young, intelligent, articulate and determined, its principles enduring, its aim to translate these principles into political action in a world which has lost its moorings and is looking about for them desperately?

One wonders why an organized conservative political youth movement was not begun before, so naturally does it fit, now that it is on the scene, and so plain is the need for it. It could be that the nonexistence of such an organization ten years ago is fortunate, for it might have piled on the rocks. It is only in the last decade that American conservatism has been freed from the exclusive hold which the narrow dogmas of vested business interests had upon it. The National Association of Manufacturers is a splendid organization that has accomplished a great deal of good; but it is wrong to suppose that it was ever equipped to generate a *Weltanschauung* which could galvanize the intellectual, creative, and moral energies of students who had been indoctrinated over thirty years by their teachers to believe that conservatism was merely a highbrow word for the profit system—that there was nothing in conservatism beyond the vaults of the Chase National Bank.

The Young Americans for Freedom have the benefit of perspectives which ten years ago could only have been intuited. In ten years much has happened. History proved the irrelevance of Liberal doctrine. The critique of Liberalism has been made, if not definitively, at least sufficiently; and it is a total critique. The word "conservatism" is accepted both by Russell Kirk and Frank Meyer as designating their distinct but complementary, even symbiotic positions. In the last ten years more important books have been written than there is time here to catalogue, books of journalistic, philosophical, economic, historical and cultural import — all of them concentrically pointing an accusing finger at the tottering idols of Liberalism. The great renewal of the last decade is reflected in the nuances in the Young Americans' statement of first principles, which is reproduced [in the next chapter]. Here is mention of the moral aspect of freedom; of transcendent values; of the nature of man. All this together with a tough-as-nails statement of political and economic convictions which Richard Nixon couldn't read aloud without fainting.

The students were called to the founding conference in Sharon, Connecticut by Douglas Caddy, until recently a student at Georgetown University, now with the McGraw-Edison Committee for Public Affairs in New York. Ninety students turned up from 24 states, representing 44 colleges. The age limits for members were set in the original draft of the by-laws at between 16 and 28; but the conference overruled the committee and with a low bow to the achievements of geriatrics, moved the old age limit up to 35, and made at least this bystander feel young again. Caddy was elected National Director, and all inquiries should be addressed to him at 343 Lexington Avenue, New York 16, N.Y. Enclose a dollar bill, if you want to help with the cost of setting the organization up. Robert Schuchman of the Yale Law School is chairman. There are six regional directors. In the Northeast it is Walter McLaughlin Jr. of the Harvard Law School. For the Central Atlantic states, Robert Harley of Georgetown University. For the South, George Gaines of Tulane University. For the West, Dick Noble of Stanford University. For the Southwest, Jim Kolbe of Northwestern University, and for the Midwest, Robert Croll, also of Northwestern University. The twelve members of the Board of Directors are David Franke (New School for Social Research), Richard Cowan (Yale), Tom Colvin (Davidson), Carol Dawson (Washington, D.C.), Carl McIntire (Shelton), Bill Madden (Holy Cross), William Schulz (Antioch), James Abstine (Indiana), Howard Phillips (Harvard), Scott Stanley Jr. (University of Kansas Law School), Lee Edwards (press assistant to Senator John Marshall Butler), and Herbert Kohler (Knox).

What will the Young Americans for Freedom do? What did the Young Socialists do? What do the Students for Industrial Democracy do? The American Youth for Democracy? The Students for Democratic Action? The Left never lacked for things to do; neither does the Right. Every chapter of YAFF in every college will shape a program rooted in the principal concerns of its own campus; except that no one will be accepted as a member who does not endorse the Sharon Statement. There will be annual meetings. Perhaps they will find the funds to publish a newsletter. They will have the help of the Intercollegiate Society of Individualists a non-political organization whose aim it is to advance an understanding of freedom at the college level.

But what is so striking in the students who met at Sharon is their appetite for power. Ten years ago the struggle seemed so long, so endless, even, that we did not even dream of victory. Even now the world continues to go left, but all over the land dumbfounded professors are remarking the extraordinary revival of hard conservative sentiment in the student bodies. It was Goldwater, not Nixon or Eisenhower, who was the hero of the bright and dominant youth forces at the Chicago Convention. It is quixotic to say that they or their elders have seized the reins of history. But the difference in psychological attitude is tremendous. They talk about *affecting* history; we have talked about *educating* people to want to affect history. It may be that, as Russell Kirk keeps reminding us, the Struggle Avalleth. No one would doubt it who talked to the founding fathers of the Young Americans for Freedom.

Chapter Twenty-one

The Sharon Statement

Adopted by the Young Americans for Freedom in conference
at Sharon, Conn., September 9–11, 1960

In this time of moral and political crisis, it is the responsibility of the youth of America to affirm certain eternal truths.

We, as young conservatives, believe:

That foremost among the transcendent values is the individual's use of his God-given free will, whence derives his right to be free from the restrictions of arbitrary force;

That liberty is indivisible, and that political freedom cannot long exist without economic freedom;

That the purposes of government are to protect these freedoms through the preservation of internal order, the provision of national defense, and the administration of justice;

That when government ventures beyond these rightful functions, it accumulates power which tends to diminish order and liberty;

That the Constitution of the United States is the best arrangement yet devised for empowering government to fulfill its proper role, while restraining it from the concentration and abuse of power;

That the genius of the Constitution—the division of powers—is summed up in the clause which reserves primacy to the several states, or to the people, in those spheres not specifically delegated to the Federal Government;

That the market economy, allocating resources by the free play of supply and demand, is the single economic system compatible with the requirements of personal freedom and constitutional government, and that it is at the same time the most productive supplier of human needs;

That when government interferes with the work of the market econ-

From *National Review*, September 24, 1960, pp. 172–173. Reprinted by permission.

omy, it tends to reduce the moral and physical strength of the nation; that when it takes from one man to bestow on another, it diminishes the incentive of the first, the integrity of the second, and the moral autonomy of both;

That we will be free only so long as the national sovereignty of the United States is secure; that history shows periods of freedom are rare, and can exist only when free citizens concertedly defend their rights against all enemies;

That the forces of international Communism are, at present, the greatest single threat to these liberties;

That the United States should stress victory over, rather than coexistence with, this menace; and

That American foreign policy must be judged by this criterion; does it serve the just interests of the United States?

Chapter Twenty-two

A Choice, Not an Echo

Phyllis Schlafly

By mid-1963, impartial observers could see that the Republican Party had one obvious, logical, deserving, winning candidate. He combined the integrity of Robert A. Taft with the glamour of Dwight Eisenhower. He had proved his ability to win against heavy odds. He was truly *a national* candidate with a demonstrated following in all the 50 states. For the first time, Republicans had a candidate with genuine appeal to the youth of America. When Senator Barry Goldwater at long last announced he would be a candidate, this was in response to a genuine grassroots movement— not the result of a publicity blitz.

This obvious candidate had been a success at everything he has tried. Like Eisenhower, this obvious candidate is a General, and like Taft he has vast political experience. He is the epitome of American constitutional principles.

He was a successful businessman. He is a successful author; his two books were best-sellers: *The Conscience of a Conservative* and *Why Not Victory?* He had a distinguished World War II record; he has risen to the rank of Major General in the Air Force Reserve, and he still pilots jet fighter planes, a remarkable feat for one of his age and position.

He has been a tremendous success in politics. He was twice elected Senator from Arizona, a state where the Democratic registrations outnumber Republicans two to one. He successfully held one of the most important jobs in the Republican Party: Chairman of the Republican Senatorial Campaign Committee. He is the most sought-after speaker in the United States today.

Reprinted by permission of Phyllis Schlafly. Copyright 1964.

The obvious nominee of the Republican Party in 1964 was Senator Barry Goldwater.

Goldwater has the magic quality of leadership that is based on independence of thought and courage. An almost-forgotten incident in his legislative career proves how the Goldwater brand of leadership can prevail even when a minority of one.

In 1959 the Senate passed what was popularly known as the Kennedy "sweetheart" labor bill by the staggering margin of 90 to 1. Senator Goldwater was the lone dissenter. He voted against the bill on the ground that it allowed Senator Kennedy, a presidential aspirant, to give the appearance of sponsoring labor reform legislation; whereas, his bill could be properly described as like a flea bite on the hide of a bull elephant. The entire press predicted that Senator Goldwater's dissent was a futile gesture and that the Kennedy bill would pass the House quickly and become law.

Then a remarkable thing happened. Because of the brilliant way that Senator Goldwater had focused attention on the issue of monopoly versus freedom, our Congressmen began to hear from their constituents back home.

As a result, it was not the Kennedy "sweetheart" bill, but a real labor reform bill called the Landrum-Griffin Act, which passed the House and ultimately became law as a substitute for the Kennedy bill.

Senator Goldwater gave us dramatic proof that conservatism is popular. He showed that a minority of one can ultimately be victorious against overwhelming odds.

Any political leader can score a win if he has the votes in his pocket, just as any general can win if he has more men and more weapons. The true test of leadership is the ability to carry your side to victory when the odds are against you. This is the kind of leadership Barry Goldwater has demonstrated in a political way in Arizona, and in a legislative way in the Senate.

This is leadership that can win elections and solve problems at home, and defeat the Communists abroad. This is the leadership for which America yearns today.

Most important, Barry Goldwater is the one Republican who can and will win—because he will campaign on the issues of 1964. He is the one Republican who will not pull his punches to please the kingmakers. He can be counted on to face the issues squarely. He will make the kind of forthright hard-hitting campaign that American voters admire. This is why he is the man the left-leaning liberals most fear. He is the only Republican who will truly offer the voters "a choice, not an echo."

As Goldwater's grassroots strength grew in 1963 and early 1964, the leftwing propaganda against him grew in geometric proportion. *Life* magazine put into words an anti-Goldwater argument that has appeared in one form or another in numerous magazines and newspaper columns. *Life* said we must beware of Goldwater because he has one-sentence solutions for national problems. According to this peculiar line of egghead reasoning, present day problems are so complex that we must have sophisticated—not simple—solutions.

Contrary to this argument, civilization progresses, freedom is won, and problems are solved because we have wonderful people who think up simple solutions! It is not the complicated, roundabout Rube Goldberg approach that accomplishes anything, but the direct approach that goes to the heart of the problem.

The man who did as much as anyone to emancipate women from their daily drudgery was the inventor of the sewing machine. His invention depended on a very simple idea; just put the eye of the needle in the point instead of in the other end.

Two brothers named Wright who ran a bicycle shop in Dayton, Ohio, had the ambition to invent an airplane. They received long letters from experts at the Smithsonian Institution and from Professors at European universities telling them that heavier-than-air flight was impossible. But the Wright brothers had two simple solutions—the curved wing to provide lift, and the propeller—and with these simple solutions, they built and flew the first airplane. Their simple solutions dominated air travel until the perfection of the jet engine.

When our infant Republic was threatened by the greatest military conquerer of the 19th century, our Minister to France said: "Millions for defense sir, but not one cent for tribute." This simple solution brought peace, not war.

When an American citizen named Perdicaris was captured and held hostage by a bandit named Raisuli, President Theodore Roosevelt had a simple solution: just send a cable reading "Perdicaris alive or Raisuli dead." It got results; Perdicaris was promptly released. Today, American servicemen are held hostage by Red bandits from East Germany to Cuba, to Red China, and no one has tried to get them out by simple solutions.

In 1958 the Chinese Reds made their big drive to take over Quemoy and Matsu. Appeasement-minded pundits at home urged that we evacuate these islands because "Why die for Quemoy?" President Eisenhower had a simple solution: he just went on television and told the world the United States would stand firm in the Formosa Straits. Shortly afterwards the Reds gave up their attacks, and for six years these islands have been secure outposts of freedom.

Likewise, there are numerous simple solutions for most of the problems that confront our country today. Barry Goldwater is the man who can cut through the egghead complexities in Foggy Bottom and solve these problems for us.

There is a very simple solution for what to do about Cuba—just reinstate the Monroe Doctrine. It would rid us of Castro and his subversion. We should not submit to the international blackmail of the false claim that using the Monroe Doctrine will start World War III. In 140 years of use, the Monroe Doctrine never brought war; it brought only peace. It would bring peace today if only we had a President with the courage to use it. Barry Goldwater is that man.

There was a very simple solution to what to do about the Berlin Wall. The Soviets started building it on Friday evening after our President had left Washington for a weekend holiday. By the time he returned to the White House on Monday afternoon, the Wall was built; the State Department wrung its hands and said: "There is nothing we can do now. What do you want to do, start World War III?" The solution was simple. A president with leadership could have made this announcement Friday night: "If the Communists close that door in Berlin, we will close the doors of the Soviet Embassy and consulates in our country." The Soviets would do anything to keep open these privileged sanctuaries which serve as the headquarters of their subversion, espionage, and propaganda in the United States.

There was a very simple solution to what to do about the Congo: let the Congolese solve it! When they had a chance, they got rid of the Communist Lumumba. They would have eliminated the rest of the Communists, if our State Department had not, in collusion with the UN, told the Congolese they had to be more democratic and admit Communist followers of Lumumba into their government.

There is a simple solution as to what to do about Southeast Asia: just follow the advice of our greatest military authority on the Far East, General Douglas MacArthur. He said that Red China's aggressions could be stopped by announcing the end of the privileged Red sanctuaries requested by Attlee, granted by Acheson and still respected. General MacArthur thought it was wrong to send American boys to die in Asia, while refusing to use any of the 600,000 trained soldiers of the Republic of China or other means available for victory.

There is a very simple solution to what to do about the problem of world Communism: just stop helping the Communists. The Soviet empire would die of its own economic anemia if Democratic Administrations didn't keep giving it massive blood transfusions, such as the sending of 64 million bushels of American wheat.

There is a very simple solution to the problem of peace and disarmament. It was given to us by the Father of Our Country, George Washington. The formula is as good today as when he said it: "If we desire to secure peace . . . it must be known that we are at all times ready for war."

Finally, there is a very simple solution to what to do about the whole "looney" mess in Washington today—elect Barry Goldwater, the man with the courage to give us simple solutions. . . .

Some Republicans may ask, why would a regular party Republican write a book which exposes the Convention intrigues of a few alleged Republicans? Should not the mistakes of our Conventions be discussed only in private? What useful purpose can be served by public discussion of our Convention shortcomings in a year when the survival of American freedom and independence may depend on a Republican victory which will turn out of office the ADA radicals in the White House, the unilateral disarmers in the Pentagon, and the "rather Red than dead" advocates in the State Department?

I have done volunteer work for the Republican Party ever since 1945. During those 19 years, I have given thousands and thousands of hours of dedicated work to the cause of good government through the medium of the Republican Party. I have traveled thousands of miles in order to speak to small groups and large, help little clubs, build stronger Republican organizations, inject enthusiasm, inspire and persuade women to work for the Party, and solve problems of many kinds.

I have done this at my own expense and at great sacrifice on my part and on the part of my family—for one purpose, because I believe in working for good government, and I believe this can be best achieved through the Republican Party. I have never sought to be appointed to any job on any level, or otherwise to gain material or personal advantage from my work for the Republican Party.

When the primary or the Republican National Convention did not nominate the candidate of my choice, I nevertheless stumped the state just as energetically and enthusiastically as when my favorites were selected.

I can look back on campaigns in which I saw Republicans on the local level working their hearts out for a cause they believed to be just, only to realize, after it was all over, that the kingmakers had given them a candidate who would not campaign on the issues. I speak with the voice of the countless Republican Party workers who don't want this to happen again; in the words of the greatest Republican slogan of this century, they have "had enough."

In the interest of Party unity, I kept silent as we sustained each tragic defeat. But as we started the crucial campaign of 1964, my loyalty to the thousands of Republicans who labor in the precincts compelled me to speak out. I believed it would have been dereliction of duty for me to fail to present the facts to our people so they could forestall another defeat like 1940, 1944, 1948, and 1960.

The decision to publish these pages was a hard one. The question was whether to try to help grassroots Republicans face the realities of 1964 politics, or whether to close my eyes, hope for the best, and run the grave risk of having to look into the eyes of hard-working Republicans in November, discouraged and disillusioned at another unnecessary defeat. I believed that the most constructive thing I could do for the Republican Party was to give our people the facts, in anticipation of the Convention, which would assist them to reject the efforts of the little clique of kingmakers who wanted to force upon us another "me too" candidate who would pull his punches and evade the vital issues. I made my decision in the light of what I believe to be the best interests of the America I love, the Republican Party I have served, and the voters to whom I owe a duty to speak the truth.

History shows that mistakes can be prevented by providing the people with facts and warnings in anticipation of a threatened event.

For example, on May 19, 1963 Republican Party Chairman William E. Miller gave public voice to persistent rumors that the State Department had made secret plans to appease Castro by turning over Guantanamo to him, and withdrawing American forces from Cuba to Puerto Rico. Because Miller revealed this in time with the appropriate publicity, the State Department did not have the nerve to consummate the "Guantanamo deal" it had hoped to slip through without the public realizing its significance. Miller halted the surrender of this important naval base for us by his advance warning.

Likewise, the nomination of Barry Goldwater by the 1964 Republican National Convention in San Francisco was a vivid demonstration of the axioms that "knowledge is power" and "to be forewarned is to be forearmed." Grassroots Republicans were on to the kingmakers' dirty tricks. Delegates were acutely aware of how the kingmakers had stolen previous Republican Conventions, and they were determined it would not happen again. Grassroots Republicans were fully prepared for the propaganda blitz, the vicious charges, the phony polls, the spurious issues, the slanted press—and they didn't crumble under the kingmakers' many-pronged attack.

Now that grassroots Republicans have succeeded in nominating Barry Goldwater and William E. Miller—two candidates who will campaign on the major issues of our time and fight hard to win—it has become more important than ever that this story be told to all voters, whether Republican, Democrat, or Independent. Only in this way will the average voter be prepared for the propaganda onslaught that will be activated by the kingmakers against Goldwater. It will be massive and it will be clever. The kingmakers are playing for high stakes—control of Federal spending—and they do not intend to lose. Americans must learn the significance of these famous lines spoken by Patrick Henry in 1775:

> I have but one lamp by which my feet are guided, and that is the lamp of experience. I know of no way of judging of the future but by the past.

The burden for Goldwater's election will fall on the same kind of dedicated volunteers who won his nomination. The $100 billion question is: Can grassroots Americans complete in November the victory they started winning in July?

Chapter Twenty-three

Extremism in the Defense of Liberty
The Republican National Convention
Acceptance Address

Barry M. Goldwater

Delivered before the Republican National Convention,
San Francisco, California, July 16, 1964

My good friend and great Republican, Dick Nixon and your charming wife, Pat; my running mate—that wonderful Republican who has served us so well for so long—Bill Miller and his wife, Stephanie; to Thruston Morton, who's done such a commendable job in chairmaning this convention; to Mr. Herbert Hoover who I hope is watching, and to the great American and his wife, General and Mrs. Eisenhower. To my own wife, my family, and to all of my fellow Republicans here assembled, and Americans across this great nation:

From this moment, united and determined, we will go forward together dedicated to the ultimate and undeniable greatness of the whole man.

Together we will win.

I accept your nomination with a deep sense of humility. I accept, too, the responsibility that goes with it, and I seek your continued help and your continued guidance. My fellow Republicans, our cause is too great for any man to feel worthy of it. Our task would be too great for any man did he not have with him the heart and the hands of this great Republican party.

And I promise you tonight that every fibre of my being is consecrated

From *Vital Speeches of the Day* 30: 21 (August 15, 1964).

to our cause, that nothing shall be lacking from the struggle that can be brought to it by enthusiasm, by devotion and plain hard work.

In this world no person, no party can guarantee anything, but what we can do and what we shall do is to deserve victory and victory will be ours. The Good Lord raised this mighty Republican, Republic to be a home for the brave and to flourish as the land of the free—not to stagnate in the swamp-land of collectivism, not to cringe before the bully of Communism.

Now my fellow Americans, the tide has been running against freedom. Our people have followed false prophets. We must, and we shall return to proven ways—not because they are old, but because they are true.

We must, and we shall, set the tide running again in the cause of freedom. And this party, with its every action, every word, every breath, and every heart beat, has but a single resolve, and that is freedom.

Freedom made orderly for this nation by our constitutional government. Freedom under a government limited by laws of nature and of nature's God. Freedom balanced so that order lacking liberty will not become the slavery of the prison cell; balanced so that liberty lacking order will not become the license of the mob and of the jungle.

Now, we Americans understand freedom, we have earned it; we have lived for it, and we have died for it, This nation and its people are freedom's models in a searching world. We can be freedom's missionaries in a doubting world.

But, ladies and gentlemen, first we must renew freedom's mission in our own hearts and in our own homes.

During four futile years the Administration which we shall replace has distorted and lost that faith. It has talked and talked and talked and talked the words of freedom but it has failed and failed and failed in the works of freedom.

Now failure cements the wall of shame in Berlin; failures blot the sands of shame at the Bay of Pigs; failures marked the slow death of freedom in Laos; failures infest the jungles of Vietnam, and failures haunt the houses of our once great alliances and undermine the greatest bulwark ever erected by free nations, the NATO community.

Failures proclaim lost leadership, obscure purpose, weakening wills and the risk of inciting our sworn enemies to new aggressions and to new excesses.

And because of this Administration we are tonight a world divided. We are a nation becalmed. We have lost the brisk pace of diversity and the genius of individual creativity. We are plodding along at a pace set by centralized planning, red tape, rules without responsibility, and regimentation without recourse.

Rather than useful jobs in our country, people have been offered bureaucratic make-work; rather than moral leadership, they have been given bread and circuses; they have been given spectacles, and yes, they've even been given scandals.

Tonight there is violence in our streets, corruption in our highest offices, aimlessness among our youth, anxiety among our elderly, and there's a virtual despair among the many who look beyond material success toward the inner meaning of their lives. And where examples of morality should be set, the opposite is seen. Small men seeking great wealth or power have too often and too long turned even the highest levels of public service into mere personal opportunity.

Now, certainly simple honesty is not too much to demand of men in government. We find it in most. Republicans demand it from everyone.

They demand it from everyone no matter how exalted or protected his position might be.

The growing menace in our country tonight, to personal safety, to life, to limb and property, in homes, in churches, on the playgrounds and places of business, particularly in our great cities, is the mounting concern or should be of every thoughtful citizen in the United States. Security from domestic violence, no less than from foreign aggression, is the most elementary and fundamental purpose of any government, and a government that cannot fulfill this purpose is one that cannot long command the loyalty of its citizens.

History shows us, demonstrates that nothing, nothing prepares the way for tyranny more than the failure of public officials to keep the streets safe from bullies and marauders.

Now we Republicans see all this as more—much more—than the result of mere political differences, or mere political mistakes. We see this as the result of a fundamentally and absolutely wrong view of man, his nature and his destiny.

Those who seek to live your lives for you, to take your liberty in return for relieving you of yours; those who elevate the state and downgrade the citizen, must see ultimately a world in which earthly power can be substituted for Divine Will. And this nation was founded upon the rejection of that notion and upon the acceptance of God as the author of freedom.

Now those who seek absolute power, even though they seek it to do what they regard as good, are simply demanding the right to enforce their own version of heaven on earth, and let me remind you they are the very ones who always create the most hellish tyranny.

Absolute power does corrupt, and those who seek it must be suspect and must be opposed. Their mistaken course stems from false notions, ladies and gentlemen, of equality. Equality, rightly understood as our founding fathers understood it, leads to liberty and to the emancipation of creative differences; wrongly understood, as it has been so tragically in our time, it leads first to conformity and then to despotism.

Fellow Republicans, it is the cause of Republicanism to resist concentrations of power, private or public, which enforce such conformity and inflict such despotism.

It is the cause of Republicanism to insure that power remains in the hands of the people—and, so help us God, that is exactly what a Republican President will do with the help of a Republican Congress.

It is further the cause of Republicanism to restore a clear understanding of the tyranny of man over man in the world at large. It is our cause to dispel the foggy thinking which avoids hard decisions in the delusion that a world of conflict will somehow resolve itself into a world of harmony, if we just don't rock the boat or irritate the forces of aggression—and this is hogwash.

It is, further, the cause of Republicanism to remind ourselves, and the world, that only the strong can remain free; that only the strong can keep the peace.

Now I needn't remind you, or my fellow Americans regardless of party, that Republicans have shouldered this hard responsibility and marched in this cause before. It was Republican leadership under Dwight Eisenhower that kept the peace, and passed along to this Administration the mightiest arsenal for defense the world has ever known.

And I needn't remind you that it was the strength and the believable will of the Eisenhower years that kept the peace by using our strength, by using it in the Formosa Strait, and in Lebanon, and by showing it courageously at all times.

It was during those Republican years that the thrust of Communist imperialism was blunted. It was during those years of Republican leadership that this world moved closer not to war but closer to peace than at any other time in the last three decades.

And I needn't remind you, but I will, that it's been during Democratic years that our strength to deter war has been stilled and even gone into a planned decline. It has been during Democratic years that we have weakly stumbled into conflicts, timidly refusing to draw our own lines against aggression, deceitfully refusing to tell even our own people of our full participation and tragically letting our finest men die on battlefields unmarked by purpose, unmarked by pride or the prospect of victory.

Yesterday it was Korea; tonight it is Vietnam. Make no bones of this. Don't try to sweep this under the rug. We are at war in Vietnam. And yet the President, who is the Commander in Chief of our forces, refuses to say, refuses to say mind you, whether or not the objective over there is victory, and his Secretary of Defense continues to mislead and misinform the American people and enough of it has gone by.

And I needn't remind you, but I will, it has been during Democratic years that a billion persons were cast into communist captivity and their fate cynically sealed.

Today—today in our beloved country we have an Administration which seems eager to deal with Communism in every coin known—from gold to wheat; from consulates to confidence, and even human freedom itself.

Now the Republican cause demands that we brand Communism as the principal disturber of peace in the world today. Indeed, we should brand it as the only significant disturber of the peace. And we must make clear that until its goals of conquest are absolutely renounced, and its relations with all nations tempered, Communism and the governments it now controls are enemies of every man on earth who is or wants to be free.

Now, we here in America can keep the peace only if we remain vigilant, and only if we remain strong. Only if we keep our eyes open and keep our guard up can we prevent war.

And I want to make this abundantly clear—I don't intend to let peace or freedom be torn from our grasp because of lack of strength, or lack of will—and that I promise you Americans.

I believe that we must look beyond the defense of freedom today to its extension tomorrow. I believe that the Communism which boasts it will bury us will instead give way to the forces of freedom. And I can see in the distant and yet recognizeable future the outlines of a world worthy of our dedication, our every risk, our every effort, our every sacrifice along the way. Yes, a world that will redeem the suffering of those who will be liberated from tyranny.

I can see, and I suggest that all thoughtful men must contemplate, the flowering of an Atlantic civilization, the whole world of Europe reunified and free, trading openly across its borders, communicating openly across the world.

This is a goal far, far more meaningful than a moon shot.

It's a truly inspiring goal for all free men to set for themselves during the latter half of the twentieth century. I can see and all free men must thrill to the events of this Atlantic civilization joined by a straight ocean highway to the United States. What a destiny! What a destiny can be ours to stand as a great central pillar linking Europe, the Americans, and the venerable and vital peoples and cultures of the Pacific.

I can see a day when all the Americas—North and South—will be linked in a mighty system—a system in which the errors and misunderstandings of the past will be submerged one by one in a rising tide of prosperity and interdependence.

We know that the misunderstandings of centuries are not to be wiped away in a day or wiped away in an hour. But we pledge, we pledge, that human sympathy—what our neighbors to the South call an attitude of sympatico—no less than enlightened self-interest will be our guide.

And I can see this Atlantic civilization galvanizing and guiding emergent nations everywhere. Now I know this freedom is not the fruit of every soil. I know that our own freedom was achieved through centuries by unremitting efforts by brave and wise men. And I know that the road to freedom is a long and a challenging road, and I know also that some men may walk away from it, that some men resist challenge, accepting the false security of governmental paternalism.

And I pledge that the America I envision in the years ahead will extend its hand in help in teaching and in cultivation so that all new nations will be at least encouraged to go our way; so that they will not wander down the dark alleys of tyranny or to the deadend streets of collectivism.

My fellow Republicans, we do no man a service by hiding freedom's light under a bushel of mistaken humility.

I seek an America proud of its past, proud of its ways, proud of its dreams and determined actively to proclaim them. But our examples to the world must, like charity, begin at home.

In our vision of a good and decent future, free and peaceful, there must be room, room for the liberation of the energy and the talent of the individual, otherwise our vision is blind at the outset.

We must assure a society here which while never abandoning the needy, or forsaking the helpless, nurtures incentives and opportunity for the creative and the productive.

We must know the whole good is the product of many single contributions. And I cherish the day when our children once again will restore as heroes the sort of men and women who, unafraid and undaunted, pursue the truth, strive to cure disease, subdue and make fruitful our natural environment, and produce the inventive engines of production, science, and technology.

This nation, whose creative people have enhanced this entire span of history, should again thrive upon the greatness of all those things which we—we as individual citizens—can and should do.

During Republican years, this again will be a nation of men and women, of families proud of their role, jealous of their responsibilities, unlimited in their aspirations—a nation where all who can will be self-reliant.

We Republicans see in our constitutional form of government the great framework which assures the orderly but dynamic fulfillment of the whole man, and we see the whole man as the great reason for instituting orderly government in the first place.

We can see in private property and in economy based upon and fostering private property the one way to make government a durable ally of the whole man rather than his determined enemy.

We see in the sanctity of private property the only durable foundation for constitutional government in a free society.

And beyond that we see and cherish diversity of ways, diversity of thoughts, of motives, and accomplishments. We don't seek to live anyone's life for him. We only seek to secure his rights, guarantee him opportunity, guarantee him opportunity to strive with government performing only those needed and constitutionally sanctioned tasks which cannot otherwise be performed.

We, Republicans, seek a government that attends to its inherent responsibilities of maintaining a stable monetary and fiscal climate, encouraging a free and a competitive economy and enforcing law and order.

Thus do we seek inventiveness, diversity, and creative difference within a stable order, for we Republicans define government's role where needed at many, many levels, preferably though the one closest to the people involved: our towns and our cities, then our counties, then our states then our regional contacts and only then the national government.

That, let me remind you, is the land of liberty built by decentralized power. On it also we must have balance between the branches of government at every level.

Balance, diversity, creative difference—these are the elements of Republican equation. Republicans agree, Republicans agree heartily, to disagree on many, many of their applications. But we have never disagreed on the basic fundamental issues of why you and I are Republicans.

This is a party—this Republican party is a party for free men. Not for blind followers and not for conformists.

Back in 1858 Abraham Lincoln said this of the Republican party, and I quote him because he probably could have said it during the last week or so: "It was composed of strained, discordant, and even hostile elements." End of quote.

Yet all of these elements agreed on one paramount objective: to arrest the progress of slavery, and place it in the course of ultimate extinction.

Today, as then, but more urgently and more broadly than then, the task of preserving and enlarging freedom at home and of safeguarding it from the forces of tyranny abroad is great enough to challenge all our resources and to require all our strength.

Anyone who joins us in all sincerity we welcome. Those, those who do not care for our cause, we don't expect to enter our ranks in any case. And let our Republicanism so focused and so dedicated not be made fuzzy and futile by unthinking and stupid labels.

I would remind you that extremism in the defense of liberty is no vice.

And let me remind you also that moderation in the pursuit of justice is no virtue!

By the beauty of the very system, we Republicans are pledged to restore and revitalize, the beauty of this Federal system of ours is in its reconciliation of diversity with unity. We must not see malice in honest differences of opinion, and no matter how great, so long as they are not inconsistent with the pledges we have given to each other in and through our Constitution.

Our Republican cause is not to level out the world or make its people conform in computer-regimented sameness. Our Republican cause is to free our people and light the way for liberty throughout the world. Ours is a very human cause for very humane goals. This party, its good people, and its unquestionable devotion to freedom will not fulfill the purposes of this campaign which we launch here now until our cause has won the day, inspired the world, and shown the way to a tomorow worthy of all our yesteryears.

I repeat, I accept your nomination with humbleness, with pride, and you and I are going to fight for the goodness of our land. Thank you.

Part VII

Libertarianism

Lyndon Johnson's staggering landslide over Barry Goldwater ensured the further development of Johnson's Great Society programs, and in the process, the continuation of the dominance of liberalism in American politics. The War on Poverty, civil rights legislation, environmental policies, education, and health—such goals represented the fulfillment of a liberal-progressive vision of society which was supported, it seemed, by the vast majority of the American people. Within a few months of the election, Johnson committed combat troops into Vietnam. By the summer of 1965, more than 100,000 troops were fighting in Southeast Asia; by August, riots in urban areas like Watts in Los Angeles helped conservatives challenge the basic tenets of liberal social policies. As Johnson found himself dragged into the quagmire of Vietnam (more than 500,000 troops would be there by the end of 1968), the Great Society faltered and died, a victim of "that bitch of a war," as Johnson called it, in Southeast Asia.

Conservatives fought against the Great Society while supporting the war in Vietnam. Their only criticism was that Johnson seemed unwilling to fight for a victory over communism. Rather, Johnson's incremental strategy and his fear of widening the war into North Vietnam, thereby drawing in communist China, contributed to a politically unpopular war at home. The emergence of an antiwar movement, mostly composed of left-wing student radicals, pacifists, and communists, combined with a growing specter of revolution in the wider society prompted by urban rioting, widespread drug use, and growing permissiveness, prompted a backlash against Johnson's liberalism that helped Republicans make crucial gains in 1966 mid-term congressional elections, and helped Ronald Reagan win election as governor of California.[1]

Conservatives never experienced the tumult over Vietnam that plagued the Left in the 1960s. Most factions of the conservative movement supported the war. However, there was one exception. A growing libertarian movement, never accepting the necessity of the Cold War, hostile to the national security state, and concerned with what such a state was doing to the republican tradition in America, reemerged in the 1960s, primarily due to Vietnam. Felix Morley, a founder of *Human Events*, told former Republican presidential candidate Alf Landon that "put baldly and bluntly, the Goldwater drive seems to me directly down the fairway towards fascism."[2] Murray Rothbard, an economist and old Right activist, wrote Morley praising his resistance to the Goldwater candidacy: "you were virtually the only one to have the fortitude to oppose the general adulation for Barry Goldwater . . . I believe I share your views on this and the major reasons for them: the abandonment by the 'conservative movement' of the older principles of 'isolationism' and the adoption instead of a suicidal crusade for a global nuclear war against the communist countries."[3]

Rothbard (1926–1995) would be instrumental in the development of libertarianism, a movement composed of individualists, classical liberals, Ayn Rand objectivists, and anarchists. Building on a rich individualist tradition in American thought, much of it important in the early conservative movement, and much of it forgotten by conservatives (John T. Flynn, Rose Wilder Lane, Robert Lefevre, Louis Bromfield, and Morley), Rothbard and assorted cohorts—primarily Leonard Liggio, a historian by training who helped found the Institute for Humane Studies in 1960, a veritable think-tank for the early libertarian movement—pushed for an alliance with libertarians in the New Left. The first step in this process was the journal *Left and Right: A Journal of Libertarian Thought*. The first editorial statement from *Left and Right*, as well as the Rothbard authored editorial "Why Be Libertarian?" are included herein in Chapters 24 and 25, respectively.

Getting the New Left and right-wing libertarians together proved a difficult task, especially as the New Left turned increasingly toward revolution and communism in the late 1960s. Yet, Rothbard, Liggio, and others persevered and allowed for the publication of a significant amount of revisionist history on the Cold War in *Left and Right*. Such revisionism threatened conservative anticommunist interpretations of the Cold War and undermined a continued necessity to wage the Cold War against the Soviet Union. Frank Meyer recognized the threat of right-wing libertarianism and in 1969, published "Libertarianism or Libertinism?" in *National Review*. Libertarian young people, prompted by Rothbard and Karl Hess, a former conservative speechwriter for Goldwater, had just recently attempted to organize a libertarian takeover of Young Americans for Freedom at a fiery national convention in St. Louis. While rebuffed in their takeover effort, many YAF chapters were sundered by libertarian students, with a few hundred leaving the organization to form the Society for ndividual Liberty (SIL). The effort to merge libertarian influence with the New Left (embodied by the increasingly paranoid, and Stalinist, remnant of Students for a Democratic Society, the Weathermen), suggested to Meyer a move away from freedom and toward libertinism, a philosophy that represented, in its "do your own thing" mentality, a threat to social order.[4]

Eventually, as the tumult of the sixties faded, libertarians organized their own think-tanks, like the CATO Institute; their own journals, like *Reason* magazine; their own book stores, like the mail-order *Laissez-Faire Books*; and even their own political party, the Libertarian Party. Determined to fight on behalf of maximum individual freedom and against the welfare state, libertarians have greatly influenced American conservatism since the 1960s, especially in helping to reconstruct conservative economic principles on free trade, regulation, and taxes. They also mellowed, forming alliances when convenient to do so and reintegrating themselves into the wider debate over what conservatism and libertarianism have to offer American society. In this spirit, Chapter 27, also written by Rothbard, attempts to explain some of the "Myths and Truths About Libertarianism." Taken from a speech at the 1979 meeting of the Philadelphia Society, a conservative intellectual society formed in 1964, Rothbard offers a far more temperate defense of libertarianism than was offered in the mid-1960s. Part of a wider panel on conservatism and libertarianism, the papers were published in the traditionalist journal *Modern Age,* another sign of growing moderation and respect for diverse views. Maybe fusionism was working after all.

Chapter Twenty-four

The Libertarian Review
Editorial Statement

A new journal of opinion must justify its existence; our justification is a deep commitment to the liberty of man. Our aim is to present articles that embody scholarship; but not a scholarship random, unfocussed, or devoted to minute examination of trivia. Ours will be a scholarship finely honed for use as a weapon in expanding, deepening, and refining the knowledge of and commitment to liberty in all its critical aspects and ramifications. It will cut across the insularity of disciplines. Above all, it will not remain on the level of glittering generalities, for anyone can pay lip-service to liberty if it entails no specific consequences in policy or action. General principles remain cloudy verbiage if they are not made systematic and applied to specific problems; and responses to such problems must stay hopelessly confused if they remain *ad hoc* and unsubsumed under guiding principle. This journal proposes to advance the integration of the general and the specific, the unity of the theory and practice of liberty. While each contributor is of course solely responsible for articles under his name, and we do not expect to agree with every point in every article, we intend each article to be fully consistent with our aims.

Liberty, then, is our thesis; reason shall be our method. Only reason can build a valid and consistent ideology, and only reason can strip unsparingly the veil of custom and habit and myth from dominant ideas and institutions and hold them up to the harsh light of truth. That reason is cold, impersonal, and unconcerned is a widespread myth; indeed, nothing is stronger than reason for redoubling one's passionate commitment and devotion to the cause of truth.

Our title, *Left and Right*, reflects our concerns in several ways. It reveals

From *Left and Right: A Journal of Libertarian Thought* 1 (Spring 1965): 1. Copyright 2002 by the Ludwig Van Mises Institute, all rights reserved. Reprinted by permission.

our editorial concern with the ideological; and it also highlights our conviction that the present-day categories of "left" and "right" have become misleading and obsolete, and that the doctrine of liberty contains elements corresponding with both contemporary left and right. This means in no sense that we are middle-of-the-roaders, eclectically trying to combine, or step between, both poles; but rather that a consistent view of liberty includes concepts that have also become part of the rhetoric or program of right and of left. Hence a creative approach to liberty must transcend the confines of contemporary political shibboleths.

There is a ferment abrewing in America, and the smug apathy of the 1950s is now virtually forgotten. And yet conservative and profoundly anti-intellectual views born amidst that apathy, linger on to hamper innovations of thought and action. Such view, for example, that an end has been put to ideology, and that doctrine and ideology can no longer have an impact on American life. The upsurge of new forms of ideology and activism since the end of the 'fifties has been increasingly refuting this counsel of passivity. Out of its confrontation with harsh reality, this new ferment has instinctively spurned the old and faulty categories; it sees that the old doctrines and the old leaders have led the world astray. This upsurge needs to develop an ideology which will be consistent with its keen insight into the realities of our time. Hopefully, the new dimensions of *Left and Right*'s creative thought will contribute substance and rigor to this decisive awakening.

Chapter Twenty-five

Why Be Libertarian?

Murray N. Rothbard

Why be libertarian, anyway? By this we mean: what's the point of the whole thing? Why engage in a deep and lifelong commitment to the principle and the goal of individual liberty? For such a commitment, in our largely unfree world, means inevitably a radical disagreement with, and alienation from, the status quo, an alienation which equally inevitably imposes many sacrifices in money and prestige. When life is short and the moment of victory far in the future, why go through all this?

Incredibly, we have found among the increasing number of libertarians in this country many people who come to a libertarian commitment from one or another extremely narrow and personal point of view. Many are irresistibly attracted to liberty as an intellectual system or as an aesthetic goal, but liberty remains for them a purely intellectual and parlor game, totally divorced from what they consider the "real" activities of their daily lives. Others are motivated to remain libertarians solely from their antic-ipation of their own personal financial profit. Realizing that a free market would provide far greater opportunities for able, independent men to reap entrepreneurial profits, they become and remain libertarians solely to find larger opportunities for business profit. While it is true that opportunities for profit will be far greater and more widespread in a free market and a free society, placing one's *primary* emphasis on this moti-vation for being a libertarian can only be considered grotesque. For in the often tortuous, difficult, and gruelling path that must be trod before

From *Left and Right: A Journal of Libertarian Thought* 2: 3 (Autumn 1966): 5–10.

254 MURRAY N. ROTHBARD

liberty can be achieved, the libertarian's opportunities for personal profit will far more often be negative than abundant.

The consequence of the narrow and myopic vision of both the gamester and the would-be profitmaker is that neither group has the slightest interest in the work of building a libertarian movement. And yet it is only through building such a movement that liberty may ultimately be achieved. Ideas, and especially radical ideas, do not advance in the world in and by themselves, as it were in a vacuum; they can only be advanced by *people,* and therefore the development and advancement of such people—and therefore of a "movement"—becomes a prime task for the libertarian who is really serious about advancing his goals.

Turning from these men of narrow vision, we must also see that utilitarianism—the common ground of free-market economists—is unsatisfactory for developing a flourishing libertarian movement. While it is true and valuable to know that a free market would bring far greater abundance and a healthier economy to everyone, rich and poor alike, a critical problem is whether this knowledge is enough to bring many people to a lifelong dedication to liberty. In short, how many people will man the barricades and endure the many sacrifices that a consistent devotion to liberty entails, merely so that umpteen percent more people will have better bathtubs? Will they not rather settle for an easy life and forget the umpteen percent bathtubs? Ultimately, then, utilitarian economics, while indispensable in the developed structure of libertarian thought and action, is almost as unsatisfactory a basic groundwork for the Movement as those opportunists who simply seek a short-range profit.

It is our view that a flourishing libertarian movement, a lifelong dedication to liberty, can only be grounded on a passion for justice. Here must be the mainspring of our drive, the armor that will sustain us in all the storms ahead: not the search for a quick buck, the playing of intellectual games, or the cool calculation of general economic gains. And to have a passion for justice one must have a *theory* of what justice and injustice are—in short, a set of ethical principles of justice and injustice which cannot be provided by utilitarian economics. It is because we see the world reeking with injustices piled one on another to the very heavens that we are impelled to do all that we can to seek a world in which these and other injustices will be eradicated. Other traditional radical goals—such as the "abolition of poverty"—are, in contrast to this one, truly Utopian; for man, simply by exerting his will, cannot abolish poverty. Poverty can only be abolished through the operation of certain economic factors—notably the investment of savings in capital—which can only operate by transforming nature over a long period of time. In short, man's will is here severely limited by the workings of—to use an old-fashioned but still valid term—natural law. But *injustices* are deeds that are inflicted by one set of men on another; they are precisely the actions of men, and hence they and their elimination *are* subject to man's instantaneous will.

Let us take an example: England's centuries-long occupation and brutal oppression of the Irish people. Now if, in 1900, we had looked at the state of Ireland, and we had considered the poverty of the Irish people, we would have had to say: that poverty could be improved by the English getting out and removing their land monopolies, but that the ultimate elimination of poverty in Ireland, under the best of conditions, would have to take time and be subject to the workings of economic law. But the goal of ending English oppression—that *could* have been done by the instantaneous action of men's will; by the English simply deciding to pull out of the country. The fact that of course such decisions do not take place instantaneously is not the point; the point is that that very failure is an injustice that has been decided upon and imposed by the perpetrators of injustice: in this case the English government. In the field of justice, man's will is all: men *can* move mountains, if only enough men so decide. A passion for instantaneous justice—in short, a radical passion—is therefore *not* Utopian, as would be a desire for the instant elimination of poverty or the instant transformation of everyone into a concert pianist. For instant justice *could* be achieved if enough people so willed.

A true passion for justice, then, must be *radical*—in short, it must at least *wish* to attain its goals radically and instantaneously. Leonard E. Read, President of the Foundation for Economic Education, expressed this radical spirit very aptly twenty years ago when he wrote a pamphlet, *I'd Push the Button*. The problem was what to do about the network of price and wage controls then being imposed on the economy by the Office of Price Administration. Most economic liberals were timidly or "realistically" advocating one or another form of gradual or staggered decontrols; at that point Mr. Read took an unequivocal and radical stand on principle: "If there were a button on this rostrum," he began his address, "the pressing of which would release all wage and price controls instantaneously, I would put my finger on it and push!"[1] The true test, then, of the radical spirit, is the button-pushing test: if we could push the button for instantaneous abolition of unjust invasions of liberty, would we do it? If we would *not* do it, we could scarcely call ourselves libertarians, and most of us would only do it if primarily guided by a passion for justice.

The genuine libertarian, then, is, in all senses of the word, an "abolitionist"; he would, if he could, abolish instantaneously all invasions of liberty: whether it be, in the original coining of the term, slavery, or it be the manifold other instances of State oppression. He would, in the words of another libertarian in a similar connection: "blister my thumb pushing that button!" The libertarian must perforce be a "button-pusher" and an "abolitionist." Powered by justice, he cannot be moved by amoral utilitarian pleas that justice not come about until the criminals are "compensated." Thus, when in the early nineteenth century, the great abolitionist movement arose, voices of moderation promptly appeared counselling that it would only be fair to abolish slavery if the slave-masters were financially compensated for their loss. In short, after centuries of oppression and exploitation, the slave-masters were supposed to be further rewarded by a handsome sum mulcted by force from the mass of innocent taxpayers! The most apt comment on this proposal was made by the English Philosophical Radical Benjamin Pearson, who remarked that "he had thought it was the slaves who should have been compensated"; clearly, such compensation could only justly have come from the slave-holders themselves.[2]

Anti-libertarians, and anti-radicals generally, characteristically make the point that such "abolitionism" is "unrealistic"; by making such a charge they are hopelessly confusing the desired goal with a strategic estimate of the probable outcome. In framing principle, it is of the utmost importance *not* to mix in strategic estimates with the forging of desired goals. *First,* one must formulate one's goals, which in this case would be the instant abolition of slavery or whatever other statist oppression we are considering. And we must first frame these goals without considering the probability of attaining them. The libertarian goals are "realistic" in the sense that they *could* be achieved *if* enough people agreed on their desirability, and that if achieved they would bring about a far better world. The "realism" of the goal can only be challenged by a critique of the goal *itself,* not in the problem of how to attain it. Then, *after* we have decided on the goal, we face the entirely separate strategic question of how to attain that goal as rapidly as possible, how to build a movement to attain it, etc. Thus, William Lloyd Garrison was not being "unrealistic"

when, in the 1830s, he raised the glorious standard of immediate emancipation of the slaves. His goal was the proper one; and his strategic realism
came in the fact that he did not *expect* his goal to be quickly reached. Or,
as Garrison himself distinguished: "Urge immediate abolition as earnestly
as we may, it will, alas! be gradual abolition in the end. We have never
said that slavery would be overthrown by a single blow; that it ought to
be, we shall always contend."[3]

Actually, in the realm of the strategic, raising the banner of pure and
radical principle is generally the fastest way of arriving at radical goals.
For if the pure goal is never brought to the fore, there will never be any
momentum developed for driving toward it. Slavery would never have
been abolished at all if the abolitionists had not raised the hue and cry
thirty years earlier; and, as things came to pass, the abolition was at
virtually a single blow rather than gradual or compensated.[4] But above
and beyond the requirements of strategy lie the commands of justice. In
his famous editorial that launched *The Liberator* at the beginning of 1831,
William Lloyd Garrison repented his previous adoption of the doctrine
of gradual abolition: "I seize this opportunity to make a full and unequivocal recantation, and thus publicly to ask pardon of my God, of my
country, and of my brethren, the poor slaves, for having uttered a sentiment so full of timidity, injustice and absurdity." Upon being reproached
for the habitual severity and heat of his language, Garrison retorted: "I
have need to be all on fire, for I have mountains of ice about me to melt."
It is this spirit that must mark the man truly dedicated to the cause of
liberty.[5]

NOTES

1. Leonard E. Read, *I'd Push the Button* (New York: Joseph D. McGuire, 1946)
p. 3.

2. William D Grampp, *The Manchester School of Economics* (Stanford, Calif.:
Stanford University Press, 1960), p. 59.

3. Quoted in William H. and Jane H. Pease, eds., *The Antislavery Argument*
(Indianapolis, Ind.: Bobbs-Merrill, 1965), p. xxxv.

4. At the conclusion of a brilliant philosophical critique of the charge of
"unrealism" and its confusion of the good and the currently probable, Professor
Philbrook declares: "Only one type of serious defense of a policy is open to an
economist or anyone else: he must maintain that the policy is good. True 'realism'

is the same thing men have always meant by wisdom: to decide the immediate in the light of the ultimate." Clarence Philbrook, " 'Realism' in Policy Espousal," *American Economic Review* (December, 1953), p. 859.

5. For the quotes from Garrison, see Louis Ruchames, ed., *The Abolitionists* (New York: Capricorn Books, 1964), p. 31, and Fawn M. Brodie, "Who Defends the Abolitionist?" in Martin Duberman, ed., *The Antislavery Vanguard* (Princeton: Princeton University Press, 1965), p. 67. The Duberman work is a storehouse of valuable material, including refutations of the common effort by those committed to the status quo to engage in psychological smearing of radicals in general and abolitionists in particular. See especially Martin Duberman, "The Northern Response to Slavery," in ibid., pp. 406–413.

Chapter Twenty-six

Libertarianism or Libertinism?

Frank S. Meyer

The development of contemporary American conservatism has been marked, on the theoretical level, by a continuing tension between a traditionalist emphasis and a libertarian emphasis. Over the years I have argued that these positions are in fact not incompatible opposites, but complementary poles of a tension and balance which, both in theory and practice, define American conservatism as it has come into being at midcentury. If anything, I have stressed the libertarian emphasis because I have felt that unmodified traditionalism, stressing virtue and order in disregard of the ontological and social status of the freedom of the individual person, tended dangerously towards an authoritarianism wrong in itself and alien to the spirit of American conservatism.

Recently, however, there have been ominous signs that the danger of a disbalance just as alien to conservatism is arising not from traditionalist quarters, but from an untrammeled libertarianism, which tends as directly to anarchy and nihilism as unchecked traditionalism tends to authoritarianism. This libertarianism can be seen at its most extreme in such dropouts from the Right as Murray Rothbard and Karl Hess and their handful of followers. While their position has become indistinguishable from that of the SDS, there are increasing signs of a more widespread, if more moderate, development in this direction, primarily among the young, but by no means restricted to them. The essential rationale of this position is so far removed from the rationale of libertarian conservatism and so completely ignores the proper foundations of liberty in the actual circumstances of the human condition that, like the position of the

From *National Review,* September 9, 1969, p. 910. Copyright 1969 by National Review, Inc., 215 Lexington Avenue, New York, NY 10016. Reprinted by permission.

anarchist wing of the SDS, its proper denomination is not libertarianism but libertinism.

A true libertarianism is derived from metaphysical roots in the very constitution of being, and places its defense of freedom as a political end in the context of moral responsibility for the pursuit of virtue and the underlying social necessity for the preservation of order. The libertine impulse that masquerades as libertarianism, on the other hand, disregards all moral responsibility, ranges itself against the minimum needs of social order, and raises the freedom of the individual person (regarded as the unbridled expression of every desire, intellectual or emotional) to the status of an absolute end.

Libertine Ideologues

The underlying issue between conservative libertarianism and libertine libertarianism is at bottom a totally opposed view of the nature and destiny of men. The libertines—like those other products of the modern world, ritualistic liberals, socialists, Communists, fascists—are ideologues first and last. That is, they reject reality as it has been studied, grasped, understood, and acted upon in five thousand years or so of civilized history and pose an abstract construction as the basis of action. They would replace God's creation of this multifarious, complex world in which we live and substitute for it their own creation, simple, neat, and inhuman—as inhuman as the blueprints of the bulldozing engineer.

The place of freedom in the spiritual economy of men is a high one indeed, but it is specific and not absolute. By its very nature, it cannot be an end of men's existence. Its meaning is essentially freedom from coercion, but that, important as it is, cannot be an end. It is empty of goal or norm. Its function is to relieve men of external coercion so that they may freely seek their good.

It is for this reason that libertarian conservatives champion freedom as the end of the *political* order: politics, which is, at its core, the disposition of force in society, will, if not directed towards this end, create massive distortions and obstacles in men's search for their good. But that said, an equally important question remains. Free, how are men to use their freedom? The libertine answers that they should do what they want. Sometimes, in the line of the philosophers of the French Revolution, he arbitrarily posits the universal benevolence of human beings. He presumes that if everyone does whatever he wants, everything will be for the best in the best of all possible worlds. But whether so optimistically qualified or not, his answer ignores the hard facts of history. For it is only in civilization that men have begun to rise towards their potentiality; and civilization is a fragile growth, constantly menaced by the dark forces that suck man back towards his brutal beginnings.

Reason and Tradition

The essence of civilization, however, is tradition; no single generation of men can of itself discover the proper ends of human existence. At its best, as understood by contemporary American conservatism, the traditionalist view accepts political freedom, accepts the role of reason and innovation and criticism; but it insists, if civilization is to be preserved, that reason operate within tradition and that political freedom is only effectively achieved when the bulwarks of civilizational order are preserved.

Libertine libertarianism would shatter those bulwarks. In its opposition to the maintenance of defenses against Communism, its puerile sympathy with the rampaging mobs of campus and ghetto, its contempt for the humdrum wisdom of the great producing majority, it is directed towards the destruction of the civilizational order which is the only real foundation in a real world for the freedom it espouses. The first victim of the mobs let loose by the weakening of civilizational restraint will be, as it has always been, freedom—for anyone, anywhere.

Chapter Twenty-seven

What Is Libertarianism?

Murray N. Rothbard

Libertarianism is the fastest growing political creed in America today. Before judging and evaluating libertarianism, it is vitally important to find out precisely what that doctrine is, and, more particularly, what it is not. It is especially important to clear up a number of misconceptions about libertarianism that are held by most people, and particularly by conservatives. In this essay I shall enumerate and critically analyze the most common myths that are held about libertarianism. When these are cleared away, people will then be able to discuss libertarianism free of egregious myths and misconceptions, and to deal with it as it should be—on its very own merits or demerits.

Myth #1: *Libertarians believe that each individual is an isolated, hermetically sealed atom, acting in a vacuum without influencing each other.* This is a common charge, but a highly puzzling one. In a lifetime of reading libertarian and classical liberal literature, I have not come across a single theorist or writer who holds anything like this position. The only possible exception is the fanatical Max Stirner, a mid-19th century German individualist who, however, has had minimal influence upon libertarianism in his time and since. Moreover, Stirner's explicit "Might Makes Right" philosophy and his repudiation of all moral principles including individual rights as "spooks in the head," scarcely qualifies him as a libertarian in any sense. Apart from Stirner, however, there is no body of opinion even remotely resembling this common indictment.

Libertarians are methodological and political individualists, to be sure. They believe that only individuals think, value, act, and choose. They

From: *Modern Age* (Winter 1980). Reprinted by permission of Intercollegiate Studies Institute, Wilmington, Del. All rights reserved.

believe that each individual has the right to own his own body, free of coercive interference. But no individualist denies that people are influencing each other all the time in their goals, values, pursuit, and occupations. As F. A. Hayek pointed out in his notable article, "The Non-Sequitur of the 'Dependence Effect,'" John Kenneth Galbraith's assault upon free-market economics in his best-selling *The Affluent Society* rested on this proposition: economics assumes that every individual arrives at his scale of values totally on his own, without being subject to influence by anyone else. On the contrary, as Hayek replied, everyone knows that most people do not originate their own values, but are influenced to adopt them by other people.[1] No individualist or libertarian denies that people influence each other all the time, and surely there is nothing wrong with this inevitable process. What libertarians are opposed to is not voluntary persuasion, but the coercive imposition of values by the use of force and police power. Libertarians are in no way opposed to the voluntary cooperation and collaboration between individuals: only to the compulsory pseudo-"cooperation" imposed by the state.

Myth #2: Libertarians are libertines: they are hedonists who hanker after "alternative life-styles." This myth has recently been propounded by Irving Kristol, who identifies the libertarian ethic with the "hedonistic" and asserts that libertarians "worship the Sears Roebuck catalogue and all the 'alternative life styles' that capitalist affluence permits the individual to choose from."[2] The fact is that libertarianism is not and does not pretend to be a complete moral or aesthetic theory; it is only a *political* theory, that is, the important subset of moral theory that deals with the proper role of violence in social life. Political theory deals with what is proper or improper for government to do, and government is distinguished from every other group in society as being the institution of organized violence. Libertarianism holds that the *only* proper role of violence is to defend person and property *against* violence, that any use of violence that goes beyond such just defense is itself aggressive, unjust, and criminal. Libertarianism, therefore, is a theory which states that everyone should be free of violent invasion, should be free to do as he sees fit except invade the person or property of another. What a person *does* with his or her life is vital and important, but is simply irrelevant to libertarianism.

It should not be surprising, therefore, that there are libertarians who are indeed hedonists and devotees of alternative life-styles, and that there are also libertarians who are firm adherents of "bourgeois" conventional or religious morality. There are libertarian libertines and there are libertarians who cleave firmly to the disciplines of natural or religious law. There are other libertarians who have no moral theory at all apart from the imperative of non-violation of rights. That is because libertarianism per se has no general or personal moral theory. Libertarianism does not offer a way of life; it offers liberty, so that each person is free to adopt and act upon his own values and moral principles. Libertarians agree with Lord Acton that "liberty is the highest political end"—not necessarily the highest end on everyone's personal scale of values.

There is no question about the fact, however, that the sub-set of libertarians who are free-market economists tends to be delighted when the free market leads to a wider range of choices for consumers, and thereby raises their standard of living. Unquestionably, the idea that prosperity is better than grinding poverty is a moral proposition, and it ventures into the realm of general moral theory, but it is still not a proposition for which I should wish to apologize.

Myth #3: *Libertarians do not believe in moral principles; they limit themselves to cost-benefit analysis on the assumption that man is always rational.* This myth is of course related to the preceding charge of hedonism, and some of it can be answered in the same way. There are indeed libertarians, particularly Chicago-school economists, who refuse to believe that liberty and individual rights are moral principles, and instead attempt to arrive at public policy by weighing alleged social costs and benefits.

In the first place, most libertarians are "subjectivists" in economics, that is, they believe that the utilities and costs of different individuals cannot be added or measured. Hence, the very concept of social costs and benefits is illegitimate. But, more importantly, most libertarians rest their case on moral principles, on a belief in the natural rights of every individual to his person or property. They therefore believe in the absolute immorality of aggressive violence, of invasion of those rights to person or property, regardless of which person or group commits such violence.

Far from being immoral, libertarians simply apply a universal human ethic to *government* in the same way as almost everyone would apply such an ethic to every other person or institution in society. In particular, as I have noted earlier, libertarianism as a political philosophy dealing with the proper role of violence takes the universal ethic that most of us hold toward violence and applies it fearlessly to government. Libertarians make no exceptions to the golden rule and provide no moral loophole, no double standard, for government. That is, libertarians believe that murder is murder and does not become sanctified by reasons of state if committed by the government. We believe that theft is theft and does not become legitimated because organized robbers call their theft "taxation." We believe that enslavement is enslavement even if the institution committing that act calls it "conscription." In short, the key to libertarian theory is that it makes no exceptions in its universal ethic for government.

Hence, far from being indifferent or hostile to moral principles, libertarians fulfill them by being the only group willing to extend those principles across the board to government itself.[3]

It is true that libertarians would allow each individual to choose his values and to act upon them, and would in short accord every person the right to be either moral or immoral as he saw fit. Libertarianism is strongly opposed to enforcing any moral creed on any person or group by the use of violence—except, of course, the moral prohibition against aggressive violence itself. But we must realize that no action can be considered *virtuous* unless it is undertaken freely, by a person's voluntary consent. As Frank Meyer pointed out:

> Men cannot be forced to be free, nor can they even be forced to be virtuous. To a certain extent, it is true, they can be forced to act as though they were virtuous. But virtue is the fruit of well-used freedom. And no act to the degree that it is coerced can partake of virtue—or of vice.[4]

If a person is forced by violence or the threat thereof to perform a certain action, then it can no longer be a moral choice on his part. The morality of an action can stem only from its being freely adopted; an action can scarcely be called moral if someone is compelled to perform it at gunpoint. Compelling moral actions or outlawing immoral actions, therefore, cannot be said to foster the spread of morality or virtue. On the contrary, coercion atrophies morality for it takes away from the individual the freedom to be either moral or immoral, and therefore forcibly deprives people of the chance to be moral. Paradoxically, then, a compulsory morality robs us of the very opportunity to be moral.

It is furthermore particularly grotesque to place the guardianship of morality in the hands of the state apparatus—that is, none other than the organization of policemen, guards, and soldiers. Placing the state in charge of moral principles is equivalent to putting the proverbial fox in charge of the chicken coop. Whatever else we may say about them, the wielders of organized violence in society have never been distinguished by their high moral tone or by the precision with which they uphold moral principle.

Myth #4: *Libertarianism is atheistic and materialist, and neglects the spiritual side of life.* There is no necessary connection between being for or against libertarianism and one's position on religion. It is true that many if not most libertarians at the present time are atheists, but this correlates with the fact that most intellectuals, of most political persuasions, are atheists as well. There are many libertarians who are theists, Jewish or Christian. Among the classical liberal forebears of modern libertarianism in a more religious age there were a myriad of Christians: from John Lilburne, Roger Williams, Anne Hutchinson, and John Locke in the seventeenth century, down to Cobden and Bright, Frederic Bastiat and the French laissez-faire liberals, and the great Lord Acton.

Libertarians believe that liberty is a natural right embedded in a natural law of what is proper for mankind, in accordance with man's nature. *Where* this set of natural laws comes from, whether it is purely natural or originated by a creator, is an important ontological question but is irrelevant to social or political philosophy. As Father Thomas Davitt declares: "If the word 'natural' means anything at all, it refers to the nature of a man, and when used with 'law,' 'natural' must refer to an ordering that is manifested in the inclinations of a man's nature and to nothing else. Hence, taken in itself, there is nothing religious or theological in the 'Natural Law' of Aquinas."[5] Or, as D'Entrèves writes of the seventeenth-century Dutch Protestant jurist Hugo Grotius:

> [Grotius'] definition of natural law has nothing revolutionary. When he maintains that natural law is that body of rule which Man is able to discover by the use of his reason, he does nothing but restate the Scholastic notion of a rational foundation of ethics. Indeed, his aim is rather to restore that notion which had been shaken by the extreme Augustinianism of certain Protestant currents of thought. When he declares that these rules are valid in themselves, independently of the fact that God willed them, he repeats an assertion which had already been made by some of the schoolmen . . .[6]

Libertarianism has been accused of ignoring man's spiritual nature. But one can easily arrive at libertarianism from a religious or Christian position: emphasizing the importance of the individual, of his freedom of will, of natural rights and private property. Yet one can also arrive at all these self-same positions by a secular, natural law approach, through a belief that man can arrive at a rational apprehension of the natural law.

Historically furthermore, it is not at all clear that religion is a firmer footing than secular natural law for libertarian conclusions. As Karl Witt-fogel reminded us in his *Oriental Despotism,* the union of throne and altar has been used for centuries to fasten a reign of despotism on society.[7] Historically, the union of church and state has been in many instances a mutually reinforcing coalition for tyranny. The state used the church to sanctify and preach obedience to its supposedly divinely sanctioned rule; the church used the state to gain income and privilege. The Anabaptists collectivized and tyrannized Munster in the name of the Christian reli-gion.[8] And, closer to our century, Christian socialism and the social gospel have played a major role in the drive toward statism, and the apologetic role of the Orthodox Church in Soviet Russia has been all too clear. Some Catholic bishops in Latin America have even proclaimed that the only route to the kingdom of heaven is through Marxism, and if I wished to be nasty, I could point out that the Reverend Jim Jones, in addition to being a Leninist, also proclaimed himself the reincarnation of Jesus.

Moreover, now that socialism has manifestly failed, politically and economically, socialists have fallen back on the "moral" and the "spiri-tual" as the final argument for their cause. Socialist Robert Heilbroner, in arguing that socialism will have to be coercive and will have to impose a "collective morality" upon the public, opines that: "Bourgeois culture is focused on the *material achievement* of the individual. Socialist culture must focus on his or her *moral or spiritual* achievement." The intriguing point is that this position of Heilbroner's was hailed by the conservative religious writer for *National Review,* Dale Vree. He writes:

> Heilbroner is . . . saying what many contributors to *NR* have said over the last quarter-century: you can't have both freedom and virtue. Take note, traditionalists. Despite his dissonant terminology, Heilbroner is interested in the same thing you're interested in: virtue.[9]

Vree is also fascinated with the Heilbroner view that a socialist culture must "foster the primacy of the collectivity" rather than the "primacy of the individual." He quotes Heilbroner's contrasting "moral or spiritual" achievement under socialism as against bourgeois "material" achievement, and adds correctly: "There is a traditional ring to that statement." Vree goes on to applaud Heilbroner's attack on capitalism because it has "no sense of 'the good' " and permits "consenting adults" to do anything they please. In contrast to this picture of freedom and permitted diversity, Vree writes that "Heilbroner says alluringly, because a socialist society must have a sense of 'the good,' not everything will be permitted." To

Vree, it is impossible "to have economic collectivism along with cultural individualism," and so he is inclined to lean toward a new "socialist-traditionalist fusionism"—toward collectivism across the board.

We may note here that socialism becomes especially despotic when it replaces "economic" or "material" incentives by allegedly "moral" or "spiritual" ones, when it affects to promoting an indefinable "quality of life" rather than economic prosperity. When payment is adjusted to productivity there is considerably more freedom as well as higher standards of living. For when reliance is placed solely on altruistic devotion to the socialist motherland, the devotion has to be regularly reinforced by the knout. An increasing stress on individual material incentive means ineluctably a greater stress on private property and keeping what one earns, and brings with it considerably more personal freedom, as witness Yugoslavia in the last three decades in contrast to Soviet Russia. The most horrifying despotism on the face of the earth in recent years was undoubtedly Pol Pot's Cambodia, in which "materialism" was so far obliterated that money was abolished by the regime. With money and private property abolished, each individual was totally dependent on handouts of rationed subsistence from the state, and life was a sheer hell. We should be careful before we sneer at "merely material" goals or incentives.

The charge of "materialism" directed against the free market ignores the fact that *every* human action whatsoever involves the transformation of material objects by the use of human energy and in accordance with ideas and purposes held by the actors. It is impermissible to separate the "mental" or "spiritual" from the "material." All great works of art, great emanations of the human spirit, have had to employ material objects: whether they be canvasses, brushes and paint, paper and musical instruments, or building blocks and raw materials for churches. There is no real rift between the "spiritual" and the "material" and hence any despotism over and crippling of the material will cripple the spiritual as well.

Myth #5: Libertarians are utopians who believe that all people are good, and that therefore state control is not necessary. Conservatives tend to add that since human nature is either partially or wholly evil, strong state regulation is therefore necessary for society.

This is a very common belief about libertarians, yet it is difficult to know the source of this misconception. Rousseau, the *locus classicus* of the idea that man is good but is corrupted by his institutions, was scarcely a libertarian. Apart from the romantic writings of a few anarcho-communists, whom I would not consider libertarians in any case, I know of no libertarian or classical liberal writers who have held this view. On the contrary, most libertarian writers hold that man is a mixture of good and evil and therefore that it is important for social institutions to encourage the good and discourage the bad. The state is the only social institution which is able to extract its income and wealth by coercion; all others must obtain revenue either by selling a product or service to customers or by receiving voluntary gifts. And the state is the only institution which can use the revenue from this organized theft to presume to control and regulate people's lives and property. Hence, the institution of the state establishes a socially legitimatized and sanctified channel for bad people to do bad things, to commit regularized theft and to wield dictatorial power. Statism therefore encourages the bad, or at least the criminal elements of human nature. As Frank H. Knight trenchantly put it: "The probability of the people in power being individuals who would dislike the possession and exercise of power is on a level with the probability that an extremely tenderhearted person would get the job of whipping master in a slave plantation."[10] A free society, by not establishing such a legitimated channel for theft and tyranny, discourages the criminal tendencies of human nature and encourages the peaceful and the voluntary. Liberty and the free market discourage aggression and compulsion, and encourage the harmony and mutual benefit of voluntary interpersonal exchanges, economic, social, and cultural.

Since a system of liberty would encourage the voluntary and discourage the criminal, and would remove the only legitimated channel for crime and aggression, we could expect that a free society would indeed suffer less from violent crime and aggression than we do now, though there is no warrant for assuming that they would disappear completely. That is not utopianism, but a common-sense implication of the change in what is considered socially legitimate, and in the reward-and-penalty structure in society.

We can approach our thesis from another angle. If all men were good and none had criminal tendencies, then there would indeed be no need for a state as conservatives concede. But if on the other hand all men were evil, then the case for the state is just as shaky, since why should anyone assume that those men who form the government and obtain all the guns and the power to coerce others, should be magically exempt from the badness of all the other persons outside the government? Tom Paine, a classical libertarian often considered to be naively optimistic about human nature, rebutted the conservative evil-human-nature argument for a strong state as follows: "If all human nature be corrupt, it is needless to strengthen the corruption by establishing a succession of kings, who be they ever so base, are still to be obeyed . . ." Paine added that "No man since the fall hath ever been equal to the trust of being given power over all."[11] And as the libertarian F. A. Harper once wrote:

> Still using the same principle that political rulership should be employed to the extent of the evil in man, we would then have a society in which complete political ruler-ship of all the affairs of everybody would be called for. . . . One man would rule all. But who would serve as the dictator? However he were to be selected and affixed to the political throne, he would surely be a totally evil person, since all men are evil. And this society would then be ruled by a totally evil dictator possessed of total political power. And how, in the name of logic, could anything short of total evil be its consequence? How could it be better than having no political ruler-ship at all in that society?[12]

Finally, since, as we have seen, men are actually a mixture of good and evil, a regime of liberty serves to encourage the good and discourage the bad, at least in the sense that the voluntary and mutually beneficial are good and the criminal is bad. In no theory of human nature, then, whether it be goodness, badness, or a mixture of the two, can statism be justified. In the course of denying the notion that he is a conservative, the classical liberal F. A. Hayek pointed out: "The main merit of individual-ism [which Adam Smith and his contemporaries advocated] is that it is a system under which bad men can do least harm. It is a social system which does not depend for its functioning on our finding good men for running it, or on all men becoming better than they now are, but which makes use of men in all their given variety and complexity . . ."[13]

It is important to note what differentiates libertarians from utopians in the pejorative sense. Libertarianism does not set out to remould human nature. One of socialism's major goals is to create, which in practice means by totalitarian methods, a New Socialist Man, an individual whose major goal will be to work diligently and altruistically for the collective. Libertarianism is a political philosophy which says: Given any existent human nature, liberty is the only moral and the most effective political system. Obviously, libertarianism—as well as any other social system—will work better the more individuals are peaceful and the less they are criminal or aggressive. And libertarians, along with most other people, would like to attain a world where more individuals are "good" and fewer are criminals. But this is not the doctrine of libertarianism *per se*, which says that *whatever* the mix of man's nature may be at any given time, liberty is best.

Myth #6: *Libertarians believe that every person knows his own interests best.* Just as the preceding charge holds that libertarians believe all men to be perfectly good, so this myth charges them with believing that everyone is perfectly wise. Yet, it is then maintained, this is not true of many people, and therefore the state must intervene.

But the libertarian no more assumes perfect wisdom than he postulates perfect goodness. There is a certain common sense in holding that most men are better apprised of their own needs and goals then is anyone else. But there is no assumption that everyone always knows his own interest best. Libertarianism rather asserts that everyone should have the *right* to pursue his own interest as he deems best. What is being asserted is the right to act with one's own person and property, and not the necessary wisdom of such action.

It is also true, however, that the free market—in contrast to government—has built-in mechanisms to enable people to turn freely to experts who can give sound advice on how to pursue one's interests best. As we have seen earlier, free individuals are not hermetically sealed from one another. For on the free market, any individual, if in doubt about what his own true interests may be, is free to hire or consult experts to give him advice based on their possibly superior knowledge. The individual may hire such experts and, on the free market, can continuously test their soundness and helpfulness. Individuals on the market, therefore, *tend* to patronize those experts whose advice will prove most successful. Good doctors, lawyers, or architects will reap rewards on the free market, while poor ones will tend to fare badly. But when government intervenes, the government expert acquires his revenue by compulsory levy upon the taxpayers. There is no market test of his success in advising people of their own true interests. He only need have ability in acquiring the political support of the state's machinery of coercion.

Thus, the privately hired expert will tend to flourish in proportion to his ability, whereas the government expert will flourish in proportion to his success in currying political favor. Moreover, the government expert will be no more virtuous than the private one; his only superiority will be in gaining the favor of those who wield political force. But a crucial difference between the two is that the privately hired expert has every pecuniary incentive to care about his clients or patients, and to do his best by them. But the government expert has no such incentive; he

272 MURRAY N. ROTHBARD

obtains his revenue in any case. Hence, the individual consumer will tend to fare better on the free market.

I hope that this essay has contributed to clearing away the rubble of myth and misconception about libertarianism. Conservatives and everyone else should politely be put on notice that libertarians do *not* believe that everyone is good, nor that everyone is an all-wise expert on his own interest, nor that every individual is an isolated and hermetically sealed atom. Libertarians are not necessarily libertines or hedonists, nor are they necessarily atheists; and libertarians emphatically *do* believe in moral principles. Let each of us now proceed to an examination of libertarianism as it really is, unencumbered by myth or legend. Let us look at liberty plain, without fear or favor. I am confident that, were this to be done, libertarianism would enjoy an impressive rise in the number of its followers.

NOTES

1. John Kenneth Galbraith, *The Affluent Society* (Boston: Houghton Mifflin, 1958); F. A. Hayek, "The Non-Sequitur of the 'Dependence Effect' " *Southern Economic Journal* (April, 1961), pp. 346–48.

2. Irving Kristol, "No Cheers for the Profit Motive," *Wall Street Journal* (Feb. 21, 1979).

3. For a call for applying universal ethical standards to government, see Pitirim A. Sorokin and Walter A. Lunden, *Power and Morality: Who Shall Guard the Guardians?* (Boston: Porter Sargent, 1959), pp. 16–30.

4. Frank S. Meyer, *In Defense of Freedom: A Conservative Credo* (Chicago: Henry Regnery, 1962), p. 66.

5. Thomas E. Davitt, S.J., "St. Thomas Aquinas and The Natural Law," in Arthur L. Harding, ed., *Origins of the Natural Law Tradition* (Dallas, Tex: Southern Methodist University Press, 1954), p. 39.

6. A. P. d'Entrèves, *Natural Law* (London: Hutchinson University Library, 1951), pp. 51–52.

7. Karl Wittfogel, *Oriental Despotism* (New Haven: Yale University Press, 1957), esp. pp. 87–100.

8. On this and other totalitarian Christian sects, see Norman Cohn, *Pursuit of the Millenium* (Fairlawn, N.J.: Essential Books, 1957).

9. Dale Vree, "Against Socialist Fusionism," *National Review* (December 8, 1978), p. 1547. Heilbroner's article was in *Dissent,* Summer 1978. For more on the Vree article, see Murray N. Rothbard, "Statism, Left, Right, and Center," *Libertarian Review* (January 1979), pp. 14–15.

10. *Journal of Political Economy* (December 1938), p. 869. Quoted in Friedrich A. Hayek, *The Road to Serfdom* (Chicago: University of Chicago Press, 1944), p. 152.

11. "The Forester's Letters, III" (orig. in *Pennsylvania Journal,* Apr. 24, 1776), in *The Writings of Thomas Paine* (ed. M. D. Conway, New York: G. P. Putnam's Sons, 1906), I, 149–150.

12. F. A. Harper. "Try This on Your Friends," *Faith and Freedom* (January, 1955), p. 19.

13. F. A. Hayek, *Individualism and Economic Order* (Chicago: University of Chicago Press, 1948), reemphasized in the course of his "Why I Am Not a Conservative," *The Constitution of Liberty* (Chicago: University of Chicago Press, 1960), p. 529.

Part VIII

New Rights

The election of Richard M. Nixon in 1968 should have meant much for American conservatives. With a Republican in the White House, opportunities for conservatives in Washington, one might think, would have broadened considerably. After years of activist liberalism, conservatives longed to roll back the Great Society and rein in the excesses of the 1960s Left. Nixon appeared to most conservatives to be the man to do this, and in 1968 he gained the widespread support of the majority of conservatives over the upstart candidacy of Ronald Reagan.[1] Throughout the 1968 campaign, Nixon promised to shift the power of the federal government back to the states, to cut back the growing intrusiveness of the federal bureaucracy, and to preserve law and order in an increasingly disruptive society. What could be more conservative than these promises?

In the end Nixon expanded the regulatory power of government far more than Lyndon Johnson and the power of the federal bureaucracy grew unchecked. His efforts to deal with revolutionary terrorists like the Weathermen and Black Panthers bordered on the unconstitutional and eventually paved the way for Watergate. His pursuit of detente with the Soviet Union and his opening to Mao Zedong's China, brilliant and innovative diplomatic strategies, led to further erosion of his support from conservatives. Conservatives had misjudged Nixon's long-term commitment to a powerful executive branch and a managerial state. They also misjudged Nixon's views of government. Nixon, as historian Robert M. Collins has labeled him, was an American Whig, a politician committed to an activist presidency who took a nonideological and pragmatic approach to government programs, deciding each on their necessity and merit.[2] By 1972 conservatives were in an uproar over Nixon and looking to back somebody else.

The more critical problem that emerged in the Nixon years was the potential political realignment that awaited the politician skillful enough to effect it. Kevin Phillips, an aide to the Nixon campaign, had recognized the potential for growing conservative influence electorally in 1968 and advocated a "southern strategy" designed to take advantage of southern white hostility to civil rights. Republicans, Phillips thought, could make headway in once solid Democratic territory. After the campaign, Phillips published *The Emerging Republican Majority* (1969) arguing for Republicans to tap southerners, westerners, and disillusioned white ethnics (former supporters of liberal policies, many of them Catholics) as potential Republican cohorts. Nixon would spend much of his effort in office trying to reach these voters, labeling them a "silent majority" and employing policies designed to attract these constituencies. Nixon's efforts to realign American politics along these lines determined, not surprisingly, his commitment to specific policies; whom they could help, or, cynically, whom they could hurt, determined more than the necessity of helping in the first place. A discussion of whether or not certain policies *were* helpful, or whether they should be created at all, was sacrificed, often, to political expediency.[3]

Many conservatives remained enthusiastic about the potential of electoral realignment. Two examples are included herein. William Rusher (1925–) was for many years the publisher of *National Review*. An ardent politico, Rusher had been instrumental in guiding YAF through many internal schisms, had helped organize the Draft Goldwater committee, and had participated in the New York Conservative Party, which succeeded in getting James Buckley, William's brother, elected senator from New York in 1970.[4] In 1972 Rusher fought for Reagan at the Republican convention, but no matter how frustrated conservatives were with Nixon, they refused to back away from the sitting president.

Rusher began immediately to recommend that conservatives form their own party. As Nixon self-destructed throughout his second term, Rusher saw opportunity for the development of a "majority party." The emergence of the social issue—divisive political issues like abortion, crime, pornography, and affirmative action—would galvanize such an opposition. During 1974 and 1975 Rusher struggled to realize his goal of a new party capable of displacing the Republicans, but when Reagan, realizing his political future would be better served within the GOP, refused to run as an independent in the 1976 primaries, Rusher's dream faded "with a whimper." The American Independent Party ran a candidate in America's bicentennial year, but it was former Georgia governor and notorious racist, Lester Maddux—not Reagan—who ran. By that time, Rusher had given up on his dream.

New constituencies did begin to vote Republican throughout the 1970s. Especially important among these new groups were Catholics and evangelical Protestants, disturbed by the growing moral threat emanating from Supreme Court decisions and growing social and sexual permissiveness. The so-called religious Right emerged out of concern for these issues, although it is questionable what influence they have had on American politics (see Part X). More important was the movement of former New Deal constituents, like white ethnics and southerners, into the GOP column. These "middle American radicals (MARs)," as conservative columnist Samuel Francis has called them, were growing in influence and importance throughout the 1970s. Whether dubbed the "silent majority" or "MARs," conservatives hoped to build an electoral coalition around these groups. They would do so, in part, with Reagan's 1980 campaign for the presidency.

Apart from the movement of former ethnics and religious groups to conservatism, there was also a movement of liberal intellectuals, many of them former communists, to the Right. The neoconservatives, as they were dubbed by socialist Michael Harrington, were policy intellectuals, academics and politicians who embraced the conservative concerns over the Cold War and the decline of American culture. The godfather of neoconservatism was Irving Kristol (1920–), who had been a Trotsky supporter battling against Stalinists while enrolled at the City College of New York in the 1930s. A longtime critic of the Soviet Union, Kristol had participated in the Committee of Cultural Freedom, a CIA-backed front group, and edited its magazine *Encounter*. In 1966, he and Daniel Bell, a democratic-socialist, founded *The Public Interest*, a policy journal that tested the assumptions of Great Society liberalism. He, and other contributors, found most of the assumptions faulty, especially concerning the war on poverty, race, and urban issues. Kristol was also troubled by the antiwar movement and its condemnation of America. As a Jew, Kristol, and other neoconservatives, like *Commentary* editor Norman Podhoretz, became deeply suspicious of the Left's anti-Americanism, cultural radicalism, and their embrace of totalitarian Third World regimes. They were also concerned with a marked rise of anti-Semitism on the Left, owed to their embrace of the Palestinian cause. Secular themselves, they came to rediscover their Jewishness and became ardent defenders of Israel.[5]

While much of the neoconservative attention in the 1970s was focused on American foreign policy and particularly the danger of a growing post-Vietnam isolationism (that reminded them of America in the 1930s),[6]

Kristol focused most of his editorial commentary on culture and the economy. The chapter contained in this section is a defense of corporate capitalism from attack by its populist critics on the Right and from the "new class" critics on the Left. It is, pure and simple, an articulation of the economic themes developed by the conservative movement since World War II, a perspective which hardly deserved the mantle "*neocon-servative.*"

Neoconservatives came to influence conservative public policy, and through their well-connected social and economic positions as New York intellectuals, they were thought by many old Rightists to have hijacked the conservative movement (see Part IX).[7] There is much truth to the charge, but it was not a conspiratorial coup. If anything, neoconservatives helped reshape conservatism through their recognition of a changing political and intellectual climate. By the 1980s, conservatives were hungry for power, and neoconservative intellectuals and their ideas on foreign policy, social issues, and the economy would help conservatives achieve such power in the person of Ronald Reagan, a neoconservative himself.

Chapter Twenty-eight

An Emerging Conservative Majority

William A. Rusher

In May 1974 the Gallup Poll reported the latest result of a survey it has taken regularly ever since the inception of the poll itself in 1936. If the parties were realigned ideologically, it inquired of a representative cross section of the American public, "which party would you, personally, prefer—the conservative or the liberal party?"

In response, 26 percent of those polled replied that they would choose the liberal party, 36 percent reported they were undecided, and 38 percent said they would prefer the conservative party. In other words, counting only those with an opinion (or assuming that those who were undecided would ultimately divide in the same proportions), 59 percent of the American people considered themselves "conservative" and only 41 percent "liberal." The percentage describing themselves as "conservative" was the highest in the entire thirty-eight-year history of the Gallup Poll.

Now these are surely remarkable figures. After all, the word "liberal" is widely and rightly identified with the administrations of Franklin Roosevelt, his Democratic successors in the presidency, and the general policies of the Democratic Party—men and policies that have triumphed repeatedly, almost monotonously, in most national elections since 1932. On the other hand, the word "conservative" broadly connotes, at least in relative terms, the candidates and policies of the Republican Party, which was the loser in those same elections, and it is identified above all with the name and policies of Barry Goldwater, who was resoundingly defeated by Lyndon Johnson in 1964, receiving only 38 percent of the popular vote.

Moreover, Dr. Gallup's poll was taken in mid-April 1974, at a time

From William A. Rusher, *The Making of a New Majority Party* (Ottawa, Il.: Green Hill Publishers, 1976 ed.) Reprinted by permission of William A. Rusher.

when the fortunes of the Republican Party were at almost their lowest ebb: only six months after Spiro Agnew, a Republican vice president, had resigned upon pleading *nolo contendere* to a charge of tax fraud, and while Richard Nixon, a Republican president, was daily sinking deeper into the morass of Watergate-related charges which were to result, just four months later, in his resignation to forestall certain impeachment. A subsequent poll by the Gallup organization, taken in July 1974, confirmed the low opinion of the Republican Party held by most Americans. While 44 percent of those polled called themselves "Democrat," and 33 percent said they were "independent," only 23 percent were willing to identify themselves as "Republican."

What, then, is going on here? Do Americans, despite the supposed longstanding identification of the Democratic and Republican parties as "liberal" and "conservative" respectively, actually perceive the Democrats as somehow the more "conservative" party? It seems most unlikely. Or are voters who adopt the "conservative" label using it in some rare and special sense that can safely be ignored? This is the solution preferred by A. James Reichley in his annual tribute to liberal Republicanism published in *Fortune*'s issue for December 1974. Reichley cites one survey that suggests "that what most self-designated conservatives identify with is a conservative 'life-style'—personal deportment, social attitudes, moral values—rather than a specific ideology." Having thus comfortingly accounted for this "otherwise puzzling phenomenon," Reichley quickly reaches the fascinating conclusion that "the most likely beneficiaries of the voters' growing identification with conservatism are the political moderates."

Despite his obvious ax-grinding for Republican liberals, Reichley has stumbled onto a corner of the truth. A good many thoughtful observers have concluded that the word "conservative" connotes, to the Americans who apply it to themselves, an entire constellation of values, including not only those assimilable under the category of "life-style" but others— values which the Republican Party, and especially its more "moderate" candidates, have represented most imperfectly. On this theory, the "conservatives" include not only most of the 23 percent who still think of themselves as Republican, but also a good many of the independents and a not inconsiderable minority of Democrats as well.

But, if this is the case, the thought rises almost unbidden: Might not a realignment of the parties be brought about, in which the "conservative" values endorsed by so substantial a proportion of the population could find expression in a party specifically designed to express them?

It is not a new idea. On the contrary, I shall demonstrate that exactly such a political movement has been on the very verge of success in this country for at least fifteen years—slouching around Bethlehem, as it were, trying to be born. Once it came to the brink of realization, only to be thwarted by the black mischance of an assassin's bullet. On another occasion conservatives themselves, momentarily yielding to the temptation of what appeared to be expedient compromise, threw away a golden opportunity. And on a third occasion the conservative majority in this country actually united at last, and promptly swept everything before it—under fortuitous circumstances not repeatable, unless we consciously build a new party to reflect the true distribution of political forces.

But the evidence is fast accumulating that the time for such a party realignment may at last be ripe. In Congress especially, the failure of the present major parties to reflect adequately the political desires of a majority of voters is painfully manifest. In the past twenty-seven years, the Democratic Party has had majorities in both the House and Senate in every year but two; yet this overwhelming predominance has resulted in few policy initiatives that can, with any seriousness, be regarded as expressing the will of a majority of the American people, or even any specific proclivities of the Democratic Party. Rather, the Democrats, with a congressional spectrum reaching from Ron Dellums to Sonny Montgomery, have stood for just about everything, while the Republicans in their generality have responded by standing for practically nothing. The result has been that neither of them, taken all in all, has stood for much of anything.

In presidential terms, the performance of the two parties has been little better. Both, with rare exceptions, have tacitly admitted their substantial interchangeability by bidding avidly for the votes of certain self-described "independents" occupying the ground where the parties most squarely overlap. The result has been to reduce real interparty differences in presidential campaigns to the lowest possible level, and to produce presidential administrations of both parties that have been indistinguishable in everything but incident and name.

Is it any wonder that the American people have responded to this state of affairs by displaying a growing indifference to both parties, and an increasing reluctance to be identified with either?

But if the Democratic and Republican parties today come very close to constituting a permanent majority and a permanent minority, both almost equally meaningless, it does not necessarily follow that the solution is to launch a frankly conservative "third party" dedicated to opposing them both, more or less in perpetuity. The genius of our political system is, or at any rate hitherto always has been, bipartisan. If a major political impulse demands expression, tradition and prudence alike command that it seek that expression within one of the two major parties. If that effort is unsuccessful however, it still has, within the bipartisan framework, two options: either consciously to accept minor-party status, hoping to influence the two major parties from outside; or to try to replace one of the two major parties altogether, as the Republican Party in the 1850s replaced the Whigs. In this book, I am proposing that America's conservatives set out to do the latter: i.e., form a new party that will replace the Republican Party *in toto* as one of America's two major parties.

Why the latter? Is it so clear that the conservative movement cannot find a home in the GOP? Don't conservatives, in fact, dominate it—especially its national conventions and its congressional caucuses—rather handily? Conservatives took control of the party in 1964, nominating Senator Goldwater for president. For better or worse it was conservatives, still dominant in the party's national convention, who nominated Richard Nixon in 1968. Even in 1972, when Nixon's departures from conservative principle had become too numerous and too painful to ignore, he was manifestly far more conservative than his Democratic opponent, and received the support of the vast majority of conservatives for both renomination and reelection. Finally, Nixon's appointed successor as president, Gerald Ford, is, on the basis of his congressional voting record, undoubtedly best described as a moderate conservative. Why should conservatives abandon an existing major party that has shown itself so susceptible to their influence?

There are two separate answers to that question. One involves the intrinsic viability (or vice versa) of the Republican Party today. The other has to do with the imperative need for a total realignment of the political forces in this country, if conservatism is not to spend an important part of its energy struggling against itself—a realignment that might, theoretically, take place under the aegis of Republicanism, but which in fact is going to be infinitely easier to bring about if conservatives abandon the GOP altogether and build themselves a statelier mansion elsewhere.

I trust it is not necessary for me to dwell at any great length on the present low estate of the Republican Party. Both major parties have been around so long that they exude the seedy, unmistakable odor of entrenched and callous old age. But in the eye (or nose) of public opinion, thanks to Watergate and various other recent disasters, the GOP has unquestionably forged into a commanding lead in this unhappy respect. No other party in our history has ever had a vice president resign after pleading *nolo contendere* to a charge of tax evasion—or any other charge. No other party in our history has ever had a president resign to avoid certain impeachment and removal for conspiring to obstruct justice—or any other conspiracy. These disasters may, even will, be forgotten or mossed over in time; but how much time do conservatives—does America—have?

Or take a different but equally serious problem: the economy. It does not take an economist to perceive that the United States today is in deep economic difficulties, or a political scientist to predict that the voters will (however unfairly) blame this state of affairs on the president and party in the White House. It took the GOP twenty years to live down the onus of the Great Depression. How long must conservatives wait for it to recover this time?

In other words, the alleged ability of conservatives to dominate the Republican Party is only part of the story. We must still ask: When and if they finally take it over in *toto*, what will they have gained? The stain of Watergate, the onus of recession, and precious little else.

There is, however, another and even greater disadvantage to the GOP from the conservative standpoint. In the three most recent Republican national conventions, to be sure, conservatives have outnumbered their relatively liberal opponents (I am referring to Rockefeller, Percy, Scranton, Scott, Hatfield, and their ilk) in a steady ratio of about 9 to 4. In the Senate and House Republican caucuses the conservative margins are far narrower, but still adequate. The conservatives have thus been strong enough to impose their will in various contexts, where there were major questions up for decision; but the liberal minority has always been large enough to compel a certain amount of compromise or adjustment *in its direction*—which just happens to be the direction 180 degrees away from that which can alone lead to a new national conservative coalition and the long-awaited triumph of the conservative majority in America.

To understand this, it is necessary to know something of the history of our two major parties, and of the issues that have divided them in the past forty-five years—matters that will consume several chapters of this book. For the moment, however, it is enough to say that the Republican Party, as at present constituted, is still designed to fight (and, one is tempted to add peevishly, to lose) a battle that ended, for most practical purposes, at least a quarter of a century ago: the battle of the Roosevelt years, which was waged between the parties largely over FDR's economic policies and their frank favoritism toward the lower economic classes of the society. On that broad subject, Republicans of all varieties and origins were united in their opposition, and it simply didn't matter—on the contrary, it was a sign of vitality and health—that the GOP opposition included a spectrum of economic and social interests, fighting side by side.

But the battles of the Roosevelt years are over, as irrevocably as Antietam and Gettysburg. The basic economic division in this country is no longer (if it ever was) between the haves and the have-nots. Instead, a new economic division pits the producers—businessmen, manufacturers, hard-hats, blue-collar workers, and farmers—against the new and powerful class of nonproducers comprised of a liberal verbalist elite (the dominant media, the major foundations and research institutions, the educational establishment; the federal and state bureaucracies) and a semipermanent welfare constituency, all coexisting happily in a state of mutually sustaining symbiosis. It is this new economic and social cleavage that has produced the imposing (though not yet politically united) conservative majority detected by Dr. Gallup; and it is the ineradicable presence in the Republican Party of a liberal minority that either belongs to or is broadly sympathetic to this new class—a minority unable to dominate the GOP itself, but always able to force it to compromise *toward* the liberal positions rather than away from them—that makes the Republican Party, all else aside, so spectacularly unfitted to be the political vector of the conservative majority in the American society.

Whenever a liberal proposal is introduced in Congress, the liberal Republican minority in both Houses can be observed supporting it energetically—and later receiving, in various liberal—dominated contexts, the political, monetary, and social rewards of doing so. Whenever a Republican national convention gathers, the liberal minority is on hand— rarely to impose its will, but always able to force the selection of candidates and the adoption of platform planks calculated to offend its sensibilities as little as possible. The recent history of the Republican Party is little more than a record of the compromises made by conservative majorities, who knew instinctively how victory could be fashioned, to appease a liberal minority whose sole effective function has been to insure the defeat of conservatism.

Yet there is nothing inauthentic about the Republicanism of these people. They are "Republican," all right; they are merely not conservative. Like the drone bee, they have (whether they realize it or not) only one function: to work for liberal principles and defend liberal interests *within the Republican Party,* and thereby to prevent it from ever uniting the conservative majority in America and leading that majority to victory.

That is why many observers believe the time is opportune for a new major party, consciously designed to replace the Republican Party altogether; and that party is what this book is about. Nothing in it is intended as dogma, so far as the organization, the platform, the candidates, or even the prospects of a new major party are concerned. My intention has been simply to point in directions that deserve thoughtful consideration. But of the broad general proposition that such a party is needed, and that the time is ripe to found it, I feel as confident as anyone reasonably can of a political intuition. In that conviction I have, at any rate, a great deal of company, and it seems almost certain that the effort will be made. If this book contributes in some small measure to the success of that effort, it will have fulfilled my hopes. . . .

The opportunity is to create a new, broadly based major party. Please note that I specify a "major" party—which is to say, a party like the Democratic and Republican parties, consisting of a nationwide *coalition* of interests and capable of capturing both the presidency and the Congress.

Since a party must have a name, and since fate appears to be beckoning this one into existence on the 200th anniversary of our country's independence, I propose to call it hereinafter "the Independence Party." I hasten to add that I don't feel strongly about the matter of a name, provided only that it is a generic one and thereby avoids the sort of fatal particularization that helped to destroy the Greenback Party and the Prohibition Party.

Conceivably the Independent Party, once brought into being, might for a time coexist precariously with the present major parties. But all the factors which are conducive to a two-party system in the United States will tend instead to force it fairly quickly in one of two directions: either toward total replacement of one of the present major parties (almost certainly the Republican Party), or toward the gradual erosion of its own major-party pretensions into typical "third party" status, whence its issues

and voters can ultimately be co-opted by one or both of the present
major parties (again, primarily the GOP). The latter fate, while not by
any means necessarily worse than death (since after all the issues and
voters thus co-opted would play a perceptible and perhaps even central
part in shaping the course of the co-opting party—as the Progressive and
Social Parties did vis-à-vis the Democrats in the decade following 1924),
is emphatically not what the founders of the Independence Party should
have in mind. Their aim should be to do to the Republican Party what
the latter did to the Whigs: namely, replace it *in toto*.

Existence of the Necessary Conditions

It will be recalled from our earlier discussion that the replacement of a
major party in the United States appears to require, at a minimum, the
following fairly rare combination of circumstances: a basic issue that
sharply (though not necessarily equally) divides the party to be replaced—
and probably the opposition party too; a fresh impulse regarding that
issue, to be found among voters both within and outside the fading party;
a counter-tendency on that issue, among certain members of that party,
who then naturally tend to gravitate toward the existing opposition party;
and finally, a strikingly weak leadership and organizational structure in
the party to be replaced.

The political situation today fulfills every one of those requirements:

1. Since at least the early 1950s, as already described, the basic economic division in the United States has been, not between the old categories of the haves and have-nots, but between those elements at all
economic levels of the society that, as the producers, still subscribe to its
original basic values, and those who are converts, voluntary or otherwise,
to the liberal world-view: a world-view that is militantly secular, heavily
guilt-ridden, and perhaps even subliminally suicidal. The new division is
based on a growing resistance to the all-too-successful attempt of a new
class of liberal verbalists, centered in the federal and state bureaucracies,
the principal media, the major foundations and research institutions, and
the nationwide educational establishment, to run the United States for
the benefit of interests (notably their own, and those of their huge welfare
constituency) conformable to that world-view.

Thus, for example, liberals are obsessed with the need to rectify, by
federal intervention, the injustices historically perpetrated by whites

against the black population of the country, as well as other wrongs allegedly committed against a whole series of newly discovered and acutely self-conscious "minorities," ranging from homosexuals and American Indians to Spanish-speaking citizens, flower people, prison inmates, and women—a guilt syndrome so familiar that the *New Yorker* some years ago ran a cartoon of one policeman saying to another, apropos a woebegone figure who has entered the station house, "He says he's a white liberal and he wants to turn himself in."

Conservatives are certainly not blind to the fact that wrongs have occured in this country, but neither are they completely driven to express their distress in the form of federal largesse, often dispensed in response to shrewd lobbying, without careful consideration of the costs or possible consequences. Accordingly they tend to oppose ever-expanding federal involvement in welfare and such grotesqueries as forced integration of the public schools (including busing, which many liberals, whose own children are so often in private schools in wealthy areas dependably white, find it easy to favor). On the other hand, a subtle animus against religion typically leads liberals to resist, on grounds of maintaining the separation of church and state, all efforts to reinforce the modest but vital religious elements in our national life, including school prayer; conservatives typically favor them.

In the field of foreign affairs, liberals are hostile to the governments of South Korea, South Vietnam, Nationalist China (Taiwan), the Philippines, Spain, South Africa, Rhodesia, Chile, and Brazil, and correspondingly warm toward Communist China, Madame Gandhi's India, "democratic" Portugal, the ex-colonial black nations of Northern and Central Africa, and Castro's Cuba. They are also détente-minded, critical of the Pentagon and the CIA, and disposed to be enthusiastic about SALTs I and II. On every score, conservatives disagree.

Finally, conservatives emphatically do not share the regnant liberal impulse to diminish this country, and indeed all mankind, by governmental efforts to achieve Zero Population Growth, by indulging in cataclysmic fantasies of the Club de Rome type, or by federal support of such widely offensive policies as abortion and euthanasia.

2. The same hostility toward the liberal world-view, and to the new class that battens on it, is widely felt within the ranks (though seldom to be found in the leadership) of the Democratic Party. It loomed large in the 1948 "Dixiecrat" rebellion of J. Strom Thurmond, who later defected to the GOP and became one of the most enthusiastic supporters of Barry

Goldwater. It is also the central theme of Alabama Governor George Wallace, who contested various Democratic presidential primaries unsuccessfully in 1968 and had already won the Democratic primaries in Florida, Alabama, Tennessee, North Carolina, and Michigan when he was shot in 1972.

3. A fresh conservative impulse, bluntly opposed to the liberal views and forces described above, has been struggling for effective political expression in America for nearly twenty years. Prior to about 1950, many of the voters who now describe themselves to Dr. Gallup as "conservative" were concerned primarily with economic issues in a society where the distribution of forces ranged them on the "liberal" side of many questions and prompted them to vote Democratic. But the outbreak of the Cold War, the issue of domestic Communism, the longer-range implications of liberalism in the field of social values, the steadily increasing size and cost of government, and its exploitation by a whole new class of nonproducing verbalists augmented by a huge and apparently permanent welfare constituency, has gradually loosened the allegiance of those voters to the Democratic Party and brought about a growing convergence between their views and those of traditional economic conservatives.

When the election of Dwight Eisenhower failed to give this conservative impulse voice and force, it began to organize itself largely outside both major parties. In 1961, however, conservative Republicans mounted a successful drive to co-opt the new impulse to capture the 1964 presidential nomination for Barry Goldwater. Unfortunately the effort fell far short of its full potential impact at the polls that November, largely because (as already noted) Lyndon Johnson's accession to the presidency briefly returned to the Democratic ranks a substantial segment of the national conservative majority.

In 1968 the conservative movement missed a key opportunity to win national power behind Ronald Reagan, because Nixon succeeded in persuading a majority of the conservative delegates to the Republican convention that the ever-present need to appease their own liberal fellow-Republicans justified his nomination instead—whereupon George Wallace pressed his third-party candidacy, got ten million votes, and thereby again divided the basic conservative constituency.

In 1972 Nixon, having abandoned almost every serious principle of conservatism save those few (notably opposition to busing) which he had reserved as necessary to compete effectively against Wallace, succeeded in winning the united conservative majority to his banner—though only because Wallace's candidacy was ended by a bullet, and because the Democrats played into his hands by nominating McGovern. These circumstances being almost surely unrepeatable, the conservative impulse must be regarded as still seeking adequate institutional expression.

4. The Eastern liberal wing of the Republican Party, drawn from the ranks of upper class WASPs and their fellow-travelers, finds itself acutely uncomfortable, yet not altogether powerless, under the domination of the GOP by its conservative majority. After Goldwater's convention victory in 1964, several of the leading spokesmen for liberal Republicanism (including Rockefeller, Lindsay, and Javits) flatly refused to pledge their support for his election. And their followers got the message: Goldwater lost heavily in just about every state, and every election district, where there was an appreciable number of liberal Republicans. The conservatives, in response, made the fatal strategic concession of consenting to the nomination of Nixon in 1968, and thereby recouped these losses for the party to some degree; but by 1970 liberal-Republican defections were under way again, led by some of their major spokesmen. New York's liberal Republican mayor, John Lindsay, who had lost his own party's nomination in 1969 and won reelection in a three-cornered race as the Liberal Party candidate, now changed his registration to Democrat. And while Lindsay's move was easy to attribute to his own strategic necessities, rather than to any deep disaffection among upper-class WASPs in general (since Lindsay's personal following in the city was largely Jewish, black, and Puerto Rican anyway) he was soon followed out of the GOP by yet another prominent Republican sprung from the party's bluest Eastern blood: Westchester Congressman Ogden Reid, scion of the family that had owned the liberal-Republican *New York Herald-Tribune.*

Of the remaining leaders of the Republican Party's relatively liberal Eastern wing, Rockefeller alone has shown the slightest tendency to drift toward the right. This (as already noted) is merely a tropistic response, on one or two cautiously chosen fronts, to the clear implications of his own private polls. If he had, as Lindsay and Reid obviously think they have, a long enough career in active politics ahead of him, he would in all likelihood be trending leftward, either within the Republican Party or (more probably) to and beyond the Democratic Party, as rapidly as they. Instead, by luck and hard work he has managed to become the vice presidential choice of a Republican president of the United States who apparently believes that he has thereby strengthened his own position with the American people.

5. Lastly, the leadership and organization of the Republican Party are today at an all-time low. In state after state it scarcely exists at all. In part this is due to the long-term shift of financial support from the party to individual candidates—but this, in turn, is squarely the result of the party's essential meaninglessness. No one can effectively lead or even work for the Republican Party today, because no one can possibly say what it stands for. It simply defies categorization—and defies it, moreover, not (like the Democratic Party) in the interests of a fructifying opportunism to which nothing human is alien, but in a sterile and futile effort to moderate the hostility of leftist blocs that have no intention whatever of voting for it, and to preserve the loyalty of a liberal-Republican minority whose only real function is to prevent any effective coalition with formerly Democratic social conservatives.

We are justified, then, in concluding that the essential preconditions for a successful new major party in the United States exist, and that the Independence Party might plausibly hope to replace the Republican Party altogether in the reasonably near future—permanently capturing from the Democrats in the process huge segments of the old Roosevelt coalition that the Republican Party has signally failed to attract or retain, and losing to the Democrats only the liberal Eastern WASP elite and its fellow-travelers. (Do not, incidentally, make the cardinal mistake of confusing these "limousine liberals" with the great bulk of middle-class Protestants in the Northeast or elsewhere. The latter bloc, which is huge but—as the triumphs of the old Roosevelt coalition conclusively demonstrated—insufficient to elect a president all by itself, shares most of the views I have described above as characteristically conservative, and should be a basic political resource of the Independence Party.) . . .

The Crisis of 20th-century Democracy

For most Americans of my generation, who came to maturity before or during World War II, "democracy" will probably always be something of a god-word. The world in those days was (or seemed) neatly divided between the "democracies" and the "dictatorships," and the war was to determine which of these two forms of government would prevail. (The presence of the Soviet Union on the side of the democracies was an embarrassing anomaly, but dismissible as little more than a historical accident.)

Of the virtues and viability of democracy itself, regarded simply as a political institution, I cannot recall that we entertained any serious doubts whatever. It was, of course, an admittedly imperfect device ("the worst form of government," Churchill declared, "except all those other forms"), but it was vastly preferable to any rival political system, and seemed to work well enough for all practical purposes. If the size of a given polity made "New England town meeting democracy" impractical, as it usually did, "representative democracy" (i.e., through elected representatives) would serve as well, or better. The majority would rule, though under strict inhibitions and with careful concern for the rights of dissident minorities—notably their right to be heard, and to seek at the polls majority status for themselves. For those who enjoyed having their political theory served up on a platter of free-market rhetoric, it was sometimes explained that democracy was really just a "market place of ideas," in which competing principles and proposals vied for the approval of the "buyer" (i.e., voter).

That the buyers in this market place might be duped into buying shoddy goods was a disagreeable notion that we pushed into a dark corner of our minds. But it was a problem that had not escaped the Founding Fathers. Madison, speaking of the need for an informed electorate, had warned, "Knowledge will forever govern ignorance, and a people who mean to be their own governors must arm themselves with the power which knowledge gives." The 18th-century solution to the problem had been a limited franchise; but by the middle of the 20th century the limitations were heavily eroded or long gone. Majorities might err now and then, we conceded, but in the long run they were very likely to be right.

Underlying our comfortable democratic faith, then, was that major untested assumption. Democracies, though never the usual form of human government, had been around for a long time; but prior to the 20th century the franchise in even the most enlightened of them was almost always severely restricted. In ancient Greece, for example, it was limited to free-born Athenians, although the Athenian state and economy largely depended on the labor of vast numbers of slaves who could not vote. It was their efforts that left the "citizens" of Athens (rarely, if ever, totaling more than 10,000) free to participate so vigorously in "democratic" politics. As late as the 19th century, and well into our own, "democracy," where it existed at all, was almost invariably based upon a franchise that in one way or another sharply confined voting rights to carefully defined categories of citizens. Sometimes it would be (as in Switzerland) only males; far more often (e.g., in the early United States) there would be a property, or at least a literacy, qualification. In all three cases, the effect was to insure that those who did the voting would have a modicum of worldly wisdom, or at least a stake in the politico-economic system they were helping to guide. It was only in this century, and largely among a group of nation-states bordering the North Atlantic, that a serious creative effort was made to extend the franchise to all native-born or naturalized individuals who could plausibly be described as adult—without regard to their economic status, their sex, their length of residence, or even their ability to read or write.

The untested assumption required us to suppose that such an electorate, or at least a majority of its members, would be capable of exercising the discrimination, the self-restraint, and where necessary the self-denial, that characterized previous successful examples of democracy. One of Athens' ten thousand citizens, after discussions with his peers, might plausibly be able (though even he all too often was not) to resist the blandishments of some demagogue who was trying to persuade the voters that he could make silk purses out of sows' ears. A property-owner in early 19th-century England or America was certainly no easy mark for such a proposition. But in America, as the 20th century nears its end, we are relying for similar skepticism and restraint on a potential electorate of at least 140 million voters, ranging in age from 18 to senility, large numbers of whom have no identifiable vested interest whatever in the prevailing social system (quite the contrary), and many of whom are functional illiterates as well.

There is nothing wrong with the heart of a society that takes such a gamble; we may even borrow Herbert Hoover's description of Prohibition and call it "an experiment noble in purpose." But it is nonetheless an experiment, and there is no blinking at the mounting evidence that the experiment isn't going very well—either here, or in the Western European democracies that have tried it too.

The central problem involves the matter of "benefits." How, precisely, does an honest politician in a democratic society run successfully against some spellbinder who has invented a new "benefit" and has pledged to confer it on the voters if he is elected? By telling the truth, of course, about the real cost and impact of the proposed "benefit." But what reason is there to believe that the voters (or at least a majority of them) will listen, or understand what they hear, or believe it if they understand it?

Being a voter these days is no bed of roses; the quality of public debate has declined shockingly since the days of Lincoln and Douglas. Bombarded on all sides by alleged experts uttering flatly contradictory advice on (say) economic policy; bewildered by the intricate ballet of such terms as "inflation," "stagflation," and "slumpflation"; knowing for sure only that he and his family are feeling the pinch—is it reasonable to expect even comprehension, let alone self-restraint, from such a voter?

Yet that is the leaky vessel in which 20th-century democracy has set sail. In Britain and Italy the storm warnings are already flying, and here at home the feeling grows, almost day by day, that we too shall not escape the blast. The mechanisms of borrowing and inflation have been used and abused by a series of profligate administrations until the interest alone on our national debt exceeds $30 billion every year, and until this country is as dependent on ever-greater stimuli through inflation as the drug addict is on ever-increasing doses of heroin. The day of economic reckoning is very near, and is bound to be painful.

In such circumstances the dangers of both demagogic folly and authoritarian counter-measures are too obvious to require elaboration. Salvation cannot come through the policies, the leaders, or (very probably) the parties that caused this whole predicament in the first place. Rescue will come—if it comes at all—through the belatedly united efforts of America's economic and social conservatives, bending their will and their immense talents to the high task of making mass-franchise democracy work.

The hour is late—perhaps too late. I do not want to pretend to an optimism I do not feel. But *if* there is still a chance, then the Great Coalition and a new major party based on it are its indispensable embodiments. It is very probably true of us, as Lincoln warned his contemporaries it was true of them, that "we shall nobly save or meanly lose the last, best hope of earth."

The Immediate Context

But whatever the strategic urgency of the problem, it is perfectly natural to wonder whether, in purely tactical terms, this is "the right time" to attempt to found a new major party. In reply, I ask when, if ever, there will be a better?

As 1975 opened, Republicans occupied the presidency and vice presidency, but their grip on the White House was pitifully weak and their prospects for retaining it after 1976 were, to say the least, not encouraging. Both houses of Congress are, as usual, overwhelmingly Democratic. President Ford is widely liked, in the sense of being regarded as a sincere and amiable man; but it is revealing no state secret to add that even among those who like him best there are many who concede that he is probably not capable of providing the kind of forceful leadership that America needs today. He may, as the months roll by, continue his practice of vetoing Democratic spending proposals, and by so doing gradually build a reputation as a (relative) foe of profligacy; but it is hard to remember the last time such a posture actually helped a politician win an election, and all too easy to recall a score of instances in which it was the big-time spenders who won the hearts—and votes—of the people. It is difficult, in fact, to picture President Ford making a really powerful bid for reelection—though the liberal media, employing their favorite broken-wing trick, may contrive to suggest that they fear him, until he is safely renominated.

Vice President Rockefeller has assuredly not gotten over his long unrequited love affair with the presidency. He is certain to try to use his new office and prominence to impress himself favorably on the public consciousness, with a view to yet another presidential candidacy in circumstances still unforeseeable. He is a restless and forceful man, with substantially limitless resources for self-promotion, and it is only prudent to assume that he may emerge as the Strong Man of the Ford administration. But he cannot accede to the presidency unless Ford vacates it, and even if Ford did resign in his favor or decide not to run for reelection, it is highly debatable whether Rockefeller could impose his own nomination on the Republican Party, or then persuade the American people to choose him as their president. In either case Rockefeller would certainly face in the Republican primaries (unless they were already past) a formidable challenge by Reagan; so the pressure on Mr. Ford will be to run again, even if his prospects for victory are not bright, "to keep the party from being torn apart" by a long and bitter preconvention struggle between Rockefeller and Reagan. And in the general election in November 1976 the Republican candidate, whether it is Ford or Rockefeller (or even Reagan), will face formidable difficulties simply by virtue of that label.

It is difficult, in fact, to conceive of a major party being in much worse shape, purely as a party, than the GOP is in at the moment. I began this book by mentioning, in its introduction, that less than a quarter of all

American voters (one recent poll says only 18 percent are willing to identify themselves with this supposedly "major" party today. The resignations of Agnew and Nixon, and the whole mass of arrogance and corruption summed up in the word "Watergate," are only a part of the reason—though, Heaven knows, an important part. But, quite apart from Watergate, the Republican Party has simply lost touch with the American people. Far from reaching out to co-opt the new conservative impulse as healthy major parties (including the Republican Party) have always done in the past, it has been forced, by the need to appease its liberal minority, to stand for as little as possible—confronting the Democratic *omnium gatherum* with a near-perfect vacuum. Still another recent poll found the American people hard put to think of a single category of government in which the Republican Party excels the Democrats—not, one hopes, because the Democrats are perceived as such stellar performers, but merely because the image of the Republican Party fails to suggest anything whatever that it can do well.

To these difficulties, intrinsic to the party, must be added those occasioned by the present state of the nation. It is only fair—but also quite pointless—to add that these are scarcely the exclusive fault of the Ford administration. America is now paying the long-deferred price of economic policies pursued, in a spirit of irresponsibility compounded by ignorance, by every administration of both parties for over forty years. There is no way out of the present crisis that is either quick or painless, and no political precedent is better established than that which decrees the defeat of the incumbent administration in retaliation for such distress, whatever its actual degree of responsibility for the distress may have been.

But even if the Republican Party is ready to expire at the administration of a vigorous push, are conservatives in any mood to give that push? More than one friend of mine, sympathetic to the general idea of a new party, has expressed the view in recent months that conservatives at present are emotionally exhausted. The collapse of the hopes they had vested in Agnew, the slow unfolding of the stomach-turning facts about Watergate, the consequent triumph of the despised liberal media, the near-impeachment and forced resignation of Nixon, the accession of Ford and his designation of Rockefeller as vice president—all these in a space of less than two years (so the argument goes), have left conservatives incapable of a fresh initiative.

In response, I can say only that I read the portents quite differently. Conservatives are indeed downhearted, and with good reason. But they are more frustrated than exhausted. It has been years since they saw light at the end of any accessible tunnel. If they are shown at last a direction they can take with pride, and with a reasonable prospect of success, and if they are presented with able candidates and managers willing to step out with them in that direction, I believe they will respond not merely dutifully but with a vigor that will attest spectacularly to the basic vitality of the conservative movement.

Toward a Healthy Society

At the opening of this chapter I spoke of the growing fear that mass-franchise democracy of the 20th-century type has been weighed in the balance and found wanting: wanting, specifically, in that quality of self-restraint that is the only possible alternative to restraints less voluntary. Now, as the chapter comes to a close, I submit that only the political coalition I have described has, in America today, both the numbers to win and the moral resources necessary to guide this country through its present crisis and, on its 200th anniversary as a free nation, rededicate it to its original principles.

The conservative coalition outlined in this book is neither new nor jerry-built. On the contrary, it has existed *de facto* for most purposes for nearly twenty years, and its impressive power at the polling-place was actually glimpsed, briefly, in 1972. In size, depth, and breadth, it qualifies as a movement fully capable of finding expression in a new major party, and leading this nation under that aegis for the foreseeable future.

It has appeared, perhaps not coincidentally, at a time when both of the old parties are plainly out of intellectual steam and badly compromised by the corrupting effects of long years of power—but also at a moment of crisis, when a fresh initiative will be especially welcome, and in a year when a nation more than normally conscious of its history and heritage will be properly concerned to preserve them.

We may even, if we wish, concede that there is in theory no reason why this impulse could not—as has happened so often before—be co-opted by one or the other of the two existing major parties and find its expression there. But the Democrats cannot possibly accomplish this without losing for good the left they have never, since the Roosevelt years, been willing (or able) to lose; and the Republican Party under Ford and Rockefeller is inherently incapable of expanding its far too narrow base in the only direction that could save it. The presence in the GOP of a liberal minority dedicated to blocking any really effective conservative coalition is the Republican Party's passport to desuetude.

What cannot and must not happen is for the conservative impulse in this nation to go inadequately expressed because our existing political leadership lacks the vision or the will or the inclination to express it. The time has come—indeed, it has nearly passed—to say the words and do the deeds that can save America. Let them be said, and done, at last!

There is no such thing as a worthwhile human objective achieved without effort, and the effort that men devote to such achievements is their principal contribution to society's well-being. To insure that such efforts are appropriately rewarded is a paramount obligation of society, in its own best interests. Sometimes the rewards will be self-generating, and society will have no affirmative role to play in the process. But often it will be necessary for society to create and protect the conditions under which a proper reward for useful effort can be realized; and sometimes society itself may even have to provide the reward. In all this there is nothing new; in one form or another these have been the assumptions, tacit or express, of every modern society, including both the capitalist and Marxist variants.

Beyond this, every humane society recognizes a minimal obligation to those unfortunates who, for whatever reason, are unable to put forth a worthwhile effort. A civilized country simply will not permit any of its people to starve, however negligible their personal contribution. This is well-trodden ground, not to be yielded.

But into our life and thought there has crept, in recent decades, a spirit of challenge to the whole concept of effort and reward. At bottom it is, unquestionably, a philosophical challenge to the entire Judaeo-Christian concept of human nature. But in programmatic terms it presents itself as a denial of the possibility, and even the propriety, of the effort-and-reward system. The focus of emphasis shifts subtly from what man can do for society to what society can do for man, and the mighty name of Science is invoked as a *deus ex machina* that will do away with the need for purposive effort.

As the attack gathers speed, successive aspects of the effort-oriented society are condemned. Monotheistic religions, with their emphasis on every human being's relation to his Creator, are deserted in favor of ambiguous Nirvanas (or even mere drugs) promising surcease from pain. Individual efforts to improve one's lot are sneered at, and corporate efforts are denounced as exploitation at home and imperialism abroad. The defensive institutions of the society—the armed forces, the national security systems, the local police, the prisons—are battered by criticism. In the name of protecting the environment, the whole healthy bias in favor of *life* is reversed, and a series of proposals for limiting it spring into vogue.

This process has reached the point where society's role is wholly re-formed, and it is seen as the omnipresent nurse, servant, and protector of the individual, who in turn is conceived as having no reciprocal obliga-tions whatever. In return for the progressive diminution of his liberty (and even ultimately of his identity); he receives from the Guardian State an endlessly proliferating series of "rights." He has a "right" to an educa-tion, up to any limit that appeals to him (including a "right" to matricu-late, regardless of his record). He has a "right" to a job—or, if he chooses not to work, a "right" to a guaranteed minimum income anyway, simply for being human. He has a "right" to free medical care, and to a dignified old age. Meanwhile he has a "right" to any lifestyle of his choosing, substantially without regard to its impact on the lifestyle of others or on the public *mores* of his community. And this whole delightful state of affairs is to be brought about without serious drains on any income he may acquire, and defended without any obligation on his part to share in the perils of the defense. On the contrary, he will often champion almost any foreign power that condemns, in terms strong enough, the nation that sustains him.

This—the whole sick contribution of liberalism to the American dialogue—is what conservatism opposes, and to stand for its precise opposite is what the Independence Party is all about.

We are (let us say to the voters of America) tired unto death of those who find nothing but blemishes on the face of this country. Of course there are blemishes, but—blemishes and all—it is by far the fairest society ever constructed by free men. We will honor those whose sweat and skill have constructed it, and maintain it. We will reject the leadership of an elite which, operating through the bureaucracy, the educational establishment, the media, and the major foundations and research insti-tutions, has persistently led this nation ever further from its moral and psychological moorings. We will defend this land against its foreign ene-mies (and they assuredly exist) whatever the cost may be.

We will restore, to generations yet to come, the old and all-but-forgotten pride in this country and its heritage. We will give still further solid and visible grounds for that pride, by making the nation's streets safe, and its air and water clean. We will make way for ability wherever it exists—and remember our obligation of compassion, where it does not.

We reject the counsels of demagogues who promise something for nothing, and will speak instead the truth, even when it hurts. Above all, we will restore to the American political process some part of the joy and optimism it has lost.

For if we succeed, we will have accomplished a mighty thing. We will have reversed, no less—and reversed moreover in America, where it counts most—the whole downward-spiraling tide of the 20th century. There is no reason why this century's great experiment with freedom *must* end in failure. It was men and women who created the opportunity, and they who have botched it; and they can rescue it, even now, if they only will. It is up to us, and the means are at hand: a large and devoted majority of the American people, and a new party, under tested leaders, ready to express their will. Together they can save, and formidably reinvigorate, our beloved and imperiled country.

Chapter Twenty-nine

Message from MARs
The Social Politics of the New Right

Samuel Francis

The label "New Right" is at best a confusing one. In the first place, what the label represents is not entirely new, since many of its themes, values, and interests have been expounded to one degree or another by the Old Right of the 1950s and 1960s. In the second place, it is not entirely "Right," since other ideals and values associated with it have seldom been expressed by conservatives of any generation. The New Right is perhaps best known for its populism and its heated contempt for elitism and "limousine liberals." Its polemical exchanges with the Left (and even, sometimes, with the Right) often display a bitterness that was lacking in the amiable sparring bouts of Mr. Buckley and Professor Galbraith. Moreover, the New Right voices no small amount of antibusiness (not to say anticapitalist) rhetoric. Bankers, multinational corporations, Big Business, and The Rich occupy a distinct circle in the New Right vision of the Inferno. The symbols of wealth are also important in its demonology: the Ivy League, the country club, and the Trilateral Commission. Orthodox conservatives of the Old Right generally deprecate, smile at, or strain themselves ridiculing such gaucherie.

Yet, if the New Right is often the victim of its own rhetoric, it can, in 1980, lay claim to something that the Old Right can never claim Political commentators will no doubt debate for years whether the Republican capture of the White House and Senate in 1980 was or was not due to New Right efforts alone, but, they have never debated, and never will, whether the Old Right elected Barry Goldwater in 1964—or Robert Taft in 1952—or Herbert Hoover in 1932. The New Right in 1981, and for some years to come, has what the Old Right could never claim: a national constituency, and the clear possibility of political victory, if not political dominance, in the United States for the remainder of the century.

Despite the incoherence of its name and sometimes of its message, the New Right represents far more than a political ideology or an electoral coalition. The New Right is the political expression of a profound social movement that reflects the dynamics of American society and promises to dominate not only politically, but also perhaps socially and culturally. The origins of the New Right in a social movement explain why its political message often appears to be incoherent, contradictory, or simplistic. What the New Right has to say is not premeditated in the inner sanctums of tax-exempt foundations or debated in the stately prose of quarterly or fortnightly journals. The contents of its message are perceived injustices, unrelieved exploitation by anonymous powers that be, a threatened future, and an insulted past. It is therefore understandable that the New Right has less use for the rhetorical trope and the extended syllogism than for the mass rally and the truth squad and that some of its adherents sometimes fantasize that the cartridge box is a not-unsatisfactory substitute for the ballot box.

The social movement that the New Right expresses and whose values, resentments, aspirations, and fears it tries to articulate is composed of what sociologist Donald I. Warren calls "Middle American Radicals"— MARs. This movement, in Professor Warren's description, is less an objectively identifiable class than a subjectively distinguished temperament, yet it possesses verifiable features that set it apart from other social groups and formations. In the mid-1970s, MARs had a family income of three to thirteen, thousand dollars. There was a strong presence among them of northern European ethnics, although Italians tended to account for more MARs than other groups. MARs were nearly twice as common in the South as in the north-central states. They tended to have completed high school but not to have attended college. They were more common among Catholics and Jews than among Protestants and among Mormons and Baptists than among other Protestant sects. They tended to be in their thirties or in their sixties and were "significantly less likely to be professional or managerial workers" than to be "skilled and semi-skilled blue collar workers."[1]

Yet these statistical features do not define MARs. What defines them as a movement is an attitudinal quality, and what Warren finds most distinctive of them is their view of government and, in a broader sense, of the "establishment" and their role in it. Unlike adherents of the Left, MARs do not regard the government as favoring the rich, and, unlike adherents of the Right, they do not regard the government as giving too much to the poor. According to Warren,

> MARs are a distinct group partly because of their view of government as favoring both the rich and the poor simultaneously. . . . MARs are distinct in the depth of their feeling that the middle class has been seriously neglected. If there is one single summation of the MAR perspective, it is reflected in a statement which was read to respondents: *The rich give in to the demands of the poor, and the middle income people have to pay the bill.*[2]

This attitude is resonant with significant social and political implications. It points to a sense of resentment and exploitation, mainly economic but also broader, that is directed upwards as well as downwards. It points to distrust of decision-makers in state and economy as well as to fear of the economically depressed. It points also to the frustration of aspirations, to an alienation of loyalties, and to a suspicion of established institutions, authorities, and values.

The economic frustrations of MARs, as represented in the above quotation, spill over into political, cultural, and moral expression. The objective features of the MAR profile, coupled with awareness of MAR political ferocity in New Right protests, from the antibusing movements of the early 1970s to the Panama Canal and anti-ERA mobilizations of 1977–1978, should substantiate the movement as social rather than political in a narrow sense. MARs form a class—not simply a middle class and not simply an economic category—that is in revolt against the dominant patterns and structures of American society. They are, in the broadest sense, a political class, and they aspire, through the New Right, to become the dominant political class in the United States by displacing the current elite, dismantling its apparatus of power, and discrediting its political ideology.

"Ruling classes," wrote Gaetano Mosca, the great Italian political scientist of the early twentieth century, "do not justify their power exclusively by de facto possession of it, but try to find a moral and legal basis for it, representing it as the logical and necessary consequence of doctrines and beliefs that are generally recognized and accepted."[3] The current elite in the United States, which has held both political and social power since the 1930s, is no exception. Its ideology or political formula by which it rationalizes its power, is generally known as liberalism—a set of ideas and values that ostensibly eschews power and upholds equality, liberty, and the brotherhood of man, but which is amazingly congruent with and adaptable to the political, economic, and social interests (the structural interests) of the groups that espouse it.

This elite seized power in the political and economic crisis of the Great Depression. The chief instrument of its rise to power, then and in the following decades, was the state, especially the federal government, and more especially the executive branch. Through the state, it made common cause with certain mass organizations—large corporations, labor unions, universities, foundations, and the media—and has generally favored their expansion and strengthening at the expense of smaller-scale units. In domestic affairs it has supported federally enforced economic planning and social engineering for the purpose (at least ostensibly) of realizing its liberal ideology. In foreign affairs, it has favored international activism through similar large-scale organizations and transnational alliances that seem to promote global fraternity and the disappearance of national distinctions and differences. In political theory it abandoned the ideal of a neutral government based on impartial laws and administering equal justice and associated itself with a concept of the state as intimately involved in social and economic processes and as an architect of desirable social change. This concept of the state has been buttressed by a variety of pseudoscientific ideologies—psychoanalysis, behaviorism, legal positivism, applied sociology, Marxism *manqué*, educational progressivism, etc.— most of which are logically incompatible with liberalism but are nevertheless abridged, distorted and popularized into congruence with current ideological fixations.

It is in its cultural and social ideologies and life-styles that the new elite has developed what is probably the clearest indicator of its dominant position. The life-styles, aspirations, and values of the current elite are bound together, rationalized, and extended by what may be called the "cosmopolitan ethic." This ethic expresses an open contempt for what Edmund Burke called the "little platoons" of human society—the small town, the family, the neighborhood, the traditional class identities and their relationships—as well as for authoritative and disciplinary institutions—the army, the police, parental authority, and the disciplines of school and church. The cosmopolitan ethic, reversing a Western tradition as old as Aesop, finds virtue in the large city, in the anonymous (and therefore "liberated") relationships of de-classed, de-sexed, demoralized, and deracinated atoms that know no group or national identities, accept no given moral code, and recognize no disciplines and no limits. The ethic idealizes material indulgence, the glorification of the self, and the transcendence of conventional values, loyalties, and social bonds. At the same time, it denigrates the values of self-sacrifice, community, and moral and social order. Its most perfect (though extreme) expression is perhaps Mick Jagger, but a more typical and vapid form is portrayed in advertisements that tell us What Kind of Man Reads *Playboy*.

The ideology or formula of liberalism grows out of the structural interests of the elite that espouses it. Liberalism barely exists as an independent set of ideas and values. Virtually no significant thinker of this century has endorsed it. Internally, the doctrines of liberalism are so contrary to established fact, inconsistent with each other, and immersed in sentimentalism, resentment, egotism, and self-interest that they cannot be taken seriously as a body of ideas. Liberalism flourishes almost entirely because it reflects the material and psychological interests of a privileged, power-holding, and power-seeking sector of American society.

In the early twentieth century, the increasing massiveness of American society appeared to demand new organizational forms of control. The imperatives of mass scale in the economy, in government and politics, and in social and cultural life gave rise to a new elite that found its principal power base in bureaucracy. In both the public and private sectors, the bureaucratic organization of power and control appeared to be the only means of ruling modern mass units. In the private sector the evolution of bureaucratic dominance followed the "separation of ownership and control" in the large corporations and took the form of managerial direction of large corporate firms. In government, modern bureaucracy developed in a more sudden and revolutionary way in the crisis of the Great Depression. Yet there was no fundamental difference between the interests of the bureaucrats of the public sector and those of the private sector. Both bureaucratic realms shared a common mentality: a rationalistic faith in administrative and manipulative techniques as a means of holding and exercising power. Both sectors, perhaps more importantly shared certain common material interests: the more massive the scale of organization, the more imperative the bureaucratic-managerial form of organization and the more power and material rewards that accrued to the elites that controlled such organizations. The same or similar interests and imperatives pertained in all mass-scale organizations, and the same dominant bureaucratic functions developed in control of the mass unions. Similarly, but more recently, the media of mass communication (in almost every form—book publishing, news reporting, entertainment, documentaries, etc.) have displayed the same dynamic of elite formation, and, most recently, the instruments of legitimate force—the armed forces and the larger metropolitan police departments—display it also. Unlike the older, more localized and personal elites of American society, the new elite possesses a more uniform mentality and a more homogeneous interest: the expansion of mass units of organization under the bureaucratic forms of governance, animated by an ideology of manipulative, administrative social engineering.

From its very nature, therefore, the new elite found liberalism a useful and indeed indispensable formula for rationalizing its existence and power. Modern liberalism justified government on a mass scale and bureaucratic manipulation of social and economic processes. Liberalism allowed for an economy led by mass corporations, themselves governed by "progressive" executives whose positions depended on merit and schooling in managerial sciences, and not on inheritance, experience, or the virtues of the Protestant ethic Liberalism championed schooling itself, especially education (also on a mass scale) that emphasized the practical disciplines of social science, public administration, and modern business management. Finally, liberalism, at its very center, articulated a vision of man that not only rationalized bureaucratic manipulation of the social environment but also laid the groundwork for the cosmopolitan ethic. The great value of this ethic in the rise of the new bureaucratic elite was its discrediting and delegitimization of the formulas and ideologies of its older rivals. Liberalism and cosmopolitanism were able, through their immense appeal to an intelligentsia, to portray localism and decentralized institutions as provincial and a mask for bigotry and selfishness; the small town, the family, class, religious, ethnic, and community ties as backward, repressive, and exploitative; the values of work, thrift, discipline, sacrifice, and postponement of gratification (on which, as values, the moral legitimacy of the older elites rested) as outmoded, absolutist, puritanical, superstitious, and not infrequently hypocritical.

A more direct connection between the material interests of the new elite and the semicollectivist ideology of liberalism exists also. The mass economy of the twentieth century requires a mass level of consumption for the financing of its productive capacities. Due to the inability of lending institutions in the Great Depression to mobilize sufficient credit for the resumption of production, the federal government undertook labor policies, transfer programs, and pension policies designed to insure sufficient demand for the mass economy to function. The immediate beneficiary of these policies, of course, was the impoverished underclass of American society, but the ultimate beneficiaries were the new managerial and bureaucratic elites in corporation and government. The stimulation of demand through government policy—a policy financed by middle-class taxpayers and consumers—insured the existence and dominance of the mass organizations of government, corporation, and union and their managerial elites. At the same time, this policy cemented an alliance, not only among the different sectors of the new elite, but also between the new elite as a whole and the proletariat of American society— against the remnants of the old elite and an exploited and excluded middle class.[4]

The new elite, following a pattern that has been repeated many times in human history, also found that the aggrandizement of the federal executive branch was conducive to its revolution. The older elites were based mainly in local and state governments and in the Congress. The Caesarist political style of the new elite made use of the presidency, under Roosevelt and Truman and their successors, to attack, wear down, usurp, and discredit the authority and powers of both state and local bodies and the Congress. In this new political style, the rising managerial elite was following a pattern evident in the careers of Pericles, Caesar, Henry Tudor, Louis XIV, and Napoleon Bonaparte. Older elites, entrenched in established institutions, are attacked by newer social formations that make alliances with charismatic leaders exercising autocratic power and with an underclass that receives material benefits expropriated from the old elite. New, centralized institutions controlled by the new elite develop in place of the localized institutions of the old rulers.

A pattern often associated with this "sandwich" attack on an old elite by an alliance of an underclass and an autocrat who represents an emerging elite is an activist and expansionist foreign policy led by the new men in opposition to the passive, often isolationist policies associated with the old ruling class. Thus, Pericles promoted Athenian imperialism through enfranchisement of the lower-class crews of the Athenian navy and against the interests of the landed, inward-looking Attic oligarchy. Caesar's revolution in Rome, made possible by his patronage of the lower classes, was to be extended in imperial-military adventures in the East, but this was cut short by his assassination. The Tudors, Louis XIV, and

Napoleon all embarked on expansionist foreign policies that sought to benefit the aspirations and interests of the new elites on which their own power was based. The older elites oppose expansionism because their own power bases are not equipped to profit from it and indeed are frequently threatened by the rise of new powers and forces in the newly acquired territories.

This pattern also was present in the revolution of the managerial elite of the depression-World War II era. The Old Guard of the Republican party, representing the old elite, was isolationist in both world wars. The new elite found both its economic and political interests benefited by an activist, globalist foreign policy. The new political structures revolving around international and regional blocs, new markets and trade arrangements, and new internal institutions for international relations and conflict were all congruent with the interests of the new elite in government, industry and finance, education, and labor.

It is against this elite—which Irving Kristol and others somewhat belatedly call the "New Class" but which James Burnham more accurately (and much earlier) called the "managerial class"[5]—that the New Right with its MAR social base operates. It would be tendentious to claim that the ideologies and institutions of the managerial elite are purely self-serving while claiming also that those of the MARs are objectively true, public-spirited, in the general interest, and morally pure. The MARs form a sociopolitical force now coalescing into a class and perhaps into a new elite that will replace the managerial elite. As a rising political class, the MARs have their own interests, aspirations, and values, and these are not intended to benefit the nation, society as a whole, or humanity. Nevertheless, the structural interests of the MARs—what is of benefit to them because of their position and functions in American society—may be beneficial to America as well. The MARs, and similar social forces now developing in the Sunbelt, promise a new dynamism in America—economically as well as spiritually—in place of the now decadent and moribund managerial elite. They offer also a discipline a code of sacrifice for something larger than themselves, and a new purpose that are beyond the reach of the jaded, self-indulgent, increasingly corrupt elite of the present day. The MARs are not better or worse than other human beings in other social formations, but the objective interests of their own formation appear to dictate a social order quite different from, and probably better than, that designed, manipulated, and misruled by the managerial class and its cohorts.

What the MARs and the New Right seek, then, is the overthrow of the present elite and its replacement by themselves. This is a revolutionary goal, no less so than the goal of the rising managers of the early part of the century. It is revolutionary not in the sense that its realization will require violent rebellion, mass liquidation, or totalitarian rule—these are not envisioned by the New Right and would be antithetical to MAR interests—but in the sense that the replacement of one elite by another almost always leads to a cultural renaissance, to new and dynamic forces that alter ideas and institutions, and to an efflorescence of material and spiritual life.

Yet the New Right will not be the spearhead of the Middle American Revolution if it is concerned only with politics in its narrow, formal sense. It must go beyond the tactics of electoral coalitions and roll-call votes and develop a strategy for the seizure of real social power. Real power is not limited to control of the formal apparatus of government but extends to the levers by which human societies are controlled—to the media of communication, the means of production, and the instruments of force. At the present time these levers of social control and real social power are almost entirely dominated by the managerial elite or are negated by it. Merely formal control of the political apparatus will not alter this fact. The New Right–MAR coalition must seek to dismantle or radically reform the managerial apparatus of social control, and this objective means a far more radical approach to political conflict and to contemporary institutions. The strategic objective of the New Right must be the localization, privatization, and decentralization of the managerial apparatus of power. Concretely, this means a dismantling of the corporate, educational, labor, and media bureaucracies; a devolution to more modest-scale organizational units; and a reorientation of federal rewards from mass-scale units and hierarchies to smaller and more local ones.

To include the large corporations in the "enemies list" of the New Right may strike many adherents of the Old Right as odd or even as subversive. Yet libertarians have long recognized that large, publicly owned, manager-dominated corporations have interests and political orientations quite different from those of small privately owned and controlled enterprises. As G. William Domhoff a radical sociologist, has recognized,

> The businesspeople who were most isolationist, antiwelfare and antilabor were more likely to be in NAM [National Association of Manufacturers] and to be associated with smaller and more regional corporations. Those

who were more moderate [i.e., more liberal] were more likely to be in CED [Committee for Economic Development] and to manage larger companies. More recently, our study of the corporate interlocks of CED and NAM leaders revealed the same large/small dichotomy. For example, NAM's directors for 1972 had only 9 connections to the top 25 banks, whereas CED had 63. Similarly, NAM had but 10 connections to the 25 largest industrials, while CED had 48. The findings were similar for insurance, transport, utilities and retails.[6]

The present managerial elite, whether in the public or private sector, has a vested interest in centralized decision making and collective organization. The dynamic of MAR interests dictates ultimately a policy of localization and privatization of real social power in both the public and private sectors. Only by unleashing the now over-regulated, overtaxed, and unrewarded MAR social and economic forces can their innovative and productive potential be developed. This unleashing of MAR forces can come about only by dismantling the managerial power structure.

To call the New Right "conservative," then, is true only in a rather abstruse sense. Its social and cultural values are indeed conservative and traditionalist, but, unlike almost any other conservative group in history, it finds itself not only out of power in a formal sense but also excluded from the informal centers of real power. Consequently, the political style, tactics, and organizational forms of the New Right should find a radical, antiestablishment approach better adapted to the achievement of its goals. Ideologically, much in the formulas and theory (in so far as there is any) of the New Right derives from exponents of the Old Right. Yet the premise of almost all Old Right publicists has been that the values and institutions they were defending were part of an establishment that was under revolutionary attack. For much of the period in which the Old Right flourished, this premise was correct. Today, however, and since at least the mid-1960s, the revolution of mass and managers has triumphed, entrenched itself as a new elite, and indeed has revealed strong signs of ossification and decadence. The Old Right failed to arrest the revolution mainly because it lacked an adequate social base. Its powerful, well-honed, but esoteric critique of liberal ideology appealed to few save the most sophisticated intellectuals and the declining entrepreneurial elite whose interests and values were reflected in conservative theory.

The New Right must consciously abandon much of the inertial conservatism of its Old Right premises. It must cease congratulating itself on its ability to raise money and win elections within the system developed by the present establishment and begin to formulate a strategy for besieging the establishment. With its MAR social base, the New Right is in a strong position to develop such a strategy, and there are signs it is doing so. Some New Right groups have successfully politicized sections of American society. Smaller businessmen, broadcasters, clergy, parent groups, and other institutional representatives have played an active and important role in New Right political campaigns. However, a key element in the success of the New Right will be its ability to focus on how the establishment uses its apparatus of power in the media, corporations, schools, etc., for political domination and exploitation. This has been made reasonably clear with regard to the bureaucracy and the unions, but other institutional supports of the liberal managerial elite need exposure as well.

In economics, the Old Right has consistently defended the free market. While there is much to be said for the renaissance of free market ideas led by Ludwig von Mises, F. A. Hayek, Milton Friedman, Arthur Laffer, and others, it is doubtful that the MAR coalition and its allies in the Sunbelt's entrepreneurial regions will continue to focus on this classical liberal principle. It is more likely that MAR-Sunbelt interests require a strong governmental role in maintaining economic privileges for the elderly and for unionized labor (where it now exists), that they will also require (or demand) subsidization of construction and perhaps of characteristic Sunbelt enterprises (energy, defense and aerospace industries, and agriculture). One New Right tactic would be payment of these subsidies and privileges out of the proceeds of taxing the Frostbelt and reorienting economic policy and legislation toward the South and West. For the New Right to embrace such a tactic openly (as well as a more favorable attitude toward protectionism) would be a frank recognition that the classical liberal idea of a night-watchman state is an illusion and that a MAR elite would make use of the state for its own interests as willingly as the present managerial elite does. MAR resentment of welfare, paternalism, and regulation is not based on a profound faith in the market but simply on the sense of injustice that unfair welfare programs, taxes, and stifling regulation have bred. The central focus of MAR–New Right political economy is likely to be economic growth, a value often confused with, sometimes encompassing, but not identical to the free market.

Clearly, economic growth involves the lifting of most legal and administrative restraints on enterprise—the demise of environmentalist legislation, OSHA, the sale of federally owned land in the Far West, etc. But it would also include government assistance to dynamic but underfed sectors of the economy—e.g., the space program and new technology forms. The role of government in stimulating growth is no less inconsistent with free market ideals than its role in retarding growth, and since the social forces of the New Right would have a strong interest in the former role, there is little value in their adherence to a strict laissez-faire ideology.

The promotion of a "no-growth" cultus by powerful elements of the current liberal managerial elite is strong evidence of its decadence and ossification. The "selective isolationism" in foreign policy, the withdrawal from the Third World and the conflict with the Soviets, and the guilt experienced for our past foreign policy are also indications of decadence. The fundamental reason for the fall of Vietnam, the U.S. retreat from Angola, the betrayal of Somoza, the desertion of Taiwan, and the collapse of the Shah (as well as the weakening of our commitments to other Third World allies) lies in the inability of our present elite to deal effectively with the often brutal realities of the Third World, in the failure of the liberal formulas of the elite to rationalize necessary and desirable policies for dealing with these realities, and in a preference by the elite to deal with other elites similar to itself in developed regions (Japan, Western Europe, and the Soviet Union). The rationalistic, administrative, and technical skills on which the power of the managerial class is based are of little value in underdeveloped regions, especially where violent resistance to planning and manipulation requires a more coercive response than managerial ideology can justify.

Moreover, the material interests of the elite, as well as its psychic interests and ideological orientation, impel it toward the developed world. Ideologically, the current elite distrusts nationalism and favors internationalist and regionalist units of organization (the United Nations, the Common Market, the British Commonwealth, the Atlantic Community, etc.). This preference is in accord with its cosmopolitan ethic, but it also is consistent with the economic interests of the large corporate entities. Free trade, the integration of international markets, and the stabilization of international relations all reflect the interests of the transnational elites that dominate in the developed countries. In contrast, smaller producers situated in the Sunbelt require protection against cheap imports and access to the raw materials and resources of the Third World, and they are less committed to international stability than to the continued predominance of the United States.

The foreign policy of the New Right, then, reflecting the interests and

values of its MAR-Sunbelt-neo-entrepreneurial base, is likely to endorse a
new nationalism that insists on the military and economic preeminence
of the United States, on international activism (and even expansionism)
in world affairs, on at least some measure of protection for domestic
producers, and for more resistance to Third World arrogance, aggression,
and barbarism. The controversy over the Trilateral Commission, whatever
its merits, reflects this conflict over foreign policy between the social
forces of the dominant elite and those of the New Right. The commission
is essentially the forum of the elite and its multinational components; as
such, it has become a symbol of the resentments of MARs and the forces
of the Sunbelt.[7] Moreover, the nationalism of the New Right will probably
replace the anticommunism of the Old Right as a focus of foreign policy.
While the Soviet Union, Cuba, and their allies remain the principal threat
to the United States and our predominance, New Right elements are
likely to focus on the threat itself rather than the ideological origins of
the threat. The distinction between the nationalist focus of the New Right
and the anticommunist orientation of the Old became clear in the opposition to the Panama Canal Treaty. While Old Right anticommunists
sought to portray Panamanian dictator Omar Torrijos as a Marxist, this
was a far less effective tactic than Ronald Reagan's New Right, nationalist
slogan on the canal—"We built it, we paid for it, and it's ours."

The nationalism of the New Right points to what is perhaps its best-
known characteristic, the rejection of the cosmopolitan ethic of the managerial elite and a thunderous defense of moral and social traditionalism.
The most offensive component of cosmopolitanism to MARs is its abstract universalism, its refusal to make any distinctions or discriminations
among human beings. The brotherhood of man, egalitarianism, the rela-
tivization of moral values, and the rejection of conventional social and
cultural identities as obsolete and repressive all derive from this universalist tendency. In its place, the central formula of the rising MAR-Sunbelt
elite is likely to form around what may be called a domestic ethic that
centers on the family, the neighborhood and local community, the
church, and the nation as the basic framework of values. The values
associated with the domestic ethic will contrast sharply with those of
cosmopolitanism: the duty of work rather than the right of welfare; the
value of loyalty to concrete persons, symbols, and institutions rather than
the cosmopolitan dispersion of loyalties; and the social and human necessity of sacrifice and deferral of gratification rather than the cosmopolitan-
managerial demand for immediate gratification, indulgence, and con-

sumption. The domestic ethic may also lay the basis for a more harmonious relationship between employer and worker, since the place of work itself can be portrayed as an institution no less central than the family or the local community. The common interest of workers and employers in opposing the restrictive, stagnationist policies of the managerial elite is one element of New Right rhetoric that could develop into this harmony, and the explicit approach to blue-collar workers by recent New Right candidates appears to confirm this trend.

Out of the structural interests and residual values of the MARs, and similar forces in the Sunbelt and in new entrepreneurial forces throughout the country, the New Right can construct a formula or ideology. This formula will reflect the demands for economic growth, a more aggressively nationalistic foreign policy, and an assertion of traditionalist ethics and loyalties. It will not be conservative although it will encompass some ideas of the Old Right and reject others. It will, in fact, be a radical formula, demanding changes not only in the formal appearance of power but also in the realities of the distribution and uses of power in its social forms. As a radical movement, representing rising social forces against an ossified elite, the New Right must abandon the political style of the Old Right. That style, based on the premise that the Old Right represented an establishment, sought to defend the intermediary institutions against the Caesarist, leveling forces of the new managerial elite. The managerial class, however, has long since become the establishment and shows signs of abandoning the executive branch as a spearhead of its power-seizure. The New Right, therefore, should make use of the presidency as its own spearhead against the entrenched elite and should dwell on the fact that the intermediary bodies—Congress, the courts, the bureaucracy, the media, etc.—are the main supports of the elite. The adoption of the Caesarist tactic by the New Right would reflect the historical pattern by which rising classes ally with an executive power to displace the oligarchy that is entrenched in the intermediate bodies.

Jeffrey Hart has suggested this idea of a New Right–Caesarist style based on the presidency, but apparently without attracting broad support.[8] While the New Right can expect to make gains in Congress and state and local governments, only the presidency—as Nixon and Agnew showed—has the visibility and resources to cut through the intractable establishment of bureaucracy and media to reach the MAR social base directly. Only the presidency is capable of dismantling or restructuring the bureaucratic-managerial apparatus that now strangles the latent dynamism of the MAR-Sunbelt social forces. The key to this Caesarist strategy is that the New Right does not now represent an elite but a subelite, that it must acquire real social power and not preserve it in its current distribution. The intermediate institutions of contemporary America—the bureaucracy, the media, the managerial hierarchies of the mass unions and corporations, the universities and foundations, the urban conglomerates—are not allies of the New Right and are not conservative influences except in the sense that they serve to protect established powers. Hence, the New Right should not defend these structures but should expose them as the power preserves of the entrenched elite whose values and interests are hostile to the traditional American ethos and as parasitical tumors on the body of Middle America. These structures should be levelled or at least radically reformed, and only the presidency has the power and the resources to begin the process and to mobilize popular support for it.

The characterization of the New Right presented in this essay is unconventional and will perhaps be controversial. The New Right is not merely an electoral coalition concerned with winning elections and roll calls; it is the political expression of a relatively new social movement that regards itself as the depository of traditional American values and as the exploited victim of the alliance between an entrenched elite and a ravenous proletariat. Viewed in this sociopolitical perspective, the New Right is not a conservative force but a radical or revolutionary one. It seeks the displacement of the entrenched elite, the discarding of its ideology of liberalism and cosmopolitanism, and its own victory as a new governing class in America. The New Right is able to aspire to these ambitions because, unlike the Old Right, it has a viable social base in the Middle American Radicals and in the dynamic economy of the Sunbelt.

If the New Right is not conservative, it should be clear that it will need a new ideology, formula, or political theory that can win the loyalties and represent the interests of its social base and rationalize its quest for social and political power. The primary justification of its quest for power must be the corruption, decadence, incompetence, oppressiveness, and alienation of the old elite that it is seeking to displace. This elite—identified here as the managerial class that rose to power in the government bureaucracy, large corporations, and other modern mass-scale organizations since the 1930s—is clearly foreign to the bulk of the nation in its lifestyle, values, and ideals. Yet these life-styles, values, and ideals cannot be simply discarded by the old elite; they represent a logical outgrowth of its own structural interests: large, social engineering government in alliance with corporations, universities, and foundations, the mass media, unions, and other bureaucracies. Only the cosmopolitan ethic and liberal ideology described above can rationalize these structural interests of the entrenched elite. The fundamental problem is not the ethic or ideology of the elite but the elite itself, and it is the elite and its apparatus of power that must be the main targets of New Right attack.

The principal values to which the New Right should appeal in this attack differ from those defended by the Old Right as well as from those articulated by the managerial elite. In place of the free market of the Old Right or the "stabilization" of the present elite, the New Right should center its economic aspirations on the concept of economic growth. Clearly, the concept of growth involves a dismantling of bureaucracy, regulation, fiscal and environmentalist policies, and a decentralization and privatization of economic forces, but this reorientation toward a freer economic climate is incidental to the central idea of economic growth, expansion, and dynamism. In place of the strictly anticommunist foreign policy of the Old Right or the selective isolationism of the decadent managerial class, the New Right should assert a foreign policy founded on a new activist and expansionist nationalism—a policy that would necessarily encompass Old Right anticommunism but would also respond to rising noncommunist threats. In place of the hedonistic, pragmatist, relativist, and secularized cosmopolitanism of the present elite, the New Right should expound without compromise the ideals and institutions of the American ethos: hard work and self-sacrifice, morally based legislation and policies, and a public commitment to religious faith. In place of the faith in congressional supremacy and established intermediary institutions that characterizes both the Old Right and the entrenched managerial elite, the New Right will favor a populist-based presidency able to cut through the present oligarchical establishment and to promote new intermediary institutions centered on Middle America.

The conflict into which the New Right is entering is a complex one. Because of its complexity, the political expression of the MARs cannot take forms that are entirely consistent in ideology or calculated to please everyone within its own ranks. Because the issues and values are real and not the product of abstract cerebration, there will probably be no monolithic movement under the New Right aegis. There will be a coalition that will often find itself split, and the opponents of the New Right will of course seek to take advantage of these splits. Hence, the political movement requires, more than is customary in American political history, a discipline, a leadership, and a formula that will promote its cohesion, its electoral advantages, and its objectives.

The late Carroll Quigley argued that new civilizations form themselves around dynamic, innovative social forces, which he called "instruments." As these instruments develop, they acquire vested interests that retard their dynamism and slow their innovative capacities. The instruments then become ossified "institutions" that oppose the rise of new forces and, unless challenged, lead to civilizational decay.[9] The managerial elite as described in this essay began its history as an "instrument" and is now in a stage of what Quigley would call "institutionalization." In its youth it was a force for much innovation, expansion, and cultural dynamism. In its senescence it is a force only for itself and for the cultivation of self-indulgence, both material and psychological. Its power is being challenged by a new force, also described above; if victorious, no doubt the MARs themselves will exploit their rivals and, like all men, have much to answer for. No doubt also the new elite that they will form will someday degenerate and itself be challenged by new dynamic forces. But the choice between the present elite and its challengers is not merely between one power and another. It is a choice between degeneration and rebirth, between death and survival, for survival is not a right or a gift freely granted by the powers that be. Survival, in the jungle or in political societies, is a hard-won prize that depends ultimately on power itself. In this world, wrote Goethe, one must be the hammer or the anvil. The essence of the message from MARs is that the messengers want to work the forge.

NOTES

1. Donald I. Warren, *The Radical Center: Middle Americans and the Politics of Alienation* (Notre Dame: University of Notre Dame, 1976), 23–29.

2. Ibid., 20–21.

3. Gaetano Mosca, *The Ruling Class (Elementi di Scienza Politica)*, ed. Arthur Livingston, trans. Hannah D. Kahn (New York: McGraw-Hill, 1939), 70.

4. The alliance of elite and underclass against the middle class—what I have here called the "sandwich strategy"—has been noted by, among others, New Right political theorists Robert W. Whitaker, *A Plague on Both Your Houses*

(Washington: Robert B. Luce, 1976), chap. 4; and William A. Rusher, *The Making of a New Majority Party* (Ottawa, Ill: Green Hill Publishers, 1975), 33.

5. See Irving Kristol, *Two Cheers for Capitalism* (New York: New American Library, 1979), especially chap. 2. Kristol's idea of the "New Class" is apparently limited to the public sector and media and does not extend to large corporations. James Burnham, *The Managerial Revolution: What Is Happening in the World* (New York: John Day Company, 1941), despite its age and problems, remains to my mind the most accurate and comprehensive account of the New Class, its ideology, interests and dynamics. For a fuller discussion of the New Class, see B. Bruce-Briggs, ed. *The New Class?* (New Brunswick, N.J.: Transaction, 1979).

6. G. William Domhoff, *The Powers That Be: Processes of Ruling-Class Domination in America* (New York: Random House, 1978), 85; see also John Chamberlain, "The New Enterprising Americans," *Policy Review*, No. 13 (Summer 1980): 36, on "the preponderance of small-scale Middle Western enterprisers on the board of trustees" of conservative Hillsdale College, Michigan, and their criticism of Big Business.

7. Thomas Ferguson and Joel Rogers, "Another Trilateral Election?" *Nation* (June 28, 1980): 783–84.

8. Jeffrey Hart, "The Presidency: Shifting Conservative Perspectives?" *National Review* (November 22, 1974): 1351–55.

9. Carroll Quigley, *The Evolution of Civilizations: An Introduction to Historical Analysis* (New York: Macmillan, 1961), 73–74.

Chapter Thirty

Why Big Business Is Good for America

Irving Kristol

The United States is the capitalist nation par excellence. That is to say, it is not merely the case that capitalism has flourished here more vigorously than, for instance, in the nations of Western Europe. The point is, rather, that the Founding Fathers *intended* this nation to be capitalist and re-garded it as the *only* set of economic arrangements consistent with the liberal democracy they had established. They did not use the term "capi-talism," of course; but, then, neither did Adam Smith, whose *Wealth of Nations* was also published in 1776, and who spoke of "the system of natural liberty." That invidious word, "capitalism," was invented by Eu-ropean socialists about a half-century later—just as our other common expression, "free enterprise," was invented still later by antisocialists who saw no good reason for permitting their enemies to appropriate the vocabulary of public discourse. But words aside, it is a fact that capitalism in this country has a historical legitimacy that it does not possess else-where. In other lands, the nation and its fundamental institutions ante-date the capitalist era; in the United States, where liberal democracy is not merely a form of government but also a "way of life," capitalism and democracy have been organically linked.

This fact, quite simply accepted until the 1930s—accepted by both radical critics and staunch defenders of the American regime—has been obscured in recent decades by the efforts of liberal scholars to create a respectable pedigree for the emerging "welfare state." The impetus behind this scholarship was justified, to a degree. It is true that the Founding

Excerpts from "Conservatism in America: Since 1930: A Reader with Documents" by Irving Kristol, as reprinted in *Neoconservatism: The Autobiography of an Idea: Selected Essays*, pp. 211–229.

Fathers were not dogmatic laissez-faireists, in a later neo-Darwinian or "libertarian" sense of the term. They were intensely suspicious of governmental power, but they never could have subscribed to the doctrine of "our enemy, the State." They believed there was room for some governmental intervention in economic affairs; and—what is less frequently remarked—they believed most firmly in the propriety of governmental intervention and regulation in the areas of public taste and public morality. But, when one has said this, one must add emphatically that there really is little doubt that the Founders were convinced that economics was the sphere of human activity where government intervention was, as a general rule, least likely to be productive, and that "the system of natural liberty" in economic affairs was the complement to our system of constitutional liberty in political and civil affairs. They surely would have agreed with Hayek that the paternalistic government favored by modern liberalism led down the "road to serfdom."

But one must also concede that both the Founding Fathers and Adam Smith would have been perplexed by the kind of capitalism we have in 1978. They could not have interpreted the domination of economic activity by large corporate bureaucracies as representing, in any sense, the working of a "system of natural liberty." Entrepreneurial capitalism, as they understood it, was mainly an individual—or at most, a family—affair. Such large organizations as might exist—joint stock companies, for example—were limited in purpose (e.g., building a canal or a railroad) and usually in duration as well. The large, publicly owned corporation of today which strives for immortality, which is committed to no line of business but rather (like an investment banker) seeks the best return on investment, which is governed by an anonymous oligarchy, would have troubled and puzzled them, just as it troubles and puzzles us. And they would have asked themselves the same questions we have been asking ourselves for almost a century now: Who "owns" this new leviathan? Who governs it, and by what right, and according to what principles?

The Unpopular Revolution

To understand the history of corporate capitalism in America, it is important to realize in what sense it may be fairly described as an "accidental institution." Not in the economic sense, of course. In the latter part of the last century, in all industrialized nations, the large corporation was born out of both economic necessity and economic opportunity: the necessity of large pools of capital and of a variety of technical expertise to exploit the emerging technologies, and the opportunity for economies of scale in production, marketing, and service in a rapidly urbanizing society. It all happened so quickly that the term "corporate revolution" is not inappropriate. In 1870, the United States was a land of small family-owned business. By 1905, the large, publicly owned corporation dominated the economic scene.

But the corporate revolution was always, during that period, an unpopular revolution. It was seen by most Americans as an accident of economic circumstance—something that happened to them rather than something they had created. They had not foreseen it; they did not understand it; in no way did it seem to "fit" into the accepted ideology of the American democracy. No other institution in American history—not even slavery—has ever been so consistently unpopular as has the large corporation with the American public. It was controversial from the outset, and it has remained controversial to this day.

This is something the current crop of corporate executives find very difficult to appreciate. Most of them reached maturity during the post-war period, 1945–1960. As it happens, this was—with the possible exception of the 1920s—just about the only period when public opinion was, on the whole, well-disposed to the large corporation. After 15 years of depression and war, the American people wanted houses, consumer goods, and relative security of employment—all the things that the modern corporation is so good at supplying. The typical corporate executive of today, in his fifties or sixties, was led to think that such popular acceptance was "normal," and is therefore inclined to believe that there are novel and specific forces behind the upsurge of anticorporate sentiment in the past decade. As a matter of fact, he is partly right: there *is* something significantly new about the hostility to the large corporation in our day. But there is also something very old, something coeval with the very existence of the large corporation itself. And it is the interaction of the old hostility with the new which has put the modern corporation in the critical condition that we find it in today.

The old hostility is based on what we familiarly call "populism." This is a sentiment basic to any democracy—indispensable to its establishment but also, ironically, inimical to its survival. Populism is the constant fear and suspicion that power and/or authority, whether in government or out, is being used to frustrate "the will of the people." It is a spirit that intimidates authority and provides the popular energy to curb and resist it. The very possibility of a democratic society—as distinct from the forms of representative government, which are its political expression—is derived from, and is constantly renewed by, the populist temper. The Constitution endows the United States with a republican form of government, in which the free and explicit consent of the people must ultimately ratify the actions of those in authority. But the populist spirit, which both antedated and survived the Constitutional Convention, made the United States a democratic nation as well as a republican one, committed to "the democratic way of life" as well as to the proprieties of constitutional government. It is precisely the strength of that commitment which has always made the American democracy somehow different from the democracies of Western Europe—a difference which every European observer has been quick to remark.

But populism is, at the same time, an eternal problem for the American democratic republic. It incarnates an antinomian impulse, a Jacobin contempt for the "mere" forms of law and order and civility. It also engenders an impulse toward a rather infantile political utopianism, on the premise that nothing is too good for "the people." Above all, it is a temper and state of mind which too easily degenerates into political paranoia, with "enemies of the people" being constantly discovered and exorcised and convulsively purged. Populist paranoia is always busy subverting the very institutions and authorities that the democratic republic laboriously creates for the purpose of orderly self-government.

In the case of the large corporation, we see a healthy populism and a feverish paranoia simultaneously being provoked by its sudden and dramatic appearance. The paranoia takes the form of an instinctive readiness to believe anything reprehensible, no matter how incredible, about the machinations of "big business." That species of journalism and scholarship which we call "muckraking" has made this kind of populist paranoia a permanent feature of American intellectual and public life. Though the businessman per se has never been a fictional hero of bourgeois society (as Stendhal observed, a merchant may be honorable but there is nothing heroic about him), it is only after the rise of "big business" that the businessman becomes the natural and predestined villain of the novel, the drama, the cinema, and, more recently, television. By now most Americans are utterly convinced that all "big business" owes its existence to the original depredations of "robber barons"—a myth which never really was plausible, which more recent scholarship by economic historians has thoroughly discredited, but which probably forever will have a secure hold on the American political imagination. Similarly, most Americans are now quick to believe that "big business" conspires secretly but most effectively to manipulate the economic and political system—an enterprise which, in prosaic fact, corporate executives are too distracted and too unimaginative even to contemplate.

Along with this kind of paranoia, however, populist hostility toward the large corporation derives from an authentic bewilderment and concern about the place of this new institution in American life. In its concentration of assets and power—power to make economic decisions affecting the lives of tens of thousands of citizens—it seemed to create a dangerous disharmony between the economic system and the political. In the America of the 1890s, even government did not have, and did not claim, such power (except in wartime). *No one* was supposed to have such power; it was, indeed, a radical diffusion of power that was thought to be an essential characteristic of democratic capitalism. The rebellion of Jacksonian democracy against the Bank of the United States had been directed precisely against such an "improper" concentration of power. A comparable rebellion now took place against "big business."

"Big Business" or Capitalism?

It was not, however, a rebellion against capitalism as such. On the contrary, popular hostility to the large corporation reflected the fear that this new institution was subverting capitalism as Americans then understood (and, for the most part, still understand) it. This understanding was phrased in individualistic terms. The entrepreneur was conceived of as a real person, not as a legal fiction. The "firm" was identified with such a real person (or a family of real persons) who took personal risks, reaped personal rewards, and assumed personal responsibility for his actions. One of the consequences of the victorious revolt against the Bank of the United States had been to make the chartering of corporations—legal "persons" with limited liability—under state law a routine and easy thing, the assumption being that this would lead to a proliferation of small corporations, still easily identifiable with the flesh-and-blood entrepreneurs who founded them. The rise of "big business" frustrated such expectations.

Moreover, the large corporation not only seemed to be but actually was a significant deviation from traditional capitalism. One of the features of the large corporation—though more a consequence of its existence than its cause—was its need for, and its ability to create, "orderly markets." What businessmen disparagingly call "cutthroat competition," with its wild swings in price, its large fluctuations in employment, its unpredictable effects upon profits—all this violates the very *raison d'être* of a large corporation, with its need for relative stability so that its long-range investment decisions can be rationally calculated. The modern corporation always looks to the largest and most powerful firm in the industry to establish "market leadership" in price, after which competition will concentrate on quality, service, and the introduction of new products. One should not exaggerate the degree to which the large corporation is successful in these efforts. John Kenneth Galbraith's notion that the large corporation simply manipulates its market through the power of advertising and fixes the price level with sovereign authority is a wild exaggeration. This is what all corporations *try* to do; it is what a few corporations, in some industries, sometimes succeed in doing. Still, there is little doubt that the idea of a "free market," in the era of large corporations, is not quite the original capitalist idea.

The populist response to the transformation of capitalism by the large corporation was, and is: "Break it up!" Antitrust and antimonopoly legislation was the consequence. Such legislation is still enacted and reenacted, and antitrust prosecutions still make headlines. But the effort is by now routine, random, and largely pointless. There may be a few lawyers left in the Justice Department or the Federal Trade Commission who sincerely believe that such laws, if stringently enforced, could restore capitalism to something like its pristine individualist form. But it is much more probable that the lawyers who staff such government agencies launch these intermittent crusades against "monopoly" and "oligopoly"— terms that are distressingly vague and inadequate when applied to the real world—because they prefer such activity to mere idleness, and because they anticipate, that a successful prosecution will enhance their professional reputations. No one expects them to be effectual, whether the government wins or loses. Just how much difference, after all, would it make if AT&T were forced to spin off its Western Electric manufacturing subsidiary, or if IBM were divided into three different computer companies? All that would be accomplished is a slight increase in the number of large corporations, with very little consequence for the shape of the economy or the society as a whole.

True, one could imagine, in the abstract, a much more radical effort to break up "big business." But there are good reasons why, though many talk solemnly about this possibility, no one does anything about it. The costs would simply be too high. The economic costs, most obviously: an adverse effect on productivity, on capital investment, on our balance of payments, etc. But the social and political costs would be even more intolerable. Our major trade unions, having after many years succeeded in establishing collective bargaining on a national level with the large corporation, are not about to sit back and watch their power disintegrate for the sake of an ideal such as "decentralization." And the nation's pension funds are not about to permit the assets of the corporations in which they have invested to be dispersed, and the security of their pension payments correspondingly threatened.

One suspects that even popular opinion, receptive in principle to the diminution of "big business," would in actuality find the process too painful to tolerate. For the plain fact is that, despite much academic agitation about the horrors of being an "organization man," a large proportion of those who now work for a living, of whatever class, have learned to prefer the security, the finely calibrated opportunities for advancement, the fringe benefits, and the paternalism of a large corporation to the presumed advantages of employment in smaller firms. It is not only corporate executives who are fearful of "cutthroat competition"; most of us, however firmly we declare our faith in capitalism and "free enterprise," are sufficiently conservative in our instincts to wish to avoid all such capitalist rigors. Even radical professors, who in their books find large bureaucratic corporations "dehumanizing," are notoriously reluctant to give up tenured appointments in large bureaucratic universities for riskier opportunities elsewhere.

So the populist temper and the large corporation coexist uneasily in America today, in what can only be called a marriage of convenience. There is little affection, much nagging and backbiting and whining on all sides, but it endures "for the sake of the children," as it were. Not too long ago, there was reason to hope that, out of the habit of coexistence, there would emerge something like a philosophy of coexistence: a mutual adaptation of the democratic-individualist-capitalist ideal and the bureaucratic-corporate reality, sanctioned by a new revised version of the theory of democracy and capitalism—a new political and social philosophy, in short, which extended the reach of traditional views without repudiating them. But that possibility, if it was ever more than a fancy, has been effectively canceled by the rise, over the past decade, of an anticapitalist ethos which has completely transformed the very definition of the problem.

The Antiliberal Left

This ethos, in its American form, is not *explicitly* anticapitalistic, and this obscures our perception and understanding of it. It has its roots in the tradition of "progressive reform," a tradition which slightly antedated the corporate revolution but which was immensely stimulated by it. In contrast to populism, this was (and is) an upper-middle-class tradition—an "elitist" tradition, as one would now say. Though it absorbed a great many socialist and neosocialist and quasi-socialist ideas, it was too American—too habituated to the rhetoric of individualism, and even in some measure to its reality—to embrace easily a synoptic, collectivist vision of the future as enunciated in socialist dogmas. It was willing to contemplate "public ownership" (i.e., ownership by the political authorities) of *some* of the "means of production," but on the whole it preferred to think in terms of *regulating* the large corporation rather than nationalizing it or breaking it up. It is fair to call it an indigenous and peculiarly American counterpart to European socialism: addressing itself to the same problems defined in much the same way, motivated by the same ideological impulse, but assuming an adversary posture toward "big business" specifically rather than toward capitalism in general.

At least, that is what "progressive reform" used to be. In the past decade, however, it has experienced a transmutation of ideological substance while preserving most of the traditional rhetorical wrappings. That is because it embraced, during these years, a couple of other political traditions, European in origin, so that what we still call "liberalism" in the United States is now something quite different from the liberalism of the older "progressive reform" impulse. It is so different, indeed, as to have created a cleavage between those who think of themselves as "old liberals"—some of whom are now redesignated as "neoconservatives"— and the new liberals who are in truth men and women of "the Left," in the European sense of that term. This is an important point, worthy of some elaboration and clarification, especially since the new liberalism is not usually very candid about the matter.[1]

The Left in Europe, whether "totalitarian" or "democratic," has consistently been antiliberal. That is to say, it vigorously repudiates the intellectual traditions of liberalism—as expressed, say, by Locke, Montesquieu, Adam Smith, and Tocqueville—and with equal vigor rejects the key institution of liberalism: the (relatively) free market (which necessarily implies limited government). The Left emerges out of a rebellion against the "anarchy" and "vulgarity" of a civilization that is shaped by individuals engaged in market transactions. The "anarchy" to which it refers is the absence of any transcending goal or purpose which society is constrained to pursue and which socialists, with their superior understanding of History, feel obligated to prescribe. Such a prescription, when fulfilled, will supposedly reestablish a humane "order." The "vulgarity" to which it refers is the fact that a free market responds, or tries to respond, to the appetites and preferences of common men and women, whose use of their purchasing power determines the shape of the civilization. Since common men and women are likely to have "common" preferences, tastes, and aspirations, the society they create—the "consumption society," as it is now called—will be regarded by some critics as shortsightedly "materialistic." People will seek to acquire what they want (e.g., automobiles), not what they "need" (e.g., mass transit). Socialists are persuaded that they have a superior understanding of people's true needs, and that the people will be more truly happy in a society where socialists have the authority to define those needs, officially and unequivocally.

Obviously, socialism is an "elitist" movement, and in its beginnings—with Saint-Simon and Auguste Comte—was frankly conceived of as such. Its appeal has always been to "intellectuals" (who feel dispossessed by and alienated from a society in which they are merely one species of common man) and members of the upper middle class who, having reaped the benefits of capitalism, are now in a position to see its costs. (It must be said that these costs are not imaginary: Socialism would not have such widespread appeal if its critique of liberal capitalism were entirely without substance.) But all social movements in the modern world must define themselves as "democratic," since democratic legitimacy is the only kind of legitimacy we recognize. So "totalitarian" socialism insists that it is a "people's democracy," in which the "will of the people" is mystically incarnated in the ruling party. "Democratic socialism," on the other hand, would like to think that it can "socialize" the economic sector while leaving the rest of society "liberal." As Robert Nozick puts it, democratic socialists want to proscribe only "*capitalist* transactions between consenting adults."

The trouble with the latter approach is that democratic socialists, when elected to office, discover that to collectivize economic life you have to coerce all sorts of other institutions (e.g., the trade unions, the media, the educational system) and limit individual freedom in all sorts of ways (e.g., freedom to travel, freedom to "drop out" from the world of work, freedom to choose the kind of education one prefers) if a "planned society" is to function efficiently. When "democratic socialist" governments show reluctance to take such actions, they are pushed into doing so by the "left wings" of their "movements," who feel betrayed by the distance that still exists between the reality they experience and the socialist ideal which enchants them. Something like this is now happening in all the European social-democratic parties and in a country like India.

The "New Class"

The United States never really had any such movement of the Left, at least not to any significant degree. It was regarded as an "un-American" thing, as indeed it was. True, the movement of "progressive reform" was "elitist" both in its social composition and its social aims: it, too, was distressed by the "anarchy" and "vulgarity" of capitalist civilization. But in the main it accepted as a fact the proposition that capitalism and liberalism were organically connected, and it proposed to itself the goal of "mitigating the evils of capitalism," rather than abolishing liberal capitalism and replacing it with "a new social order" in which a whole new set of human relationships would be established. It was an authentic *reformist* movement. It wanted to regulate the large corporations so that this concentration of private power could not develop into an oligarchical threat to democratic-liberal capitalism. It was ready to interfere with the free market so that the instabilities generated by capitalism—above all, instability of employment—would be less costly in human terms. It was even willing to tamper occasionally with the consumer's freedom of choice where there was a clear consensus that the micro-decisions of the marketplace added up to macro-consequences that were felt to be unacceptable. And it hoped to correct the "vulgarity" of capitalist civilization by educating the people so that their "preference schedules" (as economists would say) would be, in traditional terms, more elevated, more appreciative of "the finer things in life."

Ironically, it was the extraordinary increase in mass higher education after World War II that, perhaps more than anything else, infused the traditional movement for "progressive reform" with various impulses derived from the European Left. The earlier movement had been "elitist" in fact as well as in intention, i.e., it was sufficiently small so that, even while influential, it could hardly contemplate the possibility of actually exercising "power." Mass higher education has converted this movement into something like a mass movement proper, capable of driving a president from office (1968) and nominating its own candidate (1972). The intentions remain "elitist," of course; but the movement now encompasses some millions of people. These are the people whom liberal capitalism had sent to college in order to help manage its affluent, highly technological, mildly paternalistic, "postindustrial" society.

This "new class" consists of scientists, lawyers, city planners, social workers, educators, criminologists, sociologists, public health doctors, etc.—a substantial number of whom find their careers in the expanding public sector rather than the private. The public sector, indeed, is where they prefer to be. They are, as one says, "idealistic," i.e., far less interested in individual financial rewards than in the corporate power of their class. Though they continue to speak the language of "progressive reform," in actuality they are acting upon a hidden agenda: to propel the nation from that modified version of capitalism we call "the welfare state" toward an economic system so stringently regulated in detail as to fulfill many of the traditional anticapitalist aspirations of the Left.

The exact nature of what has been happening is obscured by the fact that this "new class" is not merely liberal but truly "libertarian" in its approach to all areas of life—except economics. It celebrates individual liberty of speech and expression and action to an unprecedented degree, so that at times it seems almost anarchistic in its conception of the good life. But this joyful individualism always stops short of the border where economics—i.e., capitalism—begins. The "new class" is surely sincere in such a contradictory commitment to a maximum of individual freedom in a society where economic life becomes less free with every passing year. But it is instructive to note that these same people, who are irked and inflamed by the slightest noneconomic restriction in the United States, can be admiring of Maoist China and not in the least appalled by the total collectivization of life—and the total destruction of liberty—there. They see this regime as "progressive," not "reactionary." And, in this perception, they unwittingly tell us much about their deepest fantasies and the natural bias of their political imagination.

Meanwhile, the transformation of American capitalism proceeds apace. Under the guise of coping with nasty "externalities"—air pollution, water pollution, noise pollution, traffic pollution, health pollution, or what have you—more and more of the basic economic decisions are being removed from the marketplace and transferred to the "public"—i.e., political— sector, where the "new class," by virtue of its expertise and skills, is so well represented. This movement is naturally applauded by the media, which are also for the most part populated by members of this "new class" who believe—as the Left has always believed—it is government's responsibility to cure all the ills of the human condition, and who ridicule those politicians who deny the possibility (and therefore the propriety) of government doing any such ambitious thing. And, inevitably, more ex- plicitly socialist and neosocialist themes are beginning boldly to emerge from the protective shell of reformist-liberal rhetoric. The need for some kind of "national economic plan" is now being discussed seriously in Congressional circles; the desirability of "public"—i.e., political—ap- pointees to the boards of directors of the largest corporations is becoming more apparent to more politicians and journalists with every passing day; the utter "reasonableness," in principle, of price and wage controls is no longer even a matter for argument, but is subject only to circumstantial and prudential considerations. Gradually, the traditions of the Left are being absorbed into the agenda of "progressive reform," and the structure of American society is being radically, if discreetly, altered.

"The Enemy of Being Is Having"

One of the reasons this process is so powerful, and meets only relatively feeble resistance, is that it has a continuing source of energy within the capitalist system itself. That source is not the "inequalities" or "injustices" of capitalism, as various ideologies of the Left insist. These may represent foci around which dissent is occasionally and skillfully mobilized. But the most striking fact about anticapitalism is the degree to which it is *not* a spontaneous working-class phenomenon. Capitalism, like all economic and social systems, breeds its own peculiar discontents, but the discontents of the working class are, in and of themselves, not one of its major problems. Yes, there is class conflict in capitalism; there is always class conflict, and the very notion of a possible society without class conflict is one of socialism's most bizarre fantasies. (Indeed, it is this fantasy that is socialism's original contribution to modern political theory; the importance of class conflict itself was expounded by Aristotle and was never doubted by anyone who ever bothered to look at the real world.) But there is no case, in any country that can reasonably be called "capitalist," of such class conflict leading to a proletarian revolution. Capitalism, precisely because its aim is the satisfaction of "common" appetites and aspirations, can adequately cope with its own class conflicts, through economic growth primarily and some version of the welfare state secondarily. It can do so, however, only if it is permitted to—a permission which the anticapitalist spirit is loath to concede. This spirit *wants* to see capitalism falter and fail.

The essence of this spirit is to be found, not in *The Communist Manifesto*, but rather in the young Marx who wrote: "*The enemy of being is having.*" This sums up neatly the animus which intellectuals from the beginning, and "the new class" in our own day, have felt toward the system of liberal capitalism. This system is in truth "an acquisitive society," by traditional standards. Not that men and women under capitalism are "greedier" than under feudalism or socialism or whatever. Almost all people, almost all of the time, want more than they have. But capitalism is unique among social and economic systems in being organized for the overriding purpose of giving them more than they have. And here is where it runs into trouble; Those who benefit most from capitalism—and their children, especially—experience a withering away of the acquisitive impulse. Or, to put it more accurately: They cease to think of acquiring money and begin to think of acquiring power so as to improve the "quality of life," and to give *being* priority over *having*. That is the meaning of the well-known statement by a student radical of the 1960s: "You don't know what hell is like unless you were raised in Scarsdale." Since it is the ambition of capitalism to enable everyone to live in Scarsdale or its equivalent, this challenge is far more fundamental than the orthodox Marxist one, which says—against all the evidence—that capitalism will fail because it *cannot* get everyone to live in Scarsdale.

Against this new kind of attack, any version of capitalism would be vulnerable. But the version of corporate capitalism under which we live is not merely vulnerable; it is practically defenseless. It is not really hard to make a decent case, on a pragmatic level, for liberal capitalism today—especially since the anticapitalist societies the 20th century has given birth to are, even by their own standards, monstrous abortions and "betrayals" of their originating ideals. And corporate capitalism does have the great merit of being willing to provide a milieu of comfortable liberty—in universities, for example—for those who prefer *being* to *having*. But the trouble with the large corporation today is that it does not possess a clear theoretical—i.e., ideological—legitimacy within the frame-work of liberal capitalism itself. Consequently the gradual usurpation of managerial authority by the "new class"—mainly through the transfer of this authority to the new breed of regulatory officials (who are the very prototype of the class)—is almost irresistible.

Bureaucratic Enterprise

So long as business was an activity carried on by real individuals who "owned" the property they managed, the politicians, the courts, and public opinion were all reasonably respectful of the capitalist proprieties. Not only was the businessman no threat to liberal democracy; he was, on the contrary, the very epitome of the bourgeois liberal-democratic ethos—the man who succeeded by diligence, enterprise, sobriety, and all those other virtues that Benjamin Franklin catalogued for us, and which we loosely call "the Protestant ethic."[2]

On the whole, even today, politicians and public opinion are inclined to look with some benevolence on "small business," and no one seems to be interested in leading a crusade against it. But the professionally managed large corporation is another matter entirely. The top executives of these enormous bureaucratic institutions are utterly sincere when they claim fealty to "free enterprise," and they even have a point: Managing a business corporation, as distinct from a government agency, does require a substantial degree of entrepreneurial risk-taking and entrepreneurial skill. But it is also the case that they are as much functionaries as entrepreneurs, and rather anonymous functionaries at that. Not only don't we know who the chairman of General Motors is; we know so little about the kind of person who holds such a position that we haven't the faintest idea as to whether or not we want our children to grow up like him. Horatio Alger, writing in the era of precorporate capitalism, had no such problems. And there is something decidedly odd about a society in which a whole class of Very Important People is not automatically held up as one possible model of emulation for the young, and cannot be so held up because they are, as persons, close to invisible.

Nor is it at all clear whose interests these entrepreneur-functionaries are serving. In theory, they are elected representatives of the stockholder "owners." But stockholder elections are almost invariably routine affirmations of management's will, because management will have previously secured the support of the largest stockholders; and for a long while now stockholders have essentially regarded themselves, and are regarded by management, as little more than possessors of a variable-income security. A stock certificate has become a lien against the company's earnings and assets—a subordinated lien, in both law and fact—rather than a charter of "citizenship" within a corporate community. And though management will talk piously, when it serves its purposes, about its obligations to the stockholders, the truth is that it prefers to have as little to do with them as possible, since their immediate demands are only too likely to conflict with management's long-term corporate plans.

It is interesting to note that when such an organization of business executives as the Committee on Economic Development drew up a kind of official declaration of the responsibilities of management a few years ago, it conceived of the professional manager as "a trustee balancing the interests of many diverse participants and constituents in the enterprise," and then enumerated these participants and constituents: employees, customers, suppliers, stockholders, government—practically everyone. Such a declaration serves only to ratify an accomplished fact: The large corporation has ceased being a species of private property, and is now a "quasi-public" institution. But if it is a "quasi-public" institution, some novel questions may be properly addressed to it: By what right does the self-perpetuating oligarchy that constitutes "management" exercise its powers? On what principles does it do so? To these essentially political questions management can only respond with the weak economic answer that its legitimacy derives from the superior efficiency with which it responds to signals from the free market. But such an argument from efficiency is not compelling when offered by a "quasi-public" institution. In a democratic republic such as ours, public and quasi-public institutions are not supposed simply to be efficient at responding to people's transient desires, are not supposed to be simply *pandering* institutions, but are rather supposed to help shape the people's wishes, and ultimately, the people's character, according to some version, accepted by the people itself, of the "public good" and "public interest." This latter task the "new class" feels itself supremely qualified to perform, leaving corporate management in the position of arguing that it is improper for this "quasi-public" institution to do more than give the people what they want: a debased version of the democratic idea which has some temporary demagogic appeal but no permanent force.

The Corporation and Liberal Democracy

Whether for good or evil—and one can leave this for future historians to debate—the large corporation has gone "quasi-public," i.e., it now straddles, uncomfortably and uncertainly, both the private and public sectors of our "mixed economy." In a sense one can say that the modern large corporation stands to the bourgeois-individualist capitalism of yesteryear as the "imperial" American polity stands to the isolated republic from which it emerged. Such a development may or may not represent "progress," but there is no turning back.

The danger which this situation poses for American democracy is not the tantalizing ambiguities inherent in such a condition; it is the genius of a pluralist democracy to convert such ambiguities into possible sources of institutional creativity and to avoid "solving" them, as a Jacobin democracy would, with one swift stroke of the sword. The danger is rather that the large corporation will be thoroughly integrated into the public sector, and lose its private character altogether. The transformation of American capitalism that *this* would represent—a radical departure from the quasi-bourgeois "mixed economy" to a system that could be fairly described as kind of "state capitalism"—does constitute a huge potential threat to the individual liberties Americans have traditionally enjoyed.

One need not, therefore, be an admirer of the large corporation to be concerned about its future. One might even regard its "bureaucratic-acquisitive" ethos, in contrast to the older "bourgeois-moralistic" ethos, as a sign of cultural decadence and still be concerned about its future. In our pluralistic society we frequently find ourselves defending specific concentrations of power, about which we might otherwise have the most mixed feelings, on the grounds that they contribute to a general diffusion of power, a diffusion which creates the "space" in which individual liberty can survive and prosper. This is certainly our experience vis-à-vis certain religious organizations—e.g., the Catholic Church or the Mormons—

whose structure and values are, in some respects at least, at variance with our common democratic beliefs, and yet whose existence serves to preserve our democracy as a free and liberal society. The general principle of checks and balances, and of decentralized authority too, is as crucial to the social and economic structures of a liberal democracy as to its political structure.

Nevertheless, it seems clear that the large corporation is not going to be able to withstand those forces pulling and pushing it into the political sector unless it confronts the reality of its predicament and adapts itself to this reality in a self-preserving way. There is bound to be disagreement as to the forms such adaptation should take, some favoring institutional changes that emphasize and clarify the corporation's "public" nature, others insisting that its "private" character must be stressed anew. Probably a mixture of both strategies would be most effective. If large corporations are to avoid having government-appointed directors on their boards, they will have to take the initiative and try to preempt that possibility by themselves appointing distinguished "outside" directors, directors from outside the business community. At the same time, if corporations are going to be able to resist the total usurpation of their decision-making powers by government, they must create a constituency— of their stockholders, above all—which will candidly intervene in the "political game" of interest-group politics, an intervention fully in accord with the principles of our democratic system.

In both cases, the first step will have to be to persuade corporate management that some such change is necessary. This will be difficult: corporate managers are (and enjoy being) essentially economic-decision-making animals, and they are profoundly resentful of the "distractions" which "outside interference" of any kind will impose on them. After all, most chief executives have a tenure of about six years, and they all wish to establish the best possible track record, in terms of "bottom line" results, during that period. Very few are in a position to, and even fewer have an inclination to, take a long and larger view of the corporation and its institutional problems.

At the same time, the crusade against the corporations continues, with the "new class" successfully appealing to populist anxieties, seeking to run the country in the "right" way and to reshape our civilization along lines superior to those established by the marketplace. Like all crusades, it engenders an enthusiastic paranoia about the nature of the Enemy and the deviousness of His operations. Thus, the *New Yorker*, which has become the liberal-chic organ of the "new class," has discovered the maleficent potential of the multinational corporation at exactly the time when the multinational corporation is in full retreat before the forces of nationalism everywhere. And the fact that American corporations sometimes have to bribe foreign politicians—for whom bribery is a way of life—is inflated into a rabid indictment of the personal morals of corporate executives. (That such bribery is also inherent in government-aid programs to the underdeveloped countries is, on the other hand, *never* taken to reflect on those who institute and run such programs, and is thought to be irrelevant to the desirability or success of the programs themselves.) So far, this crusade has been immensely effective. It will continue to be effective until the corporation has decided what kind of institution it is in today's world, and what kinds of reforms are a necessary precondition to a vigorous defense—not of its every action but of its very survival as a quasi-public institution as distinct from a completely politicized institution.

It is no exaggeration to say that the future of liberal democracy in America is intimately involved with these prospects for survival: the survival of an institution which liberal democracy never envisaged, whose birth and existence have been exceedingly troublesome to it, and whose legitimacy it has always found dubious. One can, if one wishes, call this a paradox. Or one can simply say that everything, including liberal democracy, is what it naturally becomes—is what it naturally evolves into—and our problem derives from a reluctance to revise yesteryear's beliefs in the light of today's realities.

NOTES

1. It must be said, however, that even when it is candid, no one seems to pay attention. John Kenneth Galbraith has recently publicly defined himself as a "socialist," and asserts that he has been one—whether wittingly or unwittingly, it is not clear—for many years. But the media still consistently identify him as a "liberal," and he is so generally regarded. Whether this is mere habit or instinctive protective coloration—for the media are a crucial wing of the "new liberalism"—it is hard to say.

2. I say "loosely call" because, as a Jew, I was raised to think that this was an ancient "Hebrew ethic," and some Chinese scholars I have spoken to feel that it could appropriately be called "The Confucian ethic."

Part IX

The Reagan Era

The election in 1980 of conservative Republican Ronald Reagan to the presidency seemed to assure the dawn of a new era in American politics. Reagan had run a campaign focused on restoring economic growth to an economy battered by inflation and high unemployment; he also promised to restore America's military strength and confidence and end detente with the Soviet Union. He would accomplish both goals. Through a policy of tax and spending cuts—generally described as supply-side economics— and by a commitment to eradicate economic inflation, a policy that provoked the worst recession since the 1930s, the economy recovered, initiating an almost twenty-year period of economic growth (with two relatively minor recessions in 1991 and 2001). Reagan's optimism regarding America's promise and his unhesitating desire to free up entrepreneurial investment and decrease reliance on government, helped engender a revolution in economic thinking and governmental policy that continues to this day. It was Democrat Bill Clinton, who, in 1996, uttered the famous phrase "the era of big government is over."

Reagan's second goal was to end detente and confront the Soviet Union. Beginning in early 1981, Reagan increased defense spending to levels not seen since Vietnam. He also refused to hold defense spending hostage to budget cuts, stubbornly resisting his budget director David Stockman's entreaties that massive budget deficits would accrue unless defense spending was curtailed. Stockman was correct, but Reagan refused to yield (over the long term, it could be argued, the lower amount spent on defense without a Cold War to fight, the so-called "peace dividend," was a product of the massive defense spending increases in the 1980s which culminated with the collapse of the Soviet Union).[1]

Reagan confronted the Soviets. He refused to meet with Soviet leaders; sponsored anticommunist resistance movements in Afghanistan, Nicaragua, Cambodia, and Angola; in spite of pressure from Europeans, he deployed Pershing-II missiles in western Europe after the Soviets deployed missiles in eastern Europe; he called the Soviet Union an "evil empire", articulated a missile defense system, known as the Strategic Defense Initiative (dubbed "Star Wars" by the media), that would cripple the Soviet economy if it tried to keep up; and he persisted in his explanation, first in China in 1983, and then in Moscow in 1987, that communism represented the antithesis of freedom, "a bizarre sad chapter in the annals of human history" whose end was in sight. Such rhetoric, combined with policy, strong backing from allies (Great Britain's Margaret Thatcher, West Germany's Helmut Kohl, and France's François Mitterand), a Polish Roman Catholic Pope, John Paul II—the first pontiff from a communist nation, and a simple yet effective faith in American institutions and ideas, contributed to the collapse of communism in eastern Europe, and then, amazingly and with terrific suddenness, in the Soviet Union as well.

Chapter 31 contains excerpts from three Reagan speeches. The first is his 1981 inaugural address; the second, his speech before a joint session of Congress, one month after an assassination attempt, outlining his economic plan that passed in July. The third is the famous "evil empire speech." All three speeches contain Reagan's essential views concerning communism, the economy, and the future of freedom.

Chapter 32 is a remembrance of Reagan written in 1989 by George Will (1941–), the syndicated conservative newspaper columnist. Will was a critic of Reagan's foreign policy, especially his embrace of detente and arms control after Soviet leader Mikhail Gorbachev took power in 1985. He was also not above criticizing Reagan's blunders, like the Iran-Contra scandal that nearly derailed the Reagan presidency in 1986 and 1987. Will recognized in Reagan, however, something historians are beginning to pay attention to: a leadership style and ability that made him a "near great" president (Will argues for the "front rank of the second rank of presidents").[2] He compared Reagan favorably to Franklin Roosevelt, "a great reassurer, a steadying captain who calmed the passengers and, to some extent, the sea." Will, who had worked initially for Buckley's *National Review,* was not well regarded by many conservatives.[3] No activist, he was more inclined to view conservatism from the perspective of Alexander Hamilton, who argued for a bigger government, than from the perspective of Ronald Reagan.[4] He was also impressed by the institutions of American government and by powerful "inside-the-beltway" political figures, despite party affiliation (he would heap praise on Daniel Patrick

Moynihan and AFL-CIO chief Lane Kirkland). He epitomized the conservative intellectual close to the font of power in Washington, a product of conservatism's growing political and intellectual influence.

Some conservative intellectuals were greatly troubled by the shift from being a movement of ideas to one of power and policy. Historian Stephen J. Tonsor (1923–), a professor of European intellectual history at the University of Michigan, was troubled by the new conservatism. In 1986, at a particularly tense meeting of the Philadelphia Society, Tonsor attacked the neoconservatives. His paper, "Why I Am Not a Neoconservative," was later published in *National Review* and is included herein (see Chapter 33). The Philadelphia Society meeting in 1986 contributed to a widening split among the intellectual conservatives—between the neoconservatives, who many believed had usurped the conservative movement, and a group of old Right figures dubbed paleoconservatives.

In 1986 *The Intercollegiate Review,* the biannual publication of the Intercollegiate Studies Institute (ISI), sponsored a symposium on the state of conservatism. Editor Gregory Wolfe, in his introduction, spoke of conservatism "adrift" in the mid-1980s. At the peak of its political success, conservative intellectuals lamented the decline of concern among conservatives with "first principles." The participants in the symposium (Russell Kirk, Gerhart Niemeyer, Clyde Wilson, George Carey, and George Panichas) were all traditionalists. Yet, they spoke to something important— the embrace of politics and policy led conservatives away from ideas and principles. Wolfe's introduction summarizes the common perspective in the symposium.

The response to the attack of Tonsor and the ISI symposium was published in *Commentary* magazine in May 1988. Dan Himmelfarb, a young assistant managing editor at *The Public Interest,* defended neoconservatives in his essay "Conservative Splits" (see Chapter 35) Arguing for unity rather than disunity and that "labels matter less than principles," Himmelfarb provides a counter perspective to the view that the conservative movement had been hijacked by well-connected and well-funded neoconservatives.

In the end, such arguments foreshadowed difficulties ahead for the conservative movement. With the collapse of the Soviet Union and the end of the Cold War, with global communism no longer a threat, what would bind the conservative movement's disparate factions together? Could fusion still work when there were very few real principles on which conservatives agreed anymore? Reagan's political and diplomatic success in the 1980s would represent, ironically, the demise of the conservative movement as it had developed since World War II. What took (or is taking) its place is still a matter of some debate and further disagreement.

Chapter Thirty-one

The Great Communicator
Three Speeches

Ronald Reagan

Inaugural Address, January 20, 1981

Senator Hatfield, Mr. Chief Justice, Mr. President, Vice President Bush, Vice President Mondale, Senator Baker, Speaker O'Neill, Reverend Moomaw, and my fellow citizens:

To a few of us here today this is a solemn and most momentous occasion, and yet in the history of our nation it is a commonplace occurrence. The orderly transfer of authority as called for in the Constitution routinely takes place, as it has for almost two centuries, and few of us stop to think how unique we really are. In the eyes of many in the world, this every-four-year ceremony we accept as normal is nothing less than a miracle.

Mr. President, I want our fellow citizens to know how much you did to carry on this tradition. By your gracious cooperation in the transition process, you have shown a watching world that we are a united people pledged to maintaining a political system which guarantees individual liberty to a greater degree than any other, and I thank you and your people for all your help in maintaining the continuity which is the bulwark of our Republic.

The business of our nation goes forward. These United States are confronted with an economic affliction of great proportions. We suffer from the longest and one of the worst sustained inflations in our national history. It distorts our economic decisions, penalizes thrift, and crushes

From *Public Papers of the Presidents: Ronald Reagan, 1981* (Washington, D.C.: GPO, 1983).

the struggling young and the fixed-income elderly alike. It threatens to shatter the lives of millions of our people.

Idle industries have cast workers into unemployment, human misery, and personal indignity. Those who do work are denied a fair return for their labor by a tax system which penalizes successful achievement and keeps us from maintaining full productivity.

But great as our tax burden is, it has not kept pace with public spending. For decades we have piled deficit upon deficit, mortgaging our future and our children's future for the temporary convenience of the present. To continue this long trend is to guarantee tremendous social, cultural, political, and economic upheavals.

You and I, as individuals, can, by borrowing, live beyond our means, but for only a limited period of time. Why, then, should we think that collectively, as a nation, we're not bound by that same limitation? We must act today in order to preserve tomorrow. And let there be no misunderstanding: We are going to begin to act, beginning today.

The economic ills we suffer have come upon us over several decades. They will not go away in days, weeks, or months, but they will go away. They will go away because we as Americans have the capacity now, as we've had in the past, to do whatever needs to be done to preserve this last and greatest bastion of freedom.

In this present crisis, government is not the solution to our problem; government is the problem. From time to time we've been tempted to believe that society has become too complex to be managed by self-rule, that government by an elite group is superior to government for, by, and of the people. Well, if no one among us is capable of governing himself, then who among us has the capacity to govern someone else? All of us together, in and out of government, must bear the burden. The solutions we seek must be equitable, with no one group singled out to pay a higher price.

We hear much of special interest groups. Well, our concern must be for a special interest group that has been too long neglected. It knows no sectional boundaries or ethnic and racial divisions, and it crosses political party lines. It is made up of men and women who raise our food, patrol our streets, man our mines and factories, teach our children, keep our homes, and heal us when we're sick—professionals, industrialists, shopkeepers, clerks, cabbies, and truck-drivers. They are, in short, "We the people," this breed called Americans.

Well, this administration's objective will be a healthy, vigorous, growing economy that provides equal opportunities for all Americans, with no barriers born of bigotry or discrimination. Putting America back to work means putting all Americans back to work. Ending inflation means freeing all Americans from the terror of runaway living costs. All must share in the productive work of this "new beginning," and all must share in the bounty of a revived economy. With the idealism and fair play which are the core of our system and our strength, we can have a strong and prosperous America, at peace with itself and the world.

So, as we begin, let us take inventory. We are a nation that has a government—not the other way around. And this makes us special among the nations of the Earth. Our government has no power except that granted it by the people. It is time to check and reverse the growth of government, which shows signs of having grown beyond the consent of the governed.

It is my intention to curb the size and influence of the Federal establishment and to demand recognition of the distinction between the powers granted to the Federal Government and those reserved to the States or to the people. All of us need to be reminded that the Federal Government did not create the States; the States created the Federal Government.

Now, so there will be no misunderstanding, it's not my intention to do away with government. It is rather to make it work—work with us, not over us; to stand by our side, not ride on our back. Government can and must provide opportunity, not smother it; foster productivity, not stifle it.

If we look to the answer as to why for so many years we achieved so much, prospered as no other people on Earth, it was because here in this land we unleashed the energy and individual genius of man to a greater extent than has ever been done before. Freedom and the dignity of the individual have been more available and assured here than in any other place on Earth. The price for this freedom at times has been high, but we have never been unwilling to pay that price.

It is no coincidence that our present troubles parallel and are proportionate to the intervention and intrusion in our lives that result from unnecessary and excessive growth of government. It is time for us to realize that we're too great a nation to limit ourselves to small dreams. We're not, as some would have us believe, doomed to an inevitable decline. I do not believe in a fate that will fall on us no matter what we do. I do believe in a fate that will fall on us if we do nothing. So, with all the creative energy at our command, let us begin an era of national renewal. Let us renew our determination, our courage, and our strength. And let us renew our faith and our hope.

We have every right to dream heroic dreams. Those who say that we're in a time when there are not heroes, they just don't know where to look. You can see heroes every day going in and out of factory gates. Others, a handful in number, produce enough food to feed all of us and then the world beyond. You meet heroes across a counter, and they're on both sides of that counter. There are entrepreneurs with faith in themselves and faith in an idea who create new jobs, new wealth and opportunity. They're individuals and families whose taxes support the government and whose voluntary gifts support church, charity, culture, art, and education. Their patriotism is quiet, but deep. Their values sustain our national life.

Now, I have used the words "they" and "their" in speaking of these heroes. I could say "you" and "your," because I'm addressing the heroes of whom I speak—you, the citizens of this blessed land. Your dreams, your hopes, your goals are going to be the dreams, the hopes, and the goals of this administration, so help me God.

We shall reflect the compassion that is so much a part of your makeup. How can we love our country and not love our country-men; and loving them, reach out a hand when they fall, heal them when they're sick, and provide opportunity to make them self-sufficient so they will be equal in fact and not just in theory?

Can we solve the problems confronting us? Well, the answer is an unequivocal and emphatic "yes." To paraphrase Winston Churchill, I did not take the oath I've just taken with the intention of presiding over the dissolution of the world's strongest economy.

In the days ahead I will propose removing the roadblocks that have slowed our economy and reduced productivity. Steps will be taken aimed at restoring the balance between the various levels of government. Progress may be slow, measured in inches and feet, not miles, but we will progress. It is time to reawaken this industrial giant, to get government back within its means, and to lighten our punitive tax burden. And these will be our first priorities, and on these principles there will be no compromise.

On the eve of our struggle for independence a man who might have been one of the greatest among the Founding Fathers, Dr. Joseph Warren, president of the Massachusetts Congress, said to his fellow Americans, "Our country is in danger, but not to be despaired of. . . . On you depend the fortunes of America. You are to decide the important questions upon which rests the happiness and the liberty of millions yet unborn. Act worthy of yourselves."

Well, I believe we, the Americans of today, are ready to act worthy of ourselves, ready to do what must be done to ensure happiness and liberty for ourselves, our children, and our children's children. And as we renew ourselves here in our own land, we will be seen as having greater strength throughout the world. We will again be the exemplar of freedom and a beacon of hope for those who do not now have freedom.

To those neighbors and allies who share our freedom, we will strengthen our historic ties and assure them of our support and firm commitment. We will match loyalty with loyalty. We will strive for mutually beneficial relations. We will not use our friendship to impose on their sovereignty, for our own sovereignty is not for sale.

As for the enemies of freedom, those who are potential adversaries, they will be reminded that peace is the highest aspiration of the American people. We will negotiate for it, sacrifice for it; we will not surrender for it, now or ever.

Our forbearance should never be misunderstood. Our reluctance for conflict should not be misjudged as a failure of will. When action is required to preserve our national security, we will act. We will maintain sufficient strength to prevail if need be, knowing that if we do so we have the best chance of never having to use that strength.

Above all, we must realize that no arsenal or no weapon in the arsenals of the world is so formidable as the will and moral courage of free men and women. It is a weapon our adversaries in today's world do not have. It is a weapon that we as Americans do have. Let that be understood by those who practice terrorism and prey upon their neighbors.

I'm told that tens of thousands of prayer meetings are being held on this day, and for that I'm deeply grateful. We are a nation under God, and I believe God intended for us to be free. It would be fitting and good, I think, if on each Inaugural Day in future years it should be declared a day of prayer.

This is the first time in our history that this ceremony has been held, as you've been told, on this West Front of the Capitol. Standing here, one faces a magnificent vista, opening up on this city's special beauty and history. At the end of this open mall are those shrines to the giants on whose shoulders we stand.

Directly in front of me, the monument to a monumental man, George Washington, father of our country. A man of humility who came to greatness reluctantly. He led America out of revolutionary victory into infant nationhood. Off to one side, the stately memorial to Thomas Jefferson. The Declaration of Independence flames with his eloquence. And then, beyond the Reflecting Pool, the dignified columns of the Lincoln Memorial. Whoever would understand in his heart the meaning of America will find it in the life of Abraham Lincoln.

Beyond those monuments to heroism is the Potomac River, and on the far shore the sloping hills of Arlington National Cemetery, with its row upon row of simple white markers bearing crosses or Stars of David. They add up to only a tiny fraction of the price that has been paid for our freedom.

Each one of those markers is a monument to the kind of hero I spoke of earlier. Their lives ended in places called Belleau Wood, The Argonne, Omaha Beach, Salerno, and halfway around the world on Guadalcanal, Tarawa, Pork Chop Hill, the Chosin Reservoir, and in a hundred rice paddies and jungles of a place called Vietnam.

Under one such marker lies a young man, Martin Treptow, who left his job in a small town barbershop in 1917 to go to France with the famed Rainbow Division. There, on the western front, he was killed trying to carry a message between battalions under heavy artillery fire.

We're told that on his body was found a diary. On the flyleaf under the heading, "My Pledge," he had written these words: "America must win this war. Therefore I will work, I will save, I will sacrifice, I will endure, I will fight cheerfully and do my utmost, as if the issue of the whole struggle depended on me alone."

The crisis we are facing today does not require of us the kind of sacrifice that Martin Treptow and so many thousands of others were called upon to make. It does require, however, our best effort and our willingness to believe in ourselves and to believe in our capacity to perform great deeds, to believe that together with God's help we can and will resolve the problems which now confront us.

And after all, why shouldn't we believe that? We are Americans.

God bless you, and thank you.

Address Before a Joint Session of the Congress on the Program for Economic Recovery, April 28, 1981

You wouldn't want to talk me into an encore, would you? [*Laughter*]

Mr. Speaker, Mr. President, distinguished Members of the Congress, honored guests, and fellow citizens:

I have no words to express my appreciation for that greeting.

I have come to speak to you tonight about our economic recovery program and why I believe it's essential that the Congress approve this package, which I believe will lift the crushing burden of inflation off of our citizens and restore the vitality to our economy and our industrial machine.

First, however, and due to events of the past few weeks, will you permit me to digress for a moment from the all-important subject of why we must bring government spending under control and reduce tax rates. I'd like to say a few words directly to all of you and to those who are watching and listening tonight, because this is the only way I know to express to all of you on behalf of Nancy and myself our appreciation for your messages and flowers and, most of all, your prayers, not only for me but for those others who fell beside me.

The warmth of your words, the expression of friendship and, yes, love, meant more to us than you can ever know. You have given us a memory that we'll treasure forever. And you've provided an answer to those few voices that were raised saying that what happened was evidence that ours is a sick society.

The society we heard from is made up of millions of compassionate Americans and their children, from college age to kindergarten. As a matter of fact, as evidence of that I have a letter with me. The letter came from Peter Sweeney. He's in the second grade in the Riverside School in Rockville Centre, and he said, "I hope you get well quick or you might have to make a speech in your pajamas." [*Laughter*] He added a postscript. "P.S. If you have to make a speech in your pajamas, I warned you." [*Laughter*]

Well, sick societies don't produce men like the two who recently returned from outer space. Sick societies don't produce young men like Secret Service agent Tim McCarthy, who placed his body between mine

From *Public Papers of the Presidents: Ronald Reagan, 1981* (Washington, D.C.: GPO, 1983).

and the man with the gun simply because he felt that's what his duty called for him to do. Sick societies don't produce dedicated police officers like Tom Delahanty or able and devoted public servants like Jim Brady. Sick societies don't make people like us so proud to be Americans and so very proud of our fellow citizens.

Now, let's talk about getting spending and inflation under control and cutting your tax rates.

Mr. Speaker and Senator Baker, I want to thank you for your cooperation in helping to arrange this joint session of the Congress. I won't be speaking to you very long tonight, but I asked for this meeting because the urgency of our joint mission has not changed.

Thanks to some very fine people, my health is much improved. I'd like to be able to say that with regard to the health of the economy.

It's been half a year since the election that charged all of us in this Government with the task of restoring our economy. Where have we come in this 6 months? Inflation, as measured by the Consumer Price Index, has continued at a double-digit rate. Mortgage interest rates have averaged almost 15 percent for these 6 months, preventing families across America from buying homes. There are still almost 8 million unemployed. The average worker's hourly earnings after adjusting for inflation are lower today than they were 6 months ago, and there have been over 6,000 business failures.

Six months is long enough. The American people now want us to act and not in half-measures. They demand and they've earned a full and comprehensive effort to clean up our economic mess. Because of the extent of our economy's sickness, we know that the cure will not come quickly and that even with our package, progress will come in inches and feet, not in miles. But to fail to act will delay even longer and more painfully the cure which must come. And that cure begins with the Federal budget. And the budgetary actions taken by the Congress over the next few days will determine how we respond to the message of last November 4th. That message was very simple. Our government is too big, and it spends too much.

For the last few months, you and I have enjoyed a relationship based on extraordinary cooperation. Because of this cooperation we've come a long distance in less than 3 months. I want to thank the leadership of the Congress for helping in setting a fair timetable for consideration of our recommendations. And committee chairmen on both sides of the aisle have called prompt and thorough hearings.

We have also communicated in a spirit of candor, openness, and mutual respect. Tonight, as our decision day nears and as the House of Representatives weighs its alternatives, I wish to address you in that same spirit.

The Senate Budget Committee, under the leadership of Pete Domenici, has just today voted out a budget resolution supported by Democrats and Republicans alike that is in all major respects consistent with the program that we have proposed. Now we look forward to favorable action on the Senate floor, but an equally crucial test involves the House of Representatives.

The House will soon be choosing between two different versions or measures to deal with the economy. One is the measure offered by the House Budget Committee. The other is a bipartisan measure, a substitute introduced by Congressmen Phil Gramm of Texas and Del Latta of Ohio.

On behalf of the administration, let me say that we embrace and fully support that bipartisan substitute. It will achieve all the essential aims of controlling government spending, reducing the tax burden, building a national defense second to none, and stimulating economic growth and creating millions of new jobs.

At the same time, however, I must state our opposition to the measure offered by the House Budget Committee. It may appear that we have two alternatives. In reality, however, there are no more alternatives left. The committee measure quite simply falls far too short of the essential actions that we must take.

For example, in the next 3 years, the committee measure projects spending $141 billion more than does the bipartisan substitute. It regrettably cuts over $14 billion in essential defense spending, funding required to restore America's national security. It adheres to the failed policy of trying to balance the budget on the taxpayer's back. It would increase tax payments by over a third, adding up to a staggering quarter of a trillion dollars. Federal taxes would increase 12 percent each year. Tax-payers would be paying a larger share of their income to government in 1984 than they do at present.

In short, that measure reflects an echo of the past rather than a benchmark for the future. High taxes and excess spending growth created our present economic mess; more of the same will not cure the hardship, anxiety, and discouragement it has imposed on the American people.

Let us cut through the fog for a moment. The answer to a government that's too big is to stop feeding its growth. Government spending has been growing faster than the economy itself. The massive national debt which we accumulated is the result of the government's high spending diet. Well, it's time to change the diet and to change it in the right way.

I know the tax portion of our package is of concern to some of you. Let me make a few points that I feel have been overlooked. First of all, it should be looked at as an integral part of the entire package, not something separate and apart from the budget reductions, the regulatory relief, and the monetary restraints. Probably the most common misconception is that we are proposing to reduce Government revenues to less than what the Government has been receiving. This is not true. Actually, the discussion has to do with how much of a tax increase should be imposed on the taxpayer in 1982.

Now, I know that over the recess in some informal polling some of your constituents have been asked which they'd rather have, a balanced budget or a tax cut, and with the common sense that characterizes the people of this country, the answer, of course, has been a balanced budget. But may I suggest, with no inference that there was wrong intent on the part of those who asked the question, the question was inappropriate to the situation.

Our choice is not between a balanced budget and a tax cut. Properly asked, the question is, "Do you want a great big raise in your taxes this coming year or, at the worst, a very little increase with the prospect of tax reduction and a balanced budget down the road a ways?" With the common sense that the people have already shown, I'm sure we all know what the answer to that question would be.

A gigantic tax increase has been built into the system. We propose nothing more than a reduction of that increase. The people have a right to know that even with our plan they will be paying more in taxes, but not as much more as they will without it.

The option, I believe, offered by the House Budget Committee, will leave spending too high and tax rates too high. At the same time, I think it cuts the defense budget too much, and by attempting to reduce the deficit through higher taxes, it will not create the kind of strong economic growth and the new jobs that we must have.

Let us not overlook the fact that the small, independent business man or woman creates more than 80 percent of all the new jobs and employs more than half of our total workforce. Our across-the-board cut in tax rates for a 3-year period will give them much of the incentive and promise of stability they need to go forward with expansion plans calling for additional employees.

Tonight, I renew my call for us to work as a team, to join in cooperation so that we find answers which will begin to solve all our economic problems and not just some of them. The economic recovery package that I've outlined to you over the past weeks is, I deeply believe, the only answer that we have left.

Reducing the growth of spending, cutting marginal tax rates, providing relief from overregulation, and following a noninflationary and predictable monetary policy are interwoven measures which will ensure that we have addressed each of the severe dislocations which threaten our economic future. These policies will make our economy stronger, and the stronger economy will balance the budget which we're committed to do by 1984.

When I took the oath of office, I pledged loyalty to only one special interest group—"We the people." Those people—neighbors and friends, shopkeepers and laborers, farmers and craftsmen—do not have infinite patience. As a matter fact, some 80 years ago, Teddy Roosevelt wrote these instructive words in his first message to the Congress: "The American people are slow to wrath, but when their wrath is once kindled, it burns like a consuming flame." Well, perhaps that kind of wrath will be deserved if our answer to these serious problems is to repeat the mistakes of the past.

The old and comfortable way is to shave a little here and add a little there. Well, that's not acceptable anymore. I think this great and historic Congress knows that way is no longer acceptable. [*Applause*]

Thank you very much.

I think you've shown that you know the one sure way to continue the inflationary spiral is to fall back into the predictable patterns of old economic practices. Isn't it time that we tried something new?

When you allowed me to speak to you here in these chambers a little earlier, I told you that I wanted this program for economic recovery to be ours—yours and mine. I think the bipartisan substitute bill has achieved that purpose. It moves us toward economic vitality.

Just 2 weeks ago, you and I joined millions of our fellow Americans in marveling at the magic historical moment that John Young and Bob Crippen created in their space shuttle, *Columbia*. The last manned effort was almost 6 years ago, and I remembered on this more recent day, over the years, how we'd all come to expect technological precision of our men and machines. And each amazing achievement became commonplace, until the next new challenge was raised.

With the space shuttle we tested our ingenuity once again, moving beyond the accomplishments of the past into the promise and uncertainty of the future. Thus, we not only planned to send up a 122-foot aircraft 170 miles into space, but we also intended to make it maneuverable and return it to Earth, landing 98 tons of exotic metals delicately on a remote, dry lakebed. The space shuttle did more than prove our technological abilities. It raised our expectations once more. It started us dreaming again.

The poet Carl Sandburg wrote, "The republic is a dream. Nothing happens unless first a dream." And that's what makes us, as Americans, different. We've always reached for a new spirit and aimed at a higher goal. We've been courageous and determined, unafraid and bold. Who among us wants to be first to say we no longer have those qualities, that we must limp along, doing the same things that have brought us our present misery?

I believe that the people you and I represent are ready to chart a new course. They look to us to meet the great challenge, to reach beyond the commonplace and not fall short for lack of creativity or courage.

Someone you know has said that he who would have nothing to do with thorns must never attempt to gather flowers. Well, we have much greatness before us. We can restore our economic strength and build opportunities like none we've ever had before.

As Carl Sandburg said, all we need to begin with is a dream that we can do better than before. All we need to have is faith, and that dream will come true. All we need to do is act, and the time for action is now.

Thank you. Good night.

Remarks at the Annual Convention of the National Association of Evangelicals in Orlando, Florida, March 8, 1983

Reverend clergy all, Senator Hawkins, distinguished members of the Florida congressional delegation, and all of you:

From *Public Papers of the Presidents: Ronald Reagan, 1983* (Washington, D.C.: GPO, 1984).

I can't tell you how you have warmed my heart with your welcome. I'm delighted to be here today.

Those of you in the National Association of Evangelicals are known for your spiritual and humanitarian work. And I would be especially remiss if I didn't discharge right now one personal debt of gratitude. Thank you for your prayers. Nancy and I have felt their presence many times in many ways. And believe me, for us they've made all the difference.

The other day in the East Room of the White House at a meeting there, someone asked me whether I was aware of all the people out there who were praying for the President. And I had to say, "Yes, I am. I've felt it. I believe in intercessionary prayer." But I couldn't help but say to that questioner after he'd asked the question that—or at least say to them that if sometimes when he was praying he got a busy signal, it was just me in there ahead of him. [*Laughter*] I think I understand how Abraham Lincoln felt when he said, "I have been driven many times to my knees by the overwhelming conviction that I had nowhere else to go."

From the joy and the good feeling of this conference, I go to a political reception. [*Laughter*] Now, I don't know why, but that bit of scheduling reminds me of a story—[*laughter*]—which I'll share with you.

An evangelical minister and a politician arrived at Heaven's gate one day together. And St. Peter, after doing all the necessary formalities, took them in hand to show them where their quarters would be. And he took them to a small, single room with a bed, a chair, and a table and said this was for the clergyman. And the politician was a little worried about what might be in store for him. And he couldn't believe it then when St. Peter stopped in front of a beautiful mansion with lovely grounds, many servants, and told him that these would be his quarters.

And he couldn't help but ask, he said, "But wait, how—there's something wrong—how do I get this mansion while that good and holy man only gets a single room?" And St. Peter said, "You have to understand how things are up here. We've got thousands and thousands of clergy. You're the first politician who ever made it." [*Laughter*]

But I don't want to contribute to a stereotype. [*Laughter*] So, I tell you there are a great many God-fearing, dedicated, noble men and women in public life, present company included. And, yes, we need your help to keep us ever mindful of the ideas and the principles that brought us into the public arena in the first place. The basis of those ideals and principles is a commitment to freedom and personal liberty that, itself, is grounded in the much deeper realization that freedom prospers only where the blessings of God are avidly sought and humbly accepted.

The American experiment in democracy rests on this insight. Its discovery was the great triumph of our Founding Fathers, voiced by William Penn when he said: "If we will not be governed by God, we must be governed by tyrants." Explaining the inalienable rights of men, Jefferson said, "The God who gave us life, gave us liberty at the same time." And it was George Washington who said that "of all the dispositions and habits which lead to political prosperity, religion and morality are indispensable supports."

And finally, that shrewdest of all observers of American democracy, Alexis de Tocqueville, put it eloquently after he had gone on a search for the secret of America's greatness and genius—and he said: "Not until I went into the churches of America and heard her pulpits aflame with righteousness did I understand the greatness and the genius of America . . . America is good. And if America ever ceases to be good, America will cease to be great."

Well, I'm pleased to be here today with you who are keeping America great by keeping her good. Only through your work and prayers and those of millions of others can we hope to survive this perilous century and keep alive this experiment in liberty, this last, best hope of man.

I want you to know that this administration is motivated by a political philosophy that sees the greatness of America in you, her people, and in your families, churches, neighborhoods, communities—the institutions that foster and nourish values like concern for others and respect for the rule of law under God.

Now, I don't have to tell you that this puts us in opposition to, or at least out of step with, a prevailing attitude of many who have turned to a modern-day secularism, discarding the tried and time-tested values upon which our very civilization is based. No matter how well intentioned, their value system is radically different from that of most Americans. And while they proclaim that they're freeing us from superstitions of the past, they've taken upon themselves the job of superintending us by government rule and regulation. Sometimes their voices are louder than ours, but they are not yet a majority.

An example of that vocal superiority is evident in a controversy now going on in Washington. And since I'm involved, I've been waiting to hear from the parents of young America. How far are they willing to go in giving to government their prerogatives as parents?

Let me state the case as briefly and simply as I can. An organization of citizens, sincerely motivated and deeply concerned about the increase in illegitimate births and abortions involving girls well below the age of consent, sometime ago established a nationwide network of clinics to offer help to these girls and, hopefully, alleviate this situation. Now, again, let me say, I do not fault their intent. However, in their well-intentioned effort, these clinics have decided to provide advice and birth control drugs and devices to underage girls without the knowledge of their parents.

For some years now, the Federal Government has helped with funds to subsidize these clinics. In providing for this, the Congress decreed that every effort would be made to maximize parental participation. Nevertheless, the drugs and devices are prescribed without getting parental consent or giving notification after they've done so. Girls termed "sexually active"—and that has replaced the word "promiscuous"—are given this help in order to prevent illegitimate birth or abortion.

Well, we have ordered clinics receiving Federal funds to notify the parents such help has been given. One of the Nation's leading newspapers has created the term "squeal rule" in editorializing against us for doing this, and we're being criticized for violating the privacy of young people. A judge has recently granted an injunction against an enforcement of our rule. I've watched TV panel shows discuss this issue, seen columnists pontificating on our error, but no one seems to mention morality as playing a part in the subject of sex.

Is all of Judeo-Christian tradition wrong? Are we to believe that something so sacred can be looked upon as a purely physical thing with no potential for emotional and psychological harm? And isn't it the parents' right to give counsel and advice to keep their children from making mistakes that may affect their entire lives?

Many of us in government would like to know what parents think about this intrusion in their family by government. We're going to fight in the courts. The right of parents and the rights of family take precedence over those of Washington-based bureaucrats and social engineers.

But the fight against parental notification is really only one example of many attempts to water down traditional values and even abrogate the original terms of American democracy. Freedom prospers when religion is vibrant and the rule of law under God is acknowledged. When our Founding Fathers passed the first amendment, they sought to protect churches from government interference. They never intended to construct a wall of hostility between government and the concept of religious belief itself.

The evidence of this permeates our history and our government. The Declaration of Independence mentions the Supreme Being no less than four times. "In God We Trust" is engraved on our coinage. The Supreme Court opens its proceedings with a religious invocation. And the Members of Congress open their sessions with a prayer. I just happen to believe the schoolchildren of the United States are entitled to the same privileges as Supreme Court Justices and Congressmen.

Last year, I sent the Congress a constitutional amendment to restore prayer to public schools. Already this session, there's growing bipartisan support for the amendment, and I am calling on the Congress to act speedily to pass it and to let our children pray.

Perhaps some of you read recently about the Lubbock school case, where a judge actually ruled that it was unconstitutional for a school district to give equal treatment to religious and nonreligious student groups, even when the group meetings were being held during the students' own time. The first amendment never intended to require government to discriminate against religious speech.

Senators Denton and Hatfield have proposed legislation in the Congress on the whole question of prohibiting discrimination against religious forms of student speech. Such legislation could go far to restore freedom of religious speech for public school students. And I hope the Congress considers these bills quickly. And with your help, I think it's possible we could also get the constitutional amendment through the Congress this year.

More than a decade ago, a Supreme Court decision literally wiped off the books of 50 States statutes protecting the rights of unborn children. Abortion on demand now takes the lives of up to 1½ million unborn children a year. Human life legislation ending this tragedy will some day pass the Congress, and you and I must never rest until it does. Unless and until it can be proven that the unborn child is not a living entity, then its right to life, liberty, and the pursuit of happiness must be protected.

You may remember that when abortion on demand began, many, and, indeed, I'm sure many of you, warned that the practice would lead to a decline in respect for human life, that the philosophical premises used to justify abortion on demand would ultimately be used to justify other attacks on the sacredness of human life—infanticide or mercy killing.

Tragically enough, those warnings proved all too true. Only last year a court permitted the death by starvation of a handicapped infant.

I have directed the Health and Human Services Department to make clear to every health care facility in the United States that the Rehabilitation Act of 1973 protects all handicapped persons against discrimination based on handicaps, including infants. And we have taken the further step of requiring that each and every recipient of Federal funds who provides health care services to infants must post and keep posted in a conspicuous place a notice stating that "discriminatory failure to feed and care for handicapped infants in this facility is prohibited by Federal law." It also lists a 24-hour, toll-free number so that nurses and others may report violations in time to save the infant's life.

In addition, recent legislation introduced in the Congress by Representative Henry Hyde of Illinois not only increases restric tions on publicly financed abortions, it also addresses this whole problem of infanticide. I urge the Congress to begin hearings and to adopt legislation that will protect the right of life to all children, including the disabled or handicapped.

Now, I'm sure that you must get discouraged at times, but you've done better than you know, perhaps. There's a great spiritual awakening in America, a renewal of the traditional values that have been the bedrock of America's goodness and greatness.

One recent survey by a Washington-based research council concluded that Americans were far more religious than the people of other nations; 95 percent of those surveyed expressed a belief in God and a huge majority believed the Ten Commandments had real meaning in their lives. And another study has found that an overwhelming majority of Americans disapprove of adultery, teenage sex, pornography, abortion, and hard drugs. And this same study showed a deep reverence for the importance of family ties and religious belief.

I think the items that we've discussed here today must be a key part of the Nation's political agenda. For the first time the Congress is openly and seriously debating and dealing with the prayer and abortion issues— and that's enormous progress right there. I repeat: America is in the midst of a spiritual awakening and a moral renewal. And with your Biblical keynote, I say today, "Yes, let justice roll on like a river, righteousness like a never-failing stream."

Now, obviously, much of this new political and social consensus I've talked about is based on a positive view of American history, one that takes pride in our country's accomplishments and record. But we must never forget that no government schemes are going to perfect man. We know that living in this world means dealing with what philosophers would call the phenomenology of evil or, as theologians would put it, the doctrine of sin.

There is sin and evil in the world, and we're enjoined by Scripture and the Lord Jesus to oppose it with all our might. Our nation, too, has a legacy of evil with which it must deal. The glory of this land has been its capacity for transcending the moral evils of our past. For example, the long struggle of minority citizens for equal rights, once a source of disunity and civil war, is now a point of pride for all Americans. We must never go back. There is no room for racism, anti-Semitism, or other forms of ethnic and racial hatred in this country.

I know that you've been horrified, as have I, by the resurgence of some hate groups preaching bigotry and prejudice. Use the mighty voice of your pulpits and the powerful standing of your churches to denounce and isolate these hate groups in our midst. The commandment given us is clear and simple: "Thou shalt love thy neighbor as thyself."

But whatever sad episodes exist in our past, any objective observer must hold a positive view of American history, a history that has been the story of hopes fulfilled and dreams made into reality. Especially in this century, America has kept alight the torch of freedom, but not just for ourselves but for millions of others around the world.

And this brings me to my final point today. During my first press conference as President, in answer to a direct question, I pointed out that, as good Marxist-Leninists, the Soviet leaders have openly and publicly declared that the only morality they recognize is that which will further their cause, which is world revolution. I think I should point out I was only quoting Lenin, their guiding spirit, who said in 1920 that they repudiate all morality that proceeds from supernatural ideas—that's their name for religion—or ideas that are outside class conceptions. Morality is entirely subordinate to the interests of class war. And everything is moral that is necessary for the annihilation of the old, exploiting social order and for uniting the proletariat.

Well, I think the refusal of many influential people to accept this elementary fact of Soviet doctrine illustrates an historical reluctance to see totalitarian powers for what they are. We saw this phenomenon in the 1930s. We see it too often today.

This doesn't mean we should isolate ourselves and refuse to seek an understanding with them. I intend to do everything I can to persuade them of our peaceful intent, to remind them that it was the West that refused to use its nuclear monopoly in the forties and fifties for territorial gain and which now proposes 50-percent cut in strategic ballistic missiles and the elimination of an entire class of land-based, intermediate-range nuclear missiles.

At the same time, however, they must be made to understand we will never compromise our principles and standards. We will never give away our freedom. We will never abandon our belief in God. And we will never stop searching for a genuine peace. But we can assure none of these things America stands for through the so-called nuclear freeze solutions proposed by some.

The truth is that a freeze now would be a very dangerous fraud, for that is merely the illusion of peace. The reality is that we must find peace through strength.

I would agree to a freeze if only we could freeze the Soviets' global desires. A freeze at current levels of weapons would remove any incentive for the Soviets to negotiate seriously in Geneva and virtually end our chances to achieve the major arms reductions which we have proposed. Instead, they would achieve their objectives through the freeze.

A freeze would reward the Soviet Union for its enormous and unparalleled military buildup. It would prevent the essential and long overdue modernization of United States and allied defenses and would leave our aging forces increasingly vulnerable. And an honest freeze would require extensive prior negotiations on the systems and numbers to be limited and on the measures to ensure effective verification and compliance. And the kind of a freeze that has been suggested would be virtually impossible to verify. Such a major effort would divert us completely from our current negotiations on achieving substantial reductions.

A number of years ago, I heard a young father, a very prominent young man in the entertainment world, addressing a tremendous gathering in California. It was during the time of the cold war, and communism and our own way of life were very much on people's minds. And he was speaking to that subject. And suddenly, though, I heard him saying, "I love my little girls more than anything—" And I said to myself, "Oh, no, don't. You can't—don't say that." But I had underestimated him. He went on: "I would rather see my little girls die now, still believing in God, than have them grow up under communism and one day die no longer believing in God."

There were thousands of young people in that audience. They came to their feet with shouts of joy. They had instantly recognized the profound truth in what he had said, with regard to the physical and the soul and what was truly important.

Yes, let us pray for the salvation of all of those who live in that totalitarian darkness—pray they will discover the joy of knowing God. But until they do, let us be aware that while they preach the supremacy of the state, declare its omnipotence over individual man, and predict its eventual domination of all peoples on the Earth, they are the focus of evil in the modern world.

It was C. S. Lewis who, in his unforgettable "Screwtape Letters," wrote: "The greatest evil is not done now in those sordid 'dens of crime' that Dickens loved to paint. It is not even done in concentration camps and labor camps. In those we see its final result. But it is conceived and ordered (moved, seconded, carried, and minuted) in clear, carpeted, warmed, and well-lighted offices, by quiet men with white collars and cut fingernails and smooth-shaven cheeks who do not need to raise their voice."

Well, because these "quiet men" do not "raise their voices," because they sometimes speak in soothing tones of brotherhood and peace, because, like other dictators before them, they're always making "their final territorial demand," some would have us accept them at their word and accommodate ourselves to their aggressive impulses. But if history teaches anything, it teaches that simple-minded appeasement or wishful thinking about our adversaries is folly. It means the betrayal of our past, the squandering of our freedom.

So, I urge you to speak out against those who would place the United States in a position of military and moral inferiority. You know, I've always believed that old Screwtape reserved his best efforts for those of you in the church. So, in your discussions of the nuclear freeze proposals, I urge you to beware the temptation of pride—the temptation of blithely declaring yourselves above it all and label both sides equally at fault, to ignore the facts of history and the aggressive impulses of an evil empire, to simply call the arms race a giant misunderstanding and thereby remove yourself from the struggle between right and wrong and good and evil.

I ask you to resist the attempts of those who would have you withhold your support for our efforts, this administration's efforts, to keep America strong and free, while we negotiate real and verifiable reductions in the world's nuclear arsenals and one day, with God's help, their total elimination.

While America's military strength is important, let me add here that I've always maintained that the struggle now going on for the world will never be decided by bombs, or rockets, by armies or military might. The real crisis we face today is a spiritual one; at root, it is a test of moral will and faith.

Whittaker Chambers, the man whose own religious conversion made him a witness to one of the terrible traumas of our time, the Hiss-Chambers case, wrote that the crisis of the Western World exists to the degree in which the West is indifferent to God, the degree to which it collaborates in communism's attempt to make man stand alone without God. And then he said, for Marxism-Leninism is actually the second oldest faith, first proclaimed in the Garden of Eden with the words of temptation, "Ye shall be as gods."

The Western World can answer this challenge, he wrote, "but only provided that its faith in God and the freedom He enjoins is as great as communism's faith in Man."

I believe we shall rise to the challenge. I believe that communism is another sad, bizarre chapter in human history whose last pages even now are being written. I believe this because the source of our strength in the quest for human freedom is not material, but spiritual. And because it knows no limitation, it must terrify and ultimately triumph over those who would enslave their fellow man. For in the words of Isaiah: "He giveth power to the faint; and to them that have no might He increased strength . . . But they that wait upon the Lord shall renew their strength; they shall mount up with wings as eagles; they shall run, and not be weary. . . ."

Yes, change your world. One of our Founding Fathers, Thomas Paine, said, "We have it within our power to begin the world over again." We can do it, doing together what no one church could do by itself.

God bless you, and thank you very much.

Chapter Thirty-two

Looking Backward at the Gipper

George Will

There is a special openness to the horizon in the Middle West, an openness that reveals no obstacle to travel in any direction. The remarkable flatness of the prairie suggests that God had good times in mind—smooth infields for countless baseball diamonds—when he designed Illinois, where Ronald Reagan spent his formative years. There Reagan acquired a talent for happiness. Since then he has traveled far and had a good time all the way.

The nation is, by and large, better off because he did. Most Americans feel that way, which is why today, for the first time in 60 years, a president is preparing to turn over his office to a successor from his party. The cheerfulness that has defined Reagan's era of good feelings has been, on balance, salutary. But it also has been a narcotic, numbing the nation's senses about hazards just over the horizon.

Most presidents come to Washington bright as freshly minted dimes and leave much diminished. To govern is to choose and choosing produces disagreements, disappointments, even enemies. Furthermore, the modern president is omnipresent in the public's consciousness and the public confuses prominence with power. Therefore too much is expected of presidents. They are blamed when it becomes clear, as it always does, that events are in the saddle, riding mankind. However, Reagan is leaving Washington more popular than he was when he arrived (having won just 50.7 percent of the 1980 vote). Like Eisenhower, he is leaving on a crest of affection.

It has not all been smooth sledding. The silly phrase "Teflon president" was coined by a Democrat and was a way of saying that the people are fools, bewitched by Reagan's magic. They are not fools and they do not cotton to a party that says they are. During the 1982 recession, Reagan was not protected by any political Teflon. His popularity plummeted, as it did four years later during the Iran-contra revelations.

One reason Reagan today is standing tall in public approval is that he is standing. He has gone the distance. The last time Americans were watching the completion of a president's second term they were reading *To Kill a Mockingbird*, listening to "Itsy Bitsy Teenie Weenie Yellow Polkadot Bikini," and watching the movie *Psycho*. It has been a long time. Too long. Reagan is not only upright at the final bell, he is bouncing on the balls of his feet. He has proven that the presidency is not such a destroyer after all.

The most common, indeed jejune criticism of Reagan is that he did not properly allow the presidency to fill his days, let alone his nights. His immediate predecessor, Jimmy Carter, proudly, even ostentatiously made the presidency seem crushing. It was Jefferson's "splendid misery" without the splendor. Reagan made being president look a little too easy for some tastes. He drained it of the aura of melodrama that journalists relish. (Melodrama enlarges them by making them participants in stirring events.)

Reagan has been president for 4 percent of the republic's constitutional history. He did not shinny to the top of the greasy pole of American politics by accident or lassitude. He first sought the presidency in 1968. He fought fiercely for the Republican nomination in 1976, losing one of life's close calls. (If 794 votes had switched in the New Hampshire primary Reagan might have been president when oil prices doubled and hostages were taken in Tehran.) In 1980 the man and the moment met for two reasons—foreign policy humiliation and domestic inflation. Both created a demoralizing sense that the nation had lost control over its destiny.

Inflation generated the fuel of political change in America, middle-class anxiety and anger. Inflation was blamed on Washington and reinforced the core conservative message of hostility toward government. Today, however, the dialectic of democracy is working. The Democratic Party has benefited from Reagan in two ways. The dampening of inflation, and the general geniality of the most visible symbol of government, has caused confidence in government to increase. That makes the future a little less forbidding to the Democratic Party. Second, the Democratic Party has moved like a tide pulled by the rise of the Reagan moon. In a democracy a leader's success can often be gauged, in part, by his effect on

the opposition party. Reagan has rendered the Democratic Party more
ready to govern in the 1990s than it was in the 1970s and 1980s. He has
done this by drawing it back toward 1960.

John Kennedy was a "growth Democrat." All Democrats were then.
His Treasury Secretary was a Republican, Douglas Dillon. The last large
tax cut for individuals before Reagan's occurred in 1964 and was Kennedy's proposal. It has been downhill for Democrats since 1964. The party
was captured by people who repudiated its postwar foreign policy of
anticommunist containment and in domestic policy, were "fairness Democrats." They elbowed aside growth Democrats and advocated programs
of distributive justice. After two drubbings by Reagan and one by his vice
president, Democrats again emphasized growth.

American politics often follows a serpentine path into the future. The
Founding Fathers fought a profoundly conservative revolution, founding
a new regime to protect ancient rights. Civil war produced the ideological,
social, and economic bonds of national unity. The Depression produced
a president who was—still is—emblematic of liberalism. He saved capitalism by beginning to build a conservative "social insurance state" that
has reconciled people to the vicissitudes of economic dynamism. And in
the 1980s the man emblematic of conservatism has caused conservatives
to come to terms with the post–New Deal role of the central
government—the welfare state. He also liquidated the Cold War.

And there are other aspects of Reagan's career. This most cheerful of
presidents is the product of the first and most consequential protest
movement of the decade of protests. Before the campus and urban unrest
of the mid- and late 1960s (both kinds of protests helped bring Reagan to
California's governorship), there was the conservative insurgency in the
Republican Party. Another oddity: The oldest president ever elected—a
president who not only remembers but reveres one of the last premodern
presidents, Coolidge—has had a sure sense of modernity, in the presidency and elsewhere.

If a 19th-century congressman were returned to Capitol Hill today, he
would be stunned (and appalled) by many changes—the swarm of staff,
the glut of legislation, the general pell-mell pace of life. However, he
would say, "Congress does essentially what we did—just more of it." But
were Coolidge returned to the White House he would not comprehend
what a modern president does. The office has been utterly transformed
by the growth of governmental responsibilities, at home and abroad, and
by the power to communicate to a wired nation.

Reagan recently said that he sometimes wonders how presidents who have *not* been actors have been able to function. I do not know precisely what he meant, and he probably doesn't either, but he was on to something.

Two of this century's greatest leaders of democracies, Churchill and de Gaulle, had highly developed senses of the theatrical element in politics. FDR did, too. So have evil leaders in the age of mass effects, Hitler, Mussolini, and Castro all mastered ceremonies of mass intoxication.

A political actor, be he good or evil, does not deal in unreality. Rather, he creates realities that matter—perceptions, emotions, affiliations. An actor not only projects, he causes his audience to project certain qualities —admiration, fear, hatred, love, patriotism, empathy. In some nations the actor's role has been assigned to a constitutional monarch. But the role is not incompatible with republican values. Reagan has been diligent about the task of making vivid the values that produce cohesion and dynamism in a continental nation. That task is central, not peripheral, to the problem of governance.

Reagan may seem like the least complicated of men, an open book that by now has been completely read to the country. But there remains one particularly puzzling aspect of his personality. It may have something to do with his having been—with his being—an actor. In any case, it is this: He is genuinely amiable but also remote. He is a friendly man with few close friends. Perhaps only one. He married her.

Reagan's White House years have been the Reagans' years. Their lives are thoroughly woven together. And Nancy Reagan, in her chosen public role, has acted on an understanding she shares with him. It can be called the sophistication of simplicity.

The media often are the last to learn things. They certainly took their time even getting a partial understanding of this good and remarkable woman. When she first came to Washington she was the victim of an extremely dumb and lazy caricature by the media. She supposedly was just another Beverly Hills lady who lunched a lot, someone with a Black Belt in shopping earned on Rodeo Drive. Then the media, in one of those pendular swings that takes them from one misjudgment to another, portrayed her as a policymaker and palace intriguer—a woman who should go shopping and leave men's work alone.

The full truth about her role is known only to her and him. It is for her to tell if she chooses. She probably will tell only a carefully calibrated portion of it. A quarter of a century at the center of serious politics has schooled her in discretion and reticence. However, this much can be said for sure. She has been *with* him, physically there and mentally engaged, every step of the way. She has been in motel corridors in the middle of the night in the middle of campaign crises. She has been upstairs in the White House, where the hum of governance is heard day and night from downstairs. Her astuteness, her quick and penetrating political intuitions, have been focused on her husband's personal fortunes.

She has made one public issue her own. Before the professional political class awakened to what the public had already discovered, she recognized that drug abuse would be the most alarming phenomenon of the 1980s. Before the bankruptcy of "supply side" drug policies—interdiction and all that—became apparent, she went to work on the demand side. She knew that the solution must come from altering the behavior of young people by changing their attitudes: "Just say no."

"Say *what?*" asked the sophisticates, much amused by yet another example of Reaganite simplicity. They were right about one thing. Nancy Reagan is Reaganite. That is, she shares her husband's understanding of the arduous patience required for democratic social change. "Even now," writes James Q. Wilson, "when the dangers of drug abuse are well understood, many educated people still discuss the drug problem in almost every way except the right way. They talk about the 'cost' of drug use and the 'socioeconomic factors' that shape that use. They rarely speak plainly— drug use is wrong because it is immoral, and it is immoral because it enslaves the mind and destroys the soul. It is as if it were a mark of sophistication for us to shun the language of morality in discussing the problems of mankind."

Sophisticates have been late learners about the wisdom of plain speaking about drugs—"Just say no." When—how—did Ronald Reagan learn what he knows about simplicity and leadership? Perhaps it is not learned; perhaps it is largely a matter of temperament.

An ancient Greek poet said, "The fox knows many things, but the hedgehog knows one big thing." Reagan is more foxy than he has contrived to seem. Like Eisenhower, he understands the advantages of being underestimated by the chattering classes. But Reagan is much more of hedgehog than a fox. He knows a few simple, powerful things. He understands the economy of leadership—the husbanding of the perishable hold any president has on the attention of this complacent, inattentive nation. He knows it is necessary to have a few priorities, a few themes. He knows how often—again, the peculiar patience of politics—you must repeat

them when building a following. He knows what Dr. Johnson knew—
that people more often need to be reminded than informed. He knows
the importance of happiness in a nation where the pursuit of it was
affirmed at the instant independence was asserted.

Reagan has been derided as a Dr. Feelgood. The description is more
warranted than the derision. Reagan believes the American people are
"lumpy with unrealized potentialities." (The phrase comes from another
Californian of simple but powerful understandings, the late Eric Hoffer.)
The fruits of American talents will be bountiful when Americans are
optimistic. When they are optimistic they make the most of freedom.
They stay in school longer, have more babies, start more businesses—
varrroooom!

It is no accident that Reagan rose to the pinnacle of power at a
moment when there was a rising wave of intellectual pessimism. Numerous theories were being offered as to why the trajectory of the American
experiment has passed its apogee. Reagan's greatest gift to his country has
been his soaring sense of possibilities. To see where he got it, look at what
he has seen in a long life.

In the six decades since he left home for college, America's real GNP
has increased sixfold, three times the rate of population growth. Since the
Second World War the world (the calculation is by Norman Macrae of
the *Economist*) has added seven times as much producing power as was
added in all the previous millennia of *Homo sapiens*. More acceleration is
certain as more societies enter the information age, an age in which
(Macrae again) a moderately competent researcher using an ordinary
computer can check more correlations in an afternoon than Einstein
could check in his lifetime.

Reagan's sunniness about future possibilities is not silly. But possibilities are not certainties, or even probabilities, unless political leaders see
the world steadily and see it whole, and tell the truth about the dangers
the future holds. In domestic affairs, meaning primarily economic management, Reagan is not recognizably conservative. He is not even a
Keynesian. He is a Panglossian. And he has presided over a debilitating
feast as the nation has eaten much of its seed corn.

Congress has passed every balanced budget he has submitted. Congress
has quarreled with him a bit about the composition of spending, but not
much about the amount. The first Reagan budget was essentially Carter's.
The eighth was a product of the Reagan-Congress "summit" following
the October 1987 stock market convulsion. The middle six budgets tell

Reagan's story. Those budgets produced deficits totaling $1.1 trillion. The budgets Reagan sent to Congress *proposed* 13/14ths of that total. Congress added a piddling $90 billion, just $15 billion a year.

As Pat Moynihan has said, something fundamental happened in American governance when a conservative Republican administration produced deficits of $200 billion—and nothing happened. Nothing, that is, dramatic and immediately visible. Much happened in the way of silent rot as we mortgaged much of our future vitality. But for the political class, the event was a splendid liberation: All the rules were repealed. It was a particularly perverse event coming from conservatives: There were no longer restraints, practical or moral, on government spending. Under Reagan the interest component of the budget has more than doubled to 14 percent. The fiscal 1989 interest cost—a regressive transfer of wealth to buyers of government bonds—exceeds $150 billion. That is more than the combined budgets of nine departments—Agriculture, Commerce, Education, Energy, Interior, Justice, Labor, State, Transportation.

By knocking the budget into radical imbalance, Reagan has placed a restraining hand on the 1990s. But it will not restrain the growth of the welfare state. The population is aging and the elderly are the principal beneficiaries of welfare state payments, particularly pensions and medical care. Instead, the restraining hand will strangle defense spending, beginning with Reagan's most cherished project, the Strategic Defense Initiative.

The last large creative act of domestic policy in the Reagan years occurred in 1986. With tax simplification government took a big step back from supervision of economic choices. Rather than use the Tax Code to fine-tune the fairness of life, the policy would be: Use the Code to raise revenue and stimulate growth. Growth will deliver rough justice and the welfare state will rub much of the roughness off that justice.

Conservatives argue, plausibly, that people at the bottom of the social pyramid benefit from policies that energize those at the top—the investing, entrepreneurial class that makes a market economy hum. Since the end of the 1982 recession the economy has hummed. The number of workers earning just the minimum wage has fallen 22 percent. But by now, after 73 consecutive months of growth, we know that growth is not enough.

John Kennedy, in the full flush of postwar confidence, said, "A rising tide lifts all boats." Now we know better. We do not know how to raise those who are stuck in the mud. Conservatives have refuted the redistributionist simplicities of those who thought they knew how to help the underclass. But it would be nice if conservatives did not think that refutation exhausts their responsibilities.

Regarding the perennial American problem—race—limited progress has been made, and it may seem paradoxical to call it progress: The civil rights era ended in the Reagan years. That is, the problems afflicting poor blacks are no longer regarded as primarily matters of race. It is broadly understood that if all the members of the urban underclass were magically given white skins, their life prospects would not appreciably improve. For decades conservatives contented themselves with saying: Liberals emphasize equality of condition, we emphasize equality of opportunity. In the Reagan years conservatives have come face to face with the fact that equality of opportunity is much more complicated than they thought. It must be, in part, a government artifact.

The Reagan years have involved a rolling referendum on government. The results are clear and they are not what conservatives wanted. Americans want low taxes and a high level of services. Big surprise. Big deficit. The deficit is the numerical expression of a cultural phenomenon—the American determination to live beyond our means, to consume more than we produce. Once upon a time conservatives prided themselves on a flinty realism about the costs of life. No more. Costs are not a cheerful subject. Costs imply limits and obstacles not suggested by that openness of the prairie horizon.

Liberals have practiced "tax and tax, spend and spend, elect and elect" but conservatives have perfected "borrow and borrow, spend and spend, elect and elect." Conservatives are supposed to have clear heads to compensate for not having warm hearts. However, in the Reagan years there has been what Moynihan calls a hemorrhaging of reality regarding the fiscal requirements for strength and prosperity. This is a consequence of the narcotic of cheerfulness.

In foreign policy, too, there has been a tendency to allow wishes to be the father of thoughts. Granted, the world seems less dangerous than it did in 1980, and Reagan is partly responsible for the improvement.

The allocation of political praise or blame often is done on the basis of the *post hoc, ergo propter hoc* fallacy: The rooster crows and then the sun rises, so the crowing causes the sunrise. Reagan did not singlehandedly cause the rise in the fortunes of freedom in this decade. Many forces have been gathering strength for many decades. Still, Reagan has been a leading participant—Margaret Thatcher has been another—on the winning side of an ideological argument. Distilled to its essence, the intellectual sea change in this decade has been recognition of this: Pluralism means progress. Modernization requires markets. Free markets require some political liberty—and they generate demands for more of it.

In May, at Moscow State University, Reagan said that mankind is emerging "like a chrysalis" from the economy of the Industrial Revolution and is entering the information age, the economy of the mind. "The key is freedom—freedom of thought, freedom of information, freedom of communication." Such freedoms cannot be tentative and tactical concessions by an uncontrolled government, they must be institutionalized. Otherwise "freedom will always be looking over its shoulder. A bird on a tether, no matter how long the rope, can always be pulled back."

How true. But how wildly wrong he is about what is happening in Moscow. Reagan has accelerated the moral disarmament of the West— actual disarmament will follow—by elevating wishful thinking to the status of political philosophy. Here he is assessing Gorbachev: "He is the first leader that has come along who has gone back before Stalin and . . . he is trying to do what Lenin was teaching . . . Stalin actually reversed many of the things . . . I've known a little bit about Lenin and what he was advocating, and I think that this, in *glasnost* and *perestroika* and all that, this is much more smacking of Lenin than of Stalin." Lenin the liberal "advocate" and teacher, Stalin the aberration? The mind boggles and the spirit sags at the misunderstandings—of Soviet history, of the 20th century. Reagan blandly says that Gorbachev has just "come along." How is it that the Soviet Union suddenly fell into the hands of such a pleasant fellow? That does not puzzle our cheerful president. Hey, good things happen to nice people.

At the United Nations in September, Reagan spoke of the "synergy of peace and freedom." He said that "history teaches" that where individual rights are respected, "war is a distant prospect." History—1914 for example—really teaches a less clear lesson. It teaches that freedom is a fragile flower. We shall see if a nation hooked on the narcotic of cheerfulness can face unpleasant facts that the future is certain to put in front of it.

The future has been called the mirror with no glass in it. The future is especially unknowable in an open society. Democratic government runs on opinion, so all its achievements rest on shifting sand. Conservatives, especially, should have a keen sense of impermanence. Even success is problematic. When, in the mid-1960s, Reagan became Mr. Conservative, it was clear what conservatism was. In foreign policy it was anticommunist and particularly anti-Soviet. There was to be no nonsense about détente. In domestic policy conservatism advocated balanced budgets, radical pruning of the welfare state, and redress of Supreme Court excesses regarding the "social issues," particularly school prayer and abortion. The fate of those last two issues tells much about Reagan and his years.

At the peak of his powers he did not get the Senate, controlled by his party for six years, to pass even the mildest constitutional amendments pertaining to school prayer and abortion. Truth be told, he did not try hard. They are hot, divisive issues. They are useful to a conservative candidate who wants to energize particular constituencies. But as president, Reagan, the cheerful consensus conservative, tried to avoid heat and division. That was understandable after the nastiness of the preceding two decades.

In his second term, speaking to an audience of intense conservatives, Reagan said that "returning civility to public life and the political discourse is a high and worthy goal." Using Jefferson's phrase, he said Americans are all "brethren of the same principle." And he said each of us should be true to Teddy Roosevelt's injunction to play fair and "be a good man to camp out with." He has been that, a happy camper.

However, a great communicator will communicate complicated ideas, hard choices, and bad news. Reagan has had little aptitude and less appetite for those tasks. But, then, communication is not really Reagan's forte. Rhetoric is.

Rhetoric has a tainted reputation in our time, for several reasons. One is the carnage produced by murderous demagogues. Another is the public's uneasiness about modern means of mass manipulation, including propaganda and advertising. But rhetoric is indispensable to good politics and can be ennobling. Ancient political philosophers, such as Aristotle and Cicero, and the best modern politicians, such as Lincoln and Churchill, understood that rhetoric can direct the free will of the community to the good. Rhetoric is systematic eloquence. At its best it does not induce irrationality. Rather, it leavens reason, fusing passion to persuasion.

Rhetoric has been central to Reagan's presidency because Reagan has intended his statecraft to be soulcraft. His aim has been to restore the plain language of right and wrong, good and evil, for the purpose of enabling people to make the most of freedom. In his long career of crisscrossing the country, practicing the exacting ethic of democratic persuasion, he has resembled a political John Wesley. For all his deplorable inattentiveness regarding many aspects of his office, he has been assiduous about nurturing a finer civic culture, as he understands it. Here, then, is the crowning paradox of Reagan's career. For all his disparagement of government, he has given it the highest possible purpose, the improvement of the soul of the nation.

When passions cool and the dust raised by current contentions settles, judicious historians are apt to place Reagan in the front rank of the second rank of American presidents. The first rank includes those who were pulled to greatness by the gravity of great crises. Washington and Jefferson were pulled by the hazardous flux of the founding era. Lincoln was pulled by disunion and the need to define the nation's meaning. Theodore Roosevelt was pulled by the need to tame the energies of industrialism, Woodrow Wilson by America's entry into the vortex of world affairs, Franklin Roosevelt by the Depression and the dictators.

Reagan is the last president for whom the Depression will have been a formative experience, the last president whose foremost model was the first modern president, Franklin Roosevelt. Roosevelt's first words as president ("the only thing we have to fear is fear itself") emphasized the tone-setting role of the office, and the need for high public morale. America was far less troubled in 1981 than in 1933, but it needed reassurance. It needed to recover confidence in its health and goodness. It needed to recover what was lost in the 1960s and 1970s, the sense that it has a competence commensurate with its nobility and responsibilities. Reagan, like Roosevelt, has been a great reassurer, a steadying captain who calmed the passengers and, to some extent, the sea.

Chapter Thirty-three

Why I Am Not a Neoconservative

Stephen J. Tonsor

I feel somewhat like Mr. Creedy in the Midas Muffler television ad. The engine of the old model of Conservatism that I drive is still running well, and, as I believe that "if it ain't broke don't fix it," I have come to view Conservatism as a perennial political philosophy which does not admit of neos or "Saturn" models.

I became a Conservative in 1954. Rather, I should say that I discovered that I was a Conservative in 1954. The event was not a conversion experience, but a moment of self-revelation. My experience was not unlike that of a Catholic acquaintance of mine who, one day, as he entered a Catholic church, dipped his hand in the holy-water fount and said with sudden clarity, "My God! What am I doing here?" He left the church, never to return. I dipped my hand in the holy-water fount of Russell Kirk and said, "Home at last!"

Whether or not one is a neoconservative is not simply a generational matter. It is not that I am an "old party comrade" and knew the Twelve Apostles, while those "neos" who came after us belong to a new and different age. After all, Irving Kristol must be nearly as old as I am. No, there are still young big-C Conservatives who enter the movement every day and are as far from neo-dom as I am.

Nor is the great divide the consequence of changing times and altered political and economic circumstances. It is not that most neoconservatives think that Barry Goldwater is "cute" and ought to be honored and revered and humored now and then, but that he belongs to the paleolithic age of

From *National Review,* June 20, 1986, pp. 54–56. Reprinted by permission of Stephen J. Tonsor.

374 STEPHEN J. TONSOR

the Conservative movement. If that indeed is the case, then I too am a paleo-conservative.

It can't simply be that neoconservatives read and often write for *Commentary* magazine, I read *Commentary* and have done so for years. I find myself often in agreement, always stimulated, and now and then put off by *Commentary*. However, I don't think *Commentary* is a reliable test; It often publishes writers I consider big-C Conservatives.

Age, changed circumstances, and an identifiable literary connection have little or nothing to do with the ideological identity of those on the Right. (There, I have uttered that awful word, usually prefaced by "far," as in far-sighted.) These differences that separate neoconservatives from Conservatives are differences that have for nearly a hundred years divided the Right.

I have made these personal references because I believe that the way in which I became a Conservative, and my starting point, were very different from the way in which one becomes a neoconservative, and the 'neoconservatives' starting point. One's starting point and the way in which one achieves an identity have very important implications for what one becomes.

These differences among Conservatives are grounded in the relationship of Conservatism to modernity. Increasingly, our culture is becoming aware that it is no longer "modern," though it is totally uncertain just what it is. This cultural break with "modernity" presents us with the preconditions for an accurate assessment of our relationship to it.

By "modernity" I mean that revolutionary movement in culture which derived from a belief in man's radical alienation, in God's unknowability or non-existence, and in man's capacity to transform or remake the conditions of his existence. The thoroughgoing secularism, the attack upon the past, religious and social, aristocratic or bourgeois, the utopian dream of alienation overcome and innocence restored are all linked together in the modernist sensibility. To be "up-to-date" was, for a hundred years, to be an alienated person. The world was viewed as anarchic chaos upon which man become God imposed his own particular dream of order. Often as not, that order was an inverted order, against the grain, against nature. Prometheanism and Satanism were one and the same order of man's invention. The Romantic Satanic hero is the same man as the Prometheus of Shelley and Mary, the Zarathustra of Nietzsche.

To pretend that the Right, that Conservatives, have been immune to modernity is self-delusion. On the whole, the Right has been much more modernist than the Left because the Right has dared to think consequen-tially, because the Right knows that he who says A must also say B. It is for this reason that the modernists of the Right have been, almost without exception, fascists and totalitarians, for they know that when things fall apart and the center does not hold, the only recourse is to an invented and imposed order.

Now that we are able to gain some perspective on this past century, we recognize that the social and political consequence of, modernity is totalitarianism. We can see that the denial of the existence of order as the ground of being, and the rejection of the transcendent, are a one-way street to Dachau. If everything is permitted and the will to power the only reality, then the Gulag is as logical as an Euler diagram. Those who do not refuse to think the unthinkable have known this for a long while. Hitler did not need to give a specific command for the "final solution." Himmler and the members of the *SS Einsatzgruppen* knew the "final solution" was implicit in their conception of reality. It is on the ground of modernity that Right and Left are merged and the differences between them are only differences of style and slogans. The Right that is born of modernity is a radical, a revolutionary Right, which cannot in any impor-tant degree be distinguished from the revolutionary Left.

Now it is a matter of fact that most of those who describe themselves as neoconservatives are or have been cultural modernists. They have been, to use Peter Berger's telling phrase, baptized in the "fiery brook." (He was making an elegant pun on the name of Ludwig Feuerbach, the Left Hegelian inspiration of Marx and the Church Father of alienation theory.) We Conservatives have been baptized in the Jordan, and there is a vast difference between the Jordan and the fiery brook.

It has always struck me as odd, even perverse, that former Marxists have been permitted, yes invited, to play such a leading role in the Conservative movement of the twentieth century. It is splendid when the town whore gets religion and joins the church. Now and then she makes a good choir director, but when she begins to tell the minister what he ought to say in his Sunday sermons, matters have been carried too far. I once remarked to Glenn Campbell of the Hoover Institution that had Stalin spared Leon Trotsky and not had him murdered in Mexico, he would no doubt have spent his declining days in an office in Hoover Library writing his memoirs and contributing articles of a faintly neocon-servative favor to *Encounter* and *Commentary*.

It is ungracious of me to suggest that political and even religious conversion does not often improve the mind's capacity for sound judgment? Whittaker Chambers, one of the most beguiling intellectuals of the twentieth century, had a flawed judgment as a Marxist and said some very silly things on the subject of Conservatism once he had become a convert.

All of which is not to say that the rejection of Marxism is unimportant and that the piecemeal rejection of various articles of faith shared with Left-liberal modernists is unimportant. Nor do I wish to imply that the assistance of neoconservatives is unwelcome in the work of dismantling the failed political structures erected by modernity. Conservatives have made common cause with classical liberals, and there is no reason why they should not make common cause with neoconservatives. When the wagon train is attacked we arm the women and children even though they may in their ineptitude occasionally mistake a friend for a foe.

Still, halfway from modernity is not far enough. Politics has always been inseparable from culture, and both derive ultimately from religion. It is absurd to believe that one can remain a modernist in culture and reject the implications of modernism in politics. Unbelief is incompatible with Conservatism. Conserve what? And to what end? Werner Dannhauser, writing in the December 1985 *Commentary,* tells us: "Too many conservatives have failed to come to terms with Nietzsche's thought, dismissing it as an embarrassing attempt to outflank them on the Right. But the challenge he represents will not go away," Dannhauser continues:

Nietzsche went far beyond Burke, who held out the hope of a time when atheism might cease to be fashionable. Nietzsche postulated an irreversible loss of naïveté in Western civilization. To put the matters crudely, he argued that the cat of atheism was out of the bag. The meanest capacities could now learn that religion was a myth, and when a myth is exposed for what it is, it can no longer serve to provide a unified horizon.

Too many conservatives whose own belief is weak or non-existent, who will privately admit that religion is "for the troops," continue to try to teach the catechism to those troops, forgetting that the latter have by now been thoroughly exposed to the Enlightenment and its lessons.

There you have it: The dividing line between conservatives is the line separating Burke from Nietzsche. Let me say parenthetically that I could never understand the reasoning processes of Jews who are Nietzscheans. Walter Kaufmann was quite unable to discern that while Nietzsche was not a biological racist he was a philosophical anti-Semite. If Nietzsche's anti-Semitism was less vulgar than that of Julius Streicher or of Nietzsche's friend Richard Wagner, it was no less deadly.

One is struck again by the true and forceful portrait Thomas Mann gives as of the Nietzschean modernist in the person of Adrian Leverkühn in *Dr. Faustus*. Adrian's music is modernist music not only as a style but in terms of the metaphysical conception out of which it is constructed. It is also demonic. It can only come into existence through the ruin of a soul, the destruction of a mind—and as the work of the composer reaches fruition, Germany is destroyed philosophically and sinks into ruin beneath the rain of Allied bombs. Mann, who made the character of Adrian Leverkühn out of a composite of Nietzsche and Arnold Schönberg, intended in this, the greatest novel of the twentieth century, to tell us something about the cultural reality of our age. The narrator, Serenus Zeitblom is a religious and pious Conservative—one, I take it, who had missed the Enlightenment.

I sometimes imagine myself and my fellow Conservatives to be of the type of Serenus Zeitblom. They have a loving regard for their age and their fellow men, and they realize that they must often forgo intervention and permit the tragic drama to play itself out. Because Leverkühn could not accept an order which, modernist that he was, he felt to be meaningless, he imposed a new order, rational and cleanly articulated as the music of Bach but lacking Bach's attachment to the divine and reconciliation to the human. Leverkühn's achievement was a great technical triumph but only a triumph of technique. It is fitting funeral music for a culture that died of pride.

Rational technique in the pursuit of irrational end; that suggests the modernist condition. That is why neoconservatives are so inventive and often correct in dealing with the realm of technique. But when push comes to shove, ends are of ultimate importance and will finally determine the appropriate technique. What the neoconservatives have done is to divorce techniques from ends in an effort to maintain their cultural modernism while rejecting its social and political implications. This, I say, is quite impossible, and in the long run dangerous. It is easy to see that the utopian social and political programs of the last hundred years have failed. It is not the cat of atheism that has been let out of the bag but the failure of the Enlightenment in all its forms. Neoconservatives are, as Irving Kristol remarked, "liberals who have been mugged by reality," but while they have been detached from their social and political myths they have not located themselves in a body of principle that makes life worth living, or that one would die defending.

It is important, also, to realize that the phrase "liberals mugged by reality" is only a part of the truth about neoconservatism. Neoconservatism is above all a transmogrification of "the New York intellectuals," in Alexander Bloom's phrase, who, in turn, reflected the instantiation of modernity among secularized Jewish intellectuals. Neoconservatism is culturally unthinkable aside from the history of the Jewish intellectual in the twentieth century. When the New York intellectuals turned from the beguilements of left-wing revolutionary utopianism, they did not in fact become Conservatives but attached themselves to positions that were neoliberal, in the sense that Mises and Hayek were neoliberals; and just as Mises and Hayek are philosophical and cultural modernists, so too New York intellectuals who now call themselves neoconservatives are modernists.

Conservatism has its roots in a much older tradition. Its world view is Roman or Anglo-Catholic; its political philosophy, Aristotelian and Thomist; its concerns, moral and ethical; its culture, that of Christian humanism. Most old-fashioned Conservatives are free of metaphysical anxiety and as happy as clams in a world that bears the unmistakable imprint of God's ordering hand. They are free of alienation, and they have absolutely no hopes of a utopian political order. They live with sin and tragedy not as a consequence of inadequate social engineering but as a consequence of man's sin and disorder. They believe that human institutions and human culture are subject to the judgment of God, and they hold that the most effective political instrument is prayer and a commitment to try to understand and do the will of God.

If neoconservatives wish us to take their conservatism seriously, they must return to the religious roots, beliefs, and values of our common heritage. They cannot dither in the halfway house of modernity and offer us technical solutions that touch the symptoms but never deal with the causes of contemporary disorder.

Chapter Thirty-four

Of What Use Is Tradition?

Gregory Wolfe

In the symposium that follows, the reader who has become accustomed to the notion that conservatism in America is at its peak in influence and intellectual rigor will be surprised to find several distinguished conservative scholars characterize the movement as "adrift" and "in trouble," suffering from "attenuation," "apostasy," and a sense of "malaise." The strength of this indictment consists partly in its very unexpectedness, for until now the paradoxical suggestion that conservatism might be experiencing internal disarray at the height of its political success has received scant notice in conservative circles. Whether the silence on this subject has been due to a reluctance to engage in seemingly "negative" criticism, or because the situation has been only partially understood, is not clear. But in recent years a number of leading conservative intellectuals have been expressing misgivings concerning the intellectual coherence and political influence of the Right. This symposium was put together in the hope that it would stimulate conservatives to begin the necessary, if unpleasant, task of self-criticism demanded by the tremendous growth of political activism marching under a "conservative" banner.

The dangers that threaten the integrity of the conservative movement can be summarized in a single term: "politicization." Ironically, conservatives launched themselves into the political sphere in an attempt to forestall the all-encompassing politicization of society that is the legacy of twentieth-century ideology. As Joseph Sobran has recently reminded us, liberalism no less than Communism aims at a political solution to the whole range of problems inherent in the human condition. We would

From *The Intercollegiate Review* (Spring 1986): 7–9. Reprinted by permission of Intercollegiate Studies Institute, Wilmington, Del.

prefer to believe that conservatives are impervious to this trend. But no community or institution is immune to temptation. For instance, we are no longer shocked by the notion that secularism has become so pervasive as to be rampant even in the churches. So too we should be willing to concede that politicization has infected the conservative movement.

In the 30th anniversary issue of *National Review* Richard Vigilante makes the following observation: "The vast and successful conservative political enterprise has become, almost overnight, subject to all the vices and temptations of power politics. That enterprise, not to be confused with the movement from which it sprang, is too large and too busy for philosophical reflection. If it does not find, or is not given, a clear, simple sense of what holds it together, it will split apart, ruptured by confusion and opportunism." According to the participants in this symposium—all leading figures in the conservative intellectual movement—the process of fragmentation and decay is already well advanced. Precisely because the label "conservative" has been undergoing a rapid inflation, these scholars are urging a period of retrenchment and renewal. The philosophical movement which gave birth to the post-war conservative renaissance— call it the Old Right, or "traditionalism," or what you will—is the only force competent to articulate the first principles which are the prerequisite for any genuine social and political reform in America.

The events which have led up to the current crisis of conservative identity and mission are complex and may well require the historian George Nash to add a second volume to his *The Conservative Intellectual Movement in America Since 1945* before they are fully understood. The contributors to this symposium are largely agreed that at least four major developments have contributed to the confusion.

First, the radicalization which took place during the sixties both in the academy and in the McGovern wing of the Democratic Party forced a number of "liberal refugees" across political borders, many of whom subsequently became known as neoconservatives. Despite the considerable polemical skills and the tactical support the neoconservatives have brought to bear on various issues of public policy, their relationship to conservatism proper was and is problematical. Essentially at peace with the welfare state, the neoconservatives continue to speak the language of social science and their policy initiatives often substitute one statist program for another. Though strongly anti-Communist, their foreign policy is plagued by a utopian temptation to promote what Paul Gottfried calls "global democratic revolution"—an idea that owes more to Woodrow Wilson than Henry Jackson.

The second factor has been the increasingly rapid decay of the American social fabric over the last two decades, evident in the rise of pornography, abortion on demand, divorce, venereal disease, and teenage suicide. To many hitherto apolitical citizens, it became clear that these scourges were the direct result of the liberal social agenda, spearheaded by the judicial fiats handed down by an activist Supreme Court. The movement that grew out of this rude awakening, populist and evangelical in character, became the New Right. In many ways closer to traditional conservatism than neoconservatism, the New Right nonetheless prefers confrontation and religiosity to a deeper and subtler understanding of the moral order embodied in the constitutional heritage bequeathed to us by the Founding Fathers. New Right populism often seems to imply that might—in the form of sheer numbers of God-fearing voters—makes right.

Third, conservative successes at the polls and in the Washington political machine, culminating in the two-term Reagan presidency, have drawn the inevitable groups of pragmatists and camp followers to the seats of power and privilege. This has entailed not only the frustration of many conservative efforts at reform, but also a continuing dilution of what conservatism actually means. As M. E. Bradford writes below: "we are in the process of forfeiting a well-developed corporate character through identification with the prudential decisions of the Reagan Administration."

Finally, and perhaps most dispiritingly, conservatives have acquiesced in, and even abetted, the redefinition of "legitimate" conservatism by the liberal-dominated media. Thus the liberals' first cousins—the neo-conservatives—are "designated . . . the official conservative opposition," according to Gottfried, while the new arch-enemy, a convenient scapegoat for liberal indignation, is the New Right. With the exception of William F. Buckley, Jr., who is now tolerantly treated as a cultural institution, the post-war conservative movement has been defined out of existence.

The contributors to this symposium are not under the illusion that traditional conservatives are the helpless victims of circumstance; that is why they are taking a stand. Neither do they believe, in gnostic fashion, that the political realm is inherently evil; the whole thrust of the conservative movement has been to reach and decisively alter the American political scene. The undeniable political achievements of recent years are given full appreciation in these pages. But traditional conservatives have always held that society is man writ large, that a fundamental understanding of human nature must precede and inform political action. That is why even the "free market" is not sufficient to justify policy: the marketplace must be seen in the context of the good. The true conservative also knows the limits of politics. He knows that long-term political change will come about only when culture itself has changed. The political victories of the present may appear insubstantial when one realizes that there have been few comparable victories in the academy, the media, the arts, or the republic of letters. Conservatism means an unrelenting commitment to man in his wholeness: man may be a political animal, but he also has an immortal soul. A vision of life which sets its sights on anything lower than this does not merit the name conservatism.

Chapter Thirty-five

Conservative Splits

Dan Himmelfarb

In his contribution to a symposium on "The State of Conservatism" in the Spring 1986 issue of the *Intercollegiate Review,* the Old Right historian and editor Paul Gottfried noted that neoconservatives "have always been open in expressing their contempt for the Old Right." Whether or not this claim is valid—and there is reason to question its validity, inasmuch as a central theme of neoconservative thought is that the enemies are now on the Left—the converse seems to be true: criticism of neoconservatism has come to be an increasingly conspicuous feature of Old Right writings.

The general complaint is that neoconservatives exert disproportionate influence within the "conservative intellectual movement," that neoconservatism is now regarded as roughly equivalent to—rather than merely a species of—"American conservatism." Thus Clyde Wilson, in the *Intercollegiate Review* symposium, wrote (of the Old Right) that "we have simply been crowded out by overwhelming numbers. . . . Our estate has been taken over by an impostor, just as we were about to inherit." And Stephen J. Tonsor took the following well-publicized swipe at neoconservatives at a Philadelphia Society meeting: "It is splendid when the town whore gets religion and joins the church. Now and then she makes a good choir director, but when she begins to tell the minister what he ought to say in his Sunday sermons, matters have been carried too far."

The tension between neoconservatism and what has come to be called paleoconservatism (i.e., the Old Right) is one of the major themes of *The Conservative Movement,* a slim book by Paul Gottfried and Old Right editor Thomas Fleming, which serves, essentially, as a postscript to

From *Commentary,* May 1988. Reprinted by permission; all rights reserved. Reprinted with permission of Dan Himmelfarb.

George H. Nash's excellent history, *The Conservative Intellectual Movement in America* (1976). While the authors of *The Conservative Movement* are considerably more evenhanded and less polemical in their treatment of neoconservatism than previous Old Right observers have been, Gottfried and Fleming's attitude toward neoconservatism remains unmistakably—albeit subtly—critical.

Why the conflict? What is (are) the difference(s) between neoconservatism and paleoconservatism? Are these differences superficial or fundamental?

There are several prevailing explanations for the split between neo- and paleoconservatives. Some are more convincing than others. None is entirely satisfactory.

One explanation holds that it is not so much the neoconservatives' conservatism that is new as their conversion to it. That is to say, neoconservatives and paleoconservatives differ only with respect to their past: as opposed to the neoconservatives, who moved—or "progressed," as some would say—from socialism to anti-Communist liberalism to conservatism, the paleoconservatives have spent their entire lives on the right half of the political spectrum. At present, according to this explanation, there is no significant difference between the two groups. Thus Nathan Glazer's definition of a neoconservative: "someone who wasn't a conservative."

While this account may apply to the neoconservative "elders"—Irving Kristol, Norman Podhoretz, and Hilton Kramer, for example—it cannot explain why younger editors and writers, who have never embraced any ideology of the Left, choose to think of themselves as neoconservatives rather than simply as conservatives. The existence of second-generation neoconservatives suggests that it is possible to have been a neoconservative all of one's life—or at least since political consciousness began.

A second explanation stresses the link between neoconservatism and social science—or more specifically sociology, the discipline of choice for, among others, Nathan Glazer, Peter L. Berger, and Seymour Martin Lipset. (Daniel Bell, another sociologist who is regularly identified with neoconservatism, continues to spurn the label.) Paleoconservatives, in contrast, are generally suspicious of social science: they eschew "tinkering," and reject the view of society as a set of "problems" for which there are coverable "solutions." Thus Gottfried and Fleming distinguish between the paleoconservatives, whose "hearts [are] in literature and theology," and the neoconservatives who "revel in statistics and computerized information." Paleoconservatives, add the authors, "rarely sought the kind of statistical confirmation that neoconservative academics produce for their positions."

While it is true that neoconservatives tend to be more respectful than paleoconservatives of the social-scientific method, the connection between neoconservatism and social science is often exaggerated—perhaps because of a tendency to equate neoconservative thought with the contents of the *Public Interest*. While it is fair to describe the *Public Interest*, with its tables, graphs, and regression analyses, as a social-science journal, such a description is inappropriate for *Commentary*, which regularly publishes essays on history, religion, and literature, among other topics outside the bounds of social science. Still less is there anything social-scientific about the *New Criterion*.

Insofar as neoconservatives do take social science seriously, more over, their approach tends to be skeptical: neoconservative social scientists have consistently argued at a large part of the solution to social problems lies in the restoration of tradition, authority, and restraint. Thus Nathan Glazer, writing in these pages in 1971,[1] argued that "the breakdown of traditional modes of behavior is the chief cause of our social problems," and prescribed "hesitation in the development of social policies that sanction the abandonment of traditional practices" and "the creation and building of new traditions." And James Q. Wilson, contributing an essay on "Private Virtue and Public Policy" to the 20th-anniversary issue of the *Public Interest* (Fall 1985), wrote: "In almost every area of important public concern, we are seeking to induce persons to act virtuously, whether as school-children, applicants for public assistance, would-be lawbreakers, or voters and public officials." Neoconservative social science is not, in the language of Max Weber, *wertfrei* (value-free), nor is it necessarily inconsistent with the paleoconservative (i.e., non-social-scientific) approach to social problems.

A third explanation emphasizes the "Jewish" character of neoconservatism. Thus Gottfried and Fleming: "Among the factors that led . . . many . . . neoconservatives to disengage from the Left, their Jewishness was certainly significant." (Stephen Tonsor has stated that "neoconservatism is culturally unthinkable aside from the history of the Jewish intellectual in the 20th century.") According to this explanation, there is something inherently Jewish about neoconservatism, while paleoconservatism is thought to be intrinsically Christian (usually specifically Catholic). Or, stated differently (and more bluntly): paleoconservatism is the conservatism of Christians, neoconservatism the conservatism of Jews.

While it is fair to argue that Judaism is a "significant" aspect of neoconservatism, it is probably an exaggeration to say that neoconservatism is "unthinkable" apart from it. The anti-Israel sentiment, to say nothing of anti-Semitism, that has become increasingly prominent in certain Left-liberal circles in the last twenty years, has indeed been an important influence on many who have broken with the Left. But this is by no means the only feature of Left liberalism that neoconservatives find objectionable; the contemporary Left's anti-Americanism, for example, is a quality that has led Gentiles as well as Jews to repudiate the Left. Brigitte and Peter Berger (both Lutherans) have observed, in these pages,[2] that "many more non-Jews identify with neoconservatism than is often supposed." And whatever causes Michael Novak (a lay Catholic theologian) and Richard John Neuhaus (a Lutheran pastor) to feel more comfortable with the neoconservative than with the paleoconservative label, it is certainly not Judaism.

A fourth explanation suggests that the distinction between neo- and paleoconservatism is a matter of placement on the political spectrum: neoconservatives are thought to be "to the left" of paleoconservatives. Gottfried and Fleming, for example, see neoconservatives as "political centrists who deplore the lack of moderation on both sides of the spectrum," and add that "neoconservatives, who may have learned from Arthur Schlesinger's book by that title the value of claiming to be the vital center, never abandon, at least rhetorically, the *juste milieu*." The view of neoconservatives as center-rightists is accurate in many respects— particularly with regard to the welfare state. Gottfried and Fleming are certainly correct when they observe that neoconservatism "is not entirely incompatible with modern state planning," and that "almost all neoconservatives . . . remain qualified defenders of the welfare state." And their distinction between the neoconservatives' plans to "trim" the welfare state and the paleoconservatives' desire to "dismantle" it is an important one.

Neoconservatives also tend to be "to the left" of paleoconservatives socially and culturally. In the preface to *The Conservative Movement*, the authors write that "one conclusion that may be drawn from this book" is that an "emphasis on progress" is a "distinctive feature of the contemporary American Right"—i.e., an American Right that has come increasingly under the influence of neoconservatism. Most of the (neoconservative) contributors to the November 1985 *Commentary* symposium,[3] as Gottfried and Fleming observe, wrote favorably about recent improvements in the areas of civil rights and economic well-being. Against neoconservatives, who emphasize social and material progress, paleoconservatives tend to see moral degeneration—itself a product of secularization—as the distinguishing characteristic of American life in the second half of the 20th century.

There is also the matter of party identification. It is probably safe to say that virtually all paleoconservatives are registered Republicans. As for neoconservatives, though the dominant branch of the Democratic party currently embraces the very ideas and policies against which they have rebelled, many neoconservatives still do not feel entirely comfortable with the Republican party—if only from an emotional or psychological standpoint. While it is likely that Robert Nisbet was exaggerating when he wrote (in the Fall 1985 *Public Interest*) that "probably only a small fraction of those who had been most prominent in the *Public Interest* and in *Commentary* voted for Reagan" in 1980 and 1984, it remains true that many—perhaps most—of the older neoconservatives, and more than a few of the younger ones, continue to think of themselves as Democrats, even while distancing themselves from the policies and candidates of the Democratic party. (Nathan Glazer, two years after his confession of his conversion to conservatism,[4] endorsed the candidacy of George McGovern, himself a founding father of the left wing of the Democratic Party.[5])

With regard to domestic policy, then, it is fair to say that neoconservatism is a center-right tendency, and that paleoconservatism is "to its right." It would be difficult to support a similar claim, however, with regard to foreign policy. If movement from left to right on the foreign-policy spectrum represents a movement from less anti-Communism to more, a case can be made for locating neoconservatives "to the right" of paleoconservatives. For in contrast to neoconservatism, a prominent feature of which is an unapologetic and unyielding anti-Communism, paleoconservatism, as Gottfried and Fleming acknowledge, "for all its professed anti-Communism, retains some of its old isolationist spirit." In foreign policy it is the paleoconservatives, not the neoconservatives, who are the "moderates."

The difference between paleoconservatives and neoconservatives, in sum, is thought to be a difference of chronology (old-timers vs. Johnnies-come-lately); a difference in attitude toward social science (hostility vs. sympathy); a difference of religion (Christianity vs. Judaism); or a differ-

ence in location on the political spectrum (right vs. center-right). Each of
these explanations is only partially correct. There is another, better way
of explaining the tension between the two conservatisms—namely, as a
tension between two distinct philosophical traditions.

Reflecting on the definition of a neoconservative, Irving Kristol has written that "the political tradition . . . which neoconservatives wish to renew
and revive . . . is the political tradition associated with the birth of modern
liberal society—a society distinguished from all others by representative
government and a predominantly free-market economy."[6] Stephen Tonsor, seeking to distinguish "real" conservatism from neoconservatism, has
argued that "conservatism has its roots in a much older tradition. Its
world view is Roman or Anglo-Catholic; its political philosophy, Aristotelian and Thomist; its concerns, moral and ethical; its culture, that of
Christian humanism."

The fundamental difference between neoconservatism and paleoconservatism is this: neoconservatives belong to the tradition of liberal-
democratic modernity, the tradition of Montesquieu, Madison, and
Tocqueville; paleoconservatives are the heirs to the Christian and
aristocratic Middle Ages, to Augustine, Aquinas, and Hooker. The principles of neoconservatism are individual liberty, self-government, and
equality of opportunity; those of paleoconservatism are religious—particularly Christian—belief, hierarchy, and prescription.

Insofar as the principles that neoconservatives embrace are rather explicitly American—they are conspicuously embodied in the Declaration of
Independence, for example—and insofar as these are not the principles
with which paleoconservatives feel most comfortable, it is fair to say that
paleoconservatism is fundamentally extra-American. That is to say, it
stands outside the American liberal tradition. Thus Gottfried and Fleming, acknowledging the premodern—indeed, antimodern—character of
paleoconservatism, locate its roots in "a civilization that went back beyond the American past, into the medieval and ancient worlds."

This philosophical division underlies the many instances in which
neoconservatives and paleoconservatives disagree even while agreeing, in
which they agree on what but not on why. Take the Founding Fathers,
for example, of whom conservatives of every stripe tend to be respectful,
if not reverent. For neoconservatives the Founders are liberals in the best
sense: they are champions of individual rights, popular government, spir-

itual equality, and cultural and religious pluralism. Paleoconservatives, in contrast, place the Founders in the Christian tradition; they regard them as defenders of the "religious heritage" of Western civilization.

Thus, in the seminal work of paleoconservatism, *The Conservative Mind* (1953), Old Right elder Russell Kirk's treatment of the Founding Fathers consists of a chapter on John Adams, by all estimates the most Burkean of the Founders. The lead author of *The Federalist,* James Madison, himself less respectful than Adams of pre-democratic ages, does not appear in Kirk's 450-page book: the index skips from James Mackintosh to Sir Henry Maine. Kirk devotes four pages to democratic capitalism which "demolished conservative ramparts"). And as for the influence of John Locke, Kirk has written (in *National Review*) that Richard Hooker, directly or indirectly, had far more to do with the fundamental opinions of the Founding Fathers than did Locke."

Or take anti-Communism, generally regarded as a common denominator of the different brands of conservatism. Neoconservatives are anti-Communist because Communism is the enemy of freedom and democracy, paleoconservatives because it is the enemy of religion, tradition, and hierarchy. For neoconservatives the relevant distinction between East and West is not the distinction between atheism and belief (as it is for paleoconservatives), nor is it the distinction between socialism and capitalism (as it is for certain libertarians). The fundamental difference, rather, is that between totalitarianism and freedom. Thus neoconservatives reject Communism in favor of some version of liberal-democratic capitalism, while paleoconservatives reject it in favor of what Gottfried and Fleming call "historic nationalities." (What is meant by "historic nationality" is not entirely clear, though presumably it implies some variety of monarchy, theocracy, or other traditionalist societal arrangement.) Paleoconservatives are critical of neoconservative anti-Communism, which Gottfried and Fleming identify with "global democratic revolution." This vision of global democracy is "secularist" and "politically and sexually egalitarian," and thus "as far removed from a traditionalist world view as from Marxist-Leninism."[7]

This philosophical division also explains the difference between neo- and paleoconservatives in their attitude toward liberalism (in the original sense of that term) and its underlying ideals. Take equality. Neoconservatives contrast equality of opportunity, a central tenet of liberalism, with equality of result, which they regard as an essentially discriminatory and coercive, and therefore *il*liberal, doctrine. Paleoconservatives are less apt to draw this distinction: they are suspicious of any principle bearing the name equality. Thus neoconservatives, by and large, are favorably disposed toward the civil rights movement of the 1960s, but are critical of affirmative action, particularly when that term implies the use of quotas. In supporting the former and opposing the latter, neoconservatives are being entirely consistent—that is, consistently liberal: in contrast to the civil rights movement, whose goals were a color-blind society and an end to legal discrimination, affirmative action requires a race-conscious society and a new form of legal discrimination.

Which is not to say that the paleoconservative view of equality is necessarily inconsistent. While neoconservatives regard affirmative action as a *perversion* of the ideals of the civil rights movement, paleoconservatives see it as an *extension:* both the civil rights movement and affirmative action have egalitarian goals; both are objectionable. Or as Gottfried and Fleming put it: "Unlike the neoconservatives, [the Old Right] remains irreconcilably opposed to . . . the principle of social equality." Thus neoconservatives tend to be respectful of Martin Luther King, Jr., whom they regard as a champion of liberal ideals, but not of Jesse Jackson, for example, whose ideas they regard as illiberal. Paleoconservatives, in contrast, for whom the relevant feature of each man is his egalitarianism (broadly defined), are respectful of neither. (Gottfried and Fleming think President Reagan's declaring King's birthday a national holiday represents a betrayal.)

If neoconservatives are defenders of the American liberal tradition, they are clearly not liberals in the sense in which that term is generally used today. For neoconservatives there are two kinds of liberals: genuine and counterfeit. The latter are men and women of the Left, who, in the last twenty-five years, have usurped the liberal label, leaving real liberals to be designated neoconservatives. These so-called liberals are illiberal in many respects: insofar as they support quotas in employment and education, they reject the liberal ideal of a society indifferent to race, gender, and ethnicity; insofar as they are inhospitable to certain views (particularly on college campuses), they show contempt for the liberal ideals of free speech and toleration of unpopular, heretical, or minority opinion; and, most important, insofar as they regard Communism as a lesser threat than anti-Communism, they betray an indifference to large-scale tyranny, the opposition to which once served as the very definition of liberalism.

Paleoconservatives, in contrast, do not distinguish between good liberals and bad; for them the phrases "great liberal tradition" and "liberal in the best sense" are merely oxymorons. Paleoconservatives regard liberalism—in all its forms—as intrinsically flawed, primarily because it is a secular and egalitarian tendency, insufficiently respectful of tradition. Thus, while neoconservatives draw a distinction between the liberalism of Franklin Roosevelt, Harry Truman, and John F. Kennedy, on the one hand, a liberalism representing a double commitment to progressivism in domestic policy and vigorous anti-Communism in foreign policy, and the anti-anti-Communist liberalism of George McGovern and his heirs, on the other, paleoconservatives see not disjunction but continuity.

A central theme of *The Conservative Movement* is that American conservatism, under the influence of neoconservatism, has, in the last two decades, moved "left." (The authors, for example, write that the emergence of neoconservatism has had the effect of "shift[ing] the parameters of conservative respectability toward the center.") Rather than arguing that American conservatism has moved left, however, it might be more accurate to say that half of American liberalism moved left and half—i.e., the neoconservatives—stayed put. Or as Gottfried and Fleming themselves put it: "Neoconservatism . . . arose in reaction to what was regarded as a betrayal of purpose. . . . Democrats and young radicals [had] corrupted the great liberal tradition." In fact, "neoconservatism" is probably a misnomer—and doubly so: it is not particularly new, and it is not necessarily conservative (at least not in the classical or medieval sense). Perhaps "paleoliberalism" would be a better term.

And just as the 18th- and 19th-century liberals opposed the Tories and *ancien régime* to their right, and the French Revolutionists and socialists to their left, so too does neoconservatism stand in opposition to both (Old) Right and (New) Left. At this point in history the fundamental challenge to liberal democracy—both externally, in the form of Communist totalitarianism, and internally, in the form of an anti-anti-Communist academic/intellectual community—comes from the Left. Thus liberal democrats (a.k.a. neoconservatives) must devote their energy to countering attacks from this quarter. In different historical circumstances, however, in which the challenge came from the opposite flank, it is entirely conceivable that the friends of liberal democracy would make ready to do battle with the Right. In this regard, it might be helpful to think not of conservatives and liberals, but of liberal democrats and their opponents, on both Left and Right.

*

An implicit thesis of *The Conservative Movement*—and an explicit thesis of previous essays by Old Right authors—is that neoconservatism is not an authentic conservatism, that it is insufficiently distinguishable from welfare-state liberalism. (Gottfried himself has written, in the *Intercollegiate Review* symposium, that one of the "common mistakes among interpreters of the current American Right" is "treating neoconservatives as genuine conservatives.") Yet neoconservatives might make a similar claim with respect to paleoconservatives. For if conservatism implies "presentism," if it means a defense of existing institutions, then there is reason to question the authenticity of a self-proclaimed American conservatism that readily identifies itself as a medieval tendency.

Indeed, it might with some justification be argued that it is neoconservatism, and not paleoconservatism, that is both genuinely American and genuinely conservative. In a brilliant 1957 essay in the *American Political Science Review,* Samuel P. Huntington, implicitly adopting the thesis of Louis Hartz's *The Liberal Tradition in America* (1955), argued that American conservatives must be liberals, that antiliberal American conservatism is an anachronism. "American institutions . . . ," wrote Huntington, "are liberal popular, and democratic. They can best be defended by those who believe in liberalism, popular control, and democratic government. Just as aristocrats were the conservatives in Prussia in 1820 and slaveowners were the conservatives in the South in 1850, so the liberals must be the conservatives in America today."

Whether or not one is "truly" a conservative, however, ought not to be a matter of fundamental importance. More significant than what one is called is what one believes: labels matter less than principles. Thus liberal democrats should be willing to regard as friends those who are generally sympathetic to the principles of liberal democracy, regardless of what these individuals are called (or call themselves). And, conversely, liberal democrats should hesitate to regard as friends those who, irrespective of how they are labeled, are uncomfortable with, suspicious of, or hostile toward liberal-democratic ideals. Such discrimination is especially necessary at a time when liberal democracy has so few friends.

NOTES

1. "The Limits of Social Policy," September 1971.
2. "Our Conservatism and Theirs," October 1986.

3. "How Has the United States Met Its Major Challenges Since 1945?"

4. "On Being Deradicalized," *Commentary,* October 1970.

5. "McGovern and the Jews: *A Debate*" (with Milton Himmelfarb), *Commentary* September 1972.

6. "What is a Liberal—Who is a Conservative?: A Symposium," *Commentary.* September 1976.

7. The authors' claim that neoconservative anti-Communism rests on the "stated or implicit assumption that American democracy with its mixed economy is the supreme human good" is at best only half right. Certainly neoconservatives prefer liberal democracy to both Communist and traditionalist societies. Few neoconservatives would agree, however, that democratic capitalism is—or, indeed, that *any* political or economic system can be—the "supreme human good." And insofar as neoconservatives embrace liberal democracy, they do so not so much because it is best as because it is least bad: with Churchill, they regard democracy as the worst political system, except for any other.

Part X

Conservatism after Reagan

Conservatism had reached its political highpoint during the Reagan years. Conservatives helped restore American power in the wake of Vietnam and helped win the Cold War; conservative economic policies helped contribute to a twenty-year period of economic growth; and conservatives helped alter the political climate in America, moving debates over public policy to the Right. Yet, for all their political success, conservatives failed to appreciably alter American culture. Believing American culture had irrevocably (and irretrievably) declined since the 1960s, conservatives lamented the "de-valuing of America." Robert Bork, a nominee for the U.S. Supreme Court, eventually rejected during tense confirmation hearings, described a nation "slouching towards Gomorrah," and in 1997 the journal *First Things* questioned whether recent Supreme Court decisions had brought about an "end of democracy."[1] Many conservatives, even in the wake of the fall of communism and with a booming economy, felt pessimistic about the American prospect.

Conservatism continued to fracture in the last decade of the twentieth century, a continuation of disputes that emerged in the Reagan era (see Part IX). Events only added to the turmoil within the conservative movement. With the collapse of the Soviet Union's empire in eastern Europe in the fall of 1989, and with the collapse of the Soviet Union itself in 1991, many conservatives felt it time to retract from global entanglements. American troops were no longer needed in Europe (or elsewhere); NATO, having served its purpose, should be abrogated; and foreign and military aid to European regimes ended. Now that the Cold War was over it was time to return to the republican virtues of nonintervention which had defined American foreign policy before World War II.

Former Nixon aide and Reagan speechwriter Patrick J. Buchanan (1938–   ), a Catholic traditionalist and diehard anticommunist, proposed a return to an America First foreign policy. Without a communist threat, America should retract; instead, it was doing just the opposite in the

1990s. America had become an empire, Buchanan argues in the essay chapter 36.

Buchanan first articulated his view of America's new imperial role in his opposition to the Persian Gulf War (1990–1991). The Iraqi invasion of neighboring Kuwait in August 1990 led to an American military buildup in Saudi Arabia, the aerial bombardment of targets in Iraq, and eventually the military liberation of Kuwait (that cost 147 American lives). George Bush scored a diplomatic and military triumph, getting Arab states like Egypt and Saudi Arabia to join a coalition with Israel against Saddam Hussein's regime. Buchanan dissented, however, telling a television audience on the PBS syndicated program, *The McLaughlin Group*, "there are a lot of things worth fighting for, but an extra 10 cents for a gallon of gasoline is not one of them." He also questioned the real motivation behind the war by arguing that "there are only two groups beating the drums for war in the Middle East, the Israeli Defense Ministry and its amen corner in the United States." Accused of anti-Semitism for this comment by A. M. Rosenthal of *The New York Times* and called an "isolationist" by *National Review*, Buchanan reasserted a nationalistic foreign policy.

His opposition to the Gulf War led Buchanan to reassert themes dormant among conservatives since Robert A. Taft's death in 1953. Buchanan opposed an activist foreign policy, fought against the global economic order coming to fruition in the 1990s, and proposed limits to immigration into the United States.[2] In 1992 he challenged Bush in the Republican primaries and while he did not win any primaries, he did force Bush to campaign against him, thereby costing the Bush candidacy quite a bit of money during primary season, and weakening the president in the fall against Bill Clinton and billionaire Reform Party candidate H. Ross Perot. At the 1992 Houston Republican convention, Buchanan forcefully drove home his view of a culture war in America, arguing "my friends, this election is about more than who gets what.... It is about what we believe and what we stand for as Americans. There is a religious war going on in this country for the soul of America. It is a cultural war as critical to the kind of nation we shall be as the Cold War itself. And in that struggle for the soul of America, [Bill] Clinton and [Hilary Rodham] Clinton are on the other side and George Bush is on our side." In 1996 he campaigned again, defeating Kansas senator Bob Dole in the New Hampshire primary, but losing thereafter. Unlike 1992, he did not appear at the Republican convention.

While Buchanan did not enjoy electoral success, some conservatives, like columnist Samuel Francis, continued to strike out against what he perceived to be the neoconservative-dominated conservative movement. Francis, a former columnist with *The Washington Times,* also wrote for *Chronicles* magazine, a journal of the paleoconservative Rockford Institute. A conservative theorist in the manner of former communist James Burnham, Francis articulated a conception of conservatism that borrowed heavily from left-wing critics of the managerial State.³ His frustration with the conservative movement's failure to build on the broad discontent of Middle American radicals (see Part VIII) is depicted in the essay "Beautiful Losers" (see Chapter 39).

The emergence of a populist-oriented conservatism in the 1990s coincided with the emergence of globalization, the election of "new" Democrat Bill Clinton in 1992, and a growing disenchantment with American institutions and distrust of government. While some liberal pundits blamed the enmity of religious traditionalists and other assorted individuals (best demonstrated by David Koresh's Branch Davidian sect, destroyed by self-set fires in Waco, Texas in April 1993 and the response of terrorist Timothy McVeigh in blowing up the Oklahoma City federal building in 1995) on Reagan's attacks on government, there was a growing distrust and cynicism with government that eschewed ready explanation. Populist conservatives like Buchanan stoked the flames of discontent in his two candidacies for president and gained little; other, inside-the-beltway conservatives saw opportunity to craft a new political agenda in 1994 by offering a program designed to challenge Clinton's new democrat agenda.

The program, Georgia congressman Newt Gingrich's Contract with America, represented a type of "conservatism-lite," aimed at electing a conservative Congress, but one which would not depart too far from the vital center of political debate. The Contract with America was a brilliant political strategy—a product of focus groups and polls—designed to link the fortunes of Republicans running in local congressional races to a national program in off-year elections (scandals among Democratic congressmen, like powerful Illinois representative Dan Rostenkowski, and within the Clinton administration, helped Gingrich's strategy). It succeeded beyond even Gingrich's wildest expectations. For the first time since 1954, the Republicans captured control of both houses of Congress. Gingrich was speaker of the House and Republicans controlled both houses of Congress the remainder of Clinton's presidency.

Yet the Gingrich revolution, as conservative Lee Edwards has called it, fell short of expectations.[4] By 1996, Bill Clinton, whose political demise was seemingly etched in stone with the results of the 1994 election, won reelection, running as a moderate against Bob Dole. Even Clinton scandals, like the Monica Lewinsky affair, could not derail Clinton, helped by a booming economy and Republican failures. Impeached by the GOP Congress in 1998, Clinton could not be convicted. Voters blamed the Republicans, and in the 1998 mid-term elections, the Democrats gained seats in both houses; in 2000, they took control of the Senate. Gingrich, a controversial Speaker of the House, was forced to resign in 1999 over violations of House rules. Before Clinton left office, a Republican Congress authorized the largest budget requests in the nation's history, capitulating to the lamest of lame duck executives. Politics seemed to be failing conservatives.

At the *fin de siecle,* conservatism was deeply troubled. Paul Weyrich, the head of the Free Congress Foundation and one of the more important conservative political organizers—he helped create the Heritage Foundation—lamented conservatism's failure to address the cultural issues in America. In an open letter to conservatives, written in February 1999, Weyrich argued that it was time for religious conservatives to withdraw from national politics in order to concentrate on problems in their own communities. He did not advocate a complete withdrawal from politics, but simply a return to more fundamental concerns of faith, family, and community.[5] Politics was not the only vehicle capable of changing society. In fact, with the Clinton scandals, politics showed how limited politics could be in addressing cultural concerns.

In a different vein, the editors of *Policy Review,* the journal of the Heritage Foundation (it has subsequently become a publication of the Hoover Institution at Stanford University), stated that conservatism represented a "completed body of ideas." The editors of *Policy Review* brazenly argued that there was little more to add to a conservative canon. Presenting their opinion as an exercise in looking backward—delineating decades of conservative intellectual and political activity—the editors were also looking forward. Clearly, to one part of the movement, the great intellectual questions had all been asked. The task now was to engage in applying the principles to America's daily problems.

Having been presented with some representative samples of the conservative canon in this book, it is imperative to allow you, the reader, to decide for yourself whether the editors of *Policy Review* are correct.

A cautionary note can be put forth, however. As events and issues have evolved, so has conservatism. A remarkably protean concept—conservatives have altered their ideas, have changed their policies, and have changed their perspective over the course of their movement's history. Whither it goes in the next century will be anybody's guess. As the foregoing essays and documents suggest, it will hardly be static.

Chapter Thirty-six

A Republic, Not an Empire

Patrick J. Buchanan

At the close of the twentieth century, U.S. foreign policy seems frozen in time. Nostalgic for the clarity and certitudes of the Cold War, our elites have resolutely refused to relinquish a single institution or commitment dating to that conflict. Yet the Soviet empire has been dead for a decade. Indeed, commitments for America to fight, in perpetuity, in defense of other nations are routinely added. Repeated incantations to America as the "indispensable nation" are made to reassure ourselves our dominance is still desired. But the world has changed since the Wall came down, and we must change with it.

Balance Sheet of an Imperial Republic

Walter Lippmann once described the "preoccupation" of a statesman as "bringing into balance, with a comfortable surplus of power in reserve, the nation's commitments and the nation's power." If a nation's power fails to cover its commitments, its foreign policy is bankrupt. While the insolvency might not be revealed until a run on the bank, as at Pearl Harbor, it will be exposed. Given U.S. military assets today, and the commitments they must cover, U.S. foreign policy is near bankruptcy.

Consider the asset side of our national security balance sheet. The Cold War Center–Right coalition has collapsed, our will to intervene has largely vanished, and U.S. power has undergone a historic contraction. Defense spending, 9 percent of GDP in Eisenhower's day, 6 percent in the Reagan era, is about 3 percent today. Under the "Proposed Active Force Levels" of the Pentagon, manpower is to be cut from 2,070,000 in 1990 to 1,453,000. Carrier battle groups, numbering fifteen during Desert Storm, are to fall to eleven; Air Force Wings are to drop from twenty-two in 1990 to thirteen.

These, nevertheless, are impressive armed forces, and, were they needed only to protect U.S. vital interests, they would be adequate. But consider the astonishing and lengthening roster of global commitments that must be covered by these dwindling military assets:

North America and Europe

Under Article V of the NATO treaty, an attack on any member state "shall be considered an attack against them all." This means the United States, in perpetuity, must respond as though America were attacked in the event of any attack on any of eighteen NATO nations: Canada, Iceland, Britain, France, Holland, Luxembourg, Belgium, Denmark, Germany, Norway, Italy, Portugal, Spain, Turkey, Greece, Poland, Hungary, and the Czech Republic.

NATO expansionists are now demanding U.S. war guarantees for Austria, Slovenia, Macedonia, Bulgaria, Rumania, Slovakia, and the three Baltic states: Estonia, Lithuania, and Latvia. There is talk of Ukraine, which ten million Russians call home, joining NATO. This would commit America to fight Europe's wars in perpetuity all the way to the Urals. On November 4, 1996, was held the first meeting of the Security Committee of the U.S.–Ukraine Binational Commission to strengthen ties between the Pentagon and Kiev's Ministry of Defense, and to promote "Ukraine's integration into European and Transatlantic security structures."

The U.S. Marines have been involved in joint maneuvers with Ukrainian troops on the Crimean Peninsula; U.S. paratroopers have practiced jumps in Kazakhstan; and Washington has been providing military assistance to Tashkent and established a United States—Uzbekistan Joint Commission to study military and political cooperation.

The Balkan Peninsula

Before President Clinton ordered air strikes on Yugoslavia in the early spring of 1999, U.S. soldiers had never fought in the Balkans. But today there are eight thousand U.S. troops in Bosnia and a U.S. presence in Macedonia. And the United States and NATO have battered Serbia to force Slobodan Milosevic to remove his army and security police from Kosovo. Yet Kosovo is part of Yugoslavia. Thus, for the first time, NATO, a defensive alliance, has taken offensive action against a country putting down an insurrection inside its own territory, and America has engaged in acts of war against a nation that did not perpetrate any act of violence against the United States or its allies. Secretary of State Madeleine Albright has been quoted as declaring that NATO must now extend its geographic reach even beyond the continent of Europe and evolve into a "force for peace from the Middle East to Central Africa."

President Clinton's original ultimatum to Yugoslavia—to attack its troops and sovereign territory if it did not remove its forces from Kosovo—was made without the formal approval of Congress.

The Middle East

While we have no treaty alliance with Israel, the United States, Britain, and France made a Tripartite Declaration in 1950, stating that they would take action if Arab nations or Israelis prepared to violate the armistice lines of 1948. "This declaration in effect supported Israel's right to exist within the frontiers established by force of arms pending a peace treaty," noted historians J. A. S. Grenville and Bernard Wasserstein. The United States signed a Mutual Defense Assistance Agreement with Israel in 1952. Under Presidents Johnson and Nixon, the United States made a moral commitment to Israeli security. That commitment led Nixon to put U.S. nuclear forces on alert when Moscow seemed about to intervene in the Yom Kippur War in October 1973.

After the Wye River meeting between Israel and the Palestinian Authority, a "memorandum of understanding" was signed committing the United States to enhance Israel's "defensive and deterrent capabilities" against chemical, biological, and nuclear weapons. Should Iran, Iraq, or Syria deploy missiles that can hit Israel, the United States will view that with "particular gravity" and consult promptly about the aid or support, "diplomatic or otherwise," it might provide. Clearly, the United States is moving toward further extension of its nuclear umbrella. As this was not a formal treaty, Senate approval was not required.

Today, U.S. troops sit on Mount Sinai to monitor an Israeli–Egyptian peace. There is talk that, in return for recognition of a Palestinian state,

Israel may be given security guarantees by the United States to come to its defense in any future Israeli–Arab war, of which there have been five. If Israel returns the Golan Heights to Syria, some Americans have suggested the United States might put its own forces there, to ensure Israel's security.

The Persian Gulf

After the Gulf War, America adopted a policy of "dual containment" of Iran and Iraq. Thousands of U.S. troops are stationed in the Gulf, and U.S. warships make routine visits to the United Arab Emirates, Oman, and Bahrain. It is understood that any attack on the pro-Western Arab nations of the Gulf would involve a U.S. response.

South Korea

After the armistice in 1953, the United States negotiated a Mutual Security Treaty with Korea. It reads, in part:

> Each party recognizes that an armed attack in the Pacific area on either of the parties in territories now under their respective administrative control ... would be dangerous to its own peace and safety and declares that it would act to meet the common danger in accordance with its constitutional processes.

Though Chinese forces left Korea forty years ago, 37,000 U.S. troops remain, and Defense Secretary William Cohen said in July 1998 that a U.S. military presence "should continue even if there is a unification of the two Koreas. . . ." The United States today spends more for the defense of South Korea than does Seoul, and if another war broke out, American soldiers would be in the thick of the fighting, and dying, from the first hours.

Japan

The U.S.–Japan Mutual Security Treaty of 1960 obligates the United States to treat any armed attack against any territories "under the administration of Japan" as "dangerous to [America's] own peace and safety. . . ." This would cover such islets as the Senkakus, also claimed by Beijing. Under the treaty, however, Japan is not obliged to treat an armed attack on the United States or its possessions as any threat to Japan. More than half a century after its defeat in World War II, Japan, which has a $4 trillion economy, spends 1 percent of its GDP on defense and relies on America to deal with any attack from Russia, China, or North Korea.

Taiwan

Though President Carter abrogated our mutual security treaty with Taiwan, signed in 1954, the United States, under Clinton, came close to a naval war with China over the island in 1996. There remains a U.S. moral commitment to Taiwan—much like that to Israel—and the United States is obligated, by a Reagan communiqué of 1982, to permit Taiwan access to American defensive weapons. Since 1996 China has engaged in a steady buildup of missiles targeted on the island.

The Philippines

Under a mutual security treaty signed in August 1951, any attack on this island nation is declared dangerous to U.S. peace and security. The treaty remains in force, though Manila years ago expelled U.S. forces from Clark Air Force Base and Subic Bay Naval Base. In late 1998, Manila, angry over China's building on disputed Mischief Reef in the Spratly island chain, suggested its U.S. pact might be invoked. "We don't think there will be a shooting war," said the Philippine defense minister, but, "[a]s far as we see it, the mutual defense treaty may still prove of value to us."

Thailand and Pakistan

Under Article V of the Manila Pact of the Southeast Asia Collective Defense Treaty of 1954, SEATO was created by Secretary of State John Foster Dulles to oppose the communist aggression and subversion in the region. Signers included the United States, Britain, France, Australia, New Zealand, the Philippines, Thailand, and Pakistan. Under Article IV, in the event of an armed attack, each member would "act to meet the common danger in accordance with its constitutional processes." De Gaulle's France withdrew from military cooperation in 1967, and Britain refused to assist the United States militarily in Vietnam. In 1972 Pakistan withdrew completely, and in 1977 SEATO was dissolved. But the Manila pact remains in force and, together with a 1962 U.S.–Thailand communiqué, constitutes the U.S. military commitment to Thailand, which remains a U.S. treaty ally.

Australia

Under the ANZUS Pact of 1951, the United States is obligated to come to the defense of Australia and New Zealand if they are attacked, but they have no obligation to come to the defense of the United States if America, or one of its other allies, is attacked. In 1985 a Labour government refused to permit U.S. ships in Wellington Harbor unless Washington stipulated there were no nuclear weapons aboard. The United States declared that New Zealand had decided to "renege on an essential element of its ANZUS participation" and suspended its security obligations to New Zealand. The ANZUS Pact between the United States and Australia, however, remains in force, and each year, under the Australia–United States Ministerial consultations, the two nations meet for high-level talks at the foreign and defense minister level.

Latin America

Under the Treaty of Rio (the Inter-American Treaty of Reciprocal Assistance) of 1947, which took effect in 1948, the United States is obliged to aid any country in the Western Hemisphere that comes under attack— with the exception of Cuba (Havana withdrew in 1960). Under Article III, signatories "agree that an armed attack by any States against an American State shall be considered as an attack against all the American States," and each signatory "undertakes to assist in meeting the attack." Under this pact, the United States must come to the military rescue of Argentina, the Bahamas, Bolivia, Brazil, Chile, Colombia, Costa Rica, the Dominican Republic, Ecuador, El Salvador, Guatemala, Haiti, Honduras, Mexico, Nicaragua, Panama, Paraguay, Peru, Trinidad and Tobago, Uruguay, and Venezuela. Article IV adds: "This article defines the region to which the treaty refers, which extends from the North Pole to the South Pole, and includes Canada, Alaska, the Aleutians, Greenland, the Falklands, the South Orkneys, and Antarctica."

Nothing can destroy this country except the overextension of our resources, Republican Senator Robert A. Taft once said. Indeed, it would be an understatement to describe the commitments above as an over-extension of our resources. In their totality, they make the nineteenth-century British Empire look isolationist; truly, this is imperial overstretch.

America has taken on the historic roles of the German empire in keeping Russia out of Europe, of the Austrian empire in policing the Balkans, of the British Empire in patrolling the oceans and sea lanes and protecting the Persian Gulf, of the Ottoman Empire in keeping peace in the Holy Land, of the Japanese empire in defending Korea and containing China, and of the Spanish empire in Latin America. Thus, we have undertaken to come to the defense of half a hundred nations around the world on a defense budget that is less than 3 percent of GDP. As Paul Kennedy (*The Rise and Fall of the Great Powers*) wrote a decade ago:

> Decision-makers in Washington must face the awkward and enduring fact that the sum total of the United States' global interests and obligations is now far larger than the country's power to defend them all simultaneously.

If not true a decade ago, it is surely true today. Our situation is unsustainable. The steady expansion of global commitments, as relative national power declines, is a prescription for endless wars and eventual disaster. . . .

The occasion was the fiftieth anniversary of the Japanese attack on the Pacific fleet. A crowd gathered on the pier overlooking the hulk of the *Arizona*. The president that day was magnanimous toward the former enemy. "I have no rancor in my heart toward . . . Japan, none at all," said George Bush, who fought in the Pacific war. But the president did have rancor for those he held responsible for the "date which will live in infamy." In a savage remark Bush declared, "[I]solationism flew escort for the very bombers that attacked our men . . . [I]solationists gathered together at what was known in those days as an 'America First' rally . . . at precisely the moment the first Americans met early, violent deaths right here at Pearl Harbor."

The president urged his countrymen to repudiate the fatal delusion that had led to the disaster, and its disciples: "[W]e stand here today on the site of a tragedy spawned by isolationism. And we must learn and . . . avoid the dangers of today's isolationism and its economic accomplice, protectionism." At his party's convention in San Diego, five years later, the ex-president thundered: "Leadership means standing against the voices of isolation and protectionism."

Yet, at Pearl Harbor, President Bush had stood history on its head. The United States found itself at war with Japan not because "isolationists" directed U.S. foreign policy but because Franklin Roosevelt, an interventionist, did. By December 1941 FDR was determined to block further Japanese expansion and was prepared to risk war to succeed. Japan attacked because it believed, correctly, that America meant to roll back its empire. The fleet was Roosevelt's weapon. As foreign policy scholar Christopher Layne wrote in response to Bush's 1991 address:

> Pearl Harbor . . . was the result of active U.S. engagement in Asian affairs, not of isolationism. America's commitment to maintaining its military presence in the Pacific and preserving its perceived political and economic interests in China put it on a collision course with a Japan determined to establish its strategic and economic predominance in East Asia. The Pacific Fleet had been deployed to Pearl Harbor for the specific purpose of dissuading Tokyo from its expansionist course. . . .

Bush's fear of a return to "isolationism" is echoed by the elites of both parties. Indeed, nothing can unite the U.S. establishment in greater solidarity than this dread specter. Which raises questions: Against what are they railing? Of whom are they afraid?

As "Munich" has become a synonym for craven and cowardly appeasement, "isolationist" is a term of abuse intended to silence an adversary, end an argument, and stifle debate. Brand an opponent an isolationist and you need not hear him out. But what is isolationism? Wayne Cole, the historian of the struggle between FDR and the America First Committee of 1940–1941, studied "isolationism" for fifty years and concludes:

> [The very term] is an obstacle to clear thinking. . . . No president or national political party in the entire history of the United States . . . ever advocated isolating the United States from the rest of the world. In the eighteenth and nineteenth centuries the term isolationism was never used to describe the foreign policies of any presidential administration.

The idea that America was ever an isolationist nation is a myth, a useful myth to be sure, but nonetheless a malevolent myth that approaches the status of a big lie. How did the term come into common usage? Cole explains:

> "Isolationism" was a pejorative term invented and applied in the twentieth century to discredit policies that the United States had followed traditionally during the first one-hundred and forty years of its independent history. The term was never an accurate label for United States policies.

The term is used today to disparage the foreign policy America pursued from the time of Washington until Wilson took us into war—and for the twenty years between the election of Harding and the third term of Franklin Roosevelt. What is today derided as isolationism was the foreign policy under which the Republic grew from thirteen states on the Atlantic into a continent-wide nation that dominated the hemisphere and whose power reached to Peking. Contrary to the impression left by the term, young America was no hermit republic. How can one characterize as a "century of isolationism" a period in American history in which:

John Adams fought an undeclared naval war with France.

Thomas Jefferson doubled the size of the country by relieving Napoleon of Louisiana, and sent ships to attack Barbary pirates.

James Madison seized West Florida from Spain, took us to war against the British Empire, and sent an army to invade Canada.

Andrew Jackson invaded Florida and packed the Spanish governor off to Havana, after which Secretary of State John Quincy Adams convinced Madrid to cede to the United States the "derelict province."

Colluding with Great Britain to prevent European powers from preying on the carcass of the Spanish empire, James Monroe declared the Western Hemisphere off limits to further colonization, an act Bismarck called an "insolent dogma" and "a species of arrogance peculiarly American and inexcusable."

John Tyler annexed Texas and asserted a preeminent U.S. interest in Hawaii when a British naval officer tried to make a protectorate of the kingdom in 1841.

James Polk invaded Mexico and seized the northern half of the country, including California.

Millard Fillmore sent Commodore Matthew Perry to open up Japan to U.S. trade; that legendary sailor succeeded, and urged the annexation of Formosa and Okinawa.

Franklin Pierce purchased a swatch of Mexico larger than West Virginia, urged the Senate to annex Hawaii and grant statehood, and tried to annex Cuba, as U.S. clipper ships opened up China.

James Buchanan won the presidency on a platform that called for the annexation of Cuba.

Andrew Johnson sent a Union army to the border to drive the French out of Mexico and help overthrow Maximilian's regime.

William Seward bought Alaska, annexed Midway, and tried to acquire Hawaii, British Columbia, Greenland, and the Virgin Islands.

Ulysses S. Grant tried to annex the Dominican Republic, threatened Spain with war over the *Virginius* naval crisis, and gave the first presidential support to an isthmian canal controlled by the United States.

Rutherford B. Hayes acquired a quasi-protectorate over the Samoan Islands, which later took us to the brink of war with Germany.

Benjamin Harrison threatened Chile with war if it refused to apologize and indemnify America for a bloody fracas involving U.S. sailors in Valparaiso.

Grover Cleveland threatened Great Britain with war over a border dispute between Venezuela and British Guiana.

William McKinley declared war on Spain; invaded Cuba; annexed Puerto Rico, Hawaii, Guam, Pago Pago, and the Philippines; put down a Filipino insurgency; sent U.S. troops to Peking to crush the Boxer Rebellion; and declared an "Open Door" for the imperial powers in China.

Teddy Roosevelt seized the Panama Canal Zone, sent the Great White Fleet to show Japan that the United States was a global power, mediated the Russo–Japanese War and the Moroccan crisis between France and Germany, and won America's first Nobel Peace Prize.

The nineteenth century witnessed a quadrupling of America's territory and its emergence as a world power. To call the foreign policy that produced this result "isolationist" is absurd. Americans were willing to go to war with the greatest powers in Europe, but only for American interests. They had no wish to take sides in European wars in which America had no stake. Our nation's ambitions always lay to the south, the west, and northwest—not to Europe. As early as the Congress of Vienna, the thrust of America's drive toward conquest was evident to the Spanish minister in Washington:

> If all Europe or its principal governments do not take steps in time against the scandalous ambition of this Republic . . . and [to obstruct] the well-established scheme of conquest which she has set for herself it may well be too late; and she may be master of Cuba and of the New Kingdom of Mexico or whatever other region suits her.

Henry Cabot Lodge would exult, even before America's "splendid little war" with Spain, "We have a record of conquest, colonization, and expansion unequaled by any people in the nineteenth century." "For really three centuries," said Frederick Jackson Turner, "the dominant fact of American life has been expansion." By 1898 America had, through diplomacy or war, eliminated all French, Spanish, Russian, and British power from the continent. As Talleyrand had predicted in the time of Napoleon: "The Americans mean to rule alone in America. Moreover, their conduct ever since the moment of their independence is enough to prove this truth; the Americans are devoured by pride, ambition, and cupidity."

Those who describe U.S. foreign policy in its first 120 years as "isolationist" should take the matter up with Mexicans, Spaniards, American Indians, and Filipinos. Isolationism, writes historian Walter McDougall, is "but a dirty word that interventionists, especially since Pearl Harbor, hurl at anyone who questions their policies." The word that best describes our earliest foreign policy tradition, he adds, is "unilateralism":

> [Unilaterism] never meant that the United States should, or for that matter could, sequester itself or pursue an ostrich-like policy toward all foreign countries. It simply meant, as Hamilton and Jefferson both underscored, that the self-evident course for the United States was to avoid permanent, entangling alliances and to remain neutral in Europe's wars except when our Liberty—the first hallowed tradition—was at risk.

The message of Washington's Farewell Address was not to isolate America from Europe but to keep it independent of Europe. Stay out of foreign wars, Washington admonished; they are the great threat to liberty, and America is about nothing if not the preservation of liberty. Look west to the mountains, the great river beyond, the plains, the Pacific. That is where our destiny lies. Europe is the past. Avoid "permanent alliances"; devote your energies to our own country. Independence, not isolation, is the American tradition. Walter Lippmann in 1952 sought to explain to the British how the term isolationism "must be handled with the greatest care, or it can do nothing but confuse and mislead":

> The word isolationist conceals the dynamic and expansionist energy of the American nation. It suggests the United States did not have a foreign policy until recently. All that is quite untrue. The United States has never been neutral in the European sense. It has always had a very active foreign policy, of which the central purpose has been the determination to expand across the continent from the Atlantic seaboard to the Pacific Ocean.

American foreign policy evolved even before independence, with colonial participation in British wars against the French and their Indian allies. Men like Washington fought in these wars for American reasons— to drive aliens and intruders out of land they themselves coveted. "Those whom we now call isolationists," wrote Lippmann, "are the true believers in the foreign policy of the men who conquered and settled the American continental domain." The controlling principle was "to keep a free hand in order to expand westward to the continental limits." Twentieth-century "isolationists," said Lippmann,

> [wanted only] to isolate American decisions and actions, to have the final word wherever Americans are involved. They carry with them the thought and feeling which has come down from those who in the eighteenth and nineteenth centuries managed in one way or another, by war and by diplomacy, to expel all the foreign powers who blocked the westward expansion of the American people.

Americans welcomed European immigrants to help build the nation, but they drove relentlessly, sometimes ruthlessly, to expel European power from the New World. We were to be masters of our own house.

Why is this dynamic, triumphant foreign policy so reviled? Because the hidden agenda of the globalists who now direct America's destiny is to harness its wealth and power to causes having little or nothing to do with the true national interests of the United States. The savagery of today's attacks on "isolationism" is a measure of the depth of establishment fear that the destiny of the Republic will be torn away from it and restored to people who carry in their hearts the great tradition of America First.

How did globalists capture the heights? As Wayne Cole writes, the tradition derided as isolationism "was not simply downed by the informed logic of a better ideology; it was quashed by every conceivable 'smear' and 'dirty trick' designed to make that once honorable approach seem to be ignorant, stupid, irresponsible, unpatriotic, evil, and even fascist or Nazi."

Victory achieved in such a fashion cannot be allowed to stand. But to overturn the regime of the globalists, Americans must be reintroduced to the history made by the great men today mocked as isolationists, to the rules that guided them as they guided America, and to the lessons they teach. For we are today on the threshold of a new century, and it is in our power to reclaim our destiny. Will we be forever ensnared in entangling alliances that will involve us and bleed us in every great new war on the Eurasian land mass until we are as diminished as the other powers of the twentieth century? Or will we recapture the freedom to decide ourselves when and where we go to war again?

America is today as overextended as any empire in history. We are committed to go to war to defend the borders of dozens of countries from Norway to Turkey, from Portugal to Poland, from Saudi Arabia to South Korea. U.S. soldiers patrol the lines between Bosnian Serbs and Bosnian Muslims, and between Macedonia and Kosovo. They sit on Mount Sinai to monitor a peace signed twenty years ago. Almost yearly, we issue new security guarantees to lock future generations into the wars of the coming century. But protest this mindless interventionism, and you are shouted down as an "isolationist!"

This transnational elite must not succeed in silencing the voices of American patriotism and enlightened nationalism. But if we are to answer insults designed to demonize us, to stifle dissent, to shut off debate, we need to rediscover the lost chapters of our history. We need to know the ideas and ideals of the Founding Fathers and America's great men, who would not believe where our leaders are taking us now.

"I think the nation-state is finished," an editor confided a few years ago. That is what is at stake. Will America endure as a free independent republic, or become the North American province of a new world order as the globalists ardently desire? To prevent us from ever going "gentle into that good night," I wrote this book.

Now, back to the beginning.

Chapter Thirty-seven

Beautiful Losers
Why Conservatism Failed

Samuel Francis

When T. S. Eliot said that there are no lost causes because there are no won causes, he probably was not thinking of American conservatism. Nearly sixty years after the New Deal, the American Right is no closer to challenging its fundamental premises and machinery than when Old Rubberlegs first started priming the pump and scheming to take the United States into a war that turned out to be a social and political revolution. American conservatism, in other words, is a failure, and all the think tanks, magazines, direct-mail barons, inaugural balls, and campaign buttons cannot disguise or alter it. Virtually every cause to which conservatives have attached themselves for the past three generations has been lost, and the tide of political and cultural battle is not likely to turn anytime soon.

Not only has the American Right lost on such fundamental issues as the fusion of state and economy, the size and scope of government, the globalist course of American foreign policy, the transformation of the Constitution into a meaningless document that serves the special interests of whatever faction can grab it for a while, and the replacement of what is generally called "traditional morality" by a dominant ethic of instant gratification, but also the mainstream of those who today are pleased to call themselves conservatives has come to accept at least the premises and often the full-blown agenda of the Left. The movement that came to be

From *Beautiful Losers: Essays on the Failure of American Conservatism.* Reprinted by permission of the University of Missouri Press. Copyright 1993 by the Curators of the University of Missouri.

known in the 1970s as neoconservatism, largely northeastern, urban, and academic in its orientation, is now the defining core of the "permissible" Right—that is, what a dominant Left-liberal cultural and political elite recognizes and accepts as the Right boundary of public discourse. It remains legally possible (barely) to express sentiments and ideas that are further to the Right, but if an elite enjoys cultural hegemony, as the Left does, it has no real reason to outlaw its opponents. Indeed, encouraging their participation in the debate fosters the illusion of "pluralism" and serves to legitimize the main Leftward trend of the debate. Those outside the permissible boundaries of discourse are simply "derationalized" and ignored—as anti-Semites, racists, authoritarians, crackpots, crooks, or simply as "nostalgic," and other kinds of illicit and irrational fringe elements not in harmonic convergence with the Zeitgeist and therefore on the wrong side of history. That is where the de facto alliance of Left and neoconservative Right has succeeded in relegating those who dissent from their common core of shared premises such as journalist Patrick J. Buchanan and anyone else who seriously and repeatedly challenges their hegemony.

"Neoconservatism" today is usually called simply "conservatism," though it is sometimes known under other labels as well: Fred Barnes's "Big Government conservatism"; HUD Secretary Jack Kemp's "progressive conservatism"; Representative Newt Gingrich's "opportunity conservatism"; Paul Weyrich's "cultural conservatism"; or, most recently, "The New Paradigm," in the phrase coined by White House aide James Pinkerton. Despite the variations among these formulas, all of them envision a far larger and more active central state than the "Old Republicanism" embraced by most conservatives prior to the 1970s, a state that makes it its business to envision a particular arrangement of institutions and beliefs and to design governmental machinery to create them. In the case of "neoconservatism," the principal goal is the enhancement of economic opportunity through one kind or another of social engineering (enterprise zones, for example) and the establishment of an ethic that regards equality (usually disguised as "equality of opportunity"), economic mobility, affluence, and material gratification as the central meaning of what their exponents often call "the American experiment."

Such goals are not conceptually distinct from those of the progressivism and liberalism athwart which the American Right at one time promised to stand, though the tactics and procedures by which they are to be achieved are somewhat (but not very) different. Indeed, much of what neoconservatives are concerned with is merely process—strategy, tactics, how to win elections, how to broaden the base of the GOP, how to make the government run more effectively, how to achieve "credibility" and exert an "impact"—and not with the ultimate goals themselves, about which there is little debate with those parts of the Left that also lie within the permissible range of "pluralistic" dialogue. Given the persistent cultural dominance of the Left, a conservatism that limits itself merely to procedural problems tacitly concedes the goals of public action to its enemies and quietly comes to share the premises on which the goals of the Left rest. Eventually, having silently and unconsciously accepted the premises and goals, it will also come to accept even the means by which the Left has secured its dominance, and the very distinction between "Right" and "Left" will disappear.

It was this kind of silent acquiescence in the premises of the Left that James Burnham identified as a salient characteristic of neoconservatism when it first began to appear in the early 1970s. In an exchange with neoconservative Peter Berger in *National Review* (May 12, 1972), Burnham noted that though neoconservatives had broken with "liberal doctrine," finding it "both intellectually bankrupt and, by and large, pragmatically sterile," they retained "what might be called the emotional gestalt of liberalism, the liberal sensitivity and temperament," the ideoneurological reflexes and knee-jerks of the Left. Since that time, those reflexes have not only not been recircuited but have been reinforced, so that today the neoconservative "Right" almost explicitly accepts and defends the New Deal and its legacy, seeking only to spruce them up and administer them more effectively and more honestly, but not to reverse them or transcend them—Old Right goals routinely dismissed by the neoconservative Right as "impractical."

But Burnham also remarked that "much of conservative doctrine . . . also is, if not quite bankrupt, more and more obsolescent," and the failure of conservatism and its eventual displacement by neoconservative formulas is closely related to its bankruptcy. The survivors of the Old Right today spend a good deal of their time complaining about their dethronement by pseudoconservatives, but those Old Rightists who survive are only the hardiest of the species, ever vigilant for camouflaged predators who slip into their herds. For the most part, their predecessors in the conservative movement of the 1950s and 1960s were not so careful, and indeed many of them failed to understand the ideological dynamics of liberalism, how the liberal regime functioned, or how to distinguish and insulate their own beliefs and organizations against the Left. That error was perhaps at least part of what Burnham meant by the "obsolescence" of conservatism. It was an error that was the principal weakness of conservatism and permitted the eventual triumph of neoconservative forces and the assimilation of the Right within the dominant cultural apparatus that serves the Left's interests.

The Old Right, composed mainly of the organized conservative resistance formed in the mid-1950s and centered around *National Review,* failed to understand that the revolution had already occurred. Conventional Old Right doctrines revolved around the ideas of a constitutionally limited central government, largely independent local and state government, an entrepreneurial economy of privately owned and operated firms, and a moral and social code of restrained or "ascetic" individualism in politics, economy, art, religion, and ethics. These doctrines reflected the institutions and beliefs of the bourgeois elite that had gained political power in the Civil War and prevailed until the dislocations of twentieth-century technological and organizational expansion brought forth a new managerial elite that seized power in the reforms of the Progressive Era and the New Deal. These reforms constituted the revolution, not only in the political power of Roosevelt, Harry Truman, and the Democratic party but also in the construction of an entire architecture of economic and cultural power, based on bureaucratized corporations and unions, increasingly bureaucratized universities, foundations, churches, and mass media, and fused, directly or indirectly, with a centralized bureaucratic state. Since the revolution occurred legally and peacefully and assimilated traditional institutions and symbols to its use, it was not immediately apparent that it had taken place at all, that the dominant minority in the United States had circulated, that the bourgeois elite no longer called the shots, or that those who continued to adhere to Old Right doctrines were no longer in a position to "conserve" much of anything. But while the Old Right of the 1950s was in principle aware and critical of the new power structure, it continued to regard itself as essentially "conservative" of an established or traditional order rather than frankly acknowledging that it had been dethroned and that a counterrevolutionary mission, not "conserving," was its mission, its proper strategy.

Hence, the entire strategy of the Old Right of the 1950s was to seek accommodation with the new managerial-bureaucratic establishment rather than to challenge it. George H. Nash writes that William F. Buckley, Jr., forcefully rejected what he called "the popular and cliché-ridden appeal to the grass-roots" and strove instead to establish a journal which would reach intellectuals. Not all conservatives agreed with this approach, but the young editor-to-be was firm. It was the intellectuals, after all, "who have midwived and implemented the revolution. We have got to have allies among the intellectuals, and we propose to renovate conservatism and see if we can't win some of them around."

Yet while Buckley seemed cognizant of the "revolution" that had transpired and was, in fact, successful in attracting a number of intellectuals, he failed to see that the new intellectual class as a whole, which had indeed "midwived and implemented the revolution," could not become conservative. It could not do so because its principal interest, social function, and occupational calling in the new order was to delegitimize the ideas and institutions of conservatism and provide legitimization for the new regime, and its power and rewards as a class depended upon the very bureaucratized cultural organizations that conservatives attacked. Only if conservatism were "renovated" to the point that it no longer rejected the cultural apparatus of the revolution could intellectuals be expected to sign up.

Moreover, by focusing its efforts in Manhattan, Washington, and the major centers of the intelligentsia and other sectors of the new elite, Buckley and his conservative colleagues isolated themselves from their natural allies in the "grass roots." While there was clearly a need for intellectual sophistication on the Right, the result of Buckley's tactic was to generate a schism between Old Right intellectual cadres and the body of conservative supporters outside its northeastern urban and academic headquarters. Among these supporters in the 1950s and 1960s there flourished an increasingly bizarre and deracinated wilderness of extremist, conspiratorialist, racialist, and even occultist ideologues who loudly rejected both the Old Right mainstream and the Old Right's new friends in the intellectual and cultural elite, but who failed to attract any but the most marginal and pathological elements in the country and exerted no cultural or political influence at all. At various times in its history, *National Review* has found it necessary to "purge" itself of such adherents, and each catharsis, no matter how prudent, has rendered its "renovated" conservatism less and less palatable to ordinary Americans and more and more acceptable to the Manhattanite intelligentsia it has always sought to attract.

In any case, the Old Right intellectuals for the most part had few links with the "grass roots," the popular, middle-class, and WASP nucleus of traditional American culture. *National Review* itself was not only Manhattanite but also Ivy League and Roman Catholic in its orientation, as well as ex-communist and ethnic in its editorial composition, and not a few of its brightest stars in the 1950s were personally eccentric, if not outright neurotic. Moreover, few of them reflected the "Protestant Establishment" that, by the end of World War II, had largely made its peace with the new regime and was scurrying to secure its own future within the managerial state, economy, and culture. Of the twenty-five conservative intellectuals whose photographs appeared on the dust jacket of George H. Nash's *The Conservative Intellectual Movement in America since 1945*, published in 1976, four are Roman Catholic, seven are Jewish, another seven (including three Jews) are foreign born, two are southern or western in origin, and only five are in any respect representative of the historically dominant Anglo-Saxon (or at least Anglo-Celtic) Protestant strain in American history and culture (three of the five later converted to Roman Catholicism). Theological meditation competed with free-market economic theory as the main interest of many Old Right intellectuals to a far larger degree than had been the case with such pre–World War II skeptics of progressivism as Albert Jay Nock, H. L. Mencken, or the "America First" opponents of foreign intervention.

The religious, ideological, and ethnic differentiation of the Old Right from the country's Protestant Establishment may have helped push its leaders in a more radical direction than they were inclined to go, but it probably also served to cut them off from both the Establishment's declining leadership and from the rank and file of Americans outside it. The Old Right could not help but remain an isolated circle of intellectuals and journalists, absorbed in rather esoteric theory, despised by the intellectual elite they hoped to impress and convert, and ignored by most Americans and their political leaders.

The Old Right's political aspirations were no less grotesque than its desire to win acceptance among the intellectuals and followed much the same strategy. Although the remnants of the bourgeois elite retained an important political base in congressional districts remote from the centers of the new regime, they could serve only as a brake on the regime's power and were unable to control either Congress or the presidency. Their inability to do so was directly related to conservatives' lack of cultural power, their lack of contact with and their not-infrequent contempt for Americans outside the circles of the national elite. Even when Old Right forces were able to capture the Republican party in 1964, the disastrous result of Barry Goldwater's candidacy was in large part due to his supporters' lack of access to the national organs of culture and opinion. Subsequent Old Right political efforts concentrated on attempts to gain influence within the political domain of the elite by means of endless searches for suitable presidential candidates who could seize national power at a single blow and through a kind of Fabian tactic of permeating the federal bureaucracy. As a result, there has now emerged an entire generation of what might be called "Court Conservatives" who devote their careers to place-seeking in the federal government and favor-currying with whatever president or satrap is able to hire them and who have long since abandoned any serious intention of challenging the bureaucratic organism they have infected with their presence.

In the absence of a significant cultural base, such political efforts not only were bound to fail but also had the effect of drawing the Right further into the institutional and conceptual framework of the liberal regime. Political maneuver by its nature is a process of bargaining, and the more conservatives have engaged in political action, the more they have found themselves bargaining and compromising with their opponents, who often do not need to bargain at all. Since their opponents on the Left, in Congress or the executive branch, have ready access to and sympathy with the mass media, they are able to discredit the men and measures of the Right that will not bend to their manipulation. Moreover, the Right's preoccupation with the presidency also forces it to seek acceptance by the national media and the dominant culture of the Left and focuses its efforts on an institution that is far less susceptible to grass roots influence than Congress. The modern presidency, as the lesson of the hapless Reagan administration shows, is less the master of the bureaucratic elite than its servant, and while a powerful president could subdue and circumvent his own bureaucracy, he could do so consistently only if he were able and willing to mobilize mass support against it from outside the elite.

The political weakness of the Old Right and its failure to understand that it really represented a subordinate and displaced elite rather than a dominant incumbent one were instrumental in its gradual assimilation by the liberal regime. The crucial episode in the assimilation occurred during the Vietnam War, which the Old Right in general supported on the grounds of anticommunism. The war itself was a result of misconceived liberal policies and was effectively lost by liberal mismanagement, and there was no good reason for the Right (even the anticommunist Right) to support it. Yet, as the New Left mounted an attack on the war and broadened the attack to include the bureaucratized university and parts of the leviathan state, the Right's response was to defend not only the war and sometimes even the liberal policies that were losing it, but also the liberal power centers themselves. The Old Right critique of containment, mounted by anti-interventionists such as Robert Taft and John T. Flynn and by anticommunist interventionists such as Burnham, was forgotten, as was much of the Old Right cultural critique of the domestic liberal regime, which mirrored its globalist regime. It was at this point that the Old Right began to join forces with emerging neoconservative elements, whose concern was entirely with defending the liberal managerial system, foreign and domestic, and which never had the slightest interest in dismantling it. The result of the coalition between Old Right and neoconservatism has been the adoption by the Right of Wilsonian-Rooseveltian globalism and its universalist premises, the diffusion of those premises within the Right in defense of what are actually the institutions and goals of the Left, and the gradual abandonment of the Old Right goals of reducing the size and scope of centralized power. By swallowing the premises of the Left's globalist and messianic foreign policy, the Right has wound up regurgitating those same premises domestically. If it is our mission to build democracy and protect human rights in Afghanistan, then why should we not also enforce civil rights in Mississippi and break down the barriers to equality of opportunity everywhere through the sledgehammer of federal power? Conservatives do not yet advocate sending the Special Forces into Bensonhurst and Howard Beach, but the story is not over yet.

To say that the conservatism of the Old Right failed is not to dismiss the important contributions its exponents made to a critical analysis of liberal ideology or all of its work in political theory, international relations, economic and social policy, and religious, philosophical, and cultural thought. The Old Right intelligentsia as a whole was a far more exciting group of thinkers and writers than the post–World War II Left produced. Nor does pointing to its failure mean that a serious Right was not or is not possible. It is merely to say that the Old Right fundamentally misperceived its own position in and relationship to the emerging managerial regime and that this misperception led it into a mistaken strategy of seeking consensus rather than conflict with the dominant elite of the regime.

It remains possible today to rectify that error by a radical alteration of the Right's strategy. Abandoning the illusion that it represents an establishment to be "conserved," a new American Right must recognize that its values and goals lie outside and against the establishment and that its natural allies are not in Manhattan, Yale, and Washington but in the increasingly alienated and threatened strata of Middle America. The strategy of the Right should be to enhance the polarization of Middle Americans from the incumbent regime, not to build coalitions with the regime's defenders and beneficiaries. Moreover, since "Middle America" consists of workers, farmers, suburbanites, and other non- or postbourgeois groups, as well as small businessmen, it is unlikely that a new Right will make much progress in mobilizing them if it simply repeats the ideological formulas of a now long-defunct bourgeois elite and its order. The more salient concerns of postbourgeois Middle Americans that a new Right can express are those of crime, educational collapse, the erosion of their economic status, and the calculated subversion of their social, cultural, and national identity by forces that serve the interests of the elite above them and the underclass below them, but at the expense of the middle class. A new Right, positioning itself in opposition to the elite and the elite's underclass ally, can assert its leadership of alienated Middle Americans and mobilize them in radical opposition to the regime.

A new, radical Middle American Right need not abandon political efforts, but, consistent with its recognition that it is laying siege to a hostile establishment, it ought to realize that political action in a cultural power vacuum will be largely futile. The main focus of a Middle American Right should be the reclamation of cultural power, the patient elaboration of an alternative culture within but against the regime—within the belly of the beast but indigestible by it. Instead of the uselessness of a Diogenes' search for an honest presidential candidate or a Fabian quest for a career in the bureaucracy, a Middle American Right should begin working in and with schools, churches, clubs, women's groups, youth organizations, civic and professional associations, local government, the military and police forces, and even in the much-dreaded labor unions to create a radicalized Middle American consciousness that can perceive the ways in which exploitation of the middle classes is institutionalized and understand how it can be resisted. Only when this kind of infrastructure of cultural hegemony is developed can a Middle American Right seek meaningful political power without coalitions with the Left and bargaining with the regime.

Eliot may have been right that no cause is really lost because none is really won, but victory and defeat in the struggle for social dominance have little to do with whether the cause is right or wrong. Some ideas have more consequences than others, and those that attach themselves to declining social and political forces have the least consequences of all. By allowing itself to be assimilated by the regime of the Left, American conservatism became part of a social and political force that, if not on the decline, is at least confronted by a rising force that seeks to displace it, even as the regime of the Left displaced its predecessor. If the American Right can disengage from the Left and its regime, it can assume leadership of a cause that could be right as well as victorious. But it can do so only if it has the wit and the will to disabuse itself of the illusions that have distracted it almost since its birth.

Chapter Thirty-eight

Contract with America

Newt Gingrich

As Republican Members of the House of Representatives and as citizens seeking to join that body we propose not just to change its policies, but even more important, to restore the bonds of trust between the people and their elected representatives.

That is why, in this era of official evasion and posturing, we offer instead a detailed agenda for national renewal, a written commitment with no fine print.

This year's election offers the chance, after four decades of one-party control, to bring to the House a new majority that will transform the way Congress works. That historic change would be the end of government that is too big, too intrusive, and too easy with the public's money. It can be the beginning of a Congress that respects the values and shares the faith of the American family.

Like Lincoln, our first Republican president, we intend to act "with firmness in the right, as God gives us to see the right." To restore accountability to Congress. To end its cycle of scandal and disgrace. To make us all proud again of the way free people govern themselves.

On the first day of the 104th Congress, the new Republican majority will immediately pass the following major reforms, aimed at restoring the faith and trust of the American people in their government:

First, require all laws that apply to the rest of the country also apply equally to the Congress;

Second, select a major, independent auditing firm to conduct a comprehensive audit of Congress for waste, fraud, or abuse;

From http://www.townhall.com/documents/contract.html.

Third, cut the number of House committees, and cut committee staff by one-third;

Fourth, limit the terms of all committee chairs;

Fifth, ban the casting of proxy votes in committee;

Sixth, require committee meetings to be open to the public;

Seventh, require a three-fifths majority vote to pass a tax increase;

Eighth, guarantee an honest accounting of our Federal Budget by implementing zero base-line budgeting.

Thereafter, within the first 100 days of the 104th Congress, we shall bring to the House Floor the following bills, each to be given full and open debate, each to be given a clear and fair vote and each to be immediately available this day for public inspection and scrutiny.

1. The Fiscal Responsibility Act

A balanced budget/tax limitation amendment and a legislative line-item veto to restore fiscal responsibility to an out-of-control Congress, requiring them to live under the same budget constraints as families and businesses.

2. The Taking Back Our Streets Act

An anti-crime package including stronger truth-in-sentencing, "good faith" exclusionary rule exemptions, effective death penalty provisions, and cuts in social spending from this summer's "crime" bill to fund prison construction and additional law enforcement to keep people secure in their neighborhoods and kids safe in their schools.

3. The Personal Responsibility Act

Discourage illegitimacy and teen pregnancy by prohibiting welfare to minor mothers and denying increased AFDC for additional children while on welfare, cut spending for welfare programs, and enact a tough two-years-and-out provision with work requirements to promote individual responsibility.

4. The Family Reinforcement Act

Child support enforcement, tax incentives for adoption, strengthening rights of parents in their children's education, stronger child pornography laws, and an elderly dependent care tax credit to reinforce the central role of families in American society.

5. The American Dream Restoration Act

A $500 per child tax credit, begin repeal of the marriage tax penalty, and creation of American Dream Savings Accounts to provide middle class tax relief.

6. The National Security Restoration Act

No U.S. troops under U.N. command and restoration of the essential parts of our national security funding to strengthen our national defense and maintain our credibility around the world.

7. The Senior Citizens Fairness Act

Raise the Social Security earnings limit which currently forces seniors out of the work force, repeal the 1993 tax hikes on Social Security benefits and provide tax incentives for private long-term care insurance to let Older Americans keep more of what they have earned over the years.

8. The Job Creation and Wage Enhancement Act

Small business incentives, capital gains cut and indexation, neutral cost recovery, risk assessment/cost-benefit analysis, strengthening the Regulatory Flexibility Act and unfunded mandate reform to create jobs and raise worker wages.

9. *The Common Sense Legal Reform Act*

"Loser pays" laws, reasonable limits on punitive damages and reform of product liability laws to stem the endless tide of litigation.

10. *The Citizen Legislature Act*

A first-ever vote on term limits to replace career politicians with citizen legislators.

Further, we will instruct the House Budget Committee to report to the floor and we will work to enact additional budget savings, beyond the budget cuts specifically included in the legislation described above, to ensure that the Federal budget deficit will be less than it would have been without the enactment of these bills.

Respecting the judgment of our fellow citizens as we seek their mandate for reform, we hereby pledge our names to this Contract with America.

Chapter Thirty-nine

An Open Letter to Conservatives

Paul Weyrich

Dear Friend:

Late last year, I had the opportunity of speaking to the Conservative Leadership Conference on the state of the conservative movement. I've given similar talks in the past, and usually they have focused on the most recent election or our situation in Congress or something similar. This time, the thoughts I offered were very different, and frankly rather radical. The strong, positive response they brought forth—which came as something of a surprise to me—has led me to think that I should share them more widely. That is the purpose of this letter.

What many of us have been trying to do for many years has been based upon a couple of premises. First of all, we have assumed that a majority of Americans basically agrees with our point of view. That has been the premise upon which we have tried to build any number of institutions, and indeed our whole strategy. It is I who suggested to Jerry Falwell that he call his organization the "Moral Majority." The second premise has been that if we could just elect enough conservatives, we could get our people in as Congressional leaders and they would fight to implement our agenda.

In looking at the long history of conservative politics, from the defeat of Robert Taft in 1952, to the nomination of Barry Goldwater, to the takeover of the Republican Party in 1994, I think it is fair to say that conservatives have learned to succeed in politics. That is, we got our people elected.

But that did not result in the adoption of our agenda. The reason, I think, is that politics itself has failed. And politics has failed because of the collapse of the culture. The culture we are living in becomes an ever-wider sewer. In truth, I think we are caught up in a cultural collapse of historic proportions, a collapse so great that it simply overwhelms politics.

That's why I am in the process of rethinking what it is that we, who still

From http://www.freecongress.org/fcf/specials/weyrichopenltr.htm. Reprinted by permission of Free Congress Foundation and Paul Weyrich.

believe in our traditional, Western, Judeo-Christian culture, can and should do under the circumstances. Please understand that I am not quarreling with anybody who pursues politics, because it is important to pursue politics, to be involved in government. It is also important to try, as many people have, to retake the cultural institutions that have been captured by the other side.

But it is impossible to ignore the fact that the United States is becoming an ideological state. The ideology of Political Correctness, which openly calls for the destruction of our traditional culture, has so gripped the body politic, has so gripped our institutions, that it is even affecting the Church. It has completely taken over the academic community. It is now pervasive in the entertainment industry, and it threatens to control literally every aspect of our lives.

Those who came up with Political Correctness, which we more accurately call "Cultural Marxism," did so in a deliberate fashion. I'm not going to go into the whole history of the Frankfurt School and Herbert Marcuse and the other people responsible for this. Suffice it to say that the United States is very close to becoming a state totally dominated by an alien ideology, an ideology bitterly hostile to Western culture. Even now, for the first time in their lives, people have to be afraid of what they say. This has never been true in the history of our country. Yet today, if you say the "wrong thing," you suddenly have legal problems, political problems, you might even lose your job or be expelled from college. Certain topics are forbidden. You can't approach the truth about a lot of different subjects. If you do, you are immediately branded as "racist," "sexist," "homophobic," "insensitive," or "judgmental."

Cultural Marxism is succeeding in its war against our culture. The question becomes, if we are unable to escape the cultural disintegration that is gripping society, then what hope can we have? Let me be perfectly frank about it. If there really were a moral majority out there, Bill Clinton would have been driven out of office months ago. It is not only the lack of political will on the part of Republicans, although that is part of the problem. More powerful is the fact that what Americans would have found absolutely intolerable only a few years ago, a majority now not only tolerates but celebrates. Americans have adopted, in large measure, the MTV culture that we so valiantly opposed just a few years ago, and it has permeated the thinking of all but those who have separated themselves from the contemporary culture.

If in Washington State and Colorado, after we have spent years talking about partial birth abortion, we can't by referendum pass a ban on it, we have to face some unpleasant facts. I no longer believe that there is a moral majority. I do not believe that a majority of Americans actually shares our values.

So, I have contemplated the question of what we should do. If you saw my predictions on the elections, you know that my views are far from infallible. Therefore, I do not represent this as any sort of final truth. It is merely my deduction based on a number of observations and a good deal of soul-searching.

I believe that we probably have lost the culture war. That doesn't mean the war is not going to continue, and that it isn't going to be fought on other fronts. But in terms of society in general, we have lost. This is why, even when we win in politics, our victories fail to translate into the kind of policies we believe are important.

Therefore, what seems to me a legitimate strategy for us to follow is to look at ways to separate ourselves from the institutions that have been captured by the ideology of Political Correctness or by other enemies of our traditional culture. I would point out to you that the word "holy" means "set apart," and that it is not against our tradition to be, in fact, "set apart." You can look in the Old Testament, you can look at Christian history. You will see that there were times when those who had our beliefs were definitely in the minority and it was a band of hardy monks who preserved the culture while the surrounding society disintegrated.

What I mean by separation is, for example, what the homeschoolers have done. Faced with public school systems that no longer educate but instead "condition" students with the attitudes demanded by Political Correctness, they have seceded. They have separated themselves from public schools and have created new institutions, new schools, in their homes.

The same thing is happening in other areas. Some people are getting rid of their televisions. Others are setting up private courts, where they can hope to find justice instead of ideology and greed.

I think that we have to look at a whole series of possibilities for bypassing the institutions that are controlled by the enemy. If we expend our energies on fighting on the "turf" they already control, we will probably not accomplish what we hope, and we may spend ourselves to the point of exhaustion. The promising thing about a strategy of separation is that it has more to do with who *we* are, and what *we* become, than it does with what the other side is doing and what we are going to do about it.

For example, the Southern Baptists, Dr. Dobson and some other people started a boycott of Disney. We may regard this boycott in two ways. We might say, "Well, look at how much higher Disney stock is than before. The company made record profits, therefore the boycott has failed." But the strategy I'm suggesting would see it differently. Because of that boycott, lots of people who otherwise would have been poisoned by the kind of viciously anti-religious, and specifically anti-Christian, entertainment that Disney is spewing out these days have been spared contact with it. They separated themselves from some of the cultural rot, and to that extent we succeeded.

I am very concerned, as I go around the country and speak and talk to young people, when I find how much of the decadent culture they have absorbed without even understanding that they are a part of it. And while I'm not suggesting that we all become Amish or move to Idaho, I do think that we have to look at what we can do to separate ourselves from this hostile culture. What steps can we take to make sure that we and our children are not infected? We need some sort of quarantine.

It is not only political conservatives who are troubled by the disintegration of the culture. I gave a speech not long ago in which I was very critical of what was on television. Several people who described themselves as liberals came up to me and said "Well, I know I don't agree with your politics, but you are absolutely correct on this and we don't allow our children to watch television any more."

Don't be mislead by politicians who say that everything is great, that we are on the verge of this wonderful, new era thanks to technology or the stock market or whatever. These are lies. We are not in the dawn of a new civilization, but the twilight of an old one. We will be lucky if we escape with any remnants of the great Judeo-Christian civilization that we have known down through the ages.

The radicals of the 1960s had three slogans: turn on, tune in, drop out. I suggest that we adopt a modified version. First, turn off. Turn off the television and video games and some of the garbage that's on the computers. Turn off the means by which you and your family are being infected with cultural decadence.

Tune out. Create a little stillness. I was very struck by the fact that when I traveled in the former Soviet Union, I couldn't go to a restaurant or any place else without hearing this incessant Western rock music pounding away. There was no escape from it. No wonder some Russians are anti-American. When they think of the United States, they think of the culture that we exported to them.

Finally, we need to drop out of this culture, and find places, even if it is where we physically are right now, where we can live godly, righteous, and sober lives.

Again, I don't have all the answers or even all the questions. But I know that what we have been doing for thirty years hasn't worked, that while we have been fighting and winning in politics, our culture has decayed into something approaching barbarism. We need to take another tack, find a different strategy. If you agree, and are willing to help wrestle with what that strategy should be, let me know. If enough people are willing to do something different, we will call a roundtable meeting here at Free Congress this year to discuss it. I hope I will see you there.

Sincerely,
Paul M. Weyrich

Chapter Forty

What's Right
Policy Review Defines the Limits of Conservatism

For better or worse, modern ideological conservatism constitutes a completed body of thought. We need not try to settle the issue of how it came
to completion, an exercise in intellectual history a bit beyond the scope
of these reflections, to note the fact. There was a time, coming to a close
perhaps a decade ago, when those of us who took an interest in the
development of conservative ideology eagerly reached for our newly arrived periodicals and newly published books in the expectation of finding
bold new insights into vexing problems, some of which we did not even
realize were problems. This was an exciting time—conservative ideology
was a work in progress, and the task had urgency, vitality, and freshness.
Part of the task was the development of a thorough critique of liberal and
radical ideology and the effects these had throughout our politics and
culture. But conservative ideology was not merely negative—merely
based in criticism. It had a positive component as well, laying claim to a
future it proposed to make-better through the defeat of radicalism, the
rejection of liberalism, and the implementation of conservative ideas in
the policy arena.

This period of intellectual ferment is over. In a way, that is a tribute to
its success. One can say of ideological conservatism nowadays that, in
general, it knows what the important questions are and it knows the
answers to those questions. There remains much detail to work out, but
the outlines are clear. Conservatives resolve arguments in favor of the
individual rather than the collective, of clear standards of judgment rather
than relativistic measures, of personal responsibility rather than the inter-
play of vast social forces, of the market rather than government economic
intervention, of international strength and self-reliance rather than empty

From: *Policy Review* (April/May 1999): 3–6. Reprinted by permission of Heritage Foundation, Washington, D.C.

promises of security. The federal government is, in general, too big, taxing too much of the wealth of Americans, doing too many unnecessary and often counterproductive things that get in the way of economic growth, to say nothing of personal liberty. Even as it has indulged in frivolity, the federal government has been neglectful of the security of Americans in its rush to disarm after the successful conclusion of the Cold War. Meanwhile, a debased high and popular culture shows few signs of recovery.

Among conservatives, one is hard-pressed to find any disagreement on these basic issues. The real questions, instead, are whether, when, and how the American political process will make good on the promises of conservatism. In certain respects, this is a tribute to the triumph of conservative ideology. In the absence of its searching critique of liberalism and its advancement of an alternative vision, it seems unlikely that the old liberal dominance would have faded as it has. The practical import of this triumph is that conservative ideology is no longer merely a theoretical matter. Conservatives would like to implement it, to substitute their ideas for the dead hand of liberalism that guided our politics for decades. The principal activity of ideological conservatism at century's end takes place not in the realm of ideas, but in the world of politics.

The Conservative Intellectual Culture

The characteristic figures of conservative intellectual culture are no longer professors and intellectuals. The characteristic figures are lawyers and journalists. This, as much as anything, is an indication of how far conservatism has come.

Making the law and reporting on how the law is or isn't getting made: In some ways, these seem the principal activities of idea-minded conservatives nowadays. Once again, this may be a product of the success of the intellectual endeavor, over the years, in asking and answering the basic questions. But there are no more basic questions to ask and answer, or so it seems, and so it seems neither inappropriate nor terribly significant that for those interested in the life of the mind these days, at least outside the academy, action consists of either a seat at the table where the big decisions are being made; or a place at the peephole into the room with the table, in order to describe it for others (and second-guess it).

The conservative intellectual culture reflects the broader media culture around us. That broader culture now worships two principal deities:

Much and Quick. Our culture produces an extraordinary volume of information for anyone interested in consuming information. Never have so many had so much access to so much, nor so quickly. What is a media culture to do in the age of the Internet and 24-hour cable programming on politics? The answer has been: Go along with it. In addition to a new breed of on-line "magazines" whose content changes from hour to hour, we have seen biweekly, weekly, and daily publications break out of their traditional "news cycle" to give us the benefit of their reporting and analysis as soon as they can post it on their websites. Conservatism, for its part, is now propagated as much by simultaneous e-mail transmission as by any other medium. To be *au courant* is to answer a liberal argument made on a morning cable show by early afternoon. It may, however, be an indication of how well-formed conservative thought is that it can propagate answers so quickly.

The Questions to the Answers

Is anything wrong with this? On one hand, no. In the first place, there is no undoing the profusion of cable or the availability of the Internet. We live in our time. It would be the height of folly to cede such powerful tools as the Internet and cable to people out to do in the conservative project. As long as these media are available, it only makes sense to seize them and use them the best one can. In the second place, the sometimes-rote quality of the propagation of conservatism and conservative positions is hardly the product of imposition of intellectual orthodoxy by some central committee taking as its charge the enforcement of discipline among the cadres. There is no such committee. Instead, the familiar quality of conservatism is a product of widespread agreement among thoughtful people. Its completed character is testimony to the sway of reason among reasonable people.

But is a swift and certain conservatism, even if such a conservatism is essential, actually sufficient? Here, there is reason to pause.

The long-term success of conservative ideology depends on how well that ideology understands and describes the world and predicts outcomes in it. If, in point of fact, conservative ideology is perfectly formed at present, then there is no particular risk in the current state of conservative intellectual culture. But if not, then what? And how will conservatives know?

The liberal experience should send a cautionary signal to conservatives. Liberalism as an ideology proved remarkably disinclined to engage in self-examination. The intellectual energy of liberalism was largely taken up in a decades-long argument between the go-fast liberals and the one-step-at-a-time liberals. Liberalism had no particular response to external pressure, either in the form of the failure of the world to act in accordance with its expectations or in the form of the conservative intellectual critique of liberalism during the heyday of the formation of conservative ideology. Liberalism, comfortable in the wielding of political power, simply did so— until there came the point at which it lost political power as a result of the bankruptcy, insufficiency, and stubborn wrong-headedness of its ideas.

Liberalism would surely have been better off had some substantial number of its most talented adherents been able or willing to take a step back from their ideological certainty and re-examine their premises in the light of real-world results. (One could say that some liberals did take this road, only to become conservatives; on the other hand, it is hardly obvious that the only alternative to liberalism is ideological conservatism.)

Conservatives should profit from this error. Some of them ought to take it as a project of some urgency to step back from the now hurly-burly world of conservative political and intellectual culture and take a long, hard, detailed look at conservatism. The alternative is merely the assumption that all is well. That is a dangerous assumption. Even if all is well, it is better to say so on the basis of serious self-scrutiny than on a whim, or worse, out of the ideological conviction that all must be well. And suppose all is not well. Suppose one or another problem becomes apparent. There is at least a possibility that such problems as arise can be addressed and corrected before their steady accretion threatens the totality of the project of conservative governance.

If ideological conservatism now is relatively self-confident in the conviction that it has the right answers to the important questions, the time has come for the right questions about the answers.

Notes

Notes to the Introduction

1. George H. Nash, *The Conservative Intellectual Movement in America: Since 1945*, 2d ed. (Wilmington, De: Intercollegiate Studies Institute, 1996; originally, 1976), xv.

2. In part, of course, it is the duty of the historian to tell a story, necessitating the use of chronological narrative. For recent works that display the "Whig interpretation of conservatism" (and note the editor's own culpability), see Gregory L. Schneider, *Cadres for Conservatism: Young Americans for Freedom and the Rise of the Contemporary Right* (New York: New York University Press, 1999); William A. Rusher, *The Rise of the Right* (New York: Wm. Morrow, 1984); Rick Perlstein, *Before the Storm: Barry Goldwater and the Unmaking of the American Consensus* (New York: Hill & Wang, 2001); Matthew Dallek, *The Right Moment: Ronald Reagan's First Victory and the Decisive Turning Point in American Politics* (New York: Free Press, 2000); and Lee Edwards, *The Conservative Revolution* (New York: Free Press, 1999).

3. For an entertaining and unrelenting examination of liberal decline, see Stephen J. Hayward, *The Age of Reagan: The Decline of the Old Liberal Order, 1964–1980* (New York: Prima, 2001).

4. For a recent intelligent analysis of intellectual conflict in the formation of the New Left, see Kevin Mattson, *Intellectuals in Action: The Origins of the New Left and Radical Liberalism, 1945–1970* (University Park: Penn State University Press, 2002).

5. Lionel Trilling, *The Liberal Imagination* (New York: Viking Press, 1950), ix.

6. Arthur M. Schlesinger, Jr., "The New Conservatism: The Politics of Nostalgia," *Reporter* 12 (June 16, 1955): 9–12; and Louis Hartz, *The Liberal Tradition in America: An Interpretation of American Political Thought Since the Revolution* (New York: Harcourt, Brace & World, 1955).

7. Daniel Bell, ed., *The New American Right* (New York: Criterion Books, 1955), updated as *The Radical Right* (Garden City, NY: Doubleday, 1963). Hofstadter's essay, "The Pseudo-Conservative Revolt," is mirrored in his later study, *The Paranoid Style in American Politics and Other Essays* (New York: Alfred A. Knopf, 1965).

Notes to Part I

1. Justin Raimando, *Reclaiming the American Right: The Lost Legacy of the Conservative Movement* (Burlingame, CA: Center for Libertarian Studies, 1993), provides a sympathetic treatment of various old Right figures. See also Ronald Radosh, *Prophets on the Right: Profiles of Conservative Critics of American Globalism* (New York: Simon & Schuster, 1975).

2. Michael Miles, *The Odyssey of the American Right* (New York: Oxford University Press, 1980), comes closest to delineating a political conservatism in the 1930s. Also see George Wolfskill, *The Revolt of the Conservatives: A History of the American Liberty League, 1934–1940* (Boston: Houghton Mifflin, 1962).

3. Jose Ortega y Gasset, *The Revolt of the Masses* (New York: W. W. Norton, 1932), symbolized to conservatives the linkage of communism and fascism.

4. For Leftist and libertarian views of the New Deal, see Ronald Radosh and Murray N. Rothbard, eds., *A New History of Leviathan: Essays on the Rise of the American Corporate State* (New York: Dutton, 1972).

5. For a history of agrarian thought during the New Deal, see Allan Carlson, *The New Agrarian Mind: The Movement toward Decentralist Thought in Twentieth-Century America* (New Brunswick, NJ: Transaction, 2000); for the effect of agrarianism on post–World War II conservatism, see Paul V. Murphy, *The Rebuke of History: The Southern Agrarians and American Conservative Thought* (Chapel Hill: University of North Carolina Press, 2001).

6. For the best history of the new Humanism, see J. David Hoeveler, Jr., *The New Humanism: A Critique of Modern America, 1900–1940* (Charlottesville: University Press of Virginia, 1977).

7. Two collections of essays provide a studied contrast to the humanist controversy. Norman Foerster, ed., *Humanism and America: Essays on the Outlook of American Civilization* (New York: 1930) and C. Hartley Grattan, ed., *The Critique of Humanism: A Symposium* (New York, 1930). For Upton Sinclair's description of Babbitt and More, see letter from Sinclair to Seward Collins, January 16, 1930, Box 11, Series I, Folder 29 (Irving Babbitt Corr.), Seward Collins Papers, Beinecke Rare Book and Manuscript Library, Yale University.

8. Michael Wreszin, *The Superfluous Anarchist: Albert Jay Nock* (Providence, RI: Brown University Press, 1971); also see Robert M. Crunden, *The Mind and Art of Albert Jay Nock* (Chicago: Henry Regnery, 1964).

Notes to Part II

1. Aaron L. Friedberg, *In the Shadow of the Garrison State: America's Antistatism and Its Cold War Grand Strategy* (Princeton: Princeton University Press, 2000).

2. F. A. Hayek, *The Road to Serfdom* (Chicago: University of Chicago Press, 1944), 1.

3. See Milton and Rose Friedman, *Two Lucky People* (Chicago: University of Chicago Press, 1999).

4. Ludwig Van Mises, *Human Action,* scholars ed. (Auburn, AL: Ludwig Van Mises Institute, 1999) is his best known work. For an introduction to Austrian economics, see the biographical sketches in Randall G. Holcombe, ed., *15 Great Austrian Economists* (Auburn, AL: Ludwig Van Mises Institute, 1999).

5. Milton Friedman and Anna J. Schwartz, *A Monetary History of the United States, 1867–1960* (Princeton: Princeton University Press, 1963).

6. One such club was affiliated with ISI at the University of Chicago. The students, primarily studying economics, published the *New Individualist Review* from 1960 to 1968. Friedman's "Capitalism and Freedom" appeared in its first issue. Friedman became a popular campus lecturer, appearing as often as a guest of the radical Students for a Democratic Society. He would tell the young radicals "your objective is the same as mine—greater individual freedom. The difference is that I know how to achieve that objective and you do not" (*Two Lucky People,* 341–342); Friedman's son, David, was a prominent libertarian member of Young Americans for Freedom in the late 1960s. See Gregory L. Schneider, *Cadres for Conservatism: Young Americans for Freedom and the Rise of the Contemporary Right* (New York: New York University Press, 1999).

7. Friedman, *Two Lucky People,* 358–359.

Notes to Part III

1. Richard M. Weaver, edited by George Core and M. E. Bradford, *The Southern Tradition at Bay: A History of Postbellum Thought* (New Rochelle, NY: Arlington House, 1968).

2. See Joseph Scotchie, *Barbarians in the Saddle: An Intellectual Biography of Richard M. Weaver* (New Brunswick, NJ: Transaction, 1997); Fred Douglas Young, *Richard M. Weaver 1910–1963: A Life in the Mind* (Columbia: University of Missouri Press, 1995); Ted J. Smith, III, ed., *In Defense of Tradition: Collected Shorter Writings of Richard M. Weaver, 1929–1963* (Indianapolis, IN: Liberty Fund, 2000); and Richard M. Weaver, "Up From Liberalism," *Modern Age* 3: 1 (Winter 1958/59): 21–32.

3. Ted J. Smith, III, ed., *Steps Towards Restoration: The Consequences of Richard Weaver's Ideas* (Wilmington, DE: ISI Books, 1998), 18.

4. For a sampling of reaction to the book, see George H. Nash, *The Conservative Intellectual Movement in America: Since 1945,* 2d ed. (Wilmington, DE: Intercollegiate Studies Institute, 1996), 34–35.

5. Frank S. Meyer, "Richard M. Weaver: An Appreciation," *Modern Age* 14 (Summer/Fall 1970), 244; and Henry Regnery, "Richard M. Weaver: A Southern Agrarian at the University of Chicago," *Modern Age* 32 (Spring 1988): 11–12.

6. See Kirk's own memoir, written in the third person, *The Sword of Imagi-*

nation: Memoirs of a Half-Century of Literary Conflict (Grand Rapids, MI: Wm. Eerdman's, 1995). Piety Hill still houses Kirk's widow, Annette, who runs the Russell Kirk Center for Cultural Renewal.

7. Ibid., 148.

8. The literature on this controversy is vast. For a sample, see Nash, *Conservative Intellectual Movement*, 64–66; and Clinton Rossiter, *Conservatism in America*, rev. ed. (Cambridge: Harvard University Press, 1982; originally published 1955), 197–234.

9. Frank S. Meyer, *In Defense of Freedom: A Conservative Credo* (Chicago: Henry Regnery, 1962).

Notes to Part IV

1. Joshua Muravchik, *Heaven on Earth: The Rise and Decline of Socialism* (San Francisco: Encounter Books, 2002).

2. See Stephanie Courtois et al., *The Black Book of Communism: Crimes, Terror, Repression* (Cambridge: Harvard University Press, 1999), for a tally of communism's victims in the twentieth century.

3. For biographies of these figures, see Ronald Radosh, *Prophets on the Right: Profiles of Conservative Critics of American Globalism* (New York: Simon & Schuster, 1975); and Justus Doenecke, *Not to the Swift: The Old Isolationists in the Cold War Era* (Lewisburg, PA: Bucknell University Press, 1979).

4. For the early history of the Cold War and the Republican Congress, see Robert A. Patterson, *Mr. Republican: A Biography of Robert A. Taft* (New York: Oxford University Press, 1972); for general histories of the Cold War and Truman, see John Lewis Gaddis, *The United States and the Origins of the Cold War, 1941–1947* (New York: Columbia University Press, 1972); Alonzo Hamby, *Man of the People: The Life of Harry Truman* (New York: Oxford University Press, 1997); and, for a new revisionist account of Truman, Arnold Offner, *Another Such Victory: President Truman and the Cold War, 1945–1953* (Stanford: Stanford University Press, 2002). For the importance of Asia to the GOP, see Michael Miles, *The Odyssey of the American Right* (New York: Oxford University Press, 1980); and Stanley D. Bachrack, *The Committee of One Million: "China Lobby" Politics, 1953–1971* (New York: Columbia University Press, 1976).

5. James Burnham, *Containment or Liberation?* (New York: John Day, 1953).

6. For a discussion of these converts from communism, see George H. Nash, *The Conservative Intellectual Movement in America: Since 1945*, 2d ed. (Wilmington, DE: Intercollegiate Studies Institute, 1996), 74–117; Gary Dorrien, *The Neoconservative Mind: Politics, Culture, and the War of Ideology* (Philadelphia: Temple University Press, 1993); John Patrick Diggins, *Up From Communism: Conservative Odysseys in American Intellectual Development* (New York: Columbia University Press, 1994; originally, 1975); Kevin J. Smant, *Principle and Heresies: Frank S.*

Meyer and the Shaping of the American Conservative Movement (Wilmington, DE: ISI Books, 2002); and Daniel Kelly, *James Burnham and the Struggle for the World* (Wilmington, DE: ISI Books, 2002).

7. See Allen Weinstein, *Perjury: The Hiss-Chambers Case* (New York: Knopf, 1978); see Sam Tanenhaus, *Whittaker Chambers: A Biography* (New York: Random House, 1997); for evidence from the Soviet archives of Hiss's culpability in espionage, see John Earl Haynes and Harvey Klehr, eds., *Venona: Soviet Espionage in America* (New Haven, CT: Yale University Press, 1999).

8. The only biography of Buckley is John B. Judis, *William F. Buckley, Jr.: Patron Saint of the Conservatives* (New York: Simon & Schuster, 1988).

Notes to Part V

1. Russell Kirk, "Apology for a New Review," *Modern Age* 1 (Summer 1957): 2–3.

2. Alan Ebenstein, *Friedrich A. Hayek: A Biography* (New York: Palgrave, 2001), 204–207.

Notes to Part VI

1. See Rick Perlstein, *Before the Storm: Barry Goldwater and the Unmaking of the American Consensus* (New York: Hill & Wang, 2001); Lee Edwards, *Goldwater: The Man Who Made a Revolution* (Washington, D.C.: Regnery, 1997); Robert Alan Goldberg, *Barry Goldwater* (New Haven, CT: Yale University Press, 1997); and Gregory L. Schneider, *Cadres for Conservatism: Young Americans for Freedom and the Rise of the Contemporary Right* (New York: New York University Press, 1999).

2. See Mary C. Brennan, *Turning Right in the Sixties: The Conservative Capture of the GOP* (Chapel Hill: University of North Carolina Press, 1995); and William A. Rusher, *The Rise of the Right* (New York: Wm. Morrow, 1984).

3. For YAF, see Schneider, *Cadres for Conservatism;* John A. Andrew, III, *The Other Side of the Sixties: Young Americans for Freedom and the Rise of Contemporary Conservatism* (New Brunswick, NJ: Rutgers University Press, 1997); and Rebecca Klatch, *A Generation Divided: The New Left, the New Right and the 1960s* (Berkeley: University of California Press, 1999).

4. Robert Welch, *The Politician* (Belmont, MA: Belmont Publishing Co., 1963.

5. For Kennedy investigations, see Andrew, *Other Side of the Sixties,* Jonathon Schoenwald, *A Time for Choosing: The Rise of Modern Conservatism* (New York: Oxford University Press, 2001), provides commentary on the fear of conservatism in the early 1960s.

6. The best chronicle of the Draft Goldwater committee is F. Clifton White, *Suite 3505: The Story of the Draft Goldwater Committee* (New Rochelle, NY: Arlington Books, 1965).

Notes to Part VII

1. See Kenneth Heineman, *Put Your Bodies upon the Wheels: Student Protest in the 1960s* (Chicago: Ivan R. Dee, 2001); Gregory L. Schneider, *Cadres for Conservatism: Young Americans for Freedom and the Rise of the Contemporary Right* (New York: New York University Press, 1999); and Matthew Dallek, *The Right Moment* (New York: Free Press, 2000).

2. Felix Morley to Alf Landon, June 20, 1964, Box 1, Names and Subject File (Alf Landon, 1958–68), Felix Morley Papers, Herbert Hoover Presidential Library, West Branch, Iowa.

3. Rothbard to Morley, December 7, 1964, Box 23, Correspondence and Subject File (Murray Rothbard), Morley Papers.

4. See John L. Kelley, *Bringing the Market Back In: The Political Revitalization of Market Liberalism* (New York: New York University Press, 1997); Schneider, *Cadres for Conservatism;* and Rebecca Klatch, *A Generation Divided: The New Left, the New Right, and the 1960s* (Berkeley: University of California Press, 1999).

Notes to Part VIII

1. William A. Rusher, *The Rise of the Right* (New York: Wm. Morrow, 1984),

2. Robert M. Collins, *More: The Politics of Economic Growth in Postwar America* (New York: Oxford University Press, 2000), 98–131; for the idea of Nixon as a liberal, see Joan Hoff, *Nixon Reconsidered* (New York: Basic Books, 1994); for a sound general history of the Nixon administration, see Melvin Small, *The Presidency of Richard M. Nixon* (Lawrence: University of Kansas Press, 1999).

3. See Patrick J. Buchanan, *Right from the Beginning* (Washington, D.C.: Regnery, 1990); Dean J. Kotlowski, *Nixon's Civil Rights: Politics, Principle and Policy* (Cambridge: Harvard University Press, 2001); Gareth Davies, "The Great Society after Johnson: The Case of Bilingual Education," *Journal of American History* 88: 4 (March 2002): 1405–1429; and Kevin Phillips, *The Emerging Republican Majority* (New Rochelle, NY: Arlington House, 1969).

4. George J. Marlin, *Fighting the Good Fight: A History of the New York Conservative Party, 1962–2002* (New York: St. Augustine's, 2002).

5. See Norman Podhoretz, *Breaking Ranks: A Political Memoir* (New York: Harper & Row, 1979), and *My Love Affair with America* (New York: Free Press, 2000).

6. Two prominent neoconservative interpretations of foreign policy are: Jeanne Kirkpatrick, "Dictatorships and Double Standards," *Commentary* 68 (November 1979): 34–45; and Norman Podhoretz, "The Present Danger," *Commentary* 69 (March 1980): 27–40.

7. Paul Gottfried and Thomas Fleming, *The Conservative Movement* (Boston: Twayne, 1986).

Notes to Part IX

1. David Stockman, *The Triumph of Politics* (New York: Avon Books, 1987).

2. For the early historical views of Reagan, see Paul Kengor, "Reagan among the Professors," *Policy Review 98* (December 1999 and January 2000): 15–7.

3. See J. David Hoeveler, *Watch on the Right: Conservative Intellectuals in the Reagan Era* (Madison: University of Wisconsin Press, 1990).

4. Will's most important work, *Statecraft as Soulcraft* (New York: Free Press, 1990), demonstrates his views most clearly.

Notes to Part X

1. William Bennett, *The De-Valuing of America: The Fight for Our Culture and Our Children* (New York: Summit Books, 1992); Robert Bork, *Slouching towards Gomorrah* (New York: Free Press, 1997); and "An End to Democracy? The Judicial Usurption of Politics" *First Things 67* (November 1996): 18–42.

2. See Patrick J. Buchanan, *The Great Betrayal* (Boston: Little Brown, 1998); *A Republic, Not an Empire* (Washington, D.C.: Regnery, 1999); and *The Death of the West* (New York: Thomas Dunne Books, 2002).

3. Paul Gottfried, *After Liberalism: Mass Democracy and the Managerial State* (Princeton: Princeton University Press, 1999).

4. Lee Edwards, *The Conservative Revolution* (New York: Free Press, 1999).

5. Weyrich's letter led to criticism that he was giving up on politics. For Weyrich's explanation of his position, see "We Need to Change Our Strategy," *World* (May 15, 1999), online at http://www.freecongress.org/fcf/specials/follow up.htm.

Index

abortion, 276, 287
Academic Freedom (Kirk), 122
Acheson, Dean, 214, 216, 235
Adams, John, 190
affirmative action, 276
Affluent Society (Galbraith), 263
Afghanistan, 337
Agnew, Spiro, 280, 295, 313
agrarian society, 14–15, 16–17
Agrarians. *See* Southern Agrarians
America First, 8, 132, 133; principles of, 395–396, 419
American ideals, 45, 47, 58–59
American Mercury, 7
American Political Science Review, 392
American Review, 7, 16–20
anarchism, 248, 260
Angola, 311, 337
anti-Americanism, 277
anticommunism, discussion of, as conservative principle, 131–134, 143–148, 233–235, 242–243, 337–338; mentioned, 8, 208, 209, 312, 381, 389
Anti-Federalists, 49
anti-liberalism, 325–327
anti-Semitism, accusations of, 277, 377, 396
antiwar movement (Vietnam), 247
Aristotle, 39, 97

Babbitt, Irving, 6, 17
Balkans, 402–403
Bay of Pigs, 239
Becker, Gary, 50
Bell, Daniel, 277, 384
Belloc, Hilaire, 6, 17, 22
Bentham, Jeremy, 75
Berger, Peter, 375, 384, 386
Bill of Rights, 49
Black Panthers, 275
Bloom, Alexander, 378
Bolshevism, 36
Bookman, 6, 17
Bork, Robert, 395

Bosnia, 403
Bourne, Randolph, 49
Bozell, L. Brent, 134, 208
Bradford, M. E., 381
Branch Davidians, 397
Brave New World (Huxley), 116
Brazil, 287
Bromfield, Louis, 248
Brown vs. Board of Education (1954), Goldwater's views of, 224–225
Buchanan, Patrick: foreign policy views of, 401–413; role as conservative discussed, 395–397
Buckley, James, 276
Buckley, William F., Jr., 93, 173, 226, 300, 338, 381; background of, 133–134; influence of, 417–419; and *National Review,* 169–170, 195–200, 201–205; speech attacking Khrushchev, 131; and Young Americans for Freedom, 208–209
Burke, Edmund, mentioned, 93, 120, 127, 172, 173, 183, 303, 376; conservative principles of, 107–112
Burnham, James, 116, 132, 134; and managerial revolution, 307, 397, 416. *See also* managerial revolution
Bush, George H. W., 396, criticism of, 406–408

Caddy, Douglas, 227
Caesar, Julius, 306
Cambodia, 268, 337
Campbell, Glenn, 375
capitalism, 20, 23, 28, 46; and bureaucracy, 331–333; and culture, 329–331; and democracy, 333–335; history of, in United States, 319–322; principles of, 80–82, 85–86
Capitalism and Freedom (Friedman), 51
Carey, George, 339
Carter, Jimmy, 363
Castro, Fidel, 234, 236, 287, 365
Catholic Church, 27, 38, 267
Catholics, as electoral constituency, 276–277

About the Editor

Gregory L. Schneider is Associate Professor of History at Emporia State University in Emporia, Kansas. He is the author of *Cadres for Conservatism: Young Americans for Freedom and the Rise of the Contemporary Right* (NYU Press, 1999). He lives in Topeka, Kansas.